level 3

OCR
nationals
ICT

www.pearsonschoolsandfe.co.uk

- Karen Anderson
- Graham Manson
- Veronica White

D1439623

PAYNE-GALLWAY
Part of Pearson

Payne-Gallway is an imprint of Pearson Education Limited, a company incorporated in England and Wales, having its registered office at Edinburgh Gate, Harlow, Essex, CM20 2JE. Registered company number: 872828

www.pearsonschoolsandfe.co.uk

Text © Pearson Education Limited 2009

First published 2009

12 11 10 09
10 9 8 7 6 5 4 3 2 1

British Library Cataloguing in Publication Data
A catalogue record for this book is available from the British Library

ISBN 978 1 905292 77 6

Edited by Caroline Low and Melanie Birdsall
Designed by Pearson Education Ltd
Typeset by Tek-Art, Crawley Down, West Sussex
Original illustrations © Pearson Education Ltd
Cover design by Pearson Education Ltd
Picture research by Pearson Education Ltd and ZOOID – Cristina
Cover photo/illustration © Digital Vision/Alamy
Printed in Scotland, by Scotprint

Acknowledgements
The authors and publisher would like to thank our independent reviewer Sonja Stuart for her invaluable advice and contributions to Units 1, 3, 5 and 6.

The authors and publisher would like to thank the following individuals and organisations for permission to reproduce photographs:

©Juniors Bildarchiv/Alamy p 3; ©Lou Linwei/Alamy p 63; ©Photofusion Picture Library/Alamy p 89; ©Photodisc p 127; ©Robert Morris/Alamy p 157; ©Capture +/Alamy p191; ©Worldthroughthelens-art/Alamy p 245; ©AP/PA Photos p 267; ©Picture Contact/Alamy p 289; ©iStockphoto/Mark Evans p 291 ©Getty Images p 307; ©Judith Collins/Alamy p 310; ©Tony Cordoza/Alamy p 312; ©toy Alan King/Alamy p 313; ©Paul Cooper/Rex Features p 319; ©Steve Allen Travel Photography/Alamy p 331; ©Peter Titmuss/Alamy p 357; ©PhotoDisc p 379.

The author and publisher would like to thank the following organisations for permission to use screenshots:

Microsoft screenshots throughout the publication: Microsoft product screen shot(s) reprinted with permission from Microsoft Corporation.
Adobe Systems Incorporated: Adobe product screen shot(s) reprinted with permission from Adobe Systems Incorporated.
Yell.com for the screenshot of the home page of Yell.com (November 2008).
Every effort has been made to contact copyright holders of material reproduced in this book. Any omissions will be rectified in subsequent printings if notice is given to the publishers.

Websites
The websites used in this book were correct and up-to-date at the time of publication. It is essential for tutors to preview each website before using it in class so as to ensure that the URL is still accurate, relevant and appropriate. We suggest that tutors bookmark useful websites and consider enabling students to access them through the school/college intranet.

Contents

Introduction

By choosing this qualification in ICT you are taking a step into one of the most exciting areas of study. As a student of ICT, you will be at the forefront of a field which is ever-changing, ever-advancing and as cutting edge as it gets.

ICT is an incredibly diverse subject, ranging from the creative areas of web design, multimedia and games design to the more hardcore interests such as programming. There is also the enterprise side of working with data and supporting business practices. It has a strong entrepreneurial streak running through it.

What is an OCR National?

The OCR National is a high quality, modern qualification aimed at providing you with specific knowledge and practical skills to prepare you for higher education or employment. Being underpinned academically, it has a strong vocational inclination which is ideal for ICT. Areas of study are practically-based and realistic to the contemporary workplace. They support the achievement of Key Skills and relate to National Occupational Standards.

There are three levels of achievement: Certificate, Diploma and Extended Diploma. For each you must complete the four mandatory units and two, eight or fourteen optional units respectively. Please refer to the OCR Centre Handbook (available from their website) for details on specific combinations of specialist and non-specialist units for each level of qualification.

Each unit is graded as Pass, Merit or Distinction, earning one, two or three points. Once all selected units are completed, these points are counted and the final total for the qualification is produced. This will then relate to the overall resulting grade for the qualification. For example, a student sitting the Diploma achieves Distinctions in all twelve units. This would be equivalent to thirty-six points and therefore a Distinction overall.

All units are assessed by the educational institution and then externally moderated by OCR. There are no examinations for these qualifications.

What units can I study?

There are twenty-nine units available in total.

The four mandatory units, which must be completed at all levels of the qualification, are included in this book:

- Unit 1: Digital Business Communication
- Unit 2: Collaborative Working
- Unit 3: Problem Solving
- Unit 4: Creating a Digital Showcase

In addition to these, there are five non-specialist and twenty specialist units available. The non-specialist units that are included in this book are:

- Unit 5 Advanced Spreadsheets
- Unit 6 Advanced Databases

The specialist areas comprise of Creative, Website and Business Enterprise. This book contains the following units:

Creative:

- Unit 14: Cartooning and Animation
- Unit 16: Programming for Computer Games
- Unit 17: Computer Games Production
- Unit 18: Computer Games Technology

Website:

- Unit 20: Web Authoring
- Unit 21: Hosting and Managing Websites
- Unit 24: Internet Past, Present and Future

How does this book work?

Each chapter begins with Learning Outcomes, which are taken directly from the OCR specification, and outline the major areas of study for that unit, which then become the headings for the sections within the chapter.

Following the Introduction to the unit there is a Scenario which outlines the case study which is used in the Portfolio Activities throughout that unit.

Each section outlines the knowledge for that particular Learning Outcome. Within each section is a Portfolio Activity and Assessment Guidance. These are practical implementations of the knowledge and tied directly to the OCR specification. There are also highlighted Key Concepts which can help you further understand particular terminology or ideas and are useful for later reference.

If all Portfolio Activities are done in full for a chapter, this could form the majority of your coursework for that unit. They allow scope for the full range of available grades. The Assessment Guidance is taken directly from the OCR specification and should help ensure that your work meets the criteria against which it is assessed.

At the back of the book there is an Index for you to quickly look up the information you need.

What do I do after this qualification?

The OCR Nationals are designed specifically to give you the knowledge and practical skills you need to study the subject further into higher education or gain employment in an ICT-related career.

If you want to study at university, the OCR National is accredited by UCAS. For example, at Certificate level, a Distinction is equivalent to 120 UCAS points which is the same as an A grade in an A level subject. The Diploma and Extended Diploma are comparable to two A levels and three A levels respectively. Pass, Merit and Distinction grades equate to E, C and A grades respectively.

If you wish to seek employment, this course gives you a strong foundation in useful skills which can be applied directly to the workplace and gives you clear evidence of your abilities and achievement in this area.

Digital Business Communication

Learning outcomes

By working through this unit you will produce evidence to meet the unit assessment objectives to show that you understand:

- the role and contribution of communication technology to business
- the aids and barriers to effective communication
- the application of a presentation style to document creation
- the use of written communication using ICT in a business context
- the effective use of email in a business context
- document and computer security in the workplace
- the use of standard ways of working to work safely, keep information secure and manage personal information.

Introduction

To complete this unit you will need to have access to the following resources:

- a web browser
- email software
- presentation software
- word-processing or desktop publishing software.

You will use a number of files that have been prepared – you will find them on the website at http://www.heinemann.co.uk/Series/Secondary/OCRNationalsICTLevel3/FreeResources/FreeResources.aspx.

Scenario

The Horse Stables is a company that provides lessons in horse riding, courses in horse care, livery services and horse feed. They offer horse breaking and horse schooling, horse clipping and trimming services. They are hoping to expand their business to include weekend and holiday breaks.

You have recently been engaged by the company to provide support to help them run the business more efficiently, and to assist in expanding the business. They need advice on the development of their computer use, so you will investigate a range of recent developments in business communications and consider their impact, both positive and negative, on organisations, so that you can help the company to understand why they should develop their business in this way. As they have not had a lot of success

attracting additional business, you will provide information on how to communicate more effectively and explain how to do this.

The company has a website for the sale of feed items only. They would like your help in increasing this side of their business. They are hoping to provide more products for the horse, such as grooming accessories, and the rider, such as hats and boots.

You will complete a variety of tasks to promote the business, including producing the following:

- a leaflet stating information about the company, including details of the horse riding lessons and promoting a special offer (book 10 riding lessons, get 2 free)
- an advertisement to be placed in horse magazines and on the website about the NVQ courses in Horse Care and Horse Care Management
- a covering letter to the magazine including the advertising copy
- an electronic slide presentation which will promote new activities that the company is about to introduce
- a report outlining why the company should expand their use of e-commerce, indicating the benefits they might expect.

While you are completing the tasks you must:

- save your work regularly
- keep backup copies on removable storage media – the backups must be completed regularly
- save your files and folders using appropriate, sensible names
- use version numbers
- ensure your work is kept securely by password protecting your files and folders.

These elements are covered in the section covering A07 on pages 56–60.

Scenario

Widespread use of business communication systems

The systems used in companies to conduct their business have changed dramatically in recent years with the introduction of new communication systems. Information and communication technology enables businesses to work more effectively by using the new facilities they offer. Among the systems most widely used in business are:

- email
- World Wide Web (WWW)
- Internet
- Intranets
- conferencing.

Email

Email predates the Internet and was a crucial part of creating it. In 1961 systems were introduced that allowed users to log into a mainframe computer from remote dial-up terminals, and to store files online. In 1965 email allowed multiple users to communicate. By 1966 network email allowed users to pass messages between different computers.

Email is a store and forward method of writing, sending, receiving and saving messages or computer files over electronic communication systems. It is a convenient method of keeping in contact with clients or colleagues worldwide. It is fast, reaching the recipient within seconds, and cheap.

Email is often used to deliver bulk unsolicited messages, or spam. Filter programs automatically block or delete some or most of these. Most email accounts offer mail filters to help stop the growing menace of spam, but one problem is that they sometimes block legitimate messages.

To send and receive emails you need an email address, which you could set up when you open an account. You can set up an account with:

- an Internet service provider (ISP)
- an organisation's own communication system, or internal mail
- a webmail server such as Lycos mail, Yahoo! mail, Gmail, and AIM email.

Internet

The Internet is a global network of computing resources. It began in the 1960s as a US Department of Defense experiment in computer networking, to allow different kinds of computers to connect and share data. By the end of the 1970s, links were developed with counterparts in other countries.

In the 1980s this network became known as the Internet. In the 1990s, the Internet grew at exponential rates. With the popularity of the World Wide Web, the number of networks connected to the Internet jumped to a total of more than 50,000 by the end of the decade.

As communication technologies have developed they have allowed greater speed of communication. This is particularly true in the case of access to the Internet. The Internet provides the facilities to enable companies to, for example:

- exchange messages and files with customers and colleagues via email
- market their products and services
- gather feedback from customers and business partners to improve their services
- provide 'current' information, with the ability to update it frequently when, for example, new products become available, or prices change.

WWW

The World Wide Web, or WWW for short, is the largest part of the Internet. It is a body of information that spans the entire Internet. Individuals and organisations provide pages of information on websites, which begin at their home page.

A webpage is a document written in a computer language called html – Hypertext Mark-up Language.

To use the Web, you need a web browser – a program that lets your computer communicate with other computers on the Internet. To tell the browser it is going to a website you enter 'www'.

So that we can find webpages, they are given a Uniform Resource Locator (URL) address. This is the location of a webpage. You reach this address by entering it into your web browser's address bar or by clicking a link to it. A common place to find links is in a search engine. Search engines allow users to surf the Internet for information using keywords. There are many search engines available on the Internet. Some common search engines are Google, Yahoo, Alta Vista and Ask Jeeves.

Intranets

An intranet is a computer network that uses the same technology and protocols as the Internet but is restricted to certain users. A business may have an Intranet which is only available to their employees. It is an internal, secure environment which operates using a local area network (LAN). It provides an interactive custom environment where the data is accessible only to people within the business. It provides quick, easy access to key company documents. It allows employees to share information, fix up appointments with each other, and circulate important documents internally.

An extranet allows selected people outside the company, such as customers or suppliers, to link to your system and access key company information. This allows them to work with you.

Conferencing

Video conferencing

Video conferencing allows two or more locations to interact via two-way video and audio transmissions. This allows individuals in different places to have meetings, thereby avoiding the time and expense of travel, as it allows face-to-face business meetings without leaving the desk. It is also used by employees working from home.

Conferencing is now being introduced to online networking websites to help companies develop relationships quickly and efficiently without leaving their place of work.

Teleconferencing

This is the live exchange of information by a group of people linked by the telephone. Conference calls can be set up so that the calling party calls the other participants and adds them to the call.

Businesses use conference calls to communicate with people who are in other locations – whether employees or clients. It is a method of cutting travel costs and allowing workers to be more productive by not having to go out of the office for meetings.

Web conferencing and podcasting

Conference calls are increasingly used in conjunction with web conferences, where presentations or documents are shared via the Internet. They are also beginning to be used in podcasting. Live streaming or broadcasting of conference calls allows a larger audience access to the call.

Instant messaging

Instant messaging (IM) is real-time communication between two or more people based on typed text. The text is transmitted via computers connected over the Internet.

Millions of the IM accounts currently in use are for business purposes. The demand for business-grade messaging and the need to ensure security have led to services which allow companies to use archiving and security products to reduce risks and provide secure instant messaging.

The risks associated with instant messaging include:

- security risks, such as messaging used to infect computers with spyware, viruses, trojans and worms, or for phishing
- inappropriate use
- potential loss of company data.

Companies need to protect themselves from inappropriate use of the informal, immediate and anonymous nature of instant messaging. They also have a legal responsibility to ensure a harassment-free work environment. Companies therefore often enforce rules for the use of IM. These vary from business to business, but are generally similar to the typical rules of chatrooms (see page 50).

Growth of Internet-based business

Business opportunities based on the Internet have grown with the number of Internet users. The World Wide Web is global – and has attracted more users in more countries than any other communication tool. Companies understand that there is still substantial growth in online sales, and that more and more people are choosing the Internet to make purchases.

e-Commerce

E-Commerce is one of the most important developments in business in recent times. It has changed the marketplace and has opened up many new opportunities. E-Commerce uses virtual shops and product catalogues that can be viewed online and provides the mechanisms for customers to place orders and pay online.

The introduction of technologies such as the Internet and credit cards, and payment systems such as PayPal have contributed to the growth in e-Commerce. High speed Internet connections such as broadband make it easier for customers to shop online. The introduction of wireless technologies and the development of handheld devices such as Blackberries, iPhones and laptops have also contributed to the growth in e-Commerce as customers can shop anywhere and at anytime.

As people become more comfortable online, they are also becoming more willing to use e-Commerce. There has been an increase in average spending and this trend is expected to continue – one of the reasons being that more offline retailers are adding online facilities.

Companies now have faster and better access to information which has led to less paperwork and improved efficiency. Orders can be placed and processed electronically. Stock control databases can be used to track items and this has meant that orders can be processed quicker and more cheaply than by paper-based methods.

For many companies, websites are essential. All types of business use this medium – post and telecommunications, wholesale, retail, catering and travel. Companies also use other forms of ICT such as Electronic Data Exchange, email, computer-based faxes and automated telephone entry, such as booking tickets.

The benefits of e-Commerce

E-Commerce has grown significantly as web accessibility, plus its interactive nature, has encouraged companies to trade online. The advantages that the technology can provide include: the removal of time and location problems with international suppliers and customers, the ability to provide constant updates to information (such as price and availability) and the ability to compare prices of a number of suppliers in one place.

It is important to keep the content accurate and regularly updated to help in promoting a positive image for the business, and attracting and retaining custom. There are many benefits, including:

- less paper and paperwork
- efficiency of integrated systems
- reduction in administrative tasks
- speedier access to information
- immediate, international sales presence
- providing services 24 hours a day, 365 days a year.

The disadvantages of e-Commerce

The growth in e-Commerce has led to a surge in the number of sites conducting e-Business and this is having an impact on the way companies do business. It has the potential to lead to growth in trade, increase markets and improve efficiency and effectiveness. However, there are potential problems connected with this form of business.

Security is important both to companies and consumers, and payment is a major issue because online methods of trading can lead to unauthorised access. Fortunately many payment facilities have been improved via encryption, but consumers remain hesitant because they do not trust that their personal information will remain private. The legislation that safeguards personal information is outlined in the Data Protection Act 1998 (see Unit 3, pages 92–93) and the Computer Misuse Act.

Some of the disadvantages include:

- The possibility of people stealing or hacking into company data (such as prices).
- The possibility of hackers stealing customer data with the intent of defrauding them by use of their financial details.
- Loss of service caused maliciously (by hackers) can affect customer confidence and result in loss of business.
- Loss of service caused by internal problems (such as equipment failure) or disasters (such as fire or flood) can affect the very existence of the business if recovery strategies are not in place.
- Companies selling customer information despite providing guarantees that it will remain private.

Communication technology and e-Commerce

Technology has contributed to the growth of e-Commerce. Customers are able to order goods over the Internet and have them delivered to their doors.

E-Commerce has benefited from communication technology as the use of the Internet has increased. More people now have Broadband access so enabling e-Retailers to provide more graphics of the goods they are selling. Websites showing stock for sale are linked to a database of the stock. This linking means that customers can find out if the item they want is in stock before it is ordered. The stock database will be updated in real time enabling accurate stock records to be held and shown. Some e-Retailers have utilised the increased use of mobile phones by sending a text, via SMS, to customers to provide details of delivery times, stock availability or special offers.

Customers can pay for the goods and services they have ordered by the use of secure payment areas (on the website). These areas enable, through encryption, customers to provide their credit or debit card details. These details are electronically sent to the customer's bank, usually via a processing company such a PayPal. The payment is then deducted from the customer's bank account and added to the company's account. An automated receipt is then sent to the customer's email account verifying and confirming that payment has been made.

Emails can also be sent to the customer notifying them of the delivery of their goods, or customers are given a unique reference number which enables them to log onto the e-Commerce website to track their order.

Mobile technology, such as Blackberrys, iPhones and mobile phones that support Internet access, also enable customers to buy goods and services wherever they are in the world. The increased availability of Internet hotspots have also, with the use of a netbook or laptop and dongle, increased customer's accessibility to e-Commerce websites.

e-Business

E-Business is a term used to describe companies run on the Internet or using technology to improve their business processes. This includes managing internal processes such as human resources, financial and administration systems, as well as external processes such as sales and marketing, supply of goods and services and customer relationships.

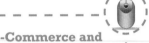

e-Commerce and e-Business
The term e-Commerce has a narrower meaning than e-Business. e-Commerce refers specifically to paying for goods and services, whereas e-Business covers the full range of business activities that can happen or be assisted via email or the Web. So e-Commerce is a subset of e-Business.

The most common implementation is an additional, or in some cases primary, place to sell. By selling products and services online, a company is able to reach a much wider consumer base. Exploiting the convenience, availability and worldwide reach of the Internet, many companies have discovered how to use it successfully. E-Business can be said to include e-Service – the provision of services and tasks over the Internet by application service providers.

Communication technology can contribute to the growth of e-Business with the use of tools such as mobile phones, personal digital assistants (PDAs), electronic data interchange, file transfer, facsimile, video conferencing, Internet, Intranets and extranets.

The benefits of e-Business

The benefits of using e-Business tools are the ability to streamline business processes and the ease of finding new markets. You also have control of the messages, images and information you send out and the company image you wish to promote.

E-Business means more than having a website – using e-Business tools can make your administrative and operational activities more efficient by:

- using the Internet to gather data about your industry, suppliers and products
- streamlining transactions by the use of online banking, financial management and stock control
- purchasing and selling using email or efax
- human resources management – by using an Intranet for news, policies, staff movements and enabling staff to apply for leave and access their personnel information online.

E-Business allows for the collaboration with other companies in production, advertising and marketing. Use of the technologies increases the throughput speed. Some of the advantages include:

- speed of communication
- consistency of message
- additional marketing capabilities
- reduction in business costs – lowering transaction costs, increasing efficient methods for payment such as using online banking, and reducing stationery and postage costs
- the opportunity to develop tailored customer support
- the ability to target specific groups – for example, a sports equipment company can place advertisements on football, rugby and athletics websites, knowing that the audience has a related interest
- cost reduction – compare the cost of a small advertisement in a magazine or the cost of printing and mailing catalogues, to the cost of a website
- increased access – there is no limitation to specific geographic areas; websites allow people all over the world to have access to the information you put online and websites can carry a much larger amount of information
- increased availability – a website provides 24-hour, 7-day information to existing and potential customers; you can display products and services to allow customers to access information immediately, and it allows you to provide up-to-date information
- interactivity – it allows you to get feedback from customers immediately; customers can communicate any concerns, complaints or questions.

The disadvantages of e-Business

One concern for e-Businesses is its dependence on technology and the potential consequences of a system failure. For example, in 2008 British Airways opened its new terminal at Heathrow Airport. Unfortunately, the baggage handling system did not operate as expected and the result was damaging for the company, not only in financial terms but also in PR terms. Other disadvantages include:

- Lack of personal service means that feedback about how people react to a product can be limited. If the only feedback is that people are buying products online, it does not help in the evaluation of product change or improvement.
- If the goods are not available locally it takes time and costs money to acquire them.
- The information about products is limited. Consumers cannot make full judgement on items as it is not possible to examine them in the same way as you would in a shop. Consumers can only see what the seller has selected, and these elements might not be those on which a consumer would base a decision.
- Returning goods online can be difficult. Questions arise about who pays for the return postage, whether the refund will be paid, and how long it will take.
- The concerns regarding the privacy and security of information and payment details. Will payment details (e.g. credit card details) be misused? Identity theft is a major concern.
- Any benefits of buying items online from a different country can be lost by delivery costs. This also means that buying individual items from a range of different companies is significantly more expensive than buying all of the items from one business because the goods can be packaged and shipped together.

Communication technology and e-Business

E-Business has benefited from communication technology as the use of the Internet has increased. With increased accessibility to the Internet more businesses are providing services to customers.

The use of the Internet has enabled more efficient research to be carried out; this is because of the increased range of information that can be found more easily. E-business also uses email to enable businesses to communicate with suppliers and customers more easily. The use of email has enabled businesses to reduce their paper and delivery/postage costs. Email, although not instant, does offer a faster delivery time than traditional methods.

E-Business has increased in use through the use of Intranets. Businesses can store company documents, policies and details on the Intranet server. This enables documents to be accessed by all staff even if they are working remotely.

The increased accessibility of the Internet has been assisted by the growth of broadband. Customers and suppliers are able to access websites more quickly as broadband offers a higher download rate. The increased use of the Internet has enabled businesses to use video-conferencing and VoIP. This technology enables businesses to reduce travel and accommodation costs.

e-Marketing

E-Marketing is also referred to as online marketing or Internet advertising. It is the marketing of products or services over the Internet. It is not as straightforward as building or promoting a website – effective e-Marketing requires a strategy for combining a company's goals with its website function. Consideration must be given to appearance, focusing on target markets, media and design.

The use of Information and communications technologies can help to support marketing as well as providing the opportunity for innovation in this field. Because the technology tools have become cheaper and more powerful, more information can be gathered, processed and delivered quickly using a variety of media formats. This can have significant financial benefits for the company.

Internet marketing has had an impact on several previously retail-oriented industries including music, film and banking, as well as the advertising industry itself. Internet marketing is now overtaking radio marketing in terms of market share.

E-Marketing allows appeal to a specific behaviour or interest, rather than a wider audience; marketing has previously divided markets according to age group, gender, geography and other general factors. E-Marketing has also had an impact on the electoral process in the USA. In 2008, candidates used Internet marketing to attract voters. Democratic candidate Barack Obama raised over $1 million a day, largely thanks to small online donors.

Companies must decide whether or not to have a separate e-Marketing plan, what it should contain, which objectives to set and how to align e-Marketing with product development.

As the importance of e-Marketing increases, the structure of marketing within a company may need to change. Developing a strategy to increase customer use requires a detailed analysis. e-Marketing should be based on knowledge of customer needs developed by researching their characteristics, behaviour, what they value and what keeps them loyal. Communications can then be delivered in tailored web and email messages, mobile phone messages and interactive digital TV.

E-Marketing is relatively inexpensive when considering the reach of the target audience. The nature of the medium allows consumers to research and purchase products and services at their own convenience. Therefore, businesses have the advantage of appealing to consumers in a medium that can bring results quickly.

The advantages of e-Marketing

The advantages of email marketing are:

■ relatively low cost – the physical costs of email are substantially less than direct mail
■ direct response encourages immediate action; email marketing encourages immediate response by an offer that can be redeemed immediately
■ lead times for producing creative aspects, and indeed the whole campaign, tend to be shorter than traditional media
■ it is easier and cheaper to personalise email
■ it is relatively easy and cost-effective to test different emails in terms of design and message
■ it allows integration – by combining email marketing with other direct media which can be personalised such as direct mail or mobile messaging, campaign response can be increased as the message is reinforced by different media.

The disadvantages of e-Marketing

The disadvantages of email marketing are:

■ the difficulty of getting messages delivered through different ISPs, corporate firewalls and web mail systems
■ the difficulty of displaying creativity as intended in the inbox
■ response – it can be difficult to keep customers engaged

Information overload
One of the major drawbacks of Internet technologies is information overload. People are bombarded on a daily basis by communications they do not want. Logging on brings information in the form of spam and pop-ups. Not attending to an inbox for a few days can result in tens of messages that can take a considerable time to check through; taking annual leave can result in hundreds of such messages!

- communications preferences – recipients will have different preferences for email offers, content and frequency, which affect engagement and response
- resource intensive – although email offers great opportunities for targeting, personalisation and more frequent communications, additional people and technology resources are required for their delivery.

E-Marketing requires customers to use new technologies and low-speed Internet connections are a barrier. If companies build large or overly-complicated websites, individuals connected to the Internet via dial-up connections or mobile devices may experience significant delays in content delivery.

Communication technology and e-Marketing

E-Marketing has seen a huge increase following the use of communication technology. E-Marketing enables a business to target their marketing campaign to a wide range of people – this is not geographically constrained.

Most websites have some form of advertising on them. Businesses are able to buy 'space' on other websites in order to advertise their company. These advertisements can be in the form of rolling banners, interactive advertisements or static text-based links.

E-Marketing utilises the details of customers who have bought goods from a business. Customer details are held in a database along with a record of the goods they purchased. When a new product is launched then an email can be sent to customers who have bought similar products.

E-Marketing is used by many different sorts of businesses. What is important to understand is that the increased use of communication technology has enabled businesses to increase their presence and enabled more people to know about their business.

Susceptibility to unauthorised access

Computer systems, networks, applications, and data can all be susceptible to unauthorised access and malicious attacks if appropriate measures are not taken to provide security. The nature of Internet communications means that your communications may be susceptible to data corruption, unauthorised access, interception and delays.

It is vital that you develop a plan to stop and deter unauthorised access to your data whether from within the company or externally. Keep the network secure with a firewall designed to protect web-enabled applications, block malicious email before it enters the network, control access and identify who is accessing data and applications. Network penetration testing is a way for companies to find out about vulnerabilities in their network security before hackers use them to break in.

Mobile and wireless security should also be considered as an unsecured, or poorly secured, wireless network and is vulnerable to accidental or deliberate intrusion. Once access is gained it can be used for illegal activities (such as data theft, system corruption and sabotage).

Threats can come from, for example, hackers, the unauthorised use of unsecured wireless Internet access, and through the manipulation of employees to obtain passwords and access sensitive data. Attacks include:

- ID spoofing in order to impersonate an authorised user or to obtain unauthorised privileges (including changing the access of a legitimate user)
- message modification by deleting, adding to, or altering content

- acceleration of data flow to assist in breaking down encryption
- monitoring transmissions for message content.

Unauthorised access to a network can be exploited to send spam or other messages, download or distribute illegal content, launch further attacks or engage in other online criminal acts. This type of activity can directly affect the security and privacy of information held on the system. The identity of a legitimate business can be assumed to carry out fraudulent or illegal transactions. This may involve the legitimate business being considered responsible for activities which may result in damage to reputation.

(For more on online threats, see Assessment Objective 6, pages 47–55.)

Portfolio Activity (AO1)

The Horse Stables is hoping to expand their use of communication systems. They currently sell horse feed through their website, but this is very limited. The owner of the Horse Stables has asked that you prepare a report to help her understand the different types of business communication systems that could be used by the Horse Stables to improve their business.

1   You need to investigate and describe at least three different types of business communication systems. You should explain, using examples, a range of benefits and drawbacks for each communication system you describe.

The owner of the Horse Stables has been told that she can increase her business by expanding into e-Commerce, e-Business and e-Marketing. However, she does not fully understand these areas or how communication technology has contributed to their growth.

2   You need to investigate and explain how communication technology has contributed to the growth of e-Commerce, e-Business and e-Marketing.

AO2: Explain the aids and barriers to effective communication

Introduction

Poor communication is the root of a large number of organisational problems; effective communication is essential for success. There are a number of things that can interfere with communication. The barriers may be in the understanding – in language and semantic problems, the ability of the receiver or the length of the communication – poor presentation, poor verbal skills or use of the wrong medium.

A company must communicate using many methods. These include:

- **internal communications** such as memos and minutes of meetings
- **external communications** with clients such as letters, reports and invoices; or advertising to prospective customers such as posters and leaflets.

The quality of the communication – judged by accuracy, clarity and presentation as well as the actual content of the message – is important because it creates a lasting impression. Using incorrect names, vague phrases, a condescending tone or including spelling errors will encourage a negative view of the company.

One of the most important aids to good communication is to be clear about what you are trying to achieve, and planning.

Purpose

When you are planning a communication, there are a number of things you need to consider – the purpose is the primary consideration. Who is this to? What is the message? What result do you wish to achieve?

Business writing has some generally accepted practices, the main one being that it is briefer and more concise than other types of writing. People in business are busy so your letter, memo or report may only get a very short time in which to be read. Get to the point quickly, support your reasoning and finish quickly.

Tables, charts, images, photographs and diagrams are often used in business documents. They are used to visually represent information in a clear, easily understood manner. They emphasise material and can present it more compactly and with less repetition than text.

Types of written business communication

Business letters

Business letters are the most common type of business correspondence. They are used to communicate with clients, to persuade or convince or to deliver information. They are a formal method of communication, so correct punctuation, an appropriate tone and good grammar should be used.

Use text that is concise, clear and well organised. State the purpose first, then explain any information you want to communicate. If you have points to emphasise, use bullets. It helps the reader if you discuss only one idea or topic per paragraph. Avoid unnecessary information and do not repeat yourself. The last paragraph is your conclusion – summarise your thoughts or make a recommendation; you could also make a request here.

Letters have a unique format. A typical business letter has the elements shown in Figure 1.1.

The remainder of the layout of a business letter usually follows these guidelines:

- body text is always single-spaced, with each paragraph aligned at the left margin
- double space (two paragraph returns) between paragraphs
- leave enough space for the written signature
- no space between the sender's name and the sender's position in the company
- notification of attachments is included at the end
- if a letter continues to a second page, do not use a letterhead. On the second plain sheet, enter the recipient's name, the page number and the date.

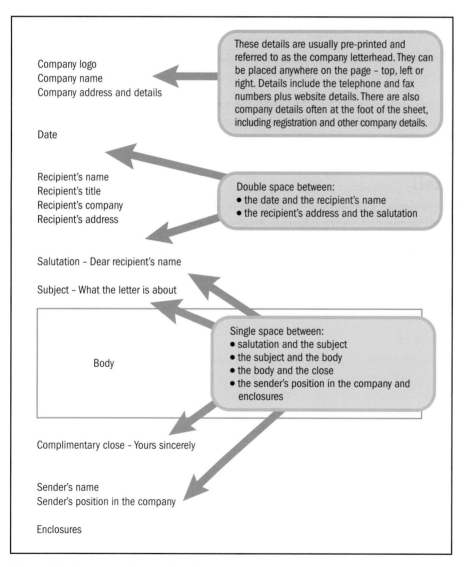

Figure 1.1 Elements to be used in a business letter

Memos

Memos are not used very often in business communication today, having been superseded by email. They are direct in style. They usually include the company logo and the word 'memo' – short for memorandum. They are to be used in the following circumstances:

- within the company
- for informal communication
- for non-sensitive communication.

Memos typically start with the following:

- From (who is sending it)
- To (who it is written for)
- Date (the date sent)
- Subject (what the memo is about).

The message is the next part of the memo and gives the information about why it has been written. Some memos contain conclusions. They are useful if you have several points to make and want to summarise them or make a recommendation, or if you want to make a request.

If attachments are to be included, this should be indicated at the end of the memo. Always identify and name your attachments.

If a memo continues to a second page, the name of the person to whom the memo is sent, the page number and the date should also be included on the second page.

Email

Email is similar to a letter or memo but it is sent by electronic means. It is quicker and usually more informal. Email messages are now the most common form of memo. For external clients, the writing style can be similar to both business letters and memos for business communication – especially so for external clients. However, there is a tendency to use more informal language in internal emails.

Reports

If you need to provide a description of a task or project, use a report to describe and summarise the activity. Reports are a standard part of business writing – the type of report is determined by the content and audience. To write a report you must plan the layout and organisation and decide what elements are useful and how to include them, so that they form an effective framework for the material and information.

Element	Description
Introduction	Brief summary of what is in the report – what is covered and the purpose. May also give some background information.
Methods	Description of how the material or information was gathered. This allows the reader to determine if your facts are reliable.
Facts	The information you have determined to be useful, necessary or important.
Discussion	How you have interpreted the facts.
Conclusions	The significance and meaning of the facts – what overall conclusions may be drawn about the project.
Recommendations	What actions the reader or company should take.

Figure 1.2 Elements of general reports

Leaflets, posters and flyers

Use leaflets, posters and flyers if you need a relatively cheap but highly effective way of attracting attention or to advertise special events. They should be informative but eye-catching and, most importantly, they should get your message across. As they are designed to capture the reader's attention, use only a few, powerful words. You do not have space to waste, but you do need to give readers enough information. For example, if you are offering a discount, let people know. You may vary the text size or colour to emphasise important points, or you may create a coupon on your flyer to encourage custom.

Invoices

Use an invoice to advise a buyer by displaying the items, quantities and prices of the goods or services provided. An invoice contains all the details of the items as well as information about the purchaser. There may be terms indicating how and when payment should be made.

A typical invoice contains:

- the word 'invoice'
- a unique reference number
- the date of the invoice
- the name and contact details of the seller
- the registration details of the seller, including the VAT registration number
- the name and contact details of the buyer
- the date the items are sold or despatched
- the buyer's purchase order number
- a description of the items
- the unit price of the items
- the total amount charged
- the VAT charged
- the payment terms – including the method of payment, date of payment and details of any late payment charges.

Agenda and minutes

If you are preparing for a meeting you will need an agenda. This is a list of what will happen in the meeting and the order it will follow. An agenda helps to give the meeting purpose and direction. The objectives of the meeting should be clearly stated.

An agenda is prepared before the meeting to identify the order in which items will be discussed and the minutes are the record of the meeting. Creating an agenda is one of the most important elements for a productive meeting. It identifies information such as the topics for discussion and the presenter for each topic.

Minutes

Minutes are a written record of a meeting. Minutes are very useful as they summarise what was discussed at a meeting, record key decisions taken and action points that were agreed. They should be concise and coherent. Minutes should include:

- the name of the organisation
- the date, time and location
- the name of the chair of the meeting
- a list of attendees
- the approval of minutes of the previous meeting
- outstanding issues from the previous meeting
- the main topics – who said what, issues discussed, major points raised and decisions taken.

Medium

Today, there are many more choices when it comes to selecting a suitable medium for your communication. You can choose to use Internet technology or traditional methods of posting and couriers. Your choice may be driven by time or cost considerations – to get a message to an employee as a matter of urgency then email or IM might be used, whereas a website can deliver your message 24 hours a day.

Email is less formal than writing a letter. It can be used as a brief and quick way of communicating. Email can also be used to send a more formal letter as an attachment. It can be cheaper than sending a letter through the traditional post. You can send documents and files as attachments and be sure they have reached their destination quickly and safely. There are disadvantages to using email too. As emails are more casual, people may not take the same care as they might do with writing an official letter. There is always a risk that your computer might catch a virus from an attachment.

If you require direct contact you should select one of the conferencing forms to exchange the communication. Communicate important, sensitive or controversial information face to face. Use the telephone to reach a quick agreement on a course of action. Use a memo or a letter to confirm agreements in writing.

The memo format is effective. You can see at a glance who wrote the memo to whom, when and about what – it makes retrieving information at a later date much easier.

A formal presentation should be concise, to the point and interesting for the audience. Use visual aids such as images or PowerPoint slides to help reinforce what you are saying. It is helpful to provide the audience with handouts that summarise your presentation.

Message

The message is what the communication is all about. What is it? Have you made it clear and will the receiver understand it? The content will determine the style, tone and language.

To effectively convey messages, regardless of the type, apply the following points.

- Identify your audience – the person or persons to whom you are writing. Think about what they know, who they are and what they want to see or hear.
- Be concise – do not use long sentences or complex constructions; keep it short and to the point.
- Cover all the information.
- Organisation is essential – if you have more than one topic or subject, use headings to make your message more readable and understandable. If you have a list of items, use bullet points.
- Limit each paragraph to one idea and try to keep the document flowing smoothly.
- Use the appropriate tone – in a business document use the first person (*I* or *we*).
- Use appropriate language – be as informal as the document allows. For example, a report will be more formal than a poster or flyer.
- Proofread your work – always check your work before sending it out.
- Identify attachments – if they become separated your reader will know that they were supposed to be there and can ask for them.

Text (font, style, size), formatting, layout

A presentation style, commonly referred to as a house style, is a set of standards for the design and writing of documents, for general use and for specific publications within a company. Styles are designed to make reading easier for the audience, and to convey the image and spirit of the company.

There is no best or easiest-to-read font, font type or font size. Typefaces have been around for about 550 years. There has been much debate regarding which font type is easier to read – serif or sans serif; research shows there is no difference in readability. There are as many experts who say to use sans serif as there are who take the opposite view. It is for you and the users to decide which typeface is easier or more difficult to read and it depends on context. No rule or guideline applies to every circumstance.

Many fonts have idiosyncrasies, and choice of font is a matter of personal preference. For example, look at the word 'Illegal' in three different fonts in Figure 1.3 (the font size is consistent at 11 point).

Serif and sans serif fonts
Serifs are the details on the end of the strokes of letters. A font with serifs is called a serif font, while a font without serifs is called sans serif (*sans* meaning without in French).

Font	What word looks like	Comments
Arial, 11 pt	Illegal	The first three letters are difficult to read owing to similarity between upper case 'I' and lower case 'l'.
Verdana, 11 pt	Illegal	Clear distinction between 'I' and 'l'
Comic Sans, 11 pt	Illegal	Much clearer distinction between 'I' and 'l'.

Figure 1.3 A comparison of letter styles in three fonts

Many fonts have similarities between two or more letters and no one notices most of the time. Notice, also, the difference in size and spacing, even though the font size is 11 point in each case.

There is a tendency to think that the bigger you make the type, the easier it will be to read, but this is not always the case. Look at the 12-point examples in different fonts in Figure 1.4.

Verdana, 12 pt	Arial, 12 pt	Times New Roman, 12 pt

Figure 1.4 A comparison of point size in three fonts

The size of the text should be suitable for the context, but generally font size smaller than 10 point is difficult for most people to read. Sentences entirely in capital letters are also considered to be hard to read, but there are always exceptions – comics traditionally use upper case in the speech bubbles.

A number of studies have been undertaken on font readability and legibility over a range of reader ages and abilities. The findings tend to show that, from a readability perspective, there is no significant difference between fonts. However, from a comfort perspective, those fonts that have been designed for viewing on-screen score higher for reading on-screen than those which have been designed primarily for print.

In terms of font readability, newspapers probably have the most experience. They have a similar approach worldwide and tend to use:

- serif fonts for close-set blocks of text
- (usually) sans serif fonts for large headlines
- a variety of font sizes, font weights (including emboldening) and capitalisation to break up the page and identify different focal points.

Language

The language used in communications depends to a large extent on the type of communication, its content and the audience. It can be formal – as in a letter, a report or minutes – or informal – as in emails, IM or memos. The important thing is that it is fit for purpose.

Communication, no matter what your intention is, may be misunderstood. Choose your words carefully. Language that describes what you want to say in your own terms may present barriers to those not familiar with your expressions and jargon, and may therefore exclude them.

Tone is also important – the tone of a letter may be cheerful, threatening, patronising, authoritative, demanding, confident, reassuring, and so on. Tone is an important stylistic term and has two broad categories – formal and informal.

Most technology and business communication is subject-centred rather than audience-centred. The focus is on products, processes, events, amounts – or on the company. Your writing should be helpful, direct and in a considerate tone – remember that you are writing for people.

Formal and informal writing

Formal writing is used when you want to convey your ideas to a wide audience. It should be clear, unambiguous and well structured. In general, it is inappropriate to write as you would speak. It requires effort to construct meaningful sentences, paragraphs and relevant arguments. Good formal writing may be difficult to write, but it is very easy to read. Paragraphs, sections, chapters, books and news reports all use the same structure – first make the topic clear, then expand upon it, and finally sum up – bringing everything back to the topic.

Speakers use informal, colloquial phrases to convey meanings other than what the words literally mean; for example, phrases such as 'at the end of the day' and 'hard facts'. Avoid this kind of imprecise phrasing in formal writing – the words you write should literally mean what they say. Among other benefits, avoiding informal language will ensure that your meaning is obvious. Writing is a permanent record of your ideas and should mean precisely what you have written. It should also be neutral to avoid causing offence, and it should never include slang or abbreviations.

Sometimes formal writing is appropriate for a subject or an audience. However, when you are writing to inform, entertain or sell, you may want to be more natural. Informal or conversational writing means writing in a way that is more similar to speech. It is not an excuse for bad writing – it means writing in a clear, concise way that anyone can understand. It may include writing to entertain or to inform people. For example, it is important when writing for the Web to write in a conversational tone – people want information and they want it fast; if your writing is stuffy and boring, they will click and go somewhere else.

Rules for formal writing	Rules for informal writing
■ Do not use contractions – for example, write 'it is' not 'it's'; 'do not' rather than 'don't'; 'he will' not 'he'll'. ■ No slang or jargon – for example, it does not 'rain cats and dogs'; an iPod is not 'cool'. ■ Avoid asking questions – this may appear conversational. ■ Avoid gender bias – use 'he or she' rather than only referring to 'he' or 'she'; use 'humanity' rather than 'mankind'. ■ Abbreviations – spell the abbreviation out the first time you use it; for example, write 'Instant Messaging (IM)' then subsequently use 'IM'.	■ Do not use exclamation marks. ■ Use contractions – you'll sound more natural if you say 'don't' and 'won't'. ■ Use *I* and *you* – it makes your writing more personal, as though you're really talking to your readers. ■ Don't be wordy – say what needs to be said, don't ramble. ■ Make sure your vocabulary is accessible to your readers; they will be put off by 'clever' words that they don't know.

Figure 1.5 Rules for formal and informal writing

Tips on using language

- Ask yourself – would I say that out loud? If the writing is filled with words that would not come naturally in conversation, it probably needs some changes.
- Say less, not more – start by saying more than necessary, then cut out anything unnecessary.
- Simple is best – make things as clear and easy to understand as possible.

Writing style

Style – the way you put together a sentence or group of sentences – is subjective. Different readers have different ideas about good writing style. However, it is always good style to keep sentences short. It is harder to spot grammatical errors in long, wordy sentences.

You should aim to say what you mean – get your point across and express your ideas directly, elegantly and persuasively. Express what you have to say in an appropriate tone – if in doubt, be conservative. Do not let the reader become distracted from what you are saying by how you are saying it.

Avoid or limit:

- wordiness – using more words than required
- clichés – write exactly what you mean (to help, ask yourself why or how)
- qualifiers such as 'very', 'often', 'hopefully', 'practically', 'basically', 'really', 'mostly'; eliminate some qualifiers and you will have a stronger, more direct point – they are necessary, but you should use them carefully
- using two words that mean the same thing (tautology), for example, 'whole entire production' – choose the more precise term and delete the other
- overuse of prepositional phrases, such as 'in', 'over', 'of', 'for', 'at'
- stock phrases you can replace with one or two words; for example, use 'professionally' rather than 'in a professional manner'.

Readability

Readability describes the ease with which a document can be read. Make your communications fit for purpose, agreeable and attractive in style, and depending on the type of communication, interesting and enjoyable. Concentrate on the ease of understanding owing to the writing – focus on content, coherence and organisation, and remember that clarity brings ease of reading.

You should be aware of the connection between the text and the reader's reading skill, prior knowledge and motivation. Successful communication is judged by the extent to which the reader understands it, is able to read it at an optimal speed and finds it interesting.

Accessibility

Because the Web is an increasingly important resource, it is essential that it provides equal access and equal opportunity to people with disabilities to participate more actively in society. Millions of people have disabilities that affect use and many sites have accessibility barriers that make it difficult or impossible for them to engage. Simple techniques such as changing browser settings can determine if a page meets some accessibility guidelines, but a comprehensive evaluation to determine if a site meets all accessibility guidelines is much more complex.

Rules of documentation writing

- Use short, simple, familiar words.
- Avoid jargon.
- Use culture- and gender-neutral language.
- Use correct grammar, punctuation and spelling.
- Use simple sentences, active voice and present tense.
- Begin instructions by starting sentences with an action verb.
- Use bulleted and numbered lists to make information visually accessible.

Accessibility
Accessibility means that people with disabilities have the right to understand, navigate, interact with and contribute to the Web. This includes people with visual, auditory, physical, speech, cognitive and neurological disabilities.

W3C

The World Wide Web Consortium (W3C) is the Internet governing body. It has issued web accessibility guidelines, which can be found on its website (www.w3c.org). When creating websites, it is important to include accessibility options, for example the ability to change text size or font colour.

Web accessibility evaluation tools are software programs or online services that help determine if a site meets accessibility guidelines. While accessibility evaluation tools can reduce the time and effort to evaluate a site, they cannot determine accessibility. Informed human evaluation is required to determine if a site is accessible.

The W3C provides a list of web accessibility evaluation tools. They do not endorse specific products as the information is provided by developers, vendors or users. The list does not provide a product quality rating nor is it presented as a complete or definitive listing.

Current legislation

By the terms of the Disability Discrimination Act (DDA) (1995, amended 2005), it is a legal requirement for websites to be accessible. (There is reference in Part III of the Act to the provision of goods, facilities and services, including websites. The DDA can be downloaded from the Equality and Human Rights Commission website – www.equalityhumanrights.com.) Companies can face legal action under the Act and the threat of unlimited compensation payments if they fail to make websites accessible.

As companies communicate with customers or employees by email, email attachments and email bulletins, they have a duty to assist those with disabilities. One thing that can be done is to consider different email formats – html, Rich Text Format (RTF) and Plain Text. They should also be aware of the principles and good practice in sending group emails. Although it may not be possible to provide for everyone who accesses electronic information, some adjustment in production can make it more suitable for a wider range of needs. This may include using appropriate styles and properties, and converting documents into portable document formats (PDFs).

Age, gender, cultural, emotional barriers

Effective communication within a company or organisation is very important as it means that messages are conveyed clearly with very little misunderstanding. Companies can often be made up of people from different cultures, different ages, different genders and different levels of experience. These differences within a company can create barriers to communication.

For example, there are many possibilities of miscommunication between cultures. A company may have employees from different countries whose first language may not be English. Many companies do business with their own company located in a different country – for example businesses based in the UK may have their IT Helpdesk in India. Businesses may also communicate with other companies and clients located in different countries.

It is important when communicating, that you are sensitive to the needs of people from other cultures whose first language may not be English. Remember to make sure your message is clear and avoid the use of colloquial speech.

Another barrier to effective communication is gender. Be careful not to use language that makes one gender seem superior to another. Use gender-neutral words such as police officer rather than policeman or salesperson rather than salesman. Try not to use gender-specific pronouns such as *he* and *she* – use *I, you* or *they* instead.

Age is another barrier to communication. Someone may look younger than they really are and their opinions may not be taken as seriously as someone who is seen to be older and more experienced. Also, someone who is older may be seen to be out of touch with modern technology or to not have the relevant skills needed in a modern technological workplace.

One of the chief barriers to open and free communication is the emotional barrier. Emotional barriers can include fear, anger, hostility and resentfulness. For example, many people hold back from saying what they think because they are scared they will look silly or will be judged.

Speed of delivery

Delivery speed will clearly depend on the method you use to send your communication. Use of any electronic method is going to be much faster than traditional methods such as the post.

Electronic communication helps companies to react much more quickly to business needs. If a quick response is required, for example to check details of an order, the location of products or the status of a delivery, electronic communication is vital to speed the response to customers. Instant messaging allows companies to provide immediate response.

Websites are available worldwide 24 hours a day, so even though they are static items they provide a fast way of communication. A website enables customers to communicate with and get information from a company outside business hours. This is of great assistance to customers located in different time zones in particular. Messages can be exchanged via a website between a company and its customers usually through email.

Again, email can be sent and received 24 hours a day, worldwide – it can provide the interactive side of a website or, more commonly, used simply as a tool for rapid exchange of a message. A message is usually received within minutes of being sent, which allows a much quicker response. It enables companies to respond to both internal and external queries and to process transactions much more quickly than by traditional means.

Conferencing – whether video conferencing or teleconferencing – allows immediate discussion and response to queries, problems and decisions. It allows all parties to exchange views, understand the current situation more clearly and clarify points immediately.

Portfolio Activity (AO2)

The Horse Stables are reviewing their current business documents. The owner is concerned that the information they contain is not being effectively communicated.

They have asked you to develop a range of new business documents and to ensure that the communication of information issues with the current documents are solved.

You need to write a report to:

- Explain the aids and barriers to effective communication. You should consider purpose, medium, message, text, formatting, layout, language, writing style, readability, accessibility, speed of delivery and age, gender, cultural, emotional considerations.

- You should provide at least four examples for each aid and barrier.

AO3: Design and create a presentation style for use in business documents

Types of written business communication

No matter the type of document, you should consider the tone, grammar, punctuation and spelling. Many businesses create house rules for spelling, italics and punctuation to provide consistency in their communications. Organisations produce style guides for their publications such as newsletters, news releases and websites – the focus is on identity and branding.

A business's house style may apply to the following types of written business communication:

- email
- report

- letter
- memo
- leaflet, poster or flyer
- invoice
- agenda
- minutes.

However, each of the above will have separate rules applied as part of the house style. For an overview of each of these document types, see pages 14–18.

Companies produce style guides (a set of standards for the design and writing of company documentation) to enable all employees to produce visually consistent work. It provides guidance, identifies writing conventions, grammar and tone. The style is chosen to demonstrate the corporate identity.

Presentation styles for business document templates

When choosing the method of communication, you need to consider the type of software to use for that type of communication. You will therefore need to think about the message you are communicating, what response (if any) you require from your audience and how the message will be delivered to your audience.

Types of software

Word processing

Word processing is the use of a computer to create, edit and print documents. It allows you to create a document, store it electronically, display it on-screen, modify it and print it. The advantage of word processing is that you can make changes without re-entering data.

There is the facility to format text – specify page size, margins, alignment, emphasis, line spacing, colour, font, font size, etc. There are also useful facilities such as find and replace, headers and footers, tables, macros, etc. There is the facility to display text in columns, as in desktop publishing.

Desktop publishing

Desktop publishing is the use of specialised software to create documents for desktop or commercial printing. It is the production of documents such as newsletters, brochures, books and other publications that were once created manually using a variety of techniques with photo-typesetting machines. It involves the assembly of digital files in the correct format for printing.

Desktop publishing allows graphic designers and non-designers to create visual communications for professional or desktop printing. There is the added component of graphic design – the process of combining text and graphics and communicating an effective message in the design of logos, graphics, brochures, newsletters, posters, signs and other types of visual communication.

The line dividing word processing from desktop publishing is constantly shifting, but desktop publishing applications have finer control over typographical characteristics, such as kerning (changing the spacing between text characters by either expanding or decreasing the amount of space), colour separation (printing one page for each colour used in black and white to determine how colours are laid out) and full-colour output.

Presentation software

Presentation software is used to create slide presentations. The purpose of a presentation is to present information, not overwhelm the audience with a demonstration of the software, which is just a tool. A presentation should have purpose, simplicity and consistency. Keep colours, clip art and templates consistent with your main objective.

Is the purpose of the presentation to inform, persuade or sell? Can it be a little light-hearted or is a more formal approach most appropriate to the subject and audience?

Webpages

Web design is a form of electronic publishing. It is the process of creating a single webpage or an entire website. It may involve design, production and creation, but the focus is on how the page or site looks and feels.

Some of the aspects included in web design are graphics and animation creation, colour selection, font selection, navigation design, content creation, html authoring, JavaScript programming and e-Commerce development.

Preparing a style guide

You should consider how you want to present the company that you are working for. Your guide for their house style may include rulings for graphic design to specify preferred layout and formatting, whereas a website section may focus on visual and technical aspects.

You may want to specify the programs to be used for documents in production, such as word-processing, desktop publishing or presentation software. The design rules that form the basis of your house style might include which colours to use, fonts and font sizes to use, how to format text, how to display text and the position of the logo. Below is an example of a house style showing the range of elements that need to be considered. An example has been given for each element.

Font	Use Arial, point size for text is 11 point.
Alignment	All text, including headings, should be left aligned and the right-hand side should be ragged.
Spacing	Paragraph spacing: one line space between paragraphs. Two line spaces above every heading. Use one space only after all punctuation marks.
Page numbering	For all documents over two pages use Arial, 10 point, centred at the foot of the page.
Emphasis	Use sparingly for maximum impact. If a word or phrase does need emphasising, use **bold** only.
Headings	Use initial capitals only, align left, kept as short as possible, do not end in a full stop. Bold, no underlining.
Acronyms	No full stops between letters e.g. ISP not I.S.P. Spell out in full on first use, with the abbreviation following in brackets. Subsequently, use the abbreviation.
Dates	Use the form 20 May 2009, (day, month, year) without commas.
Numbers	In text, write numbers from one to nine as words and 10 and above as figures. In tables and charts, use figures.
Colours	Use Yellow (or Pantone 109C) and Blue (or Pantone 2746C).

Logo	Insert logo at the top right of the page.
Numbered paragraphs	If using numbered paragraphs, be consistent with the numbering and avoid too many levels. Do not use brackets or full stops after the number. Example:

1   First level (indent measurements are 0cm and 1cm)

      1.1   Second level (indent measurements are 1cm and 2cm)

           1.1.1   Third level (indent measurements are 2cm and 3cm)

Bullets	Use round bullet points only. If you are including a bulleted list after a statement ending with a colon:

- use lower case for the first letter of the first word
- end the last bullet point with a full stop.

If the bullet points do not follow a colon, for each point use an initial capital and a full stop at the end of the point.

Diagrams and illustrations	• Include diagrams wherever possible, they add meaning to the text.

- Diagrams should be produced at an early stage, with explanatory labels in plain English.
- Use no more than 4 colours in total.

A style sheet is very important. This forms the basis for the house style of a company, by using the house style all documents produced by a company will look the same. When the style sheet has been created, it must be used every time the template for a document is created.

Create document templates

You can create templates in word-processing, desktop publishing, presentation and webpage software. In all the applications you can include page layout, text flow, paragraph formats, graphics (including lines and borders) and images (including logos). Depending on the application you are using, and what you are using it for, it is also possible to incorporate a corporate signature; this is mostly used in letters and emails. Style sheets are generally incorporated into the templates, particularly in word-processing, desktop publishing and webpage software.

To add an image such as the company logo or the logo of partner companies into templates in word-processing, desktop publishing, webpage creation and presentation software, the process is the same. On the Insert menu, select Picture and then go to the image location and click Insert. The image will be placed in your current file. You can then manipulate it by changing the position and size.

You can also create a corporate signature for email messages. This is covered on pages 41–42.

Word processing templates and styles

When you create a document that contains a lot of specialised formatting, you can save those settings as a template to use in documents in the future. A template is a style guide for documents – it can contain formatting, styles, headers, footers and macros, in addition to dictionaries, toolbars and auto text entries.

Before you create a template, decide what you want to include. You can edit your template or make changes to elements in documents created from the template, but it will save time if you plan it carefully. You might want to consider the following points:

- If creating a template to use as a letter, insert a date field that will update automatically each time the template is opened.
- On letters, include the company letterhead details, the salutation, the close and signature details.
- On headers and footers, use auto text for information that may change, such as the date, time and page numbers, as well as the document title, file path, etc.
- Add any text that will be included in all documents based on the template.
- Establish columns, margins, tabs, endnotes, footnotes, etc.
- If you want to use specific macros, include them with the template.
- If your document contains different areas with different formatting, use a descriptive name as placeholder text such as 'title', 'heading' and 'body'.

When you have planned what you want to include in the template and have created a blank document containing all the elements, you can save it as a template.

Alternatively, you can create a template based on an existing template. For example, in Microsoft Word you can click on File, New and it will give you the option of choosing a blank template in various formats such as XML, webpage or email message.

Creating a style

Although there are a variety of pre-defined styles, you can create your own. Styles help you to apply consistent formatting to your document.

1 To open the Styles and Formatting task pane, click the Styles and Formatting icon on the Formatting toolbar.

2 Click New Style. The New Style dialogue box will be displayed (Figure 1.6). You can now define the style – apply the font and other formatting such as bold, italics, underline, colour and size; and apply alignment, margins, line spacing, and indents.

3 Enter a name for the style in the Name box and click OK. Repeat to define any further styles you require.

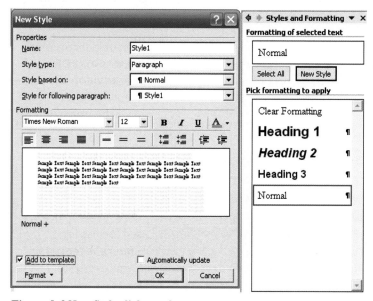

Figure 1.6 New Style dialogue box

When you have defined a style you can apply it to any section of your document. To apply any style to text, select the text that you want in a specific style. The Styles and Formatting task pane will display the style applied to it. You can change the style by clicking the style you require from the list.

You can also update a style when you make changes to text by selecting Automatically update in the New Style dialogue box.

You can also change paragraph formatting such as alignment, indent a paragraph or change the line spacing to single, 1.5 or double by going to the Formatting menu and then selecting Paragraph.

When you are setting the styles, you must refer back to the style sheet. This will ensure that the document is consistent with the house style. You will also need to consider the document you are creating. For example, if you are creating a letter then only one style will be needed as the justification, font, size and style of writing used in a letter must be the same throughout.

However, if you are creating a report then you will use a range of styles. These styles will relate to the different components of the report e.g. body text, bulleted and numbered list and different levels of headings. The style sheet must be referred to at all times.

Borders and shading

Add borders, shading and fills to emphasise elements of your work. They can be added to pages, text, tables, cells within tables, objects, images and web frames.

1 Select the text, table or section you want to add shading to.
2 Click Format, Borders and Shading. The Borders and Shading dialogue box will be displayed.
3 Select any of the Borders, Page Border or Shading tabs and apply your options.
4 Alternatively, use the Borders icon on the toolbar.

Options are displayed, including to apply to any or all sides of each page in a document, to pages in a section, etc. You can add page borders in many line styles and colours, as well as a variety of graphical borders.

Colour

When preparing written communications for a company you should incorporate their company logo and the corporate colour scheme. If you are involved in preparing the style guide for a corporate identity you should consider these points regarding use of colour:

■ Use a limited range of colours; selective use of colour enhances text, too much distracts.
■ Select colour that enhances the company logo.
■ Limit the use of colour in formal documents.
■ Use coloured borders, bullets and blocks to draw attention to specific details.
■ Use a wider range of colours that compliment the corporate colours in advertising copy, such a leaflets, flyers and posters.
■ Use a colour scheme that is appealing to the eye. Look at the combinations in Figure 1.7 and see which you prefer, then experiment with your own.

Purple on yellow	Green on white
White on black	Black on orange
White on green	Yellow on black
White on red	White on purple
Black on white	Red on white
Purple on white	Orange on black

Figure 1.7 Colour combinations

Desktop publishing templates and styles

A template is a master copy of a publication used as a starting point to design new documents. It may be as simple as a blank document in the desired size and orientation or as elaborate as a nearly complete design with placeholder text, fonts and graphics that need only a small amount of customisation of text.

Templates can be used to create business cards, brochures, greeting cards or other desktop documents. You can also design your own templates.

Page layout

Page layout or page composition is the process of arranging text and graphics on the page. A good composition is one that is pleasing to look at and effectively conveys the message. To achieve this, place each text or graphic element on the page so that they have a visual connection to each other. Use horizontal or vertical alignment, align objects along the same edge or centre them – a grid can help you to do this.

In order to create effective and pleasing compositions, you should plan how many colours, font sizes and columns of text to use and whether images will appear next to each other or be spread out.

To create a template

1   Create the publication you want to use as a template, including all the points above.
2   On the File menu, click Save As.
3   In the File name box, type a name for the template.
4   In the Save as type box, click Publisher Template. Click Save.

Changing templates

You can personalise an existing template if it is not quite right for your needs by changing the fonts, text formatting and colours as well as the layout. You can use the designs held within your software. For example, if you want to create a leaflet or brochure you can use the template Brochure design in Microsoft Publisher. If you like the overall layout of a template, you could alter it in any of the following ways:

■   changing the colours used can cause dramatic changes – turn a three-colour scheme to black and white
■   move elements around, turn the entire template upside down or flip it horizontally

- change the graphics – add your own in place of any pre-selected graphics
- change the lines or boxes – change the size or placement to fit your text
- alter the font or font size, but be careful to select one that is appropriate to the design – layouts and fonts have a casual or formal tone
- change the leading or alignment of the text
- add text embellishments such as dropped capitals or bullet lists.

Presentation templates and styles

Existing templates can force you to fit your ideas into an unsuitable structure. They often contain distracting backgrounds and bright colour combinations. It is useful to be able to create your own distinctive look.

On the task pane, click General Templates to open the Template dialogue box. You will find three tabs: General, Design Templates, and Presentations.

- The Design Templates tab offers slide designs.
- The Presentations tab offers complete presentations, ready for you to fill in the blanks. There are templates for everything from a business plan to a company meeting to a marketing plan. Just double-click a design or a presentation to launch a new presentation using the template's settings.

Creating your own presentation template

To create your own template, particularly if you have company logos or other graphics created especially for your presentations, follow these steps:

1. To create a custom template, open the file you want to save as a template. On the task pane under the 'New from existing presentation' section, click Choose presentation. Alternatively, create one from scratch.
2. Choose File, Save As.
3. In the Save as type drop-down list, choose Template (*.pot). The template will be saved in the Templates folder automatically.
4. Choose a name for your template, making sure to preserve the .pot file extension, and click Save.

You'll find your new template on the General tab in the Templates dialogue box.

Webpage templates and styles

As with word processing and desktop publishing, there are many pre-made page templates to assist you in creating page designs.

1. To select one, click File, select New then Page or Web. The New Page or Web panel will be displayed (Figure 1.8).
2. Look for the 'New from template' section, and click Page Templates.
3. FrontPage will open the Page Templates dialogue box. On the General tab you can select a template to use (Figure 1.9).
4. To help you decide which template is best suited for your needs, single-click on a template. It will be displayed in the Preview window with a short text description above.
5. When your decision is made, highlight it and click OK. FrontPage will open with a new webpage in that template for you to edit.

On the Style Sheets tab you can select a style that you wish to use (Figure 1.10). To help you decide which one is best suited for your needs, single-click on a style. It will be displayed in the Preview window with a short text description above.

Figure 1.8 New Page or Web panel

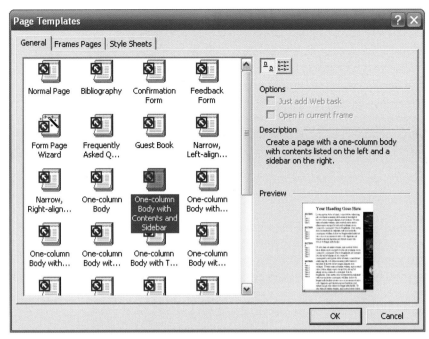

Figure 1.9 Selecting a template in Page Templates

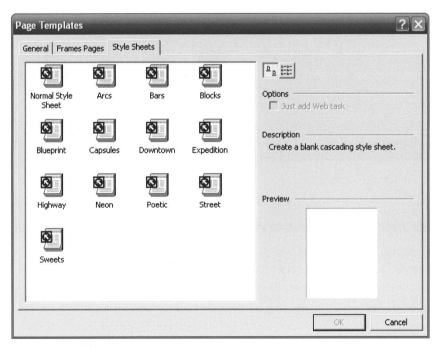

Figure 1.10 Selecting a style

The different types of software that can be used to create documents all contain pre-loaded templates. When a business is creating its own set of documents the first step is to develop a house style (corporate image). Once this has been created then a style sheet should be developed. This will ensure that all documents follow the house style. Although the pre-loaded templates are available on the software, it is not advisable to use these. The use of these pre-loaded templates to create the documents will not ensure conformity to the house style. The pre-loaded templates are very useful for getting ideas, but the templates must be created from scratch if they are to be unique to a business and follow the house style.

Portfolio Activity (AO3)

The Horse Stables have asked that you design and create a new house style. They have also asked that, based on the documents below, you create templates using this house style. The documents you need to create templates for are:

- A4 three-column leaflet
- An advertisement
- Covering letter to magazines regarding the advertisement
- Electronic slide presentation
- Report.

1 Design a house style for The Horse Stables.
2 Create a style sheet for The Horse Stables. This must be based on the house style you have already designed.
3 Create templates using at least three different types of software for the defined documents. The templates will be applied to the documents you will produce in the next task. You should consider:
   - page layout
   - text flow
   - graphic style, including lines, borders and shading
   - paragraph formatting
   - images, such as the company logo.

You need to make sure that the templates you create are usable for the Horse Stables.

You are able to present the evidence for this Assessment Objective in an electronic format..

AO4: Demonstrate the effective use of written communication using ICT in a business context

Language and writing style

For this section you will prepare five different documents – a leaflet, an advertisement, a letter, a presentation and a report. You should use the templates that you prepared in Assessment Objective 3. You will have the opportunity to use both formal and informal language and presentation. You should be able to explain your choices to the company.

For each document, consider your objectives and audience. What do you want your readers to remember or do? Is your audience internal (i.e. within the same company) or external (i.e. customers, or representatives of other companies)? What is your audience's level of understanding of the message – does it need explaining in detail, or will they already know a lot about the subject?

Make sure that your style is appropriate for your audience. If you are communicating with internal peers (i.e. colleagues at the same level as yourself) you can use a more informal style. If you are presenting information to a client or senior management, you need to use a more formal style. (See also Assessment Objective 2, pages 14–24.)

Formatting

When presenting information in a written document, you should consider the formatting you use. Make sure that it helps convey the message and doesn't hinder it (see Assessment Objective 2, pages 19–20).

Tables and numerical data

Tables are used to identify exact values – they arrange data in a way that makes it easy to read and understand. Before using tables and numerical data, check the source and accuracy.

If you use a table, chart or diagram to explain or illustrate a point, place it close to that text.

Appropriate layout and styles

When you are selecting a suitable style, consider the company and the image they want to portray. You should also think about how the style can be adapted for all the different types of communication you will prepare.

- Too much variation detracts from the information – keep the number of fonts to a minimum, but you may, for example, use a different font size for headings.
- Use different techniques to emphasise text – but not too many.
- Use a logo – it will let people know, before they even look at the rest of the information, who it belongs to.

- Avoid the use of 'all capital letters', which makes most words look the same. Words are read by the shape of the word not by individual letters, so using lower case will aid word recognition.
- The chosen layout should be appropriate to the document.
- Use white space to lead the reader to important information.
- Photographs, illustrations, diagrams and charts can present the same information in different ways; labels must be close to diagrams.

Borders and shading

Add borders, shading, and fills to emphasise elements of your work. They can be added to pages, text, tables, cells within tables, objects, images and web frames. Use the AutoFormat feature to apply a variety of borders, fonts and shading to tables, text boxes and sections of text.

Text boxes

A text box is a container for text or graphics that can be positioned on a page and sized. You can create text boxes and link them together to make text flow from one part of a document to another. They can be moved and re-sized.

Columns

Use this feature to display your work in more than one column. It is used mostly in publications, such as newspapers and magazines. It is widely used in leaflets. You can use columns for an entire document, part of a document or a section of a document. You can select the number of columns you want to use.

Bullets and numbering

Use bullets and numbering to clarify points and make it easier for the reader to identify important information.

To use these features in Word, click on the Format menu, then Bullets and Numbering. The Bullets and Numbering dialogue box will be displayed.

You can select the Bulleted tab or the Numbered tab to apply the chosen feature. You also have the facility to customise the feature in your chosen style. Alternatively, use the Bullets or Numbering icon on the Formatting toolbar.

Accuracy checking

Spelling and grammar checkers

Check spelling and grammar automatically as you enter text, and then use the spell check facility. When the spell checker encounters a word it does not recognise, it identifies similar words in its dictionary and displays a list with the most likely match highlighted.

The grammar checker identifies potential problems by analysing the text. It is designed to identify the most typical or frequent problems.

You can customise the way spelling and grammar is checked by:

- setting preferences such as skipping text during a spelling and grammar check or choosing a preferred spelling for a word
- selecting the grammar and style rules used during a grammar check

- showing or hiding the wavy underlines used to mark possible spelling and grammar problems
- using custom dictionaries for technical terms, acronyms or other specialised terms that might not be included in the main dictionary.

Checking case

To enable capital letters to be displayed appropriately, ensure that the options in the AutoCorrect dialogue box are ticked (Figure 1.11).

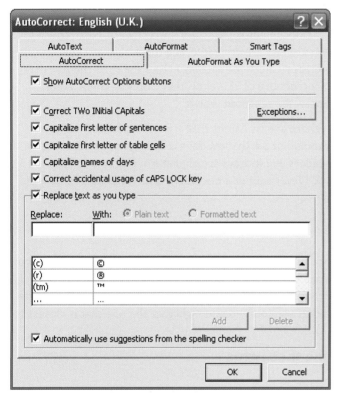

Figure 1.11 The AutoCorrect dialogue box

1 On the Tools menu, click AutoCorrect Options.
2 To set the capitalisation options, ensure that boxes 2 to 6 are ticked.
3 Click OK.

You also have options when amending text.

1 Highlight the text you want to change.
2 On the Format menu, select Change Case.
3 The Change Case dialogue box will be displayed (Figure 1.12).
4 Select the option you want to apply to amend your text.
5 Click OK.

Figure 1.12 The Change Case dialogue box

Proofreading, checking consistency and layout

If your communications have incorrect spelling, grammatical errors or poor formatting, this will be very distracting for the reader and indicate your lack of care and interest in getting the documents right, whereas they should reflect positively on you and the company. You need the tools of the trade to be effective – a dictionary, a thesaurus and a style manual – and you have actually got to use them.

Most programs have a spell checker, but these are not perfect. There will also be a thesaurus. Using it will help with alternatives for repeated words, making your text less repetitive and hopefully more interesting.

It is your responsibility to identify style problems. Your program can be set up to alert you to incorrect spacing between sentences, punctuation in or outside quotation marks and punctuation within lists, but you must be familiar with the company style guide and ensure it is applied consistently.

One of the most effective ways of proofreading is by working from the outside – make sure the margins are correct, check the headings are formatted appropriately, check that the document is paginated correctly, etc. Next, check for content, for example that sentences are complete, and make sure any corrections have not introduced new errors. Check for spelling errors the spell checker may not identify, such as the incorrect use of 'there' or 'their', double-check every questionable word, and review for repeated words.

When you are happy that there are no names that are not capitalised or words that are capitalised that should not be, that the font is appropriate, your margins, paragraph indentations, headers and footers are all uniform and correct, you are ready to submit your work. Never submit a document until it has been proofread completely.

Thesaurus

A thesaurus is a useful tool for writing. Repeating the same words and phrases can jar with the reader and make the information less interesting. A thesaurus will help you choose suitable alternatives to make your message more readable. It provides a list of synonyms for the text you look up, and highlights the one that is closest to what you have typed.

To look up text in the thesaurus

1 Highlight the text.
2 On the Tools menu, point to Language, and then click Thesaurus (Figure 1.13).
3 The Thesaurus dialogue box will be displayed. Make your selections, then click Close.

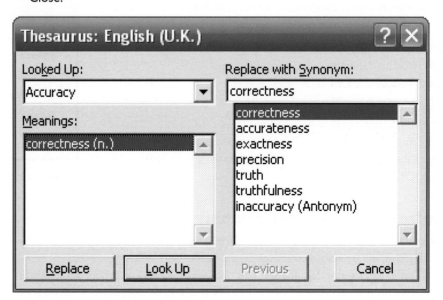

Figure 1.13 The Thesaurus dialogue box

Portfolio Activity (AO4)

The Horse Stables are happy with the house style and style sheet you have created. They have asked that you use the templates you have already created for AO3, to produce at least four of the documents. All the documents you produce must follow the house style and style sheet.

You need to:
1   Create a least four of the documents using the templates, house style and style sheet you created for AO3. You must ensure that you include the following in your documents:
    - tables
    - bullets
    - auto-numbering
    - columns
    - text boxes.
2   Use software tools to ensure that the final copies of your documents are well-structured and formatted, and contain no errors.
3   Justify the purpose and suitability of each document for the Horse Stables.

Assessment Guidance

Pass – Candidates use at least two different types of written communication. They will use at least two features from: tables, bullets, auto-numbering, columns and text boxes. The documents will be appropriately formatted using the housestyle designed as part of AO3 with few inconsistencies. The documents will contain few errors and be mainly fit for purpose.

Merit – Candidates use at least three different types of written communication using templates they have created. They will include the effective use of at least three features from: tables, bullets, auto-numbering, columns and text boxes. The documents will be appropriately formatted using the housestyle designed as part of AO3 with few inconsistencies. The documents will contain few errors and be fit for purpose.

Distinction – Candidates use at least four different types of written communication using templates they have created. They will justify the suitability of each document for that purpose. They will include the effective use of at least four features from: tables, bullets, auto-numbering, columns and text boxes. The documents will be well structured and appropriately formatted using the housestyle designed as part of AO3 and will be of near-professional business quality.

Most companies now use email for communication, so it is important that you understand how to use it and the main functions of the systems. You should be aware of these features, even though they may vary from one system to another.

Standard features

Use of cc and bcc

These features are used to include a copy of an email to another person (cc) and a silent copy to another person (bcc). The email address should be entered in the cc box of the email message, see Figure 1.14.

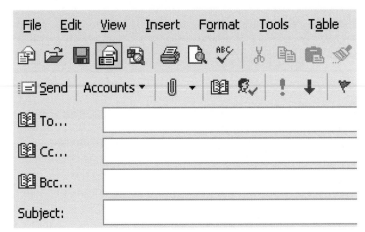

Figure 1.14 Using cc and bcc

The cc feature lets you send the same email to more than one person. This can of course be done by just sending the email to more than one person via the 'To' feature, however, you would use the cc feature rather than 'To' if the email was, for example, for information only. If you cc someone into an email, then a reply from that person, or people, is not really necessary or expected.

The bcc feature enables you to send the same email to more than one person, but only the email address in the 'To' box is shown. This feature can be used to protect email addresses. If you are using the bcc feature then it is good netiquette to put your own email address in the 'To' field.

High and low importance

Use this feature to identify those messages that are, literally, more important.

The importance level is set to normal. To change the level on a new message, click the appropriate icon on the toolbar (Figure 1.15).

Alternatively, click on the Options icon on the toolbar (Figure 1.16). The Message Options dialogue box will be displayed (Figure 1.17). Under Message settings, Importance, make your selection from Low, Normal and High.

Figure 1.15 High and Low importance icon

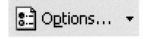

Figure 1.16 Options icon

This feature can be used to denote to the receiver if the information in the email is urgent/important. Important emails can be 'flagged' or marked by the receiver's email provider and appear with a marker/flag next to them.

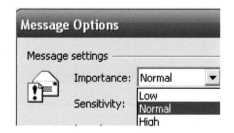

Figure 1.17 Setting importance levels

The feature may relate to the information itself being of significance, or it may be that you want to pass on the information quickly i.e. there is an urgency to get the information to the recipient.

Level of confidentiality

Use this feature to identify a message as private, personal or confidential:

1 In the message where you want to set the sensitivity, click the Options icon on the toolbar.
2 The Message Options dialogue box will be displayed (Figure 1.18). Under Message settings, Sensitivity, make your selection.

This feature could be used if personal information is contained within the email. For example, if the human resources department of a large company need to email a member of staff their pay details then the confidentiality would be set to Private.

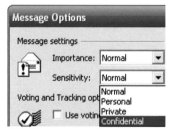

Figure 1.18 Setting confidentiality

Address book

Use the address book feature to store the email addresses of your contacts. Whenever you want to send a message, rather than having to remember the email address, you can select it from your address book. You can view, edit, search or print contact information from it.

Creation and use of a professional signature

You can set up a signature to add to an email you are sending. It can contain your name, address, phone number, company details such as your job title and the company web address. Outlook enables you to store email signatures and will also add an email signature to every outgoing message, ensuring that the signature is consistent in all email communications.

Creating an email signature

You may want to create a signature that will appear on all your emails.

1 Click on Signatures (or your system's equivalent) – Figure 1.19.
2 Select Setup Signatures. The Setup Signatures dialogue box will be displayed (Figure 1.20).

Figure 1.19 Setting up a signature

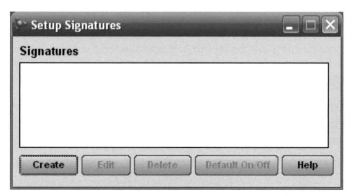

Figure 1.20 Setup Signatures dialogue box

3 Click Create. The Create Signature dialogue box will be displayed (Figure 1.21). Enter a name for the signature.

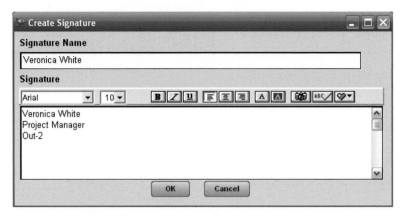

Figure 1.21 Create Signature dialogue box

4 In the bottom box, set up the actual signature – enter your name, title, company details, etc. Click OK.
5 In the Setup Signatures dialogue box, the name of the signature you have created will be displayed (Figure 1.22). Click on Default On/Off. This signature will be placed on all emails that you send.
6 Close the dialogue box.

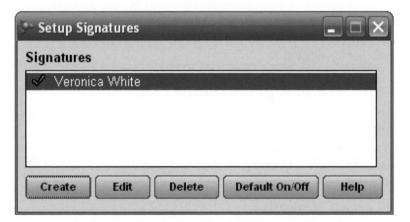

Figure 1.22 Setup Signatures dialogue box showing signature

It maybe that people create and use more than one signature. For example, the details, such as address of the business, contained within a signature used within that business will be less than those needed for external emails.

Managing your account

Very few people who use email have any training on how to organise the accumulated messages. An effective email system is easy to establish and maintain, as long as it is not too complicated.

■ The inbox should only contain emails that need some sort of action or response – a reply, further investigation or some other procedure. They will form your action list.

- Put as much information as possible in the subject line of your emails to clarify the message. This will also assist in locating the email later on.
- You may want to set up a personal account with a webmail provider.
- You may need to change the name on the account. The username related to an email account may not be recognisable as your name. You can change the account settings so that your correct and recognisable name is shown on your emails.
- Account settings may also have to be changed if you accessing your email account through a broadband dongle and a laptop, or an iPhone.

Email etiquette

When sending email there are points you should be aware of, such as using an appropriate subject – one that describes the content clearly. When attaching files to email messages you should consider the amount of time it will take to download, particularly if it is an image file. For example, an image saved in .jpg format will be about 30 per cent of the size of the same image saved in .gif format. Try to select a file type that is more helpful to the recipient, particularly if they do not have a high speed connection. Some companies have restrictions on the size of files they will accept, and if your file is too big it will not be delivered.

Netiquette is a term referring to good practice while using Internet facilities such as individual websites, emails, newsgroups, message boards or chatrooms. Some examples of netiquette include:

- Do not use someone else's name or masquerade as another person.
- Do not post or distribute illegal material.
- Do not use abusive or threatening language.
- Do not post remarks regarding people's gender or race.
- Do not spam message boards or chatrooms with repeated messages.
- Do not try to obtain or use someone else's password.
- Do not try to obtain personal information about someone.

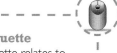

Netiquette
Netiquette relates to online behaviour. It requires people to post constructive and relevant messages. Posting messages on a different topic to the requested subject is seen as bad netiquette. Reading your messages for bad spelling and grammar is seen as good netiquette.

Advanced features

Multiple attachments, zipped files, embedded files

In business you may need to exchange documents, drawings or other data with clients or colleagues. When sending email, it is possible to add any number of attachments in any number of formats, for example documents, workbooks, presentations, etc. You can also embed files within the email rather than sending them as an attachment.

Zipped files allow many files to be placed into one zipped folder. This means that when the folder is attached to the email it can be sent and received as one attachment. When the zipped folder is received all the files contained within the folder can be downloaded at one time. This saves space in the receiver's inbox and can also save time when downloading. Zipped folders can be password protected.

Folders to organise mail

Most systems store emails for a specified period of time – once opened, they will generally be stored automatically in a separate folder. You may also need to keep email messages for future reference. You can keep emails in your inbox or create and name folders within the mailbox structure. You can set up individual folders for people with whom you communicate often or folders relating to specific topics.

Email rules

Applying rules to the messages helps you to organise and manage your emails. You can apply specific actions to messages. You can add exceptions, so that the rule is not applied if any of the exceptions is met. The rules are automatically applied when messages arrive or when you send a message. For example:

- set up a rule so that all emails from one specific person are stored in a folder as soon as they are received.
- assign the category Stables to all messages you send that have the word 'stables' in the Subject box.

You can run rules manually. This allows you to apply them to messages already in your inbox or in another folder.

To set a rule, click Tools, Rules Wizard. The Rules Wizard is displayed. Click New. You can now start creating a rule from a template, or start from a blank rule (Figure 1.23).

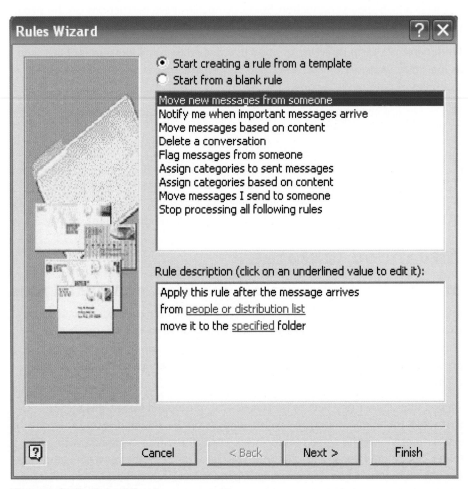

Figure 1.23 The Rules Wizard

Using this wizard allows you to automate actions for messages. The top box contains common types of rule. If you do not find the rule you want to apply, click 'Start from a blank rule' then 'Check messages when they arrive' or 'Check messages after sending', depending on when you want the rule applied. A sentence is displayed in the Rule description box that describes what the rule does.

Groups/distribution lists

If you regularly send email to the same group of people, you can create a group/distribution emailing list in your address book. This saves you having to add each email address individually every time you send an email to the group.

To create a group emailing list

1 In the Address Book window, click the Group Options then Add Group to create a new group list.
2 In the Manage Group window, enter the name of the new group.
3 Select contacts to add to the group from the Contact List – a list of all names in your Address Book – and click Add.
4 Enter any additional email addresses that are not already in your Address Book, but that you want to add to the group.
5 Click Save.

Distribution lists can be used if a group of people regularly receive the same email. For example, a large company who have lots of shops may need to send the same email to all the shop managers. If a distribution list is set up, this can contain all the email addresses of the shop managers. The list can be given a name, and when an email needs to be sent the named distribution list is used to provide the addresses in the 'To' field.

Archiving

To keep your mailbox manageable, you need another place to store (archive) old items that are important but not frequently used. You also need a way to move old items to the archive location and discard items that have expired and are no longer valid or required. There are facilities available to carry out these processes for you. They run automatically at scheduled intervals, clearing out old and expired items from folders. Old items are those that reach the archiving age you specify, and may include such things as emails you receive.

You can decide what will happen in the archive; for example, whether to permanently delete expired items or delete or archive old items to an archive file (a special type of data file). After the first time you use the archive facility, you can access items in the file directly. You can also have separate archive files for individual folders – your existing folder structure is maintained. If there is a parent folder above the folder you chose to archive, the parent folder is created in the archive file, but items within the parent folder are not archived. This means that an identical folder structure exists between the archive file and your mailbox.

Archive settings can be changed based on date, file type or sender. For example a rule can be set to delete all emails received from a specified sender after a specific time delay. How these settings can be changed will depend on your email provider.

Folders are left in place after being archived, even if they are empty. You work with the items in the same way that you work with items in your main mailbox. If you decide you want archived items moved back into your main mailbox, you can import all the items from the archive file into their original folders or into other folders you specify, or you can manually move or copy individual items.

Archiving could be used, in business, to keep an audit trail of emails. If a query or problem has been dealt with then the emails could be archived for a specified time. This will create a 'trail' which can be referred to at a later date, maybe, for training purposes or to improve customer relations.

Spam filters

Most ISPs provide spam filters with their software. You can set up features which help you take control of your mailbox and provide protection from spam. You can also set preferences; for example, to show only emails that are from people already in your address book.

ISPs have now made it much easier to report spam so that the problem is dealt with at a higher level. Reporting spam you receive enables the ISP to update their automatic spam filters more efficiently and stop junk email before it reaches you in future.

Autoreply

If you are not available to receive emails, you can set up an autoreply or an email away message by turning it on or off and choosing the type of message you wish to send.

1 Under 'Your Email Away Message is' – select the 'On' option.
2 You can now select the message you wish to use.
3 Click OK. You will then see an example of your away message and have the option to click OK if you wish to proceed, Edit if you would like to change it, or Turn Off if you no longer wish to set it.

The autoreply, also known as 'out of office' can only be activated if you are accessing email through a server. The 'out of office' is used if someone is not available to answer emails with the autoreply usually giving details of when they will be back in the office and who to contact if the email is urgent.

Portfolio Activity (AO5)

Following the creation of the documents for the Horse Stables you have been asked to email them to the owners and staff.

You need to:

1 Add the contact list to your address book.
2 Set up a distribution list for all the people in your address book whose job title is Owner.
3 Set up an electronic signature with your professional contact information. This signature must be used on all emails you send.
4 Create two folders within your inbox – one to store emails from the Horse Stables and one to store emails from your tutor. You should set up rules automatically saving emails in the appropriate folder when they arrive.
5 Send the five documents you have created, in a zipped folder, to the owners of the Horse Stables.
6 Create a document detailing email netiquette guidelines. Send this document to the staff who work at the Horse Stables. Copy the owners of the Horse Stables into the email.
7 Set up an autoreply to advise people you will be on holiday for one week. Provide details of alternative contacts during your holiday.

You will need to, for assessment purposes, provide a screenshot evidence of all tasks.

Pass – Candidates will use at least four standard features of email appropriately. Candidates set up and use at least three advanced features of email. Their emails will mainly be fit for purpose.

Merit – Candidates will use at least four standard features of email appropriately. Candidates set up and use at least four advanced features of email to good effect. Their emails will be fit for purpose and appropriate to business use.

Distinction – Candidates will use at least five standard features of email appropriately. Candidates set up and use at least five advanced features of email to good effect. All emails will be fit for purpose appropriate to business use. Candidates will show an organised approach to the management of their own email system.

AO6: Demonstrate an understanding of document and computer security in the workplace

Document and computer security

It is essential for companies that they are able to keep their computer systems safe and secure. In order to do so they must understand the potential threats to both hardware and software.

Computer security is the protection of systems and data from theft or corruption. Typical approaches to improving security can include physically limiting access to computers, employing operating system mechanisms to impose rules on programs, and the use of software to resist sabotage.

Security should not be an all or nothing issue. Designers and operators of systems should assume that security breaches are inevitable and keep full audit trails, so that when a security breach occurs they can see what caused it and what damage was done.

A company's level of security and assurance of customer protection can have a large impact on the company's reputation. Major online payment mechanisms – such as credit cards and PayPal – provide buyer protection systems to address problems if they do occur.

It is equally important to ensure document security, which can include the following:

- Abide by the correct procedures for logging on and off, and ensure that all programs and files are closed down correctly to avoid damage to them and the system.
- Use passwords to secure your working area and files from misuse. In some cases several passwords are needed to access strictly confidential data, in order to provide additional security. Files can also be password-protected. Use a password that is not easy for anyone to guess and do not give your password to anyone.
- Carry out virus checks on any files being loaded – this will protect your computer from being infected by programs that can cause damage to the system and your files.

- Back up files – you will normally have a copy of the system software, and the backups you make will be of the files you create. You should store backups in a safe place away from your computer.

Hacking

Hacking is an attempt to defeat or exploit the security of a computer system. When connecting to the Internet, you must realise that there are security risks – the main one being hackers. There are three main ways a hacker can launch an attack against your system:

- *Internal* – where an employee accesses the company network to cause damage. This can only be stopped by physical measures, not by software.
- *External* – where a hacker tries to access systems over the Internet. This can be stopped by installing security software such as a firewall.
- *Social* – where a hacker poses as a system administrator asking for your password. No software can stop a hacker with accurate stolen information.

Spoofing

Spoofing is the technique of misleading a computer network – making it think that something is happening which is not. Email spoofing is a popular form where a hacker sends email to people from a false email address. It usually involves making messages appear as if they are sent from an authorised source. One trick is to send emails as if from the network administrator, asking for passwords as the network is experiencing errors and has deleted the password file.

Mail bombs

A mail bomb is when a hacker sends a large amount of email messages to a single email address. The inbox may be filled and no more emails are permitted. The best way to deal with a mail bombing attack is to contact the email address administrator who may be able to track where the emails came from.

One of the problems with the Internet is that the original developers did not consider privacy and data, but now computers hold data on credit card numbers, account numbers, business contacts, and other confidential information for online commerce, banking or trading. Even if your system does not hold credit card numbers, a hacker can use it to obtain this information from others, so it is essential to use software to protect it.

Sniffers

A computer network sniffer is a security program designed to monitor information being transferred over a computer network. A hacker, pretending to be an employee, may attack the company network using this type of program. This is extremely dangerous as they could install a sniffer to steal vital information that could be sold to business competitors. When a sniffer is successfully installed on a network, it can be very hard to find and can remain there for years. It is essential to have up-to-date sniffer protection.

Botnets

In order to coordinate the activity of many infected computers, hackers use coordinating systems known as botnets. In a botnet, the malware – or malbot – logs into a chat system. The hacker can then give instructions to all the infected systems simultaneously. Botnets are also used to send upgraded malware to the infected systems, keeping them resistant to anti-virus software or other security measures.

The best way to protect your system from unauthorised access is by installing a firewall. A good firewall package will analyse each individual packet received or sent and detect and identify attacks by hackers.

Data misuse, unauthorised transfer, copying and distribution

Unauthorised access to a computer is illegal under the Computer Misuse Act 1990 – and similar laws in other countries. It is a crime for anyone other than the owner or operator of a computer to install software that alters web-browser settings, monitors keystrokes or disables computer-security software.

Owners of computers infected with spyware often claim that they did not authorise installation. It is important, therefore, to be vigilant when installing software to avoid loading spyware at the same time. Be sure to read the end user agreement to identify whether other programs are included.

The Computer Misuse Act 1990

This Act became law in August 1990. Under it hacking and the introduction of viruses are criminal offences. The Act makes it illegal to gain unauthorised access or make unauthorised modification to computer material. For the Act to apply either the person or the computer has to be in the home country when the unauthorised action is carried out. A conviction may lead to a fine and a prison sentence for the following:

- *Unauthorised access to computer material – hacking.* It is an offence to perform any function on a computer to gain unauthorised access to any program or data. The particular program, data and computer are not significant.
- *Unauthorised access with intent to commit or facilitate commission of further offences* – it does not matter if a further offence is to be committed on the same occasion as the unauthorised access or in the future, even if that turns out to be impossible.
- *Unauthorised modification of computer material* – it is an offence to: try to cause an unauthorised modification of the contents of a computer; impair the operation of the computer by a modification, e.g. to prevent access to a program or data; to stop a program from running; or to affect the reliability of data. This is the case for any computer, any program or any data. It does not matter whether the change – and any effect – is permanent or temporary. This includes planting viruses.

Unauthorised transfer or copying

Company information is a valuable asset. Programs written by companies and the data they contain are referred to as intellectual property (IP). Personal data is protected by law against unauthorised disclosure, but all company data should be kept confidential.

Companies should have policies in place to protect their own IP and data, as well as third party IP. Unauthorised transfer and copy of confidential material or company data can be prevented by a combination of contractual obligations (contracts of employment including appropriate confidentiality provisions), internal codes of practice (outlining data access and use, when data can be transferred and to who, etc) and training, so that all employees understand what is acceptable use of company property, data and information.

Unauthorised copying or distributing of software

All software users (individuals, companies, educational establishments, etc) have the same responsibility when using software - to use it in accordance with terms and conditions of the licence. Companies should be aware of the software in use, and ensure that the employees using it are aware of the licensing obligations.

Copyright is the exclusive right to control copying. The illegal copying of software is known as software piracy. In the workplace, employees might install a program on their computer even though the license agreement was purchased for only one computer. At home, software may be shared with a friend. Both are breaking the law and could result in fines or a prison sentence.

Many people want to use a second copy of software on a computer at home or on a laptop computer. Some software companies, knowing that many people use more than one computer for their work, have changed policy to meet these needs.

Copying of company software for personal use is a misuse of company assets, and is considered theft, which is a serious offence. The unauthorised copying of software puts both the individual and the company at risk. In some companies, use of unauthorised software or the copying of software can lead to disciplinary action.

Legislation

The Copyright, Designs and Patents Act (1988) makes it an offence to copy or steal software, or to use software beyond the terms of its licence. In three main areas it is illegal to:

- copy software without the owner's permission. When you buy software, you buy the licence and permission to use your copy, you do not own the software
- use pirated software
- send copied software by use of the Internet or over a phone line.

Email and chatroom abuses

Most chatrooms have rules to help ensure that they are a welcoming and useful resource for everyone who participates. These are general rules that apply to *all* chatrooms and outline what is deemed acceptable and unacceptable behaviour.

Companies cannot and do not review every message before it appears, but some operate a 'notice and take-down' policy which means that if they note or are made aware of a message that contravenes their rules, they have the right to amend or remove it. They encourage participants to contact them if a post violates the rules. However, they leave the responsibility for message content to the participants and do not accept any liability for the content or accuracy of messages.

Chatrooms can be protected by moderators who monitor activity. Typical rules in a chatroom include:

- Do not disrupt dialogue by causing a screen to scroll faster than other users are able to type – known as flooding.
- Do not type in block capitals – known as shouting.
- Do not victimise, harass, degrade or intimidate anyone on the basis of age, disability, ethnicity, gender, race, religion or sexual orientation. No racial or abusive comments will be tolerated.
- Do not use profanities and do not post libellous or defamatory comments.
- Do not impersonate or represent any person or entity in an attempt to deceive, harass or otherwise mislead.
- Do not pretend to be a representative of the company.
- Do not solicit personal information – this includes full name, home address, home telephone number or other identifying information.
- Do not infringe intellectual property rights, including copyright, trademark, rights of publicity, rights of privacy or other proprietary rights.
- Do not attempt to collect member information, including screen names.
- Do not advertise or solicit.

Adware, malware and spyware

Adware

Adware, or advertising-supported software, is any software which plays, displays or downloads advertisements whether or not the user has consented. It creates unwanted effects on a system, such as pop-ups and general degradation in either network connection or system performance. It is a form of spyware as it displays advertisements related to what it finds out from spying on you. Visited websites frequently install the adware in a surreptitious manner, and it directs revenue to the installing site and to the spyware company by displaying advertisements.

Adware is often bundled with spyware and each supports separate functionality – spyware gathers information about Internet behaviour, while adware displays targeted advertisements corresponding to that data. It is frequently installed as a separate program with free software. Users inadvertently agree to install adware by accepting the end user license agreement on free software and may then be given the option to pay for a registered or licensed copy to remove the advertisements. You need an anti-adware program to remove it.

Malware

Malware is software designed to gain access to a computer, without the user's permission, in order to carry out tasks, or routines, that the hacker has designed. The word is a combination of the words malicious and software.

While most malware is designed to cause damage or destroy the system or data, some have been used simply to see how widespread an infection would become. It can be very serious, causing irreversible damage to applications, files and data.

Malware is loaded by downloading software or swapping files such as music files, pictures or screen savers. It can also be included via spam, when you open a malicious message or attachment. Malware includes spyware, Trojan horses, some adware, rootkits, dialers, key loggers, botnets, viruses and worms.

Viruses and worms are best known for the way they spread. For example, if an infection is attached to an email it must be opened for it to spread, and is therefore, a virus. A worm spreads independent of user intervention. A Trojan horse is used to spread malware by concealment, for example, in an executable file.

Examples of the malware that can be installed include programs to:

Virus
A virus is a program which has infected some executable software and which causes that software to spread the virus to other executable software.

Worm
A worm is a virus that can replicate itself and infect thousands of computers. Worms are among the most dangerous viruses to affect the Internet.

- Change system settings, such as your home page settings.
- Redirect web searches to another search engine which can result in unrequested and offensive results.
- Interfere with dial-up settings, dial new numbers that result in you having to pay for the calls.
- Monitor and record keystrokes (loggers). These present a danger not only to your privacy, but also to your security as they can log your account numbers, user names, passwords, etc. This collection of your personal information can be passed to third parties who can use it for identity theft or fraud.
- Deliver spam or advertisements. If your surfing activity is being monitored, it can display advertisements considered appropriate to your interests. Although the advertisement may only be an irritation, the fact that it is relevant to your activity implies you are being monitored and your privacy is being invaded.

Spyware

Spyware is any data collection program that gathers information about you without your consent. When you are on a website, site operators can identify your computer, which webpage you have come from, use cookies to gather your profile and install spyware on your computer – all without your knowledge.

Spyware can interrupt your control by redirecting web browser activity. The information they collect is passed to advertisers and other interested parties, and is used for marketing.

Spyware does not usually copy itself, nor does an infected system try to copy the infection to other computers, but it can alter your system settings by creating unwanted CPU activity, disk usage, and network traffic. This can result in slow connection speeds, loss of Internet functionality, freezing of applications, failure to boot, and system crashes.

Changes are often difficult to reverse, so it is essential that you protect your system. Use security tools to block, detect, and remove unwanted software. It is better, however, to avoid downloading spyware. To do so you can:

- Keep protection programs up-to-date and use their auto-protection feature.
- Only download programs from websites you trust. If you are not sure you can enter the name of the program into a search engine to identify whether it has been reported as containing spyware.
- Be wary of free programs and make sure you understand any bundled software by reading disclosures, including the license agreement and privacy statement when installing software.
- Reduce your use of cookies to sites you trust.
- Avoid clicking links in advertisements.
- Avoid clicking unsolicited links in IM software, even if the message appears to be from someone you know.
- Click the red Close box in the corner of a window to close. Do not click "agree" or "OK" to close a window.

Pornography

Most companies have an Internet User policy that will outline what is considered to be acceptable use of the company Internet services, the risks that the policy is attempting to avoid and the penalties that arise from misuse. It should specify any activities that are not permitted. Unacceptable activities should be outlined, which might include downloading offensive material or using of the Internet to view, access, upload, download, store, transmit, create, or otherwise manipulate pornographic or other sexually explicit materials.

A company policy might also identify how the company monitors use, the privacy employees are permitted, and if and when, employees may use the Internet for personal use, such as breaks or in their lunch hour.

There are tools available to help prevent employees from misusing the Internet. Programs can be installed on an employee's computer that log keystrokes, capture screenshots to identify exactly what is being viewed, and keep a log of websites visited.

Online threats

Phishing

Phishing is the sending of electronic mail that claims to be from a legitimate and well-established company or individual. The message typically asks for sensitive data such as credit card details or passwords to online accounts. The email message is usually professionally designed with logos and fonts which appear to be genuinely from those companies.

The most serious phishing emails claim to be from banks or credit card companies as they pose a much more significant financial security risk. Online users should always remember that legitimate companies will never ask for any sensitive data by email.

Identity and financial abuses

Identity theft is a crime of which we should all be aware – it is the taking of personal details and using them fraudulently resulting in direct financial loss. Whether it is called identity theft, phishing, skimming or social engineering, all these activities are fraud and the increasing use of electronic systems has extended the scope and the potential profits.

One of the most dangerous methods of identity theft used online is keylogging. This type of malware copies keystrokes when a password, credit card number or other personal data is entered. This is transmitted to the malware creator enabling credit card fraud and other theft. Another method of causing financial problems is to take control of the communications and dial expensive international, premium rate and other telephone numbers – charging the call back to the owner of the infected system.

Email provides the opportunity for personal contact with millions of people to be exploited. It has also allowed potentially devastating crimes such as phishing, where online banks, in particular, have been targeted.

Phishing is when an email is sent to a user falsely claiming to be a legitimate enterprise in an attempt to get the user to disclose private information that can be used for identity theft. The email may direct the user to visit a website that asks the user to update personal information such as passwords, bank account numbers and credit card details. These websites are fake websites and are only set up to steal the user's information.

To protect system, documents and yourself from identity and financial abuses:

■ Ignore unsolicited email – if the source is unknown check it against previous correspondence and if you remain unsure, delete it.
■ Reduce risk – store documents with personal data in securely, shred any documents being disposed of, use security features on all systems, and do not allow sensitive data and documents to be removed from the workplace.
■ If there is a request for urgent action, stop. Think about it and check with the company originating the request.
■ Check financial statements carefully – a common tactic is to make small but regular withdrawals rather than one-off larger amounts. Check all accounts regularly.
■ If telephone requests are made for personal information, take the caller's number and then call them back via the main switchboard number.

Types of viruses

A virus attaches itself to a computer program. There are many different types of virus and they attack different parts of the computer, such as the boot sector. The most common indications that your computer has been infected are:

- deleted files and data
- the computer takes longer to load programs or applications
- items and images on-screen are distorted
- unusual images and text appear
- unusual noises come from your keyboard or hard disk
- the hard disk operates excessively or is inaccessible
- disk space and file names change for no reason
- system tools such as Scandisk return incorrect values.

Virus name	What it does
Polymorphican	An encrypted virus which hides in encrypted data and then decrypts itself to spread through a system. It generates a new decryption routine each time it infects a new executable file. The virus signature differs every time, making it hard for anti-virus software to detect.
Stealth	This virus hides modifications made to files and boot records by modifying and forging the results of calls to functions – the programs believe they are reading the original file. It will attempt to hide in memory when anti-virus software is run.
Slow	This virus is difficult to detect as it only modifies and infects files when they have already been modified or copied – the original file will not be infected by the copied file.
Retro	Attacks the anti-virus software designed to delete it. Attempts to attack data files such as the virus signature store which disables the ability of the anti-virus software to detect and delete viruses.
Multipartite	Attacks and infects both the boot sector and executable files simultaneously.
Armoured	Makes itself difficult to trace and disassemble to protect itself from anti-virus software.
Companion	Creates a companion file for each executable file that it infects. It may save itself as a utility file so every time a user executes that utility, the computer will load the companion file and infect the system.
Phagea	A very destructive virus that rewrites an executable program with its own code. It usually tries to delete or destroy every program it infects.
Revisiting	A worm virus that attempts to copy itself within the computer memory and then copy itself to another linked computer.

Figure 1.24 The most common types of virus

Virus detection, prevention and protection

Programs have been developed to detect, quarantine and remove spyware, adware or malware. They are designed specifically for spyware detection and will not detect viruses, although some commercial anti-virus software can also detect adware and spyware or offer a separate spyware detection package.

Anti-spyware programs combat spyware in two different ways:

■ They can provide real time protection against the installation – the software scans all incoming network data for spyware and blocks any threats.
■ They can be used solely for detection and removal of spyware already installed. This type is usually much easier to use – you can schedule daily, weekly or monthly scans to detect and remove any spyware installed. The program scans the contents of the windows registry, operating system files and installed programs, and provides a list of threats found. You then choose what you want to delete or keep.

Both methods require an up-to-date database of threats. As new spyware programs are released, they are evaluated and defined, allowing the software to detect and remove them. Without a regular source of update, anti-spyware software is of limited use. In some cases you pay for the update service, while others provide free updates.

The best way to protect against viruses is to use good anti-virus software and keep installing the latest updates. These packages may not always protect you against the latest virus, but they offer the best possible solution. You can also ensure that you:

■ use operating system updates to patch security holes
■ do not open email messages that look suspicious
■ do not click on email attachments you were not expecting.

Protecting your system

To ensure the security of your system and defend it from attack by hackers, viruses, etc., there are a number of steps that can be introduced:

■ *Use of firewalls* – these can be hardware devices or software programs. They provide some protection from online intrusion, but they allow some applications, such as web browsers, to connect to the Internet.
■ *Data encryption* – this scrambles data so it is unreadable during transmission, but the recipient can unscramble the message.
■ *Backing up data* – this secures the data. Backups should be kept in another location, which should be fireproof, waterproof and heat proof, and preferably in a separate, offsite location. Some are kept in safe deposit boxes or are located on a file hosting service that backs up files over the Internet. Backups are also important in case of natural disasters, building fire or explosion; having a backup at an alternative secure location not subject to the same potential danger is important.
■ *Access authorisation* – this restricts user access to protect either the whole computer, such as through an interactive log on-screen, or individual services, such as a server. Identifying and authenticating users may be via the use of passwords, identification cards, and more recently, smart cards and biometric systems.
■ *Use of intrusion detection systems* – these scan a network for users who should not be there or who are doing things that are a danger, such as trying many passwords to gain access.
■ *Keep employees aware* of the dangers of breaches of the network and servers.

Portfolio Activity (AO6)

The Horse Stables has not been using communication technology systems and are not certain how they should keep their systems secure. They require information about any potential threats to both hardware and software.

1 Demonstrate your understanding of the threats to computer systems by providing a guide for the company outlining how it can protect itself.
2 Demonstrate your understanding of the threats to document security by preparing a guide for the company outlining how to protect files from threats.
3 Provide the company with a guide to viruses and virus protection.

AO7: Use standard ways of working to work safely, keep information secure and manage personal information

Organising your work

Work in compliance with company policy

Companies usually have policies outlining the responsibilities of their employees when using the computer system. They often provide a guide outlining how work is to be carried out to keep information secure. It might include:

- information regarding safe working practices that must be used
- how documents must be organised to enable other employees to locate them quickly and easily
- how file names must be used and what should be included in them (such as the path or version number)
- use of passwords to protect documents from unauthorised access
- use of permissions to protect confidential information
- advice on how to handle classified and commercially sensitive data
- frequency of file backups
- rules for the physical protection of the computer equipment.

Work in compliance with health and safety legislation

Everyone has the right to work in a safe, comfortable environment to avoid tiredness, illness and injury. The company should provide appropriate equipment, as well as suitable lighting, temperature, rest facilities, ventilation and first aid.

Employees have the responsibility of taking care of themselves and ensuring that their workspace is safe. Employees should:

- be aware of emergency procedures and make sure there is a clear, safe route to exits, in case of fire
- check that cables are secured safely to avoid tripping
- ensure that power points are not overloaded
- use power surge protectors to prevent equipment being damaged by sudden voltage increases caused, for example, by lightening
- keep liquids and food away from equipment to avoid accidental damage
- keep workspace and equipment clean
- never use faulty equipment, and report faults and hazards immediately.

Keeping information secure

One of the most important aspects of computer security, data and system care, is the importance of regular, reliable data backup. It cannot be guaranteed that your data will be safe if it exists in only one place. The risks are huge.

Saving work regularly

It is important to save your work regularly, and most programs have a variety of ways in which this can be done:

- Save the document you are working on – whether it is new or already exists.
- Save all open documents at the same time.
- Save a copy of the active document with a different name.
- Save a copy of the active document in a different location.
- Save a document as a template if you have text or formatting you want to reuse in other documents you create.

To save all open documents at the same time, hold down SHIFT and click Save All on the File menu. All open documents and templates will be saved at the same time. If any of them have never been saved, the Save As dialogue box appears so that you can name them.

Regardless of how and when you save work, it is critical that you do so. Set up your system to save your files automatically while you work. This will help because the more frequently your files are saved, the more information is recovered if there is a power failure or similar problem while a file is open.

Keeping backup copies on removable media and automatic backups

There are many different methods that you can use to back up data. The main difference between these methods is the device and medium that is used to store the backup. Different media have different characteristics, such as capacity, speed, ease of use, etc.

There are various backup alternatives: programs that back up your email only or those that restore an entire hard drive in case of a crash – these take a snapshot of your disk, compress it to a single file and save it for quick recovery later. When deciding which method of backup and what type of media is suitable for you, the areas you should consider include:

- Capacity – how much does the media store?
- Is it possible to fully automate the backup?
- Cost – does the method allow additional backups at a reasonable cost?
- Reliability varies widely depending on the type of device – if you have a disaster and need to restore from the backup, will it work?
- Simplicity and convenience – how easy is the method to use? Is there any difficulty associated with the method that would tend to discourage the use of backups?
- Performance – how fast is the hardware and software used for the method? How much time will it take to do a backup?

To provide maximum safety for your data, it is important to plan a backup schedule that will allow you the most flexibility and reliability in recovering from potential disasters. In general, data files should always be backed up – they cannot be replaced. Selecting a time to perform backups depends on how the computers are used and how long it will take. Most companies prefer to do backups at night.

Your data backups are only as safe as the physical media that contain them. If you do a backup and then leave the media lying around, you are defeating the purpose – protection against risks like theft, disaster or sabotage is lost.

As well as physically protecting and securing drives, if you have concerns regarding securing the data on your drives, one solution is to encrypt and password-protect removable and fixed drives, including USB drives, memory sticks and public partitions. Once encrypted, the files cannot be opened.

Automatic backups

Microsoft Windows provides utilities to perform different types of backup. The utilities provided vary with the version of Windows. You must have the required permissions or user rights to initiate backups.

To perform the backup you can select:

- the items (files, folders and drives) you want to back up
- the type, place, and name of the backup
- how you want the backup carried out (specify verification, compression, and shadow copy options)
- whether to overwrite data
- access restrictions
- when to run the backup.

You can select Advanced Mode and the Schedule Jobs tab, to specify when the backup should be scheduled. When you have entered your requirements you will be presented with an outline showing the backup details.

In the latest versions of Windows the utilities available include automatically scheduled backups using the Windows Backup and Restore Center. Automatic Backup backs up your files and data to an external hard drive, secondary hard drive, CD, DVD or a network location. Backups can be made automatically on a schedule that you specify. Complete PC Backup backs up everything on a PC, including the operating system and applications. It is of particular use if you need to perform a disaster recovery as it can restore a PC to its original state. Some virus protection software also includes automatic backup utilities.

Virus protection software, such as Bullguard, has an option to schedule automatic backups. This means that the user can set the software to backup files to an online drive, usually provided by the vendor of the software, or to a local drive such as a removable/external hard drive.

- The benefits of using the online facility include:
- the backup is unlikely to be lost
- if the computer is lost/stolen then the data will still be safe
- online backup enables files to be accessed from anywhere – this would be useful if a person travels for their work.

Access permissions

Companies use secure network drives that allow access only to employees or those with authorisation to access the company networks. This allows businesses to maintain complete control of access to company resources: who can log on to the network, when this can be done, and where it can be done. An authorised user will usually be given a user name and password to log onto secure drives and networks. Companies may limit the number of log on attempts and have security programs in place to monitor logging on attempts and unauthorised activity.

Employees working away from the main site may also be able to log on remotely. This may require a user to have a password and a unique access code.

Access permissions can also be used to set what can be done with a file. The main access permissions are:

- none
- read/write
- read
- amend
- delete
- full.

The access permissions can be set so that different groups of users or a single user can carry out different tasks. The permissions granted should reflect the information held in the file and the user's job role. For example if a file held personal details then it could be accessed by the person whose details are held in that file, read, but the human resources department could have full access meaning they are able to read, write, amend and delete.

Password-protecting files

You can provide password protection in many ways, including using a password to protect files and to stop modification to files. You can install a password which allows others to open the document but only allows authorised users to make changes to it. If an unauthorised person changes the document, they can only save the document by giving it a different file name.

A password can contain any combination of letters, numerals, spaces and symbols, and it can be up to 15 characters long. If you select advanced encryption options, you can make a password even longer. Passwords are case-sensitive, so if you vary the capitalisation when you assign the password, users must type the same capitalisation when they enter the password.

Managing personal information

Suitable folder structure

First, set up a system by creating folders to hold your files and documents. You may want to create folders for the various types of work that you do, or you might want to separate your folders by the type – the client or company.

A folder may contain other folders or subfolders. For example, if you have created a new folder called Finance, you may have subfolders for Bank, etc. Do not create too many subfolders. Limit the number of documents you keep in each folder. The fewer files you have in a folder, the faster a file can be found.

Every time you write a letter or create a spreadsheet or a presentation, you are creating a file. When you save that file, unless you state otherwise, the program you are using puts the file into a default folder for the application that you are using. Many windows programs use a folder called My Documents as the default folder. It is a good idea to keep your files in the My Documents folder and simply create subfolders in My Documents to suit your needs.

Using appropriate names for files and folders

Windows folder and file names can contain up to 215 characters, including spaces. Keep your file names to 20–30 characters, as short file names are easier to use and some programs may have trouble interpreting long file names. Use file names that are descriptive to make them easier to locate at a later date.

File names are followed by a full stop and three letters, called an extension. The program that you are using will automatically add the extension.

Version numbers

To keep track of changes you have made to documents, you can save versions within the same document. Only the differences are saved. You can review, open, print and delete earlier versions.

If you want to save a document as it is, save a version of the document. You may then continue to work and save another version. Word can automatically save a version of your document each time the document is closed – do so if you need a record of who made changes and when.

If you save versions in one file, there are two instances when you may want to save a specific version as a separate file:

- to send only the most recent or a specific version to another person
- to compare different versions – use the Compare and Merge Documents command on the Tools menu to do this.

Saving multiple versions is different from saving a backup copy of a document, which is designed to ensure against data loss or against unintended changes.

Portfolio Activity (AO7)

You should create and name new folders and subfolders and use suitable file names to store the files which you will create for all the tasks in this unit. Files downloaded from the Internet should also be stored within this file structure.

You should demonstrate that your work is held safely and securely, that safe working practices are followed and personal information is managed well with appropriate attention to confidentiality of the information.

1 *Organising your own work* – you must demonstrate that you have carried out your work in compliance with company policy and health and safety legislation.

2 *Keeping information secure* – you must demonstrate that you have set up and adhered to methods of:
   - saving your work regularly
   - keeping backup copies on a suitable removable medium which could be to a flash pen, CD-ROM, floppy disk or a different network location
   - making automatic backups
   - securing drives
   - setting up access permissions
   - using passwords to protect files.

3 *Managing personal information* – you must demonstrate that you have set up and adhered to a suitable folder and file structure. All folders must be appropriate for your work for this unit. You may wish to create one folder for each assessment objective. You should provide evidence of:
   - your initial folder structure and your completed folder structure
   - the creation and naming of new folders to store the files
   - the creation and naming of the files downloaded from the Internet
   - locating and opening existing files
   - naming files and folders
   - version numbers.

Collaborative Working

Learning outcomes

By working through this unit you will produce evidence to meet the unit assessment objectives to show that you understand how to:

- ■ plan a project as part of a group
- ■ investigate ICT tools to support collaborative working
- ■ investigate how search engines work
- ■ carry out research for the group project
- ■ create your allocated part of the group task containing information from a range of sources
- ■ work collaboratively with others to review the results of the research and produce the final product
- ■ review and evaluate the project and collaborative tools used.

Introduction

Being able to work with other people is one of the most important skills a businessperson can possess. Team work is a crucial part of all industries, whether it is being able to follow orders, communicate ideas, cooperate towards a common goal or lead a group of people to successfully complete an objective.

Collaboration can involve disparate people needing to be united. They may have different opinions, different ways of working and different motivations, but to succeed a group effort has to be made. Compromise is a key factor in collaboration. Without it, opposing ideas can remain steadfast and solutions can never be reached.

Team leader is a key role in a group of people who are collaborating. They give direction, inspire and ensure that progress is being made, and in the right direction. However, they are not the only important member of a group. Each individual who is involved has a responsibility to contribute and a duty to give their best to the team. Only then can they share the reward when the team is successful.

Scenario

Working in a team, you will create a magazine that would be suitable for a 16 to 19-year-old readership. It must have at least one article from each person in the team and have a consistent theme throughout. This means that although articles may be written individually, collaboration is needed to produce the whole product.

Each member of the team will be allocated a role and must perform that responsibility to the best of their ability. There will be tasks to be carried out as a team and some which will be separate.

You will need to make decisions about the overall structure of the magazine, the subjects of the articles and the design of each page.

In terms of assessment, although you will be working in a team to produce a group product, each member will be assessed individually. In order for that to happen, you will need to keep a detailed log of every contribution made to the project, for example how you were involved in meetings and which parts of the magazine you developed. In addition, you should ask your teacher to observe your group work and to complete a witness statement where you feel it is appropriate. For example, you may ask them to observe your team meeting and write a witness statement to explain each member's contribution.

Portfolio Activity

Organise your team.

1 Get into a team of around five or six people. You are advised to try to work with people who you do not normally work with. This will allow for a better exchange of ideas and evidence of collaboration. All team members should brainstorm writing down all ideas on a piece of paper.

2 Discuss a name for your magazine. The team leader must minute the meeting.
   a) Once all ideas are exhausted, discuss the list and eliminate all but five.
   b) Discuss the five ideas and decide which you will use. You may wish to use debate or a vote to make your final decision.

Submit your magazine name to your teacher for approval.

Product to be produced

When working in a team, there must be a clear focus and direction. This ensures that all members move towards a shared goal and do not go off at a tangent to the original purpose of the group. After all, teams are formed in order to reach an objective.

The product to be made may have already been agreed before the team was formed, possibly in great detail, in which case roles are allocated and work is carried out.

However, teams are often given quite an open brief or problem to solve. For example, a team may be assembled to create a new breakfast cereal or to work out how a company can save money when buying from suppliers. Within this brief, many things will need to be decided by the team in terms of defining their final goal; in other words, what the result of their collaboration will be and how they will know when they are finished.

Generating ideas

Having to come up with fresh, original ideas, especially if this has to be done on a regular basis (as in the design industry), can be an incredibly difficult task. When generating ideas in a team, it can be even more difficult as people may not want to share ideas they feel are 'silly', although these can sometimes be the innovative inspirations needed to solve a problem. A current buzz phrase is 'blue-sky thinking', where nothing is out of the scope of the project team. (For example, if the team was to create a new breakfast cereal, inventing a new type of grain would be a blue-sky approach to problem solving!)

Everyone has their own method of coming up with ideas. Below are a few techniques you may find useful.

Mind maps

Mind maps are known by many names, but essentially they are a way of tracking ideas focused on a central concept. A keyword is placed in the middle and from that lines are drawn with words at the end of each line. Each 'layer' of lines should refine that avenue of thinking.

Listing

By writing lists, ideas can be prioritised and additional information can be noted by each idea such as resources needed or time to complete.

Thought showers

This technique is similar to a mind map, but without a structure. It is literally getting as many ideas down on paper as possible, usually within a specified time frame, without worrying about where each should go or how it might fit in with other ideas. A common way of doing a thought shower is for each person to have a pack of sticky notes and a pen, and to write each idea on a note and stick it to a board. Once the time period is over, the group then eliminate unsuitable ideas by removing the sticky notes from the board.

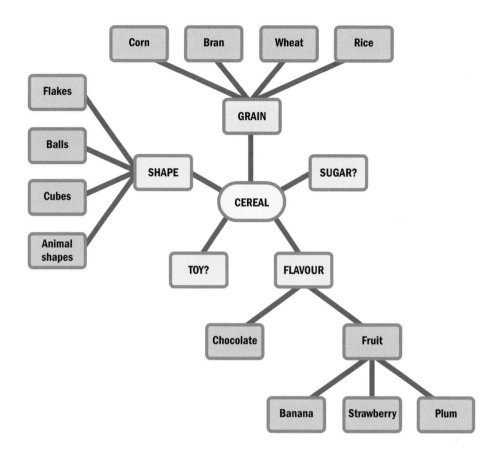

Figure 2.1 Mind map for creating a new cereal

Allocation of tasks

Once an idea is decided and a purpose set, it cannot be tackled as a whole. It must be broken into individual tasks. Deciding which team members undertake each task should ideally be based on the best person for the job. Each person should have a clearly defined role and know how his or her task fits with all the others.

By dividing the whole task into smaller, individual tasks it becomes more manageable, and it will also be known when each individual task is complete. As each smaller task is allocated to a member of the team, he or she can take responsibility for it to see it is completed on time and to the expected quality. If there is a problem, that nominated person can then be looked on as the one who will resolve it. Likewise, any successes for that individual task can be attributed to the person who took responsibility for it.

Setting and working to deadlines

In order to ensure the final product is completed by the overall deadline, each individual task must be finished in a timely fashion. This means that separate deadlines should be set for each task. Some tasks may be dependent on others, so team members cannot work in isolation and need to communicate to make sure that linked tasks flow well.

Gantt chart

A Gantt chart is a method of sharing tasks, deadlines and resources required in a diagram so it is easy to refer to. It resembles a bar chart plotting tasks against duration and can show where tasks overlap and which are dependent on each other, meaning where one task has to be completed before another can begin.

	Jan	Feb	Mar	Apr	May	Jun	Jul	Aug	Sep
Design characters	█	█							
Design environment	█	█							
Program characters			█	█					
Program landscapes			█	█					
Combine characters and landscapes						█	█	█	
Test									█

Figure 2.2 Gantt chart for computer game production

To draw a Gantt chart

■ Break the project into as many tasks as possible and list them in order down the left-hand side.

■ Divide the horizontal axis into time periods as appropriate depending on the length of the project (days, weeks, months, etc).

■ Identify which tasks are dependant on others, for example task A must be complete before task B can be started.

■ Starting with the first task, draw a bar for the length of each task, observing the dependencies which have been identified.

Critical path

Dependencies in tasks are clearly illustrated to highlight the critical path.
The critical path shows the shortest time in which a project can be completed.

To create a critical path

■ Divide the project into individual tasks.

■ Put the tasks in order, identifying any dependencies, for example those which cannot be started until previous tasks are completed.

■ Number the tasks and begin to draw the diagram. Start with task 1, then draw an arrow from task 1. For any dependant tasks, have a second arrow coming from the task, e.g. task 4 and 5 are carried out at the same time, so they are both connected to task 3.

■ For each task, estimate the duration of the task. For more detailed diagrams, estimate the minimum and maximum durations.

■ The critical path can then be estimated following the shortest path through the project, ensuring all tasks are completed.

Critical path analysis
This is a method of identifying the most important tasks and dependencies within a project highlighting the tasks that are critical to the schedule (e.g. those that will delay the project if they take longer than expected).

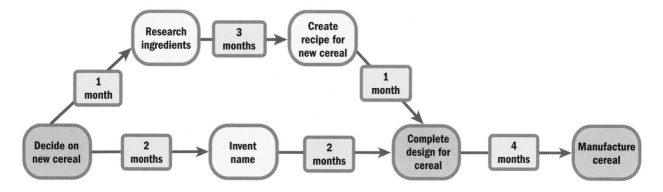

Figure 2.3 Critical path diagram for creating a new cereal

In the diagram, the project has been divided into six tasks. All tasks, except the first, are dependent on previous tasks being completed before they can start. The purple tasks are critical activities which create the critical path, which define the core timeline of the project. The yellow tasks are carried out simultaneously, but it is only once they are all completed that the second purple task can be started.

The aim of a critical path diagram is to show pictorially the order of the tasks and the formation of the activities in a project. Usually estimated timescales are also added to each branch of the diagram. For tasks which are carried out simultaneously, the longest amount of time forms the critical path. For example, in the above diagram, the critical path would be nine months, this being the shortest possible time in which all parts of the project could be carried out. There is one month of 'float' where the tasks are carried out simultaneously, as one path takes four months and the other takes five, leaving one month floating on one path while there are other tasks to be completed on the other path.

Identifying success criteria

In order to know whether individual tasks and the whole product have been completed entirely, success criteria need to be identified at the beginning of the project. For example, for a newspaper article it may be that a certain number of words have to be written or that a product receives a good reaction from a focus group of members of the target audience.

It is possible that success criteria may change during a project, as may the brief, but at the outset both must be defined clearly. This means that when the project is being planned, it will be clear when it will be finished and how the end of the project will be identified.

Success criteria should follow the SMART rule of thumb:

> **S**pecific – criteria should not be vague and should pinpoint exactly what is to be done
> **M**easurable – so that it can be clearly known when it is complete
> **A**chievable – there is no point setting a criteria which is impossible
> **R**ealistic – using the resources you have available
> **T**ime – criteria should have a definite deadline and timescale

If criteria meet these guidelines, they will be easier to fulfill and to determine when they are completed.

Portfolio Activity (AO1)

In your team meeting, plan how you will create your magazine. The editor should organise the date and time with other members and ensure everyone attends.

1 All members of the team should take detailed notes of the content of the meetings and each person's contribution. Make sure every person in the team takes a turn to minute each meeting that is held. You may wish to ask your teacher to observe and write a witness statement.

2 Discuss the product to be created. Think about the aim of the magazine, the target audience and their needs.

3 Create a mind map on a large piece of paper of your plans for the magazine. Start with the name of the magazine in the middle and then from that add ideas for each page, which should be broken down further into articles and features.

4 For each task on your mind map, allocate a member of the team to be responsible for its implementation and completion.

5 Beside the name of the magazine in the centre, write the final deadline when you would like the whole product to be completed.

6 Estimate how long each task will take and which can be done simultaneously.

7 For each task, also add a deadline. This should be realistic and achievable. Take other commitments into consideration, including additional studies, extra-curricular activities and personal obligations. The tasks should all finish well before the magazine deadline so the whole thing can be compiled. Try to leave room for unforeseen events, if possible.

8 Beside each task and deadline, add a success criterion. For example, beside the magazine title in the centre you may wish to say it will be successful if it is completed on time to a standard suitable for distributing to your target audience. Each success criterion should be appropriate and measurable so that it is clear if it has been met. Ensure all tasks have criteria so there is a comprehensive range.

9 Use mind-mapping software to produce a clear and organised version of your plans. Ensure each member of the team has a copy (for example, via email). If you do not have mind-mapping software available, photocopy your mind map so each member has a copy and keep the original safe so that it can be referred to by the team.

10 Draw a critical path diagram, as part of your planning documents, using your mind map tasks and deadlines to calculate estimated timescales.

11 Submit your mind map plan to your teacher for feedback of the content of your magazine.

12 Revise your plan based on your teacher's comments.

13 Draw a Gantt chart to show a detailed time plan. This should contain all details from the mind map, including clear and appropriate deadlines for each task. You may wish to use software such as Microsoft Project to create this.

Pass – Candidates will give brief information about the final product to be produced. They will contribute effectively to the work of a group, some of the time, to produce basic planning documents, for example mind map, brainstorm, thought-shower, showing the allocation of tasks. Some deadlines will be set. Some success criteria will be given.

Merit – Candidates will give detailed information about the final product to be produced. They will contribute effectively to the work of a group, most of the time, to produce detailed planning documents, for example mind map, brainstorm, thought-shower showing the allocation of tasks. Clear deadlines will be set with some use of a Gantt chart. A range of appropriate success criteria will be given.

Distinction – Candidates will give comprehensive information about the final product to be produced. They will consistently work effectively as part of a group to produce comprehensive planning documents, for example mind map, brainstorm, thought-shower showing the allocation of tasks. Clear and appropriate deadlines will be set with effective use of a Gantt chart. A comprehensive range of appropriate success criteria will be given.

AO2: Investigate ICT tools to support collaborative working

Communication methods

When working in a team, establishing and maintaining communication is key. Without clear, open channels of communication, team members can drift away from the original purpose or new ideas cannot be circulated. A team leader can also use communication methods to monitor the progress of the individual parts of the product to make sure they are on schedule to meet the final deadline.

Methods of sharing information

As well as communicating directly with one another, team members will also need to share information. There are several tools which provide this facility.

Collaborative editing

This is where a document is reviewed and edited by several people. This can be done by emailing the document to each other and using software tools to make the changes.

Microsoft Word provides such a facility in its Reviewing toolbar. Amendments can be tracked in different colours to identify the reviewer. Comments can also be made; these are inserted beside the text without affecting its layout and formatting. These can be printed or omitted from a print. If more than one person is reviewing the document, the software can compare different versions of the same document and merge them based on user requirements such as highest word count or latest amendments.

Alternatively, there are programs which will save one copy of a document and allow several people to view and change it. For example, Google Docs provides editing and formatting tools and access through a web browser.

Communication method	Description
Email	Distribution lists allow one email to be sent to several people at the same time. You can also keep a record of decisions by saving emails.
Forums	An online forum can be set to private so only the members of the team can post messages about the project.
Chatrooms	These can also be set to private and allow team members to chat one-to-one or as a group in real time.
Virtual learning environments (VLEs)	VLEs are systems which support learning and collaborative activities and usually are accessible online to registered members. They provide a wide range of tools for allowing communication between members, including: ■ the sharing of resources ■ digital communications in forums and chatrooms ■ a central place for project matters ■ connection to the project team from any Internet-enabled machine in the world.
Instant messaging	This allows team members to talk one-to-one with each other in real time.
Voice over Internet Protocol	VoIP is a relatively new technology which allows users to make phone calls over the Internet.
Intranet	This is a network which is restricted to certain users, usually within one company. It can allow files to be shared, storing them in a central area for authorised users to access.
Extranet	Similar to an Intranet, this also allows some connectivity to external parties, usually through a website.
Web conferencing	This enables communication via the Internet using sound and vision through a webcam and microphone. Web conferencing is also known as browser-based conferencing.
Online whiteboard	This allows users to write messages to each other, including drawing pictures which can be useful when discussing designs and ideas. An example of this is www.skrbl.com, which allows users to 'scribble'.
Online collaborative organiser	Most diary programs will allow users to give permission for others to view their appointments. This can be useful when trying to organise meetings with several different people. Microsoft Outlook has this facility as does Google Calendar.

Figure 2.4 Different communication methods

Sharing diaries

Each team member needs a diary that can be used to allocate deadlines and schedule meetings. If ICT is used, the diaries can be shared so that all those with access can see team members' commitments and available time. Programs like Microsoft Outlook provide facilities like this. They can save a great deal of time working out when all required delegates are available to meet, although – as with most ICT – it is only reliable if the users keep them up to date.

Wikis

Wikis are user-created webpages. These often hold glossaries, research data or other crucial information for a team which is constantly being updated. The collaborative approach means that all members of the team can update and access the information. It also provides a single location for the latest data which would otherwise be difficult to distribute.

Blogs

These are online journals which can be used to explain the progress each team member has made. They are written individually and can be set so only the team may read them. There is also the facility on most blog entries for readers to comment on what they have read. This can be useful in a team as the blog may have given someone an idea or sparked a discussion point.

Content management system (CMS)

A content management system is a computer system which can be used to share documents and information between team members working on a project. Usually there will be one system for a whole company, with each person having a username and password, and the system having a section for each project within the company being carried out at that time.

Being able to share materials over the Internet is very useful, especially if the team is spread around the country or the world. For example, when creating a book, a cover design could be uploaded to the CMS and the publisher, editor and author can view it separately and add comments. It allows a document or image to be reviewed and discussed much quicker and allows all messages to be seen by everyone involved, so communication is clearer and more effective.

Portfolio Activity (AO2)

Task 1

Individually, research the range of communication methods available to your team.

Research at least six methods of communicating. For each:
a) find three sources which give information about each method
b) using these sources, write an explanation of each method in your own words
c) give at least three examples of where the method could be used in collaborative working
d) explain how it could or could not be useful for your team's project.

Task 2

In your team, discuss your research and agree which you will use.

a) One member of the team should take detailed notes of the content of the meeting. Make sure every person in the team takes a turn to contribute to the discussion.
b) Discuss the methods of communicating, arguing for and against each one. Decide on at least three which you will use in this project.
c) Discuss the methods of sharing information, arguing for and against each one. Decide on at least two which you will use in this project.
d) Create a document stating how you will communicate within the team during this project.

Note: you will be using these communication and information-sharing methods throughout this unit. Keep a record or copy of when you use them, as you will need to produce evidence of them for AO6.

AO3: Investigate how search engines work

Different types of search engine

The World Wide Web contains a wealth of information, so much so that without search facilities it could be impossible to find what you were looking for. The first search engine was Archie in 1990 which indexed pages and held around 150 gigabytes of data, compared with the daily 20,000 terabytes that Google can process today.

Web crawlers

Web crawlers are the most popular type of search engine, examples of which are Google and Ask Jeeves. They have **automated bots** called 'spiders' which crawl through the Internet looking at each page they encounter. If they find one they have not seen before they will take certain information from it, such as the URL. If the site has **meta tags**, they will record them; if not, they will use the content on the site to best-guess keywords. They will then relay this data back to the main search engine database, where it is added to the records. The 'spider' will then continue looking for more new websites or ones which it has recorded previously but have changed. When a user searches, it is in fact that database which is searched and produces results. This is how it can operate so quickly.

Directories

These include search engines such as Yahoo! and Yell.com. Websites register with the search engine in order to be listed in the directory. The directory is divided into topics then broken down further and further. Websites can choose which heading, or headings, it is most appropriate for them to be listed under. This means that the search is more accurate, unlike web crawlers where websites can be sorted under incorrect keywords. However, directories are falling out of fashion for two reasons:

Automated bots
Complex software usually run on powerful machines that can **intelligently** carry out tasks without human control. In this context they are also known as 'web crawlers' or 'spiders'.

Meta tags
Part of the html of the website that describes the content of each page, usually in keywords, used for being listed by search engines. They are not shown on the pages.

- They require the website to register itself. This can be time-consuming, especially when web crawlers do this automatically.
- Searches are restricted to the directory headings, unlike web crawlers where you can type in any words or even full questions.

Hybrid

These include search engines such as Yahoo!, which provide both a web crawler and directory service. In this type there may be cross-over of its website collection method. For example they may use 'spiders' to find listings themselves, but also to invite websites to register manually to ensure they are in their desired category. The websites registered for the directory listing may automatically be entered into the web-crawling section, knowing that they will be correctly listed, and vice versa, although web-crawled sites that are then listed under the directory risk being under the incorrect headings. This type of search gives the user a choice of search styles.

Meta search engines

These include www.dogpile.com and www.surfwax.com. They allow the user to enter their keywords into the search bar and then will search several search engines to find the answer. These became popular in the early days of web crawlers when coverage was limited, as it took time for the 'spider' bots to register the millions of pages on the Internet. Meta searches were a way to compensate by using several search engines at once. However, they have fallen out of fashion as web crawlers have caught up with the Internet's rapid speed of growth and an engine like Google will have almost all sites registered, therefore removing the need to wade through meta search engine results, which could be quite complex as they report which engine has produced each website result.

Children's search engines

These include www.ajkids.com, which is Ask Jeeves for children. Because the Internet is unregulated there is a myriad of sites which are highly unsuitable for young people and which can turn up in a search which is quite innocent. For example, a search on healthy eating could result in finding a site promoting anorexia and other unhealthy eating.

In a children's search engine the websites may be registered or crawled, but each will be checked to ensure the content is suitable for children. These are popular in primary schools and in homes with young children. However, they have not gained a wider audience as new sites take a long time to be listed due to the checking process, therefore searches may produce fewer results than an ordinary search engine.

Speciality search engines

Examples of these include About.com, Rightmove.co.uk and MedicineNet.com. Each of these search engines will produce results in a certain field. For example, About.com will find answers to questions posed by the user with listings of websites as well as further information. Rightmove.co.uk will find only websites about houses for sale and to let by searching the estate agents' websites. These are useful if the user is sure of the topic he or she wants and they can make the search faster, since there is no need to wade through irrelevant results.

How search engines work

Search engine optimisation (SEO) is the process of getting the best out of directory registration and web crawling. Recently, web designers have not only needed to design and create the desired pages, they have also needed to provide facilities such as SEO to make themselves more competitive in a highly popular market.

Some search engines, such as directories, require the site to be registered before it is listed. This means additional work. Search engines which use web crawlers will automatically find and register new or changed sites. This happens for each page soon after they appear on the Internet and inclusion in the search engine is automatic.

Crawlers will register a site based on what they find. The 'spiders' will search out the homepage of the site and then read the code for that site from top to bottom. They may not read the code for the entire page, just enough for the search engine database entry. Therefore, if there are any keywords that a site should be specifically found under, it is best that they are near the top. Similarly, meta tags, as well as being specific and accurate, should be listed in the <head> section of the site (see Unit 20: Web Authoring, page 334, and Unit 21: Hosting and Managing Websites, page 360). Also in the <head> is the title which can be displayed when that website is found in a search, making it easier for the user to see what the site is about and therefore more likely to visit.

How search engines ignore keywords

Meta tags can be added as keywords or a description for a website and should relate directly to the content of that website. For example, the keywords on the OCR website are 'qualifications, GCSE qualifications, A level qualifications, exam board, CLAiT, awarding body, OCR, key skills, basic skills, exams, examinations' and the description is 'OCR Qualifications are nationally recognised and represent the most respected names in education'. Meta tags can also be used to define other features of the site, such as the language it has been written in.

The practice of keyword stuffing is putting too many meta tags in a page or repeating them several times. This is considered unethical for search engine optimisation because users are trying to find something specific and these websites are trying to poach them and gain extra visitor numbers. There are also some sites which stuff their keywords with the names of their competitors to try and steal their customers, which is also unethical. Search engine software can now recognise the procedure and will either exclude a page from its database or give it a lower ranking, therefore it is becoming an outdated practice.

How search engines rank websites

Websites can be ranked in many ways and each engine does it differently. In Google's case, it will primarily include a site in search results if the keywords logged in its database for that site match the search terms entered by the user. From that point it works on several factors to determine the site's height in the listing. Websites which have paid for sponsorship will appear at the top of the search or in the side bar of sponsored links. Those which have not paid are linked based on a system called PageRank. Each page is ranked based on the number of other websites which have linked to it. The system will also analyse the sites which have linked to the one being listed and looks at their profiles.

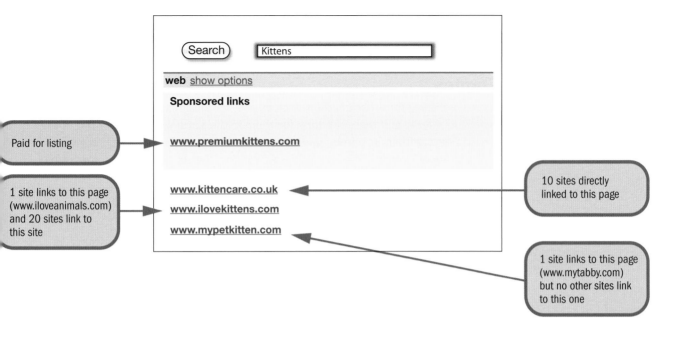

Figure 2.5 Example of page ranking for keyword search "kittens"

Therefore a site is ranked based on its own profile and the profiles of those which link to and from it. The process is very complex but is proving successful for Google which is easily the most popular search engine in the world.

Use of search engines

Using a search engine is easy, but using it well can be quite a skill, as each engine has options to make searches bear more useful fruit than many people realise. Most search engines, except directories, will allow the following refinements to a search.

Keywords

Search engines will carry out a basic search for one or more keywords. Words are entered into the search bar and then the user can press Enter or click a button to start the search. For example, if you were researching a project on Egypt you may use the keywords **egypt**, **ancient egypt**, **egypt pharaohs pyramids** or **who is Tutankhanum**. When choosing keywords for a search, it is usually best to choose the nouns in your topic. Full questions can be entered, but remember that all words in a search count and your results might be better by being more selective with your search words, for example it would be better to use **pyramids built** or **pyramids built year** than the fuller sentence **When were the pyramids built?**

Effective searching is achieved by entering the search terms which will produce the most appropriate and accurate results. Try to choose words which are precise, for example instead of **Kings of Egypt** try searching for **pharaohs**. Consider the terms which may be used on the website, for example **how did the ancient Egyptians live?** would not be a likely phrase on a website, but **daily life in**

ancient Egypt is more probable. Principally, keep your search as simple and straightforward as possible using as few search words as you can, making sure they are accurate.

Quotes

When searching for a phrase, the search engine will automatically treat each word individually and therefore look for them in the same website entry but not necessarily together. By putting quotes around the keywords, the search engine will look for the words only when they appear together in that order, in that exact phrase. For example "**the Great Wall of China**".

Boolean operators

A search can be refined further by using Boolean operators. Boolean means conditions which can be true or false. A Boolean operator determines how the true or false will be worked out. For example, using an AND operator will only allow results which fulfill both criteria. There are a few available, as shown in the table below.

Boolean operator	Example
AND / +	**rugby +league** finds results where both words are present
OR	**league OR union** finds results where either word is present
NOT / -	**rugby -union** finds results where the keyword union is not present
NEAR	**rugby NEAR league** finds results where the words are within a close proximity, usually no more than five or ten words apart

Figure 2.4 Boolean operators

Wildcards

Using a wildcard means only part of a word needs to be entered in a search. The wildcard symbol varies between search engines but is often an asterisk (*). For example, Brit* would search for all words beginning with Brit such as Britain, British, Britannia, Brittle, Britney, etc. This can be useful when the user is unsure of the whole term or perhaps the correct spelling of a word.

Advanced search options

Most search engines now provide advanced search options which can create very specific searches. These can include searching for:

■ all words entered, exact phrasing or listings not containing certain words
■ pages in a specific language, such as French
■ websites uploaded in a certain time period
■ content which is available to be used (e.g. does not fall under copyright law).

Advanced searches usually produce a much more specific set of results and can reduce searching time as the sites found are targeted more explicitly.

Portfolio Activity (AO3)

1   Research the following types of search engine. For each, explain how they work, how websites become included in their listings, why they are useful (in comparison to others) and give at least one existing example:

    a) web crawler

    b) directory

    c) hybrid

    d) meta search engine

    e) children's search engine.

2   Choose a key topic from your allocated articles for your magazine. Use four search engines to search for this topic. The four must include a web crawler, a directory and a children's search engine. You may wish the fourth to be a meta search engine.

3   Repeat the four searches for two more key topics.

4   Compare the results of these searches, explaining the positives, negatives and uses of each type of search engine.

5   Explain the following search techniques. For each, explain what it is, the effect it has and give at least three specific examples where it would be useful:

    a) keywords

    b) quotes

    c) Boolean operators

    d) mathematical signs

    e) wildcards

    f) advanced options.

Assessment Guidance

Pass – Candidates will describe the main features of two different types of search engine, giving at least one example of each. They will explain the appropriate use of two techniques when using search engines. They compare the results of searches using these techniques in two different types of search engine.

Merit – Candidates will describe the main features of three different types of search engine, giving at least one example of each. They will explain the appropriate use of at least three techniques when using search engines. They will compare the results of searches using these techniques in three different types of search engine.

Distinction – Candidates will describe the main features of four different types of search engine, giving at least one example of each. They will explain the appropriate use of at least five techniques when using search engines. They will compare the results of searches using these techniques in four different types of search engines.

Investigate a given topic, using appropriate, advanced search techniques

Research is crucial to most projects as it provides a background and foundation to the particular task at hand. It may prove that a solution already exists or that a particular method has been tried and found unsuccessful. This can save time by avoiding redoing what others have done before.

Identify the information required

When creating a brand new product, research can show you what is already available so you avoid creating something too similar. You may also get ideas from your research, identify a gap in the market or find out what your target audience wants. By clearly isolating what is to be researched, your time can be used more efficiently.

Find information from a range of sources

There is a myriad of sources of information available, both online and in hard copy.

- Do not dismiss the printed word as it provides a vast, invaluable range of interesting and useful data. This includes books, magazines, journals and newspapers. Your local library is a brilliant source of information, especially reference books. Glossaries and indexes can make searching for information simple, and often you will find more resources many of which are more reliable than information from the Internet.
- The Internet is not the only digital information source; there are also CD-ROMs, Intranets and film.
- Interviews and questionnaires can provide a wealth of information from a range of people that offers a different insight into a topic.

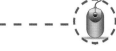

URL
Universal Resource Locator. This is the term for the specific address of any web page. It usually begins http://www.

Create an organised set of bookmarks/favourites to useful information sources

Bookmarks/Favourites are URLs that have been logged so you can visit them again later, without having to search for them again.

When you decide to bookmark a website, you will be given the option of allocating a name and putting it in a folder. The default name will be taken from the URL and the title of the site, so it is advisable to enter a different name that will instantly remind you of the reason you bookmarked the site. The default folder will be the root folder in the bookmarks list. As you collect more and more sites, it is best to save related sites in specifically named folders. The browser will usually allow you to go into your bookmarks list to organise them at any stage, for example to rearrange the order, rename them or create new folders.

When working in a team it might also be useful to use social bookmarking sites, such as Digg.com and Delicious.com, which allow users to share their bookmarks. Team members could then easily distribute research sites without having to email hyperlinks to all team members or copy out large amounts of information.

Evaluate the suitability, reliability and trustworthiness of information found

When carrying out research you will often find a great deal of information, but it cannot be taken at face value. This is especially true on the Internet as there is no regulation of content.

First, research must be evaluated for suitability. This should be based on whether the information is appropriate for the purpose. For example, when carrying out market research with the target audience it is important not to waste their time by collecting information that you do not need and that may distract you from your purpose. When finding information on the Internet, it is easy to get diverted by the vast quantity of information available.

Second, the research must be reliable and trustworthy. By using well-respected sources, such as the BBC or government websites (identifiable by the extension gov.uk), you are more likely to access trustworthy information. Another method can be by finding information from three different sources which corroborate the information.

There are some modern websites that are inherently trusted without the user really considering whether this trust is well placed. Wikipedia is one of these – the content is compiled by users and it may be considered that it is true through consensus. However, as the regulation of the information is again done by the users, incorrect information can be uploaded onto the site and it should be treated with great care.

Investigate copyright of information found

Copyright is a legal protection for any creative work such as a piece of writing, an artwork, music or a website. As soon as the work is created, it is protected under the Copyright, Designs and Patents Act 1988, which regulates against the original work being copied without the owner's position.

When carrying out research, copyright must be understood for each source so that you know how to use it appropriately. Information that has been gathered from a first-hand source belongs to the person or organisation that has carried out the research. Some information may be copyright-free, either because the owner has chosen for it to be so or because copyright has expired following the death of the owner for a stated number of years (usually 50 or 70 years under the terms of the Copyright, Designs and Patents Act 1988). Information that is protected under copyright law can be used under certain circumstances, such as if the source is referenced correctly and permission of the owner has been obtained.

Create a bibliography of sources

Each source which you have quoted or referenced must be included in a bibliography. The bibliography should appear at the end of a piece of work or sit separately in a supporting document. For example, if a piece of music has been used in a computer game, it will be credited in the manual or in the credits.

Bibliographies can take many formats, but a well-recognised method is the Harvard Referencing System. To cite a book using this method, the information is presented in the following order:

- Author (date), title, place of publication, publisher. For example:
  Anderson, K. et al (2009), *OCR National ICT Level 3,* Oxford, Heinemann

To cite a website using this method, the information is presented as follows:

- Author (only include author if applicable), URL: www.websiteaddress.com, (date accessed). For example:
  Anderson, K. et al, www.heinemann.co.uk/Series/Secondary/ OCRNationalsICTLevel3/FreeResources/FreeResources.aspx (June 2009)

Portfolio Activity (AO4)

Individually carry out all the research you require for your contribution to the magazine, considering the quality of the sources and information you obtain.

1 Write a list of all the topics you will need to research. Take care to be thorough, including at least ten or more topics if possible.
2 Beside each topic, write the method you will use to find the information. This must include searching the Internet and using books, but may also include other methods such as carrying out interviews and taking photographs.
3 Carry out all of your research.
   a) For Internet searches, take screenshots of search criteria, results pages and several bookmarks you have created.
   b) Put all of your findings into a research folder, including printouts of websites and scans of pages from books.
   c) Keep a detailed, accurate list of all the sources where you have found information.
4 Create a bibliography of all your sources. For each source, evaluate its suitability, reliability and trustworthiness, and comment on the copyright. You can choose how you format this, but the following column headings are a suggestion of what to include in a table.

- Source type
- Name (title/URL)
- Author (if applicable)
- Date
- Reason for use of source

- Suitability of source (and why)
- Reliability of source (and why)
- Trustworthiness of source (and why)
- Copyright information
- Implications of copyright (and why)

Pass – Candidates will identify a limited range of information required. They will carry out research using the Internet and at least one non-Internet source. They will list their sources and evaluate the suitability and reliability of some of them. They will comment on the copyright of some of the information found. They will create bookmarks/favourites to store useful web links.

Merit – Candidates will identify a range of information required. They will carry out research using the Internet and at least two non-Internet sources. They will list their sources and evaluate the suitability and reliability of most of them. They will comment on the copyright of most of the information found. They will create and organise bookmarks/favourites to store useful web links.

Distinction – Candidates will identify a wide range of information required. They will carry out research using the Internet and at least two non-Internet sources. They will list their sources and evaluate the suitability and reliability of all of them. They will comment on the copyright of all the information found and describe the implications of this for their use of the information. They will create and organise appropriate bookmarks/favourites to store useful web links.

AO5: Create the allocated part of the group task containing information from a range of sources

Carry out the tasks allocated at the group planning stage

At the beginning of the task, each team member should have been allocated a specific role and responsibility in the project. Once the research and the planning have been completed, the actual creation of the product can be carried out.

Use information from a range of sources

When carrying out research, try to find and use as many sources of different types as possible. These could include articles and information from the Internet, paper sources such as books or newspapers, and primary sources such as interviews or surveys.

The information required and how it is to be used are always dependent on the product which is being produced. It may be directly included within the product, for example an interview that will be used in an article in a magazine. Alternatively, it may be that the research will influence the product, such as identifying a gap in the market with market research. Review your research carefully and only include what you absolutely need.

You may wish to incorporate some of the research you have carried out directly into your product. This may involve you downloading or scanning in text or graphics. If so, ensure you have acknowledged your sources.

Portfolio Activity (AO5)

Individually create your contribution to the magazine, using your research.

1 Using at least five of your sources (including one which is not a website), write the text for your article(s) for the magazine. You should aim for it to be highly professional.
2 Check that the text is free from factual, spelling and grammatical errors.
3 Add at least three images you have taken, created or obtained from the Internet to your text. Insert captions to acknowledge the source of these images.
4 Include in your article a quote you have obtained from a person or the Internet and reference it appropriately.
5 Create a bibliography detailing the sources you have used.

AO6: Work collaboratively with others to review the results of the research and produce the final product

Use knowledge gained of communication methods to produce the final product

While the product is being created, team members should be in continual contact with each other. There are a range of communication methods available to achieve this, as described in Assessment Objective 2: Investigate ICT tools to support collaborative working (see pages 69–71).

Team members' discussions will be wide-ranging, covering all aspects of the product. These may be one-to-one or involve several people and discussions with different combinations of people will be frequent.

These discussions may be to discuss research or gain feedback on work done. This should always be done constructively, meaning honestly but positively. The aim should be to solve problems or move onto further discussions. Members of the team should regularly share the progress they are making so everyone, especially the team leader, has a clear and accurate picture of how the project is progressing against the schedule.

Discussion in a collaborative project is often the best method for producing new ideas, especially as changes are needed throughout a project. If a team member has been working on a particular section that requires a major change, it can be difficult to objectively assess the necessary alterations. Conversing with other team members who are working towards the same goal can often provide different perspectives that may lead to new ideas and solutions.

Produce final product using appropriate methods of sharing and collating information

Communication methods provide channels for discussion which can be especially useful when team members are spread around the country or even the world. If a face-to-face meeting is required, shared electronic diaries can be used to organise a time when all who need to attend can be present. Although technology is a fantastic enabler and can allow communication from all sides of the globe, there are situations where face-to-face meetings must take place and the value of them should not be forgotten. For example, the proofing of a document could be done over the Internet, but coming up with new ideas is much more effective when people get together and discuss their thoughts.

As the product progresses, collaborative editing can take place. For example, reviewing and track-changes tools can be used when producing a document such as a magazine.

Portfolio Activity (AO6)

In your team, communicate and share information in order to review each other's work before compiling it into the final product.

1. In your team, hold a meeting. At least one team member should take detailed notes of the content of the meeting and each person's contribution. You may wish to ask your teacher to observe and write a witness statement. In the meeting, discuss who will review each member's work and how this will be done (for example, how they will communicate, how they will share information). Refer to the methods you decided upon for Assessment Objective 2.

2. Carry out the review, with each team member reviewing someone else's work (articles and research). For example, person A could email their work to person B. Person B could then use the reviewing tools in Microsoft Word to add comments and track changes before emailing the work back to person A. Person A could then make changes and send it back to person B, or could discuss the feedback via email.

3. Provide evidence of the original work, the suggestions made and the amendments carried out. There should be justification for any changes not made.

4. Once all work is reviewed and amended to the satisfaction of the team, compile the magazine into one complete product. This should be done as a team and everyone should keep a record of each team member's contribution.

Assessment Guidance

Pass – Candidates will share their document electronically for review. They will review work from colleagues using ICT tools to give feedback. The candidate's individual document will be incorporated into the final group product.

Merit – Candidates will share their document electronically for review. They will make some appropriate use of document versions. They will act on feedback received or explain why suggestions were not followed. They will review work from colleagues using appropriate ICT tools to give feedback, including tracked changes **or** comments. Their feedback will be helpful. The candidate's individual documents will be incorporated into the final group product.

Distinction – Candidates will share their document electronically for review. They will use document versions appropriately. They will act on feedback received or explain why suggestions were not followed. They will review work from colleagues using appropriate ICT tools to give feedback, including tracked changes **and** comments. The candidate's final product will be of near professional standard and will be submitted with all reviewing information removed. The individual document will be incorporated into the final group product.

Measure project against success criteria

During the planning stage of the project, you should have defined success criteria for the whole project and for each of the sub-tasks. Now, in the final review stages of the project, it is time to test your product against these criteria. This will tell you whether it is complete and successful.

Your success criteria may involve testing your product thoroughly for errors, spelling mistakes or bugs, depending on the product created. Alternatively – or in addition – you may need to assemble a focus group made up of members of the target audience, to try the product and give their opinions.

If any success criteria have not been met, the team must decide whether they need to be fixed, so requiring further work on the product. If many changes are required, another plan may be required, with tasks again being allocated to team members.

Evaluation

At the end of a project it is important to look back at how it was executed and the final result. It is also vital to learn from both the things that went well and the areas that could have been improved upon. Even if your specific team will not work together again, each member can learn about his or her own team-working skills and develop for the future.

By evaluating the research phase, the team can identify – with the beauty of hindsight – the effectiveness of the search engines used and the quality of the information found. They can also look at the range of search techniques and information sources utilised. They can decide what worked well and what they would do differently next time.

This can then lead onto an examination of how the information has been used in the actual product, in turn becoming an analysis of the whole product, including whether it has satisfied the success criteria. The team should identify both good points and bad points; from the bad points, areas for improvement can be identified.

After examining the product, the final part of the evaluation should concern the team itself. The contribution of each team member can be assessed, individually and by each other. If it is felt that one person has not contributed as much as the others, then this is something which he or she can rectify in future team projects. It is better for a person to know, so that he or she can resolve issues, than to remain unaware of problems.

After looking at each person's involvement, the team should be considered as a whole. If it was an effective group that produced a successful product on time, what elements of this team contributed to this outcome? If the group was ineffective, what errors were made and what could have been done differently?

Finally, the communication methods which the team used throughout the project should be appraised – were they helpful or did they hinder the communication process and in what ways?

Portfolio Activity (AO7)

Individually assess and evaluate the whole project.

1 Look back at the success criteria you outlined in your planning. Describe how your final product has or has not achieved each criterion.

2 Describe the good and bad points of your final product. Comment upon its suitability and appropriateness in terms of target audience.

3 Explain changes you would make to the project as a whole if you were to create a similar product in the future.

4 Evaluate your individual research in terms of the effectiveness of the search engines chosen, the search criteria used and the sources of information found. Compare your web and non-web sources. Were some more useful than others? Discuss the quality of the information you found from your research.

5 Describe the effectiveness of the collaboration tools you used, including methods of communicating and methods of sharing information. Did they help or hinder?

6 Consider and explain your contribution to the group. Do you feel you were valuable? What do you consider your personal strengths and weaknesses within a team? What areas could you improve as a team member?

7 Analyse the contribution and effectiveness of the group. Discuss each member's contribution fairly.

Pass – Candidates will comment on the effectiveness of the search engine(s) used, the search criteria used and the sources of information used. They will compare their Internet and non-Internet sources. They will comment on the suitability of the final group product. They will comment on the collaborative tools used stating any changes they would make when attempting a similar task in the future. They will comment on the contribution of other group members, the effectiveness of the group and their own effectiveness.

Merit – Candidates will make detailed comments on the effectiveness of the search engine(s) used, the search criteria and the sources of information used, as well as the quality of the information found. They will compare their Internet and non-Internet sources. They will make detailed comments on the suitability of the final product. They will comment on the effectiveness of the use of collaborative tools and describe changes they would make when attempting a similar task in the future. They will review the contribution of other group members, the effectiveness of the group and their own effectiveness.

Distinction – Candidates will carry out a thorough evaluation of the effectiveness of the search engine(s) used, the search criteria and the sources of information used, as well as the quality of the information found. They will compare their Internet and non-Internet sources. They will evaluate the suitability of the final product. They willl evaluate the use of collaborative tools and explain changes they would make when attempting a similar task in the future. They will evaluate the contribution of other group members, the effectiveness of the group and their own effectiveness.

Problem Solving

Learning outcomes

By working through this unit you will produce evidence to meet the unit assessment objectives to show that you understand how to:

- define a statistical problem to be investigated
- design and carry out a data collection activity
- collect data and use spreadsheet software to store the data
- use spreadsheet software for data analysis
- create suitable graphs and charts
- present the results of the study.

Introduction

This unit is about investigating a 'problem'. You will consider what you are going to investigate, set a hypothesis, collect data and analyse it before presenting the results of your investigation.

One approach to problem solving is clarifying the description of the problem, analysing the causes, identifying alternatives, assessing each alternative, choosing one, implementing it, and evaluating whether the problem is solved or not. Another approach is hypothesis testing – assuming a possible explanation to the problem and trying to prove the assumption.

Scenario

Recently there has been a great deal of discussion regarding the health of populations in the developed world. In the UK there is concern regarding child health in terms of diet and exercise.

One current initiative is the National Child Measurement Programme. This is for children aged 4–5 years (Reception) and 10–11 years (Year 6). A trained member of staff, such as a school nurse, weighs and measures each child who has chosen to take part in the study. The more children who participate, the clearer that picture will be. This initiative is part of a national effort to improve the health and well-being of children. The information will help local health services decide on the best way to use their resources for children's health.

Children need at least 60 minutes of physical exercise a day. It is thought that many children do not take this amount of exercise each day, and some do not take any exercise at all. Indeed, children are less involved in physical activities than they were in previous generations. This will, of course, have implications on the health of the country in the future.

You have been commissioned by your local health trust to produce a study into this area. Having carried out your initial investigation, you will set your hypothesis. You should then outline your method of gathering data to prove or disprove that hypothesis and present the results of your study.

Scenario

AO1: Define a statistical problem to be investigated

Identify the problem

The first step in your project is to identify the problem and describe it. Consider what may have caused the situation to have come about, and if there are any contraindications.

The local health trust needs more information on the amount of exercise children are engaged in because of the effect this may have on their health now and in the future. You should carry out initial investigations.

No matter how you do your background research, you must record your sources and make notes. One way to start is by looking on the Internet to find out some of the main issues. Read the information you locate and note any further sources on related sites. Gather more information from existing surveys and publications.

When identifying the problem for this project you should consider if, or how, factors such as location, education, gender and age group affect the result. You should consider activities that children engage in such as swimming, horse riding and scouting, as well as clubs such as athletics clubs and martial arts clubs.

Explain the background to the problem

When you have carried out the background research you need to identify the main points of what has happened to bring about the new set of circumstances that you will examine.

When explaining the background to the problem you should consider why the local health trust believe that children are not getting sufficient exercise – outline their concerns. Are more children being seen by the health trust? Why? Are there any links or trends?

To determine the present situation, knowing what happened in the past will enable you to explore and understand the issues and relationships. This should not, however, lead you to generalise about results, findings or theories that may impact on your study. What was the situation in the past? Were there differences in specific areas, such as age or gender?

You may examine the issue of the amount of exercise taken. You should explain the purpose of the research and include an explanation of what is known now.

Set a hypothesis

Once you have decided on the area you want to consider, you should set your hypothesis. This is a statement that proposes a possible explanation to some fact, event or trend. It consists of a suggested explanation for the fact, event or trend or a reasoned proposal suggesting a possible relationship.

The hypothesis should be written before the data collection and analysis, its value being that it forces you to think about what results you should look for in a test. The keyword is testable. In considering a problem the question should be simplified into two competing claims between which there is a choice. You will then carry out data collection and analyse it. It is important that you do not know the results already and that you can independently find an answer.

Consider the formulation of your hypothesis carefully. For example, consider the hypothesis 'Children who participate in sports may be healthier'. This uses the tentative word 'may'. However, it is not particularly useful as it does not suggest how you would go about proving it. The best way to produce a hypothesis is to specify it clearly. A hypothesis should contain two variables – an independent variable, that you control, and a dependent variable, that you observe and test.

When setting a hypothesis, use statements containing the words 'if' and 'then'. State a tentative relationship, followed by a prediction of what will happen. When you identify that one thing is related to another you should be able to test it, for example: 'If the frequency of winning is related to frequency of training, then those who train more will win more often.'

Identify project objectives and success criteria

First, you have to decide what you are trying to do by carrying out this project. Limit the number of objectives to keep your project focused. Next, outline the criteria for identifying whether the outcomes of the objectives have been achieved and the project has been a success.

A project objective should be written so that it can be evaluated at the end of a project and used in the presentation of your results. A popular rule for writing good objectives is that they be SMART objectives.

Identify data to be collected and the methods of processing

When defining the objectives and the data you should be careful to include as wide a range and variety as possible, so that you do not simply gather data to prove your point. It is better to gather data, analyse that data and then make your point.

For example, you may wish to gather information from those who run the activities for young people on factors such as:

- Have the numbers participating increased or decreased?
- How are these figures broken down?
- Do more boys participate than girls?
- Does the participation change with age?
- Are there reasons for this drop off?

Do you want to calculate the average for each group or summarise the results in some other way such as percentages? Or is it better to display your data as individual data points? You also have to consider the spreadsheet that you will use to process your data – what will it be required to do? Think about the input, the processing and the output.

Hypothesis
A hypothesis is based on some previous observation, such as noticing that there are fewer children playing in streets, parks and other open spaces and more children are spending their leisure hours playing on computers. Are these two connected? How?

SMART objectives
Specific – specifies what, where, and how the problem is to be addressed.

Measurable – outlines how much, how many, etc.

Action-oriented – uses action-oriented verbs such as deliver, establish and supply.

Realistic – ensures a result that can be achieved.

Time-bound – includes a specific date for achievement.

In order to define the data and the processing of that data, you also need to give some consideration to how you want to present the results. Your conclusions will summarise whether or not your results support or contradict your original hypothesis. How will you include key facts from your background research? Will you use charts and graphs to help you analyse the data and patterns?

Demonstrate an awareness of the Data Protection Act 1998

You are going to collect and use data from people in the course of this unit. It is important that you know how you must deal with this data in terms of the Data Protection Act 1998. This Act sets out rules for use of personal information, not only on computers but also on paper records. It allows individuals the right to know what information is held about them. It defines a legal basis for the handling in the UK of information relating to living people. It is the main piece of legislation for the protection of personal data. It does not mention privacy, but it does provide a way for individuals to control the information about them. Organisations in the UK are legally obliged to comply with this Act, but there are exemptions.

The independent government authority, the Information Commissioner's Office, provides help and guidance about the Act and ensures that companies comply with it. You can find their website at www.ico.gov.uk.

The Data Protection Act uses definitions you should be aware of, including:

Data subject: a living individual who is the subject of the personal information (data).

Data controller: a person who determines the purposes for which, and the manner in which, personal information is to be processed. This may be an individual or an organisation and the processing may be carried out jointly or in common with other persons.

Notification: the requirement for organisations to supply the details of how they process personal information to the Information Commissioner's Office (ICO).

Personal data: data which can be used to identify a living person. This could include: date of birth, names, addresses, telephone numbers, fax numbers and email addresses.

The Act defines eight principles of information handling, and regulates the way that businesses act in terms of who can be contacted for marketing purposes, not only by telephone and direct mail but also electronically.

Key principles

There are eight principles to ensure that information is handled properly. The personal data must be:

- fairly and lawfully processed – your personal data must not be disclosed to other parties without your consent, unless there is legislation or an exemption to share it such as the prevention or detection of crime
- processed for limited purposes – personal data may only be used for the specific purposes for which it was collected
- adequate, relevant and not excessive in relation to the purpose or purposes for which it is processed
- accurate and, where necessary, kept up to date

- not kept for longer than necessary
- processed in line with your rights – individuals have a right of access to the information held about them, subject to certain exceptions
- not transferred to other countries without adequate protection – personal information may not be transmitted outside the European Economic Area unless you have consented or adequate protection is in place
- secure – those holding personal information must have adequate security measures in place. Appropriate technical and organisational measures should be taken against unauthorised or unlawful processing of personal data and against accidental loss or destruction of or damage to it. Technical measures might include use of firewalls and organisational measures might include staff training.

Rights

The Data Protection Act gives the individual rights if their personal data is stored, and places responsibilities on those who collect or store personal data.

If your personal data is stored you have the right to:

- view any data a company holds on you; there is a fee to view this data, referred to as 'Subject Access Requests'
- have any incorrect data corrected (if this is not done the company can be ordered by a court to correct or destroy it; in some cases you may be awarded compensation)
- specify that it is not used in a way which causes damage or distress
- specify that it is not used for direct marketing.

There are exemptions, which are mainly what could be considered as 'official'. They depend on how the data is held, and the subject of the data. There are exemptions to the Data Protection Act, these are shown on Information Commissioner's Office (ICO) website (www.ico.gov.uk).

While collecting the data you require for your investigation you will need to consider the Data Protection Act to ensure that you are not breaking any of the principles.

There are also special exemptions that apply to some personal information relating to health, education and social work.

Personal data processed for research purposes has exemption if two conditions are satisfied. These conditions are:

- the data is not processed to support measures or decisions with respect to a particular individual
- the data is not processed so that substantial damage or distress is, or is likely to be, caused to any data subject.

Portfolio Activity (AO1)

The local health trust would like to know your findings to date. Prepare a report outlining your hypothesis and how you will go about proving or disproving it.

1 Identify a problem, explain the background to the problem and set your own hypothesis by:
   a) carrying out initial investigations and explaining the background to the problem
   b) using sources such as the Internet to outline the main issues
   c) setting your hypothesis with reference to the scenario.
2 Identify the objectives you are hoping to achieve by carrying out the project.
3 Set the criteria you will use to judge the success of the project.
4 Identify the data to be collected.
5 Identify the methods of processing – you should decide what the spreadsheet is required to do in terms of:
   a) the input
   b) data processing
   c) required output, such as the type of graphs or charts that would be most suitable

6 Explain how you will comply with Data Protection legislation.

Assessment Guidance

Pass – Candidates will describe the background to the problem. They will set a simple hypothesis and list some criteria to be used to test it. They will identify some of the data that needs to be collected and briefly explain how it will be processed. They will demonstrate an understanding of Data Protection legislation and give a brief explanation of how they will comply with this.

Merit – Candidates will clearly describe the background to the problem. They will set a complex hypothesis and clearly describe criteria that will be used to test it. They will identify the data that needs to be collected and explain how it will be processed. They will demonstrate an understanding of Data Protection legislation and explain how they will comply with this.

Distinction – Candidates will explain thoroughly the background to the problem. They will set a complex hypothesis and clearly describe and justify the criteria that will be used to test it. They will identify the data that needs to be collected and explain clearly how it will be processed. They will demonstrate an understanding of Data Protection legislation and explain how they will comply with this.

AO2: Design and carry out a data collection activity

Introduction

Data is gathered all the time – by government, by banks, by businesses such as supermarkets and by information we provide about ourselves on the Internet. For example, a cookie is a small text file sent to your computer when you visit some websites which is used to store information about you for the next time you visit that site – information such as where you went on the site and what you did. They store your purchasing information and record your preferences.

For the purposes of this unit, data collection is how your data is gathered. There are various methods, including questionnaires, interviews and observation.

A formal data collection process ensures that the data you gather is both defined and accurate, and that any decisions based on arguments in your findings are valid.

Research methods

Quantitative research

Quantitative research is about numbers and measurement in the collection and analysis of data. It is used to establish relationships between two or more variables. For example, research has established a consistent and strong relationship between the amount of alcohol consumed and developing liver problems.

Quantitative research begins with the collection of data based on a hypothesis. Usually a large volume of data is collected, which requires validating, verifying and recording before analysis. For example, in opinion surveys, respondents are asked a set of questions and their responses are recorded.

Your quantitative approach might be to generate a hypothesis, develop methods for measurement, collect data, analyse the data, and finally, evaluate the results. Statistics, tables and graphs are often used to present the results.

Qualitative research

Research should be logical and without bias. However, complete objectivity is difficult as researchers may unconsciously taint data by applying their ideas or beliefs to the information while it is under observation. This is of particular importance when carrying out qualitative research, which is subjective. As the information gathered is descriptive rather than statistical it is more open to researcher bias.

The focus of qualitative research is on feelings or opinions. For example this could involve ranking, on a scale of 1–10 (1 being **dislike**, 10 being **really like**) a series of pictures.

It can be very difficult to analyse qualitative research as people have different likes and dislikes. One method by which qualitative research could be analysed is through the use of graphs and charts. This method will provide useful data on which objective analysis can be made. However, remember that qualitative research is based on opinions and is not always reliable.

Quantitative and qualitative research

To differentiate between quantitative and qualitative research:

- Quantitative research is more focused and aims to test a hypothesis – qualitative research is hypothesis-generating.

- Quantitative research is objective, so the data gathered is not influenced by personal bias – qualitative research is subjective so there is the possibility of distortion due to researcher bias.

- Quantitative research produces numeric data that is easier to analyse and display – qualitative research produces descriptive information making it more difficult to analyse and display graphically.

Data collection methods

Questionnaires

Questionnaires are a popular means of collecting data. They can be difficult to design and may require a lot of work before an appropriate questionnaire is produced.

When your questionnaire is being designed, it is essential that you consider how the questionnaire is to be used. If a questionnaire is to be completed by an interviewer asking the questions then the format, layout and instructions will be different than if the questionnaire is being completed, for example, online by the individual alone.

It is also important that the information collected enables successful analysis to be completed. The way of ensuring that all the data needed is collected is to pilot the questionnaire. This means that the questionnaire is used by a small group of people with the results being analysed. Comments from the pilot group can also be used to amend the questionnaire and make it, if needed, more appropriate to the research being completed by changing question wording, question types or layout to enhance the logical flow of the information being collected. Remember, the results from the questionnaire will form the basis of your research. If the data you collect is not appropriate then you may not be able to successfully prove your point.

You should be aware of the importance of different questions. Consider the questions with care:

- keep them short, simple and to the point; avoid unnecessary words
- use words and phrases that are unambiguous and familiar to the subject
- ask only questions that the subject can answer
- avoid questions that require use of the memory
- use quantitative statements such as 'at least once a week'
- address only a single issue in each question.

Try to ensure that your questionnaires will be completed. Do not make them too long or too complex, and do not make them too personal. To conform with the Data Protection Act you must consider if you need to collect personal data, such as name.

Advantages of questionnaires	Disadvantages of questionnaires
■ They can be used in their own right or as the basis for personal or telephone interviews. ■ They can be posted, emailed or faxed. ■ They can cover a large number of people or organisations. ■ They can provide wide geographic coverage. ■ They allow the subject to consider their responses. ■ They provide anonymity for the subjects.	■ There can be low response rates – reminders may be required. ■ There can be a time delay waiting for responses to be returned. ■ There is no control over who completes it, unless present. ■ It is not possible to give assistance, unless present. ■ They may be incomplete.

Figure 3.1 The advantages and disadvantages of using a questionnaire

Data logging equipment

Data logging is the process of collecting data through sensors, analysing the data, saving and presenting the results. It also includes control of how the data is collected and analysed. Data logging is commonly used in monitoring systems where there is the need to collect information faster than a human can, and in cases where accuracy is essential. There is a wide range of data logging hardware and software to provide input for test, monitoring and control programs.

A data logger is an electronic instrument that records information over a period of time for later use. Sensors convert a physical quantity into an electrical signal which is translated into numerical values. The type of information recorded is determined by the user. Examples of the types of information collected include temperatures, sound frequencies, times, light intensities and pressure. A data logger collects measurements at periodic intervals and records them in chronological order. They can collect up to 1000 items of data in a regular, synchronised manner from each sensor.

This type of data gathering is carried out in real time. Many operating systems and computer programs include some form of logging subsystem. An example of a physical system with a logging subsystem is the black box recorder in an aircraft.

The advantages of using data logging equipment are:

- measurements can be collected from several sensors simultaneously
- measurements are fast and regular
- measurements can be stored and presented immediately
- data can be collected over specified time periods (hours or days)
- the data can viewed retrospectively
- the collector is not directly involved
- it can be used in difficult situations where safety may be at risk
- subjects can be observed and measured in greater detail, allowing patterns which might otherwise be invisible (too small, too sudden or too slow) to be observed.

Most data logger software allows the user to view data in different formats. The most common are graphical and tabular. The graphical format allows for an overview of what is happening and observing trends. The tabular format provides raw data. Data in this format can be exported to a spreadsheet for further analysis.

Data loggers can be used if the data to be collected does not solely relate to people. For example, if the data to be collected relates to traffic use on a motorway it would be very difficult to collect data using a questionnaire. A data logger could be used to collect data about the number of cars and lorries passing a given point over a period of time. This data could then be enhanced by qualitative research to gather information about how people feel about traffic or motorways.

Sampling

The purpose of sampling is to obtain information about the characteristics or parameters of a population. This information can be gathered by taking a sample.

This includes:

1 Defining the target population – this is the collection of elements that possess the information you are looking for, in this case children.
2 Determining the sample – this is a representation of the elements of the target population, in this case selecting a group or groups of children.

3   Selecting a sampling method – this is making a decision on the type of sample method that is appropriate for your study (e.g. random, cluster, quota or stratified) to get the best possible coverage of the population.

Random sampling

A simple random sample is a subset of items chosen from a larger set. It gives each member of the population an equal chance of being chosen. In your study you might decide to allocate a number to each child in your population, and then use random numbers to select the required sample.

Random sampling avoids bias and is useful for statistical purposes, but the main disadvantage is that you require a large population from which to select your sample.

Cluster sampling

Cluster sampling is a sampling technique in which the entire population is divided into groups or clusters. A random sample of these clusters is then selected. An example of this would be to divide a large geographical area into smaller areas, or clusters. A random selection of the clusters is then selected at random and individuals from this cluster are selected for interview. For example, you can divide the British population into postcodes. 100 postcodes are then chosen at random. Then 100 addresses from these postcodes are chosen at random to select households to interview.

One of the main disadvantages of this method is that the groups that you are selecting may be very similar and so are less likely to represent the population as a whole.

Quota Sampling

Quota sampling is a method of sampling that is widely used in market research or opinion polling. An interviewer will be given a specified subject and number to interview – say, 20 teenage boys and 20 teenage girls on the subject of their favourite sport.

The problem with this technique is that the sample is not a random sample. As it is not a random selection, not everyone has the same chance of being selected. It is more open to bias, as you might only select teenage boys or girls who look sporty to be interviewed.

The main advantage is that it is quick and relatively easy to organise. However, it is not representative of the population as a whole.

Stratified sampling

Stratified sampling is used when the population can be placed into a number of groups with similar characteristics. For example, you might want to divide a population into men and women. When deciding on the variables (like gender) to separate groups or strata, you need to make sure that the variables are mutually exclusive i.e. they cannot be both men and women. Another important factor when deciding upon variables is that everyone in a population must be able to be included in a group. Other examples of variables that could be used are age, ethnicity or religion.

The advantages of using this method are that it is a useful way of identifying groups within a population, and the results from each group can be analysed separately. However, identifying appropriate groups can be more difficult, and analysing the results more complicated.

Determining the sample size

Sampling is a way of using a smaller group of people to learn information about a larger group or population. The main question is how large a sample group should you choose to represent the larger group? Determining sample size is a very important issue because samples that are too large may waste time, resources and money, while samples that are too small may lead to inaccurate results. There are several approaches that are used to determine the sample size. For example, a professional survey such an opinion poll may use published tables that already exist to determine the appropriate sample size. There are also formulas to calculate the appropriate sample size. For example, the web site http://www.surveysystem.com/sscalc.htm provides researchers with a simple calculator to estimate the size of the sample needed to get the best results.

Selecting the most appropriate sample size should produce more reliable and valid results. You should report on how you decide on your sample size so that it is possible to judge whether your assumptions and procedures are reasonable.

Potential errors

No matter how reliable sample size and the method of collection are, there is always the potential for errors to occur. There are different types of errors that can occur, and these are explained below.

Sampling errors

The sample selected could be too small to get the range of data needed. If this occurs then you may decide to expand your sample and collect more data. The sample you have selected may not be representative. Again, you may decide to collect more data with an increased sample. Another possibility is that when you were selecting your sample you may have selected an inappropriate sample method. If this occurs then you may choose to begin the data collection again using a different method or increase the sample.

Design errors

Errors can be introduced when you are designing your collection method and considering the sample. The questions, and as a result the answers you get, may not produce the data you require. When you are carrying out your analysis, you may also get errors. This may also be as a result of inappropriate analysis methods or incorrect calculations/functions.

Human errors

If the data is being collected by a person then there is the potential for very many errors to occur. For example, the answers given could be recorded incorrectly or the questions may be asked incorrectly. The person collecting the data may, despite being given the sample breakdown required, select inappropriate people to interview.

Respondent error

If you are collecting your data through a questionnaire by post or email, then the biggest issue is people not returning the completed questionnaire. This issue could be taken into account by increasing the proposed sample size to cover those people who do not respond. If people are completing the data gathering method in isolation then they may not understand the questions. This kind of error could be reduced by including comments or a help sheet.

Hardware and software required

You should outline requirements in terms of the hardware and the software that you need to carry out your project. Remember that you have to store your data in a spreadsheet and, if you wish present the findings using presentation software. You may also require word-processing or desktop publishing software to prepare your work for the data collection activity.

Collect data

Collecting data is time-consuming even for relatively small amounts of data, so it is unlikely that you will investigate a complete population. Because of the time and cost elements, the amount of data you collect will be limited and the number of people or organisations you contact will be small in number. You will probably have to take a sample, and usually a small sample.

The majority of the data you will use should come from your own primary research, such as questionnaires and interviews. When you have decided what data you need to gather, you have to collect it. Decide who, and how many subjects you are going to target for each set and subset in your study, and identify the specific subjects.

Portfolio Activity (AO2)

The local health trust needs to know that your data collection design and method meet with their requirements and your hypothesis. They would like to be sure that your sample selection and data collection methods are satisfactory and that you have the equipment to carry out your activities.

1   Prepare a report outlining:
    a) The design of your data collection activities, including:
- your research method – you should indicate what you will be doing, how you will do it and the depth of the research you will carry out
- your data collection methods, such as questionnaires and interviews
- a definition of the data you need to gather in order to support or disprove your hypothesis. In defining your sample, include the:
  - method, i.e. how you will select your sample, e.g. cluster, quota, random, stratified
  - frequency and interval size should also be considered if this is appropriate to the method of data collection that you used.

    b) The areas of potential error in your sampling regime, and explain the steps you have taken to eliminate bias from your study. You should also describe any constraints that affect the reliability of your study.
    c) The hardware and software required to carry out the task.
2   Create your data collection method and use it to collect the data.

Pass – Candidates will plan and carry out a data collection activity to gather some suitable data for their investigation. The plan will include a suitable sampling method. Candidates will list some of the constraints that could affect the reliability of their study. They will collect some useful data.

Merit – Candidates will plan and carry out a data collection activity to gather a range of suitable data for their investigation. The plan will include a suitable sampling method and size. Candidates will describe most of the constraints that could affect the reliability of their study and identify some areas of potential error in their sampling regime. They will collect the data identified.

Distinction – Candidates will plan and carry out a data collection activity to gather the data that is necessary for their investigation. They will make appropriate use of research and data collection methods. The plan will include a suitable sampling method and size, and frequency/interval if appropriate, with justification of choices. Candidates will describe the constraints that could affect the reliability of their study and identify areas of potential error in their sampling regime. They will explain the steps they have taken to eliminate bias from their study. They will collect the data identified.

AO3: Collect data and store it using a spreadsheet

Create a spreadsheet interface to collect the data required

In order for you to continue with the next phase of your project, you will need a way to help you collect, collate, store and analyse your data. Spreadsheet software is ideal for helping with these activities. You will need to decide what data you need to capture and how you will do this. You should also consider how you will keep your data secure while you are carrying out these activities, and your obligations under UK legislation when capturing personal data.

Data forms

Microsoft Excel provides forms to help you enter data in a worksheet list (a series of worksheet rows that contain related data, such as a set of names, addresses and phone numbers, with the first row containing the column labels).

Excel can generate a built-in data form – a dialogue box that displays one complete record. Use this to add, amend, change, locate and delete records in your list. All the column labels are shown in one box with blank spaces for you to enter the data. You can also find rows based on cell contents, update existing data and delete rows from the list. The built-in forms are of most use when you require a simple form and to make data entry easier.

Worksheet forms and templates

You can create a form for people to fill out online or in printed form. Worksheet forms are particularly useful when you want individual printable copies of your forms.

Template Wizard forms

If you are using Microsoft Office 2007 then you can create a form template in Excel and then use the Template Wizard to set up a separate Excel list to collect the data entered in the forms created from the template. You can use this method, for example, when multiple users will each fill in a copy of a form. If you are using a spreadsheet package other than Microsoft Excel then you may need to create macros to create and customise the interface.

Use the Template Wizard when you want both a workbook copy of each filled-in form and a separate record of all the entries. When you use Template Wizard forms, Excel maintains your list automatically and keeps an individual printable copy of each filled-in form in a separate workbook.

You should ensure that the input on the form that will be entered on the spreadsheet matches the data you have collected.

Creating a form

One method of creating a form is to:

- Highlight the row that contains the fields that need the data filling in. This is usually row 1 or the first row.
- From the menu bar, select Data and then Form.

This will create a basic form that can be used to fill in the data.

But, you must remember to set validation rules before you create the form. The form can be tailored. For example the font styles and sizes and colour used can be chosen.

Set validation to reduce data entry errors

When entering data you must try to ensure that the spreadsheet is kept error-free. Data validation can limit errors by restricting what data can be entered into a data field.

When creating a spreadsheet you can enter your own data-entry messages based on the data validation that you are introducing. You can set validation checks on cells and ranges of cells. The validation rules apply when new data is entered. See Unit 5 Advanced Spreadsheets page 156.

Use suitable tools to protect the collected data

The results of your data collection must be kept confidential. You should indicate the security you will use at both hardware and software levels, such as password protection and access rights.

You can also protect cells or ranges from all user access, or you could grant individual users access.

Protecting/locking cells

All cells in a spreadsheet can be locked. To protect all the data in a single worksheet the Protect Sheet option can be used.

If you have collected data then when it has been input into the worksheet some of it will need protecting. Protecting and locking cells can be achieved by using passwords. Cells can be protected, or locked, to ensure that the data they contain cannot be changed. For example any formulas you have input or cell-referencing, must be locked to maintain their integrity.

Password-protecting files

You will need to ensure that the collected data is kept secure. This could be achieved by password-protecting your files. This means that only the people who have the password are able to access the data. By password-protecting the files you are able to limit the access to the data, so complying with Data Protection legislation.

You can restrict who can open and use a file by requiring a password to view or edit the data. You can set two separate passwords, one to open and view the file and another to allow editing and saving of changes.

Protect a file

1 On the Tools menu, click Options, then select the Security tab.
2 Do either of the following:
   ■ If you want users to enter a password before they can view the workbook, type a password in the 'Password to open' box, and click OK.
   ■ If you want users to enter a password before they can save changes to the workbook, type a password in the 'Password to modify' box, and click OK.
3 When prompted, retype your passwords to confirm them.

By password protecting a file to define if users can view or amend data, you are setting access rights. As the creator of the file you should have full access rights. That means you can amend, delete and view the data. The access rights you set will depend on what the users need to do. For example an access right can be set so that a user can just view the data held in the spreadsheet. Other access rights include edit and write. If you are collecting your data through the use of an online method you should consider the access rights carefully. You may need to consider protecting or setting access rights for a spreadsheet workbook, worksheets or individual cells.

Back up files

Once you have stored your collected data in your spreadsheet it is important to keep it safe. To do this you should keep a backup of your work.

Backing up your work means that you make a copy of it in case something happens to the original version. You should ensure that every time you amend your original file, you make another backup copy. This will mean that any work you have completed since the last backup is saved as well.

The most important factor is that you should store backups in a safe place away from your computer. Your backup is only as safe as the media on which it is held. If you backup your work and do not place it in a secure place you are not protecting against risks such as theft or disaster (such as fire).

To further protect the security of your data, encrypt and password protect the storage media, such as USB drives, and memory sticks.

Portfolio Activity (AO3)

The local health trust has provided the hardware and software you requested to carry out your study. You should now:

1 Create a spreadsheet interface, such as a data form, to collect the data for your project.
2 Use suitable tools to protect the data collected such as:
   - locking/protecting cells
   - password-protecting files.
3 Incorporate methods of maintaining the anonymity of the data subjects and the integrity of the data you collect.
4 Set validation to reduce data entry errors.
5 Enter the data you have collected into the spreadsheet.
6 Store the data securely using password protection at data and file levels.

Note: your evidence could be word-processed documents and spreadsheet printouts. If the spreadsheet is provided electronically, then password protection or cell protection can be checked online, but if hard copies are provided, screen prints must be produced to show how the cells have, for example, been locked or protected.

Assessment Guidance

Pass – Candidates will create a simple interface for entering data into a spreadsheet. They will include at least one suitable validation routine to limit data entry errors. They will store some useful data.

Merit – Candidates will create an effective interface for entering data relevant to their research into a spreadsheet. They will include suitable validation routines to limit data entry errors for most items of data where this is appropriate. They will store the data collected and take at least one measure to ensure its security. They will demonstrate an understanding of the need for security measures.

Distinction – Candidates will create an effective and easy-to-use interface for entering data relevant to their research into a spreadsheet. They will use a range of effective validation methods to minimise data entry errors wherever possible. They will store the data collected and protect it from unauthorised access and from accidental and deliberate change and loss. They will demonstrate a thorough understanding of the need for security and the range of measures that are needed.

AO4: Create a suitable spreadsheet to analyse the data

Choose an appropriate layout

Now that you have gathered and entered the data for your project, you need to decide on the layout of the spreadsheet that you will use to display the results and analyse that data. Think about these points:

- Analysis and reporting is simpler if you limit the number of sheets that you use; place your raw data on one worksheet in one workbook.
- Avoid blank rows and columns – many of the built-in features will assume a blank row or column is the end of your data; it can also help with formulas.
- Sort data where possible – many of the Lookup and Reference formulas rely on data being sorted; it also increases the speed of the calculation process.

Let your data determine the layout of your spreadsheet. There is never just one design that is right; the size of the spreadsheet, the complexity of formatting and many other factors must all be considered.

Label the spreadsheet appropriately

To bring clarity to your design and layout, you should label the spreadsheet appropriately with titles, labels, a header and a footer. Make the title and headings explicit in describing the data held in the row or column they refer to. Apply bold font when entering headings – this will help them to be recognised as such when you use functions such as Sort.

You can use the header and the footer to hold information including a page number, the date and time, the file name and sheet name or the pathname, as shown in Figure 3.2. You can also enter your own details and information. Any of this data can be placed left, centre or right.

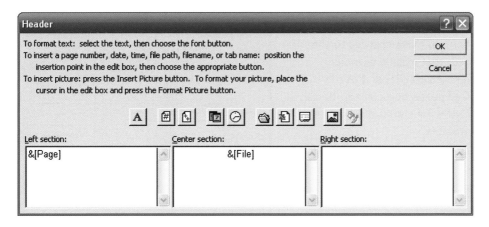

Figure 3.2 Adding information to a header

Apply appropriate formatting

Formatting refers to the way data is presented. You can format each cell or ranges of cells in any chosen format. You can format by row or column, set autoformatting for tables, apply conditional formatting and apply styles. You can format data in a variety of ways – determine the alignment, font and font size as well as applying a border or pattern. It should make your work easier to read and can highlight important data.

Formats include:

- number formatting – change the appearance of numbers, including dates and times
- cell colours; to identify specific data you can apply shading
- text formatting such as size and bold
- the appearance of text in cells – you can change the alignment, orientation or wrap the text
- conditional formatting – for example, you can apply a text colour to the cell if a specified condition is met.

Formatting worksheets

To format sheets:

1 Click the sheet to which you want to add a background pattern.
2 Select Sheet from the Format menu (Figure 3.3).

You can change the Background and Tab Colour. To change the background:

3 Click Background.
4 Select the graphics file to use for the background pattern.
5 Click OK.

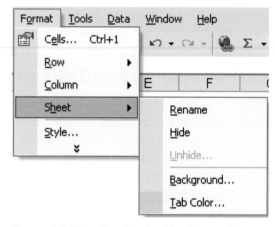

Figure 3.3 Changing the sheet background

The selected graphic is repeated to fill the sheet.

Formatting cells

You can make changes to the cells that include alignment, font (size, style) and borders. Cell protection can also be set. Figure 3.4 shows the options available.

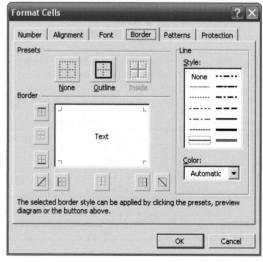

Figure 3.4 The Format Cells dialogue box

Changing the appearance of numbers

Use the Number formats to change the appearance of numbers (including dates and times). The number format does not alter the actual value used to perform calculations. There are a number of built-in number formats you can use, including the Special category. This includes formats for postal codes and phone numbers.

Autoformat

Use this feature to format a particular range of cells containing, for example, totals or summary information. Autoformat applies your chosen format to different elements in the range.

1   Highlight the cells to be formatted.
2   On the Format menu, select Autoformat.
3   The Autoformat dialogue box will be displayed (Figure 3.5).
4   Select the format you want to apply and click OK.

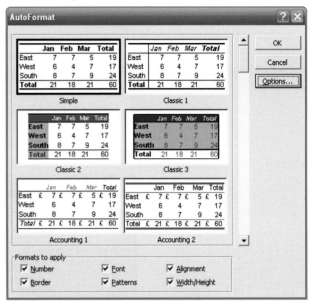

Figure 3.5 The Autoformat dialogue box

Defining a Style

To apply several formats you can combine them and apply a style. By using the Style option you can set all the options (Number, Alignment, Font, etc) at the same time.

1   Select Style from the Format menu. The Style dialogue box is displayed (Figure 3.6).
2   To change any of the options, click Modify.

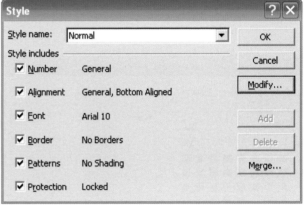

Figure 3.6 Defining a style

3   The Format Cells dialogue box will be displayed (Figure 3.7). Go to the tab of the option you wish to modify.
4   Make your changes. Click OK.
5   Go to any other tabs where you want to make changes. Make the changes and click OK.
6   When you have made all the changes click OK again to close the Style dialogue box.

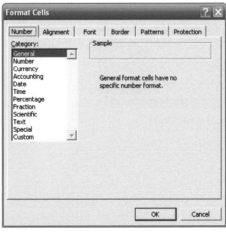

Figure 3.7 Building a style

Add conditional formats

When setting the formatting criteria in selected cells you have a choice to either use values or a formula. The formula looks at data or a condition other than the values in selected cells.

1 Select the cells for which you want to add conditional formatting.
2 On the Format menu, click Conditional Formatting. The Conditional Formatting dialogue box will be displayed (Figure 3.8).
3 You can now set Condition 1. To use values as the formatting criteria - in the first box, click Cell Value Is, in the second box, select the comparison phrase you want to use, and in the third box, enter a constant value (one that does not change) or a formula (starting it with an equal sign).

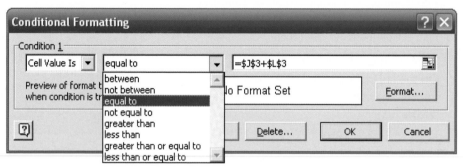

Figure 3.8 Setting a condition in the Conditional Formatting dialogue box

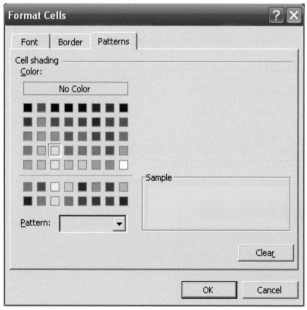

Figure 3.9 Setting the format in the Format Cells dialogue box

You can now set the format that will be used when the condition is true.

4 Click Format. The Format Cells dialogue box will be displayed (Figure 3.9)
5 Select the formatting you want to apply when the cell value meets the condition.
6 To add another condition, click Add, and repeat steps 1 to 5.
7 Click OK to finish.

You can specify up to three conditions. If none is true, the cells keep the existing format.

To use a formula as the formatting criteria: at step 3 – in the first box, click Formula Is, and in the second box enter the formula that provides a logical value of TRUE or FALSE.

Hiding and unhiding rows and columns

In some instances, you may not want to display specific information. In your project, for example, you may want to protect the identity of those participating, or you may just want to reduce the amount of data visible so that you can focus on specific data. To protect data, you can hide it. Data in a hidden row or column can still be used and referenced in your work, but it gives you control over what others have access to in your spreadsheet.

To hide a single column or row
In this case, column A is to be hidden (Figure 3.10).

1 Right-click on the header of column A.
2 Select Hide from the menu. Column A will be hidden.

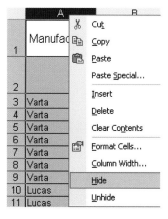
Figure 3.10 Hiding a column

To hide adjacent rows and columns
In this case, rows 3 to 9 will be hidden.

1 Highlight rows 3 to 9, and right-click.
2 Select Hide from the menu. Rows 3 to 9 will be hidden.

To hide separated rows or columns
In this case, columns A, C, D and E will be hidden (Figure 3.11).

1 Left-click on column A.
2 Press and hold down the CTRL key and left-click on columns C, D and E.
3 Right-click on one of the selected columns and choose Hide from the menu.
4 Columns A, C, D and E will be hidden.

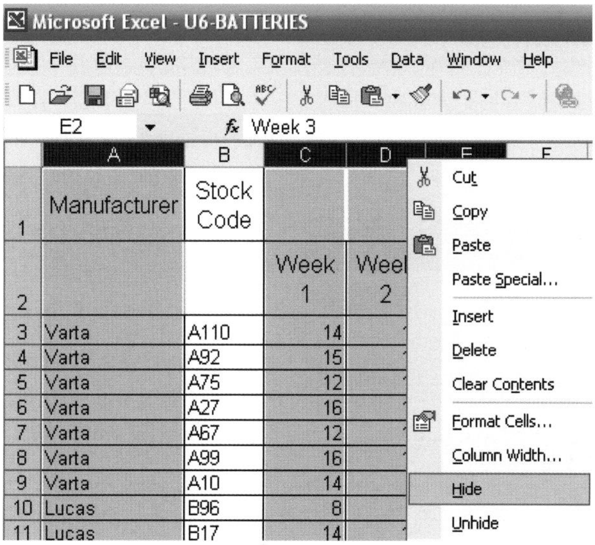

Figure 3.11 Hiding separated columns

To unhide a single row or column
In this case, column B will be unhidden (Figure 3.12).

1 Highlight the columns on each side – A and C.
2 Right-click and select Unhide. Column B will be displayed again (Figure 3.13).

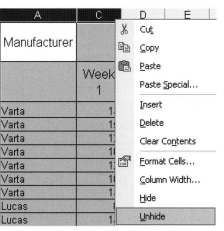
Figure 3.12 Unhide a column

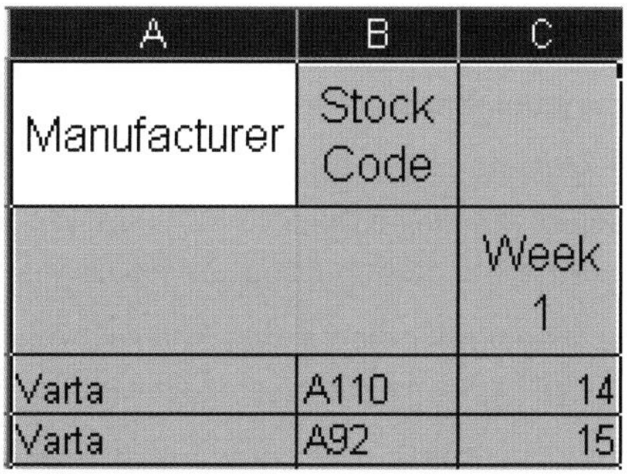

Figure 3.13 Column redisplayed

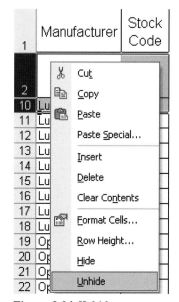
Figure 3.14 Unhide rows

To unhide multiple rows or columns

In this case rows 3 to 9 will be unhidden (Figure 3.14).

1 Highlight the rows each side – 2 and 10.
2 Right-click and select Unhide. The hidden rows will be displayed.

To hide and unhide data held in one cell

■ Select the cell and go to Format, Cells, and select the Numbers tab, then Custom. Enter three semicolons and click OK. The information will disappear.
■ To redisplay cell information, select the cell, go back to Format, Cells, and select the Numbers tab. Select General, click OK.

Setting the row height

The default row height is 12.75 points or 17 pixels. The font size default is 10 point. If you change the font size the row height is increased automatically to accommodate it.

Figure 3.15 Setting row height

To alter the row height

1 Highlight the rows, click Format, and select Cells, Row, Height (Figure 3.15).
2 Enter the height you want to use and click OK.

Alternatively, you can carry out this action manually. See pages 101–102 for forms, page 107 for defining a style and page 102 for setting validation.

Setting the column width

The default column width is 8.43 characters or 64 pixels. The font size default is 10 point. If you change the font size the column width does not alter.

Figure 3.16 Setting column width

To alter the column width

1 Highlight the columns, click Format, and select Cells, Column, Width (Figure 3.16).
2 Enter the width you want to use and click OK.

Alternatively, you can carry out this action manually. See pages 101–102 for forms, page 107 for defining a style and page 102 for setting validation.

Setting the background and text colours to hide data

You may not want certain information to be displayed, such as names that you want to keep confidential. As an alternative to hiding the columns or rows, you can set the background and text colour to hide the data. Simply set the fill and text colour to be the same and the text will not be visible.

Grouping

A group is a number of objects that are brought together as one item so that you can move, resize or rotate them together. Groups can be created within groups to build complex drawings.

You can change, for example, the line fill or text colour of all the shapes in a group at one time – in fact, anything that can be carried out by using the drawing tools and menu commands.

You may want to group objects such as a table, a chart or an equation. You are still able to select any single object within the group by selecting the group then clicking on that object. You can ungroup the items at any time and later regroup them.

To group shapes or objects, select them while holding down the Shift key. Under Draw on the Drawing toolbar, select Group.

To ungroup the items, select the group, return to Draw on the Drawing toolbar, and select Ungroup.

Use tools to improve efficiency

Linking cells between different worksheets

A link is a reference to another spreadsheet or worksheet. If the data in the first sheet is changed, the data in the second sheet is updated to reflect that change. This ensures that all data is up to date.

You can link cells in different worksheets to combine data. For example, you could lay out the detail of sales in different departments on separate worksheets, then, display only the total for each department on another sheet. In this way, you can see a summary of all departments. Linking cells in this way helps to avoid data entry errors. A change made in any of the department sales details, results in the automatic update of the data in the summary sheet linked to it.

Absolute and relative cell referencing

A reference identifies a cell (e.g. F2) or a range of cells (A1:C8) – where the letter refers to the column and the number refers to the row.

In a formula a reference identifies where the formula will find the values to carry out the calculation. For example, in the formula =SUM(A3:D3) the formula will total the values in cells A3 to D3.

You can use cell references to cells on the same sheet, on other sheets in the same workbook or to cells in other workbooks.

When you enter a formula, relative references are used by default, for example, =SUM(A3:D3). If you copy the formula, the reference automatically adjusts.

An absolute cell reference is identified by placing a dollar sign ($) before the column or row reference, or both, for example, $F$2. This type of reference identifies a cell in a specific location – F2. If you copy a formula containing an absolute reference this does not change.

For example a worksheet in a workbook could contain the static values related to the workbook. The static values will be used for calculations. As you already know cells can be given names. For example **Postal charge**, **VAT_RATE**. These cells' names can be defined as being used across multiple worksheets.

When the content of the cell needs to be used then they are referred to by their name. An example of this is:

= B4*VAT_RATE

If cells are not named then the formula would be:

=B4*$A$1

This shows that B4 is to be multiplied by the contents of cell A1.

By using cell-referencing the potential of errors occurring are reduced. This is because values have already been input and are just referred to rather than having to be input again.

Macros

If you perform a task repeatedly you can automate it with a macro. A macro is a series of commands and functions that can be run whenever you need to perform the task. It will always carry out the same steps in the same order with no chance for user error.

Use of macros improves efficiency and accuracy – you are not required to carry out the steps of the task repeatedly, thereby introducing the possibility of input or sequence errors by the user.

A macro can be activated by selecting it from a list in the Macro dialogue box. It is also possible to activate a macro by assigning it to a particular button or key combination. A macro can be assigned to a toolbar button, a keyboard shortcut or a graphic object on a worksheet.

Filter and autofilter

Filtering is a method of finding a subset of data in a list. A filtered list displays only the rows that meet the criteria you specify. There are two commands for filtering lists:

- AutoFilter, which includes filter by selection, for simple criteria
- Advanced Filter, for more complex criteria.

Filtering does not rearrange a list. It temporarily hides rows you do not want displayed. When rows are filtered, you can edit, format, chart and print your list subset without rearranging or moving it.

You can apply filters to only one list at a time. You can filter for the smallest or largest number in a list, for rows that contain specific text, for numbers greater than or less than another number, for a number equal to or not equal to another number, for the beginning or end of a text string, and for the top or bottom numbers by per cent.

Use appropriate formulas

Simple mathematical formulas

Formulas are used to achieve specified results. These may be simple calculations such as adding, subtracting, dividing and multiplying.

Using complex formulas

There are more complex calculations into which you may incorporate the use of percentages, use of brackets, two-stage calculations and functions.

Use appropriate functions to summarise and analyse the data

Functions are used to achieve specified results. They are formulas that have been set up to perform specific calculations. They use specific values (arguments) in a particular order. They can be used for simple or complex calculations.

The structure of a function begins with an equal sign (=), followed by the function name, an opening parenthesis, the arguments for the function separated by commas, and a closing parenthesis.

There are many functions available. The table in Figure 3.17 lists some from the **statistical** category.

Function	Use
SUM	Returns the sum of its arguments – it is a method of adding up rows or columns of figures. The AutoSum feature is a shortcut to using the SUM function. Up to 255 arguments can be entered.
AVERAGE	Returns the average of its arguments – used to find the average of a list, which can be numbers, named ranges, arrays or cell references. Up to 255 arguments can be entered.
MIN	Returns the minimum value – used to find the smallest value in a given list of arguments, which can be numbers, named ranges, arrays or cell references. Up to 30 arguments can be entered.
MAX	Returns the maximum value – used to find the largest value in a given list of arguments, which can be numbers, named ranges, arrays or cell references. Up to 30 arguments can be entered.
COUNT	Is used to total the number of cells in a selected range – the group of cells the function is to count. It counts only those cells that contain numbers, ignoring empty cells or those containing text. If a number is later added to an empty cell, the function will include this data automatically.
COUNTIF	Is used to count the number of cells in a selected range that meet certain criteria.

Figure 3.17 Functions – statistical category

These functions can help you to analyse your data. You must make sure that the functions you use are appropriate and help you prove your hypothesis.

For example, data has been collected relating to the number of GCSEs, grade A*-C, achieved by a class of 30 pupils. The column headings are in row 1, with the first names in column A and whether they are girls or boys in column B.

Sum: could be used to add up the total number of GCSEs achieved by the class. The formula would be written as:

=sum(C2:C31)

Average: could be used to work out the average number of GCSEs each pupil achieved. This is the total divided by 30 pupils. The formula would be written as:

=average(C2:C3)

Min: could be used to find the smallest or minimum number of GCSEs achieved by one pupil. The formula would be written as:

=min(C2:C3)

Max: is the opposite of min and could be used to find the highest, or maximum, number of GCSEs achieved by one pupil. The formula would be written as:

=max(C2:C3)

Count: could be used to count the number of pupils who achieved GCSEs. If a pupil achieved 0 GCSEs and the cell was left empty it would not be counted. The formula would be written as:

=count(C2:C3)

Countif: this could be used to count the number of girls in the class, remember column B contains the data "boy" or "girl". The formula would be written as:

=countIf (B2:B31,"girl")

The functions in Figure 3.18 are in the **logical** category. Logical functions give only a TRUE or FALSE answer.

Function	Use
IF	Specifies a logical test to determine if a certain condition is true or false. The first component is the value or expression that is tested, the second component is the value that is displayed if the test result is true, and the third component is the value that is displayed if the test result is false.
OR	Returns true if any argument is true. To determine the output, the OR function evaluates at least one mathematical expression located in another cell in the spreadsheet. Logical refers to the cell reference that is being checked. Up to 255 logical values can be used.
AND	Returns true if all its arguments are true. To determine the output, the AND function evaluates at least one mathematical expression located in another cell in the spreadsheet. Logical refers to the cell reference that is being checked. Up to 255 logical values can be used.

Figure 3.18 Functions – logical category

The IF function

Use the IF function to test whether a value in one column is, for example, greater than the value in a second column. If it is, the IF function will place chosen text in the column where the formula is entered; if it is not, the IF function will display different chosen text. To add this text to the function you must enclose it in quotation marks.

The comma is used as a separator between each argument, and identifies when each argument ends and the next begins. The arguments are:

1 the logic test
2 the value if true
3 the value if false

The logic test is always a comparison between two amounts. You use a comparison operator between the two values. The operators that can be used in the IF function are: equals (=), less than (<), less than or equal to (<=), greater than (>), greater than or equal to (>=), not equal to (<>).

Following the comma separator, you add the value if true argument. This is the text you want to display if the 'value is true', followed by another comma separator. The last section to add to the IF function is the 'value if false' argument – the text you want to display if the 'value is false', followed by the closing bracket. To copy down the function use the Fill Handle.

If you have not used the function before, you can try this simple example.

1 Enter this data into a spreadsheet, in the cells shown:

2 Go to cell C2 and enter the equal sign followed by IF and an opening bracket: **=IF(**

3 You will now enter the three arguments:

	A	B
1		
2	25	20
3	30	45
4	45	40
5	65	75

- You want to know if the value in cell A2 is higher than the value in cell B2, so enter the 'greater than' operator between the two cell references: **A2>B2** followed by a comma.
- Enter "Met" followed by a second comma.
- Enter "Make" followed by a right bracket ")".

In cell C2 you should see the completed IF function: =IF(A2>B2,"Met","Make") – Figure 3.19.

4 To complete the example, you will add the IF function to cells C3, C4, and C5. To copy the IF function in cell C2 to the other cells:

- Click on cell C2. Place the mouse pointer over the black square in the bottom right corner. The pointer will change to a plus sign.
- Click the left mouse button and drag the fill handle down to cell C5.
- Release the mouse button. Cells C3 to C5 will be filled with the IF function.

Note that the cell references in the IF function have been changed (Figure 3.20).

C2	▼	fx =IF(A2>B2,"Met","Make")
	A	B	C
1	IN STOCK	ORDERED	
2	25	20	Met
3	30	45	Make
4	45	40	Met
5	65	75	Make

Figure 3.19 The IF function

C2	▼	fx =IF(A2>B2,"Met","Make")
	A	B	C
1	IN STOCK	ORDERED	
2	25	20	=IF(A2>B2,"Met","Make")
3	30	45	=IF(A3>B3,"Met","Make")
4	45	40	=IF(A4>B4,"Met","Make")
5	65	75	=IF(A5>B5,"Met","Make")

Figure 3.20 The IF function showing formulas

The OR function

The output from the OR function is either the word **TRUE** or the word **FALSE**. To determine the output the function tests at least one mathematical expression located in another cell on the spreadsheet.

Example :

The function is entered in cell B1 (Figure 3.21). If any of the three cells (A1, A2, or A3) contains a value greater than 75, the output in cell B1 will be TRUE. If all three cells have numbers less than or equal to 75, the output will be FALSE.

The OR function is of limited use, so it is frequently combined with other functions, one of which is the IF function. This is referred to as nesting – placing one function inside another (Figure 3.22).

=IF(OR(A1>75,A2>75,A3>75),"Within limits","Out of bounds")

B1	▼	fx =OR(A1>75,A2>75,A3>75)
	A	B	C	D
1	50	TRUE		
2	75			
3	100			

Figure 3.21 The OR function

The function is located in cell B1. If any of the three cells (A1, A2, or A3) contains a value greater than 75, the IF function will display the text **Within limits** in cell B1. If all three cells have numbers less than or equal to 75, the IF function will display the text **Out of bounds** in cell B1.

B1	▼	fx =IF(OR(A1>75,A2>75,A3>75),"Within limits","Out of bounds")
	A	B	C	D	E	F	G	H
1	50	Within limits						
2	75							
3	100							

Figure 3.22 The OR function combined with the IF function

The AND function

The output from the AND function is either the word **TRUE** or the word **FALSE**. To determine the output the function tests at least one mathematical expression located in another cell in the spreadsheet.

Example:

The function is entered in cell B1 (Figure 3.23). If all three cells (A1, A2, and A3) contain a value greater than 75, the output cell B1 will be TRUE. If any of these cells have numbers less than or equal to 75, the output will be FALSE.

B1	▼	f_x =AND(A1>75,A2>75,A3>75)		
	A	B	C	D
1	50	FALSE		
2	75			
3	100			

Figure 3.23 The AND function

The AND function is of limited use, so it is frequently combined with other functions, one of which is the IF function (Figure 3.24).

=IF(AND(A1>75,A2>75,A3>75),"Within limits","Out of bounds")

The function is located in cell B1. If all three cells (A1, A2, and A3) contain a value greater than 75, the IF function will display the text **Within limits** in cell B1. If any of the three cells contain a number less than or equal to 75, the IF function will display the text **Out of bounds** in cell B1. The function returns a TRUE value only if the data in all three cells is greater than 75.

B1	▼	f_x =IF(AND(A1>75,A2>75,A3>75),"Within limits","Out of bounds")					
	A	B	C	D	E	F	G
1	50	Out of bounds					
2	75						
3	100						

Figure 3.24 The AND function combined with the IF function

Check and test the spreadsheet to ensure that it works effectively

You should prepare a plan of the tests you want to perform. Your test plan is a means of checking that your spreadsheet meets its requirements, and also provides an opportunity for identifying errors. Testing will be more effective if you:

- write a test plan setting specific goals
- cover all aspects of your spreadsheet
- prioritise the tests
- write the tests in detail
- evaluate the tests.

A test is an input and an expected result. Your test plan should include tests on the formulas, functions, macros and validation. Review your test results carefully. Did you get the results you had expected? What did you find out? Examine the results and ensure they are accurate.

See Unit 5 Advanced Spreadsheets, Assessment Objective 5: Test the spreadsheet, page 186.

Portfolio Activity (AO4)

The local health trust has provided you with spreadsheet software to use in analysing the data you have collected. You should use it to lay out your data using appropriate techniques and tools so that you can present your results to the trust at a later date. You must ensure that it produces the results that you require, appropriately formatted.

1   Create and use a spreadsheet to enter and analyse the results of your study.

- Select an appropriate layout and create a suitable spreadsheet to analyse your data. Label the spreadsheet using titles and both a header and a footer.
- Use appropriate formulas.
- Use tools to improve the efficiency of the spreadsheet.
- Use appropriate functions to summarise and analyse the data.
- Apply appropriate formatting to display results clearly on-screen and when printed.

2   Check and test the spreadsheet to ensure that it works effectively.

Assessment Guidance

Pass – Candidates create a structure to analyse and present the results of their study. They will apply appropriate titles, labels and formatting to display most information clearly. They will use appropriate functions to analyse some of the data, providing some useful data relevant to the hypothesis. They will carry out at least one test of their spreadsheet and use the results to make changes, if appropriate.

Merit – Candidates create an effective structure to analyse and present the results of their study. They will apply appropriate titles, labels and formatting to display most information clearly. They will use appropriate functions to analyse the data, providing a range of useful data relevant to the hypothesis. They will devise a test plan and use it to ensure that the spreadsheet works effectively.

Distinction – Candidates create an effective and efficient structure to analyse and present the results of their study. They will apply appropriate titles, labels and formatting to display all information clearly. They will use appropriate functions to carry out a thorough analysis of the data, providing a range of useful data relevant to the hypothesis. They will devise a comprehensive test plan and use it to ensure that the spreadsheet works effectively.

Appropriate use of a range of chart types

Charts and graphs make information clearer and easier to analyse. Taking statistics, which are often intimidating or confusing, and presenting them graphically, makes them easier to understand; patterns and trends can be difficult to see, but when they are illustrated in the chart, they are clearly identified.

When deciding on the type of chart, you should consider the type of data you are using and the variables in your data. Do you have continuous or discrete data? Are the data variables independent or dependent?

Continuous data

Continuous data is information that can be measured on a scale. You can count, order and measure continuous data. It can have almost any numeric value and can be subdivided. Length, width, temperature, the time required to get to school, are all examples of continuous data. This type of data contrasts with discrete data.

Discrete data

Discrete data is information that can be categorised into a classification. It is typically based on counts, the results are whole numbers, and it cannot be broken down into smaller units to add additional meaning. Population data is discrete because you are (generally) counting people and putting them into various categories – and there is no such thing as 'half a person'.

Independent and dependent variables

A variable is any category you want to measure, such as an object, event or time period. The two types of variable are independent and dependent.

An independent variable is one that stands alone, and is not changed by other variables you are measuring. For example, in your study you may be using population age. This is an independent variable because other variables, such as how much they exercise, what they eat, or how much television they watch, do not change the age.

When you are trying to establish a relationship between variables, you are trying to see if the independent variable causes change in the other (dependent) variables.

A dependent variable depends on other factors. For example, your project result could be a dependent variable because it could change depending on several factors such as: how much work you put into it, the amount of time you have to complete it, how much other work you have to complete.

When you are trying to establish a relationship between variables, you are trying to find out what makes the dependent variable change in the way it does.

You should use of a range of chart types, ensuring that they are appropriate to your data. They will be clearer if you minimise the use of lines, segments, colours and textures.

All charts and graphs need a data series. The data series are the parts that need to be plotted on the chart or graph. These are the contents of the cells. You can have a data series from one worksheet or taken from more than one. A data series can be selected by highlighting the cells or by typing the data series into the chart dialogue box. The easiest method is to highlight the cells.

Pie charts

Pie charts show the components of a 360-degree whole segmented into slices which represent a percentage of that whole. As it is in the form of a circle it displays the relative sizes of the shares very clearly.

Bar charts and column charts

These compare unique data sets using a bar for each. They are useful for plotting data that spans time periods (days, weeks or years) or for comparing different items in a related category (comparing the number of visitors to different hospital departments).

Comparative bar or column charts allow comparison between amounts of several items in a series, with each quantity represented by a column, its height indicating the number of units being counted. Bar charts run horizontally on the page; column charts run vertically.

Line graphs and charts

Line graphs are often used to plot changes in data over time, such as changes in prices or monthly profits. Each line in the graph shows the changes in the value of one item of data. If you are plotting changes in data over time, time is plotted along the horizontal or x-axis and your other data is plotted as individual points along the vertical or y-axis. When the individual data points are connected by lines, the changes are clearly displayed.

A line-column chart plots the line series and the bar series on the same axis.

A comparative line graph shows the changes of one or more variables over a period of time. Line graphs are most suitable when you are comparing one value as it changes with another value.

Charts and graphs
A chart is any graphic representation of information. A graph is a more specific kind of chart that represents a series of changing quantities.

Scatter graphs

A scatter graph is a statistical diagram drawn to compare two sets of data. It provides a visual display of the relationship between two variables, and can be used to look for connections or a correlation between the two sets of data.

In your project, each point would represent one person. Points are plotted but not joined. The resulting pattern describes the relationship:

- The more the points cluster around a straight line, the stronger the relationship between the two variables.
- If the line around which the points cluster runs from lower left to upper right, the relationship between the two variables is positive.
- If the line around which the points cluster runs from upper left to lower right, the relationship between the two variables is negative.
- If there is a random scatter of points, there is no relationship between the two variables.

Chart presentation techniques

Choice of legend and heading

When creating charts and graphs, you can enter an appropriate heading and legend using the Chart Wizard. A legend identifies the colours or patterns that you use on the categories or the data series in your chart. A data series is a set of related data points that are plotted in a chart. Each has a unique colour or pattern. Each is represented in the legend. Apart from a pie chart, which has only one data series, you can plot any number of data series in a chart. At step 3 you are able to:

1 Enter titles, including the chart title and axis labels.
2 Select the placement of the legend and whether it will be displayed (Figure 3.25).

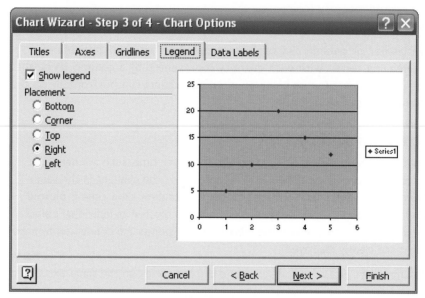

Figure 3.25 Selecting titles and the legend

The series label, shown in Figure 3.25 as Series 1, must be given a useful name. This could be, for example, in our scenario of the number of GCSE's achieved, **Number**. A series label does not have to be included on a graph. It may be better to not have a series label rather than have an inappropriate label.

Formatting and labelling

To format and label axes, data series and data points you can enter suitable data using the Chart Wizard. However, if you want to change any of these items, double-click on the item you wish to change and make your amendments.

Double-clicking on the data series will result in the Format Data Series dialogue box being displayed. This allows you to amend all of the items shown in Figure 3.26.

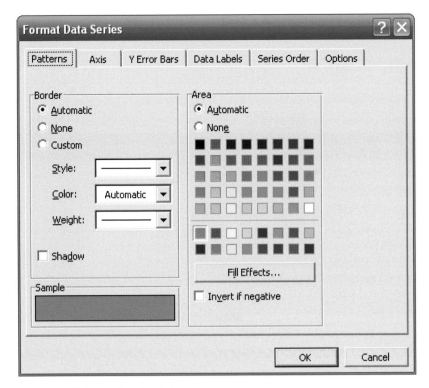

Figure 3.26 Amending the data series

Applying scale to numerical axes

To alter the scale applied to numerical axes to give them more precision for your data, double-click on the axis you want to amend. This will result in the Format Axis dialogue box being displayed. This allows you to amend all of the items shown in Figure 3.27.

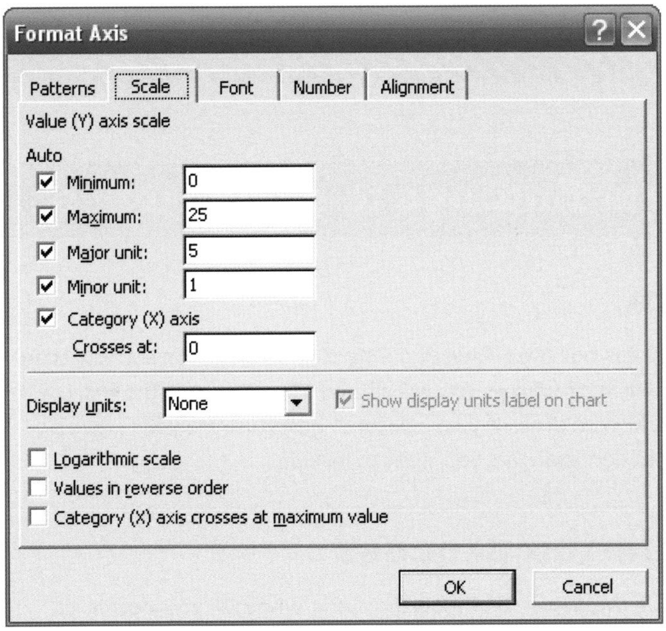

Figure 3.27
Amending an axis

Portfolio Activity (AO5)

The local health trust expects you to present the findings of your study. It is important to display these findings in the form of suitable graphs and charts in your presentation. Therefore, you should produce charts and graphs that are appropriate to the data being analysed and your hypothesis.

1   You should select the appropriate chart to display your data from:
    - pie charts
    - comparative bar or column charts
    - line-column charts
    - comparative line graphs
    - scatter graphs
    - trend lines.
2   You should apply appropriate chart presentation techniques, such as:
    - choice of legend, heading and titles
    - formatting and labelling of axes, data series and data points.

AO6: Present findings to an audience

Introduction

You should now use the data you have collected during your investigation and stored in your spreadsheet to present your findings. You will also be able to include the charts you have created. Think about how to present your results to best illustrate your material. Plan the layout and organisation and what you want to include.

The Presentation process

The process of preparing the material will be the same whether you decide to present the material as a written report, as a website, or as a talk, illustrated using presentation software.

To produce a good presentation planning is essential. It should be carried out in a systematic manner. Planning will help to provide clarification, and focus on the main factors.

Decide how much material will be included, making sure that you cover all aspects of your study. Decide on the structure, content and style, and consider your audience – this will determine the information that is presented, how it is presented, and why it is presented. Language must be appropriate, concise and well considered. This will enhance the audience's understanding and help to clearly communicate the message. The output should be easy to understand. Use charts and graphs to make data easier to visualise and understand.

Identify the main points to address and select related material. It is very important to ensure that the audience is not overwhelmed with information. Consider the way the material is structured. Use sections to separate different elements. Include:

Introduction what is in the report – the problem you were asked to research, your hypothesis, your project objectives, and your success criteria.

Methods details of how the data was gathered (including sample size, frequency and interval). This will allow the audience to determine the level of reliability of your study.

Facts the information you have determined to be useful, necessary, or important. Evidence must be presented to support the main points. This evidence will be the research you have carried out and the statistical evidence you have produced and examined as a result. Discuss how the data was processed and analysed.

Findings how you have interpreted the facts – describe the project, summarise the results and include key facts from your research to explain them. The material should be arranged so that it supports your main points. You should include appropriate tables, charts and graphs to illustrate the key findings.

Conclusions explain the results (the significance and meaning of the facts) and the overall conclusions that may be drawn about the project. Summarise how your results support or contradict your hypothesis. If the results did not support your hypothesis, do not change or manipulate them to fit it – simply explain why things did not go as expected. You may want to include recommendations that could be put in place.

The method you select to deliver your presentation will determine how you structure and present the material you have prepared. If you are going to use presentation software you should first decide on a design. Using a template helps simplify slide creation and provides consistency. A template incorporates the elements you want to include, such as font and colours. Think about how graphics, drawings or other objects might improve your presentation. Proofread carefully. Errors are distracting and give the audience the impression that you do not care about them or the material.

Think about these points when preparing your presentation:

- Use bullets and numbers to organise ideas in lists.
- Slides need to be clear from a distance, so text should be large.
- Use simple sans serif fonts.
- Limit text to about five lines per slide and about six words per line.

- Font size should reflect the importance of the points – the more important the point, the larger the font size.
- Capitals are harder to read.
- Use emboldening rather than underlining to emphasise a word or phrase.
- Keep colour simple – limit your colour choices to two or three on a contrasting background. Avoid red and green combinations; they do not offer enough contrast and if any members of your audience are colour blind they will be unable to read them.

You should include tables, charts and graphs to help illustrate the results of your findings. You will have already created these when you analysed the data you collected. You can include these in your presentation but they may need to be adapted. This adaptation may include a change in size, colour of text or font used.

If you are using an onscreen presentation to present the results of your findings then you may need to provide some notes, or a commentary, to provide more detail to accompany the text presented onscreen. You can either use the note feature on the software, or provide a word-processed additional document. The method you choose will depend on, and must be appropriate for, the size of the audience.

How well the results of the study supported or disproved your hypothesis

In defining your study, you were required to outline a hypothesis. Based on this hypothesis, you should analyse your data and present **facts** identifying whether the hypothesis is proven correct or incorrect. You can do so by the use of the data you collected and you can present that data in the form of charts and tables. Use the Notes pages for your commentary.

How well the results of the study met the identified success criteria

You need to evaluate if the analysis you have done supports or disproves your hypothesis. You set project objectives and success criteria at the beginning of the project. You must refer back to each of these stating clearly the results you found and if they were proved or not.

Portfolio Activity (AO6)

You will now produce a report of your findings for the local health trust, providing full details of your study and the results.

1 Present the findings of your study appropriately for the purpose and the audience. You should include:
   - data tables
   - graphs and/or charts
   - text
   - how well the results of the study supported or disproved your hypothesis
   - how well the results of the study met the identified success criteria.
2 Your presentation should be effectively formatted and presented. Check the presentation carefully for style and use spelling and grammar checkers.
3 Provide evidence of your evaluation of the spreadsheet model you created and used. Summarise your testing, outlining success and effectiveness.

Creating a Digital Showcase

Learning outcomes

By working through this unit you will produce evidence to meet the unit assessment objectives to show that you understand how to:

- specify requirements
- design a solution
- create and edit multimedia elements
- optimise multimedia elements for use in the target environment
- author an interactive multimedia product
- test and review a preliminary version of your multimedia product in order to produce the final product
- create a user guide.

Introduction

This unit covers the production of a digital showcase. This showcase will cover a subject of your choice, but it is your responsibility to make sure that the subject on which you focus allows you to cover all seven assessment objectives. As you work, you must also produce a portfolio of evidence, on which your work for this unit will be assessed.

Scenario

The Food and Market Group is a small organisation made up of organic fruit producers. The aim of the organisation is to advertise the benefits of organic fruit and vegetables. The main target audience is the restaurant and retailing industries.

The Food and Market Group likes to stress the small scale and traditional nature of its members in any materials it uses. Each member of the group is committed to local farming and using only organic farming methods. All materials therefore have a traditional feel, combined with a clear message that they believe that organic farming methods produce food that is both healthier and better tasting than food produced using non-organic methods.

You have been asked to produce an interactive non-linear multimedia product to be used at forthcoming trade fairs. This product should showcase the three key areas listed below, as well as include an introductory section.

You should include the following sections in your multimedia product:

- Introduction
- Organic farming methods
- Organic farming and health
- The benefits of using organic fruit.

Delegates at the trade fairs will be able to use the completed product to look at the key areas that interest them. The completed product should use a range of multimedia elements. You may use elements that you find elsewhere, but you should also include elements that you have created. The Food and Market Group has specifically asked you to include a spoken section, welcoming viewers. They have also asked that you use suitable sound effects throughout the product.

The Food and Market Group has stressed that it is happy for you to make decisions about the final design and structure of the multimedia product. However, they have asked you to take account of the following design considerations:

- the logo of the organisation uses Times New Roman font
- the logo of the organisation uses three strong colours – red (192,0,0); blue (0,0,192); yellow (247,255,9). (The figures in brackets are the RGB values for each colour.)

As delegates are to be allowed to select and view different elements, you have also been asked to create suitable navigation elements, such as buttons. The Food and Market Group has asked that the multimedia solution as a whole, as well as all elements included within it, fits the traditional and healthy image that the organisation has used in all advertising thus far.

As the completed multimedia product is to be used at many different locations, you have been asked to produce a user guide for the product. This user guide should include information on:

- how to install the multimedia product
- how to use the multimedia product
- any system requirements.

Your multimedia product should be fully tested before it is submitted to the Fruit and Market Group. If your testing identifies any changes that need to be made, these changes should be completed before the final multimedia product is submitted.

Scenario

AO1: Specify project requirements

This section is about planning a multimedia solution to a brief that has been set for you or one that you have designed. The focus of this – and every other section – will be the multimedia solution for the Food and Market Group. You should work through the stages explained here, but remember that your final submission for this unit must be your own work.

Produce specifications

Before you begin to plan your multimedia solution, you must make sure that the work you are going to produce will actually meet the needs of the client or those that you have set yourself. Each of the following topics is an area about which you need to make decisions before you begin working on your multimedia solution.

Intended audience

This should be quite an easy one to answer, as this is usually given by the client or implied in your own initial plans. Almost as soon as you think of a project to complete, you must consider who that project is for.

It is important to be clear about the intended audience, as this is possibly the biggest decision you will make. Your completed work for this assessment objective should identify the intended audience for your product, and how each design consideration has been made to ensure that the completed product fits with the needs of the intended audience.

The intended audience for your product can be defined in many ways. However, the following could all be used to describe a group of people – when you describe your intended audience, you should be using at least some of those criteria:

- age
- gender
- location
- religion
- social class
- income bracket
- education level.

For example, an audience for a teenage magazine would generally be defined by the age of the target audience, while we may use age, income bracket and even gender to define the target audience for some cars.

When creating a product for target audiences, you will need to be aware of these factors. For example, a teenage group may have very different needs from a group made up of people between the ages of 46-64 years old. These differences would appear in the design of the product. For example, a teenage audience is going to be more attracted to a magazine that has a good deal of colour on the front, an exciting font for the title and any subtitles, and a photograph that suggests fun. A more mature audience may have very different needs and so would be more interested in a cover of a magazine that was more sedate and suggested that the content was more traditional and factual.

Purpose of the product

Every product is created for a purpose. This is as true for multimedia products as it is for products you might buy in a shop or online. The following is a short list of possible purposes for multimedia products:

- to inform
- to entertain
- to generate sales
- to increase sales
- to publicise.

Main topics and key features

You will also need to decide on what you are going to include in your multimedia product. A good starting point is to think about what must be included and then add other elements that could be of use.

The elements that must be included are those that, if they were not in the completed product, would affect the suitability of the product for the intended task. This may be, for example, a clear introduction, a video clip or an important audio message. Once you have decided on these elements, then you can begin to add the extra bits and pieces that will make the completed product even more effective.

The key features are the main messages that you want your multimedia product to include. Again, these may be set by the client or may come from your own initial thoughts about your product. To some extent, the key message is very similar to the purpose of the product. It should be very clear what the key message should be for the Food and Market Group multimedia product from the scenario information.

However, if you are working for a client and do not feel that the key message has been made explicit, ask for clarification. It would probably be a good idea for you to suggest what you think the key message should be at this stage, as the client may feel that the message is clear from the instructions given.

Conditions/scenarios in which the product will be used and any usage constraints that need to be taken into account

This is a quite straightforward section and, again, could be given by the client. It is probably best to consider this as two separate subsections:

- where the product will be used
- what the implications are for where the product is to be used.

The first subsection is your chance to explain the scenarios in which your product will be used. If you are going to create a multimedia product to be used in a major shopping centre, then this is your scenario. The fact that you will then be dealing with many different sounds and other stimuli all competing for people's attention is the implication of where the product is to be used. Similarly, if you are creating a multimedia product that allows the user to interact with the product, the need for a clear navigation process is an implication of this design scenario.

A further consideration would be the format in which the completed presentation is to be presented. Not only would the format require specific hardware, but the choice of storage device on which the completed product was distributed would have an impact on the file size of the completed product. For example, a CD can hold approximately 750 MB of data, whilst a single sided DVD can hold 4.7 GB of data. Clearly, the DVD can hold more!

It may be that your completed product is to be downloaded. If that is the case, then your main consideration is probably going to be download speed. As you should know from other units within this qualification, the speed of download will be affected by how much data needs to be transferred. If your end product has a very large file size, the download speed will be longer than if you had created a relatively smaller file.

Success criteria

The final stage of your initial design process should be to decide on how you will assess the success of your completed product. At the most simple level, this could be 'it will work'. However, this is not only an unclear statement, there is also far more that could be said about a product.

Rather like the other areas in this assessment objective, the success criteria for your completed multimedia product could be set by the initial brief. If you have been asked to create a multimedia product that uses animation and text to explain the key concepts of the Green Cross Code in a way that is accessible for young children, then your success criteria could be:

- product created
- includes animation
- includes text
- young children can follow the instructions
- young children find the content suitable
- young children can learn from the instructions.

You will note here that you are not assessing whether the Green Cross Code increases road safety – the quality and effectiveness of the product advertised are different from the quality and effectiveness of the multimedia product itself.

Portfolio Activity (AO1)

You have been asked to specify the project requirements for the Food and Market Group project. You should consider each of the following areas:

- the intended audience
- the purpose of the product
- the main topics and key features within the product
- the scenario within which the completed multimedia product will be used and any implications of that scenario
- how you will measure the success of the completed product.

When creating your report project requirements, you must include the following:

- an identification of any usage constraints that may need to be taken into account at this stage
- an assessment of the main topics and features you intend to include, in order to show that these are consistent with the purpose of the product
- a justification of the content and key features in relation to the audience of the product and the purpose for which it has been created.

Pass – Candidates will identify the purpose and intended users of the multimedia product, describing briefly at least one scenario in which it will be used. They will provide a basic description of the content and key features. They will identify how the audience and purpose has affected the choice of content and key features. They will provide a brief outline of points that can be used to measure the effectiveness of their final product.

Merit – Candidates will clearly describe the purpose and intended users of the multimedia product, describing in detail at least one scenario in which it will be used. They will provide a detailed description of the main topics and key features of their product. They will explain how the audience and purpose has affected the choice of content and key features. They will provide a clear set of criteria to measure the effectiveness of their final product.

Distinction – Candidates will describe thoroughly in detail the purpose of the multimedia product and its intended users, describing fully at least one scenario in which it will be used. They will identify any usage constraints that may need to be taken into account at the design stage. They will provide a comprehensive description of the main topics and key features, and these will be consistent with the purpose. They will justify the choice of content and key features in relation to the audience and purpose. They will provide a comprehensive and realistic set of criteria to measure effectiveness of their final product.

AO2: Design a solution

Design notes

Interface design

This first stage of the design process is designing the layout of the pages that your users will meet when they use the product. Your design should suit the intended audience, therefore each design decision you take at this stage should be based on how well the intended audience could use the resource.

For example, for some users, you may need a very simple layout with few elements on the page. For a different intended audience, you may need large text on the page and on any buttons.

Structure and navigation

This design area is linked into the previous one, in that your choice of navigation tools and where these are to sit on the page will be linked to the interface design. If you are working to distinction level, your interface design needs to be comprehensive and incorporate an appropriate navigation system and structure.

Your second design consideration is how the multimedia product itself is organised. You have three choices at this stage. Your choices are:

- linear
- mesh
- hierarchical.

Linear structure

In a linear structure, the pages in the multimedia product are linked one after another. This means that each page is accessed from the previous page, so that you control the order in which the user sees the information included on the multimedia product. A linear structure allows you to provide a clearly defined pathway through your information.

While you may enjoy having this control over the multimedia product, some users can find their own lack of control a problem, as many users prefer to work through a multimedia product in their own way.

Mesh structure

At the opposite end of the spectrum, there is the mesh structure, which allows the user to access each and every page of the multimedia product from every other page. This allows the user full access to each page in any order. The best way to imagine this structure is rather like having a huge room with many doors off it. Each door leads to one room and each room has a door to each and every other room.

Using a mesh structure means that you can no longer control the order in which the user accesses the information included in your multimedia product. If you choose such a structure, you will need to think carefully about how you lay out each page of your multimedia product, so that the user can make informed choices about which pages to access.

Hierarchical structure

In the middle, is the hierarchical structure. This has a combination of linear links to sections, with a mesh structure below this. Imagine visiting a school with corridors leading to groups of rooms. Once you are in the groups of rooms, each room is accessible from the others. This combines the organised procession of information of the linear structure with the free-form structure of the mesh. You should consider using this structure if you want to organise how the user visits blocks of information, but allow free access to the information included within each block.

Script, storyboard and timings

Once you have designed the interface and structure of your multimedia product, you should be ready to plan how the different elements of your multimedia product interrelate.

Script

The easiest way of planning how the different elements of your multimedia product interrelate is to use a script. This could simply be a list of things that happen on each page. The list below could be used to describe how the different elements on a page are used. This is quite a simple script, but it does describe the process well.

- Page opens.
- Main title appears as animation.
- Main title tweens into subtitle (See pages 139–140 for more on Tweening).
- Video plays twice.

Script writing is a very useful way of describing events in an animation or on a page, and therefore makes a good starting point for a plan. However, you will also need to include a storyboard as part of your completed plan.

Storyboard

A storyboard is a series of pictures representing what is happening at key stages during a sequence. This could be used for the stages of an individual animated sequence or for individual pages in a multimedia product.

A section from a sample storyboard is shown below. This shows a key stage during a multimedia product. This scene holds a lot of detail, but this level of detail makes the plan very clear to a third party who may be asked to work on the product. You should remember that when you produce your own storyboard, you will need to include as many scenes as you need to plan your story.

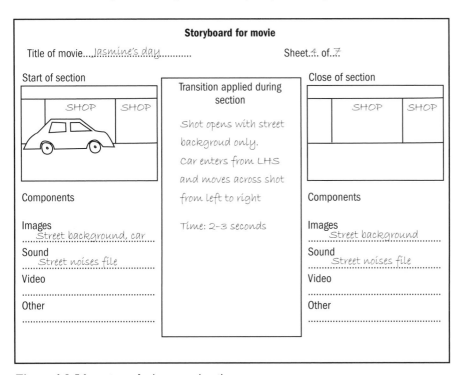

Figure 4.1 A key stage during an animation

Timings

This deals with the time that each stage takes. The list in Figure 4.2 is the same example of how a script could be used to describe what happens when a page is opened, but now the timing of each event has been added.

Event	Start time (seconds)	Finish time (seconds)
Page opens	0	2
Main title appears as animation	3	6
Main title tweens into subtitle	7	21
Video plays twice	22	56

Figure 4.2 The key stages during an animation, showing start and finish times

As you can see, each stage of the animation has a start and finish time. An alternative would be to simply show the total time for each stage to occur. However, this may cause confusion if two separate events overlap on the timeline. If you are planning to have different events overlapping, you will probably find it easier to add the timings at the storyboarding stage. In this case you may decide simply to show the amount of time that has passed overall as each frame of the storyboard becomes relevant.

If you do choose to link what happens in your multimedia product to specific times during the work, you are beginning to consider the use of a timeline to plan your work. A timeline is simply a line with key events shown along it. Usually, this line goes from left to right, with time represented by the distance moved along the line.

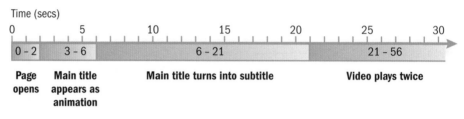

Figure 4.3 A completed timeline

Interactive elements

Your multimedia product will need to be interactive. This means that you will need elements that the user can control.

At the simplest level, these could be buttons that control how the user moves through the completed presentation. You could also choose to have videos or animations that can be controlled by the user.

As well as these relatively simple interactive elements, more complex options would include rollover images. These are images that change when a mouse moves over them. This is an extremely powerful way of giving further clues or directions to the user or to provide further instructions or advice. You could of course, just use it to show an "up" button and a "down" button. You could also consider using a rollover image to make the current image grow or shrink.

Portfolio Activity (AO2)

You should now use the techniques described above to plan your product for the Food and Market Group. This should include clear indication of how you intend to address specific design considerations that the Food and Market group have asked you to include.

When planning your project, you must include the following:

- evidence that your plan clearly meets the project requirements
- a wide range of structural elements using an appropriate navigation system and structure
- a comprehensive list of elements, including timeline-based events and a range of interactive elements.

The evidence you provide could be a tick list with commentary, for example. This would then allow you to show why you think your plan meets the requirements or the navigation system is appropriate. If you use this method, try to include clear justification of the choices you have made. You need to remember that every decision you make during the design stage should be based on the needs of the target audience. Use these needs to justify the decisions you make.

The storyboard will need to include interactive and timeline-based elements. These should be detailed in your design, so that if an event occurs over a set amount of time, the event should be seen to be happening as you progress through the timeline. Think of a clock in the corner of the scene, if you showed that on a timeline, the time shown on the clock should change as you progress along the timeline. Similarly, if you intend to run a video in the background, for example, you could show how different scenes will appear as time goes by.

Assessment Guidance

Pass – Candidates will produce a clear design plan that shows how the main project requirements will be met. They will produce a clear interface design that incorporates clear navigation and structure. They will produce a clear storyboard for the product, which will include at least one interactive element.

Merit – Candidates will produce a detailed design plan that shows clearly how most of the project requirements will be met. They will produce an effective interface design that incorporates an appropriate navigation system and structure. They will produce a detailed storyboard for the product, which will include some timeline-based events and a range of interactive elements.

Distinction – Candidates will produce a comprehensive design plan that shows clearly how all the project requirements have been met. They will produce a highly effective interface design that incorporates an appropriate navigation system and structure. They will produce a comprehensive storyboard for the product, which will fully depict a range of timeline-based events and the operation of a range of interactive elements.

Produce and/or source elements

Your completed multimedia product must include elements you have created yourself and elements you have found elsewhere and have edited. For all elements, your work should include comments about:

- suitability
- reliability
- copyright.

(See Assessment Objective 4 in Unit 2: Collaborative Working, pages 78–80.)

You will also need to correctly acknowledge all sources (see Assessment Objective 5 in Unit 2: Collaborative Working, page 81).

Create, format and edit text

Whichever software title you use to create your digital showcase, you should know how to create text, as this is probably about the most straightforward task you can complete. In most cases you will have to choose the text entry tool (usually shown by a large letter; normally an A) and then enter the text you require.

The format of text is how the text on the pages looks. This can refer to the style of text on the page – whether it is underlined or in italics, for example – or the style of individual text characters. The style of individual text characters is better known as font, but if you think about what a font is, you should quickly realise that a font is just a group of similarly styled letters. See pages 19–20 for more on fonts.

As with creating text, editing text is very straightforward and is simply a case of changing text that already exists. With most software titles, this is a case of clicking on the text item and either overwriting the text or deleting it and starting again. Remember that editing text can be making small changes, such as changing 'she' to 'he', but can also be the process of making large changes – perhaps rewriting huge sections of an article, for example.

Create drawings, diagrams and charts

Many software packages allow you to create drawings, diagrams and charts. Alternatively, you can create these in other packages and then import them into the package. If you are using a software package such as Adobe Flash, you may choose to import these items into the library so that each item can be used many times over.

There are some advantages to creating drawings, diagrams and charts in specialist packages, as these will usually provide you with more specialist tools than may be included in the animation software. For example, if you use a spreadsheet package to create a graph, you are likely to be able to add far more special effects than if you used the animation software to create the graph. The same is also true of graphics; many graphics software titles will provide you with a wide range of different effects that you may apply.

However, before you decide to ignore any of the drawing tools that are included with your package, do take a look at the options. More complex multimedia software packages do include some excellent tools that you should consider using. This is particularly true if you think you may need to resize a graphic, as this may influence your decision to create a graphic using vector or bitmap software.

Finally, there is one further advantage of using the multimedia software to create your graphics. This is to do with the overall file size of your completed product. If you create an object in your digital showcase, then you will define the size of the object on the page at the time that the object is created. However, if you create the object in another piece of software and then import it, the object may need to be resized on-screen. Resizing an object does not always change the impact on the file size, as the actual size on the screen is smaller, but the digital size – the impact of the object on the overall file size – is the same, however it is represented on-screen.

Take digital photographs, scan images and retrieve clip art

Your digital showcase is going to need some real life images. The originals of these may be digital photographs, hard copies of pictures (whether taken with a digital camera or a traditional camera using film) or images taken from clip art. Any of these elements may be imported into your digital showcase.

Digital pictures may be imported in the same way as drawings, diagrams and charts. One obvious source of digital pictures is the digital camera. However, you need to be aware that the actual physical size of digital pictures captured with a digital camera may be huge. This may not be obvious if you use the picture-viewing software that came with your computer, but if you open the digital photograph in a graphics package, such as Corel Paint Shop Pro, and then choose to look at the image size, you may be surprised when you see the actual physical size of the image.

As well as being physically huge, these graphics may well have a very large file size. Before you decide to use such digital pictures, you should consider the size that you wish these graphics to be on your completed product. If you do wish to use a final graphic that is physically smaller than the original graphic, you will find that using a graphics package to change the size of the graphic will not only make the digital picture smaller, but will also reduce the overall file size of the graphic and, by implication, that of the completed product.

As well as using digital photographs which are already digitalised, you can also use a scanner to create a digital copy of pictures which you have as hard copies. The process of using a scanner to do this is called digitalising, as the scanner is creating a digital copy of the original photograph.

A scanner will create a copy that is the same physical size as the original. However, most scanners will allow you to change the quality of the scan. This is achieved by changing the **resolution** of the scan before the scan is carried out. The screenshot shown in Figure 4.4 is an example of how this may be set.

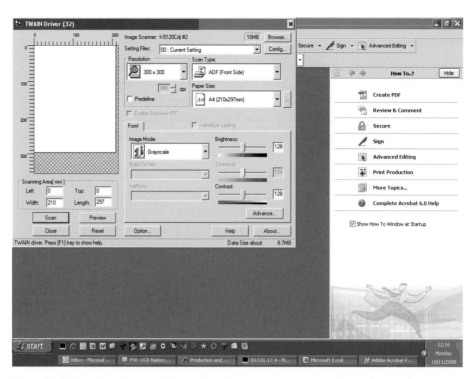

Figure 4.4 Changing the resolution of a scan

Resolution is an important consideration, especially if your completed digital showcase is to be a resource that may be downloaded from a website. If size is not an issue, then you do not need to give resolution too much thought. However, in most cases you will need to take account of file size. A good rule of thumb is to consider the use to which the scan is to be put. If your scan is to be used on a website, you will need to consider the resolution of monitors. In this case, a relatively low resolution would be sufficient. However, if you want to print the work out, you will need to use a higher resolution. For example, a resolution of 300 dpi is usually considered sufficient for most printed graphics.

Clip art

Clip art is a very wide term. One good working definition for clip art is graphics that are provided with software. However, clip art can also be downloaded from online clip art galleries. Perhaps you should consider clip art to be electronic graphics that are held as part of a collection and from which you may select graphics to use.

Clip art can be in many formats. It can be, for example, either a vector or a bitmap graphic, with all the associated implications of each format. Vector graphics resize without the inherent distortion of bitmap graphics, but this may not be too much of a problem unless you intend to use a very large canvas size for your completed product.

Edit and retouch images

Editing and retouching images is the process of making changes to your images or graphics to suit their intended use. For example, you could have taken an excellent digital photograph that was extremely well suited to your task, apart from the fact that your completed project has to use only monochrome graphics. Changing a graphic from colour to monochrome is a simple task, and in most graphics manipulation packages it is a matter of clicking a button. This is, nonetheless, one example of editing a graphic and may be evidenced by presenting the graphic in its original state and then in the edited state.

However, editing and retouching can be much more. Retouching is generally considered to be making small changes to a graphic to remove a small mistake or defect, such as removing red eye on a digital photograph, without fundamentally changing the graphic. Editing is the process of making large, substantial changes. However, there is a grey area between the two and you would be advised to include examples of where you have made small changes, such as removing red eye or perhaps removing a small area of the graphic that you do not want, as well as examples of making large changes, such as applying some of the many tools that can be applied when using a graphics manipulation package.

Produce and/or source multimedia elements

Create animations

Animation is the process of adding movement to an object; the literal meaning is 'to add life to an object'. However, creating animations should not be confused with applying an animation effect. Creating an animation is the process of adding movement to an element you have created or imported.

Frame-based animation

How you create your animation will depend on the type of software you are using. Some animation software creates **frame-based** animation. Frame-based animations are very much like films, in that your final product is a series of frames that flash on-screen. Each frame may only be on-screen for a tenth of a second or less. If each frame has subtle differences from the one which preceded it, then the illusion of movement may be achieved. This may, for example, be achieved by having a dog slightly move its head in a series of frames. As each frame is then played, so the movement in each frame adds together to form an overall impression of a dog looking from left to right.

Tweening

Frame-based animations can be very time-consuming to create. Each frame has to be drawn and, at a rate of ten frames a second, even a one-minute animation may take many hours to create. Alternatively, you could use **tweening** software, such as Adobe Flash. Tweening software is so called because it asks you to create key points in the animation and fills in the gaps between. Tweening is actually short for 'in betweening', because tweening works with the parts in between the parts you create.

There are generally two types of tweening.

■ **Motion tweening** is the movement of an object from point A to point B. This is a simple form of tweening and, while the object does move from point A to point B, the object itself does not change. (If the object was a dog, for example, there would be no suggestion that the legs were moving.)

■ **Shape tweening** is where the software compares the object at the start of the tween and at the end of the tween. The tween will then control the change from the initial state (the object at the start of the tween) and the final state (the object at the end of the tween). This is called shape tweening because the shape itself changes.

Tween
The term 'tween' is used to describe the flow of one shape into another. Tween is short for 'in between' and describes breaking down the change from one shape to another into small steps – steps that are in between the one shape and the other.

It should be clear that tweening animation software may be more complicated than frame-based animation software. However, once you have got to grips with the software, effective animations may be created far more quickly and with less effort than when using frame-based software. In both cases, there is still the need for you to create or capture starting graphics, but the actual work required to give the illusion of movement is far less for tweening software.

Record and edit sounds

As well as creating animations to go in your completed product, you will need to record and edit sound. This may be a piece of music that will play as the digital showcase opens or runs, or may be a piece of commentary that goes with the graphics that are on-screen.

There are three ways in which you could create your sound clip:

- create a new recording
- create a digital copy of an analogue (non-digital recording)
- edit and merge already existing digital sound recordings.

Of these three options, probably the easiest would be to record your own sound, as most computers will include sound recording software. Digital microphones are now supplied with computers or may be bought relatively cheaply. If you wanted to create a digital copy of previously recorded material, you could also use this method to record these, but will need another device on which to play the original materials. You should, however, be aware of the implications of the Copyright, Designs and Patents Act when doing so (see page 79).

The final option will allow you to work with already existing digital sound recordings. These may be music files or speech files and you should, as with non-digital recordings, be aware of copyright issues when working with these files. However, there are many sources from which you can download non-copyright materials and you may wish to explore these before considering using resources that may be covered by copyright regulations.

There is a range of software you could use to edit your sound files. Relatively simple software, such as Microsoft Sound Recorder, does not offer many opportunities to edit sound but does includes simple effects. Whether it could be used to create sound files that would be considered suitable is debatable, however.

You may have already used **audacity** software. If you have not, this entirely free product may be downloaded from http://audacity.sourceforge.net/. The audacity software includes a full range of tools and effects you can use to edit existing tracks, and is very easy to use. However, as with all such software, the range of effects can often lead you astray, so remember that your target is to produce a sound file that is suitable for purpose.

Record and edit video clips

You will need to include video clips in your digital showcase. The focus of these video clips will, obviously, depend on your brief, but could include any of the following:

- interviews with key speakers or members of the public
- shots of a location or building
- shots to set a theme.

Any video clips you use will need to be both created and edited. You could use a digital video camera for this task. Alternatively, many digital cameras now include video features and these may be used to record clips of a suitable quality. Similarly, many mobile phones can be used to record clips, though at present the quality of these clips is unlikely to be of the required standard.

As well as capturing your own videos, you could also work with video clips that already exist. Again, you would need to be aware of copyright issues, although there are many sources of copyright-free clips.

When it comes to editing your clips, you could consider using Microsoft's Movie Maker software. This is a free download that breaks clips down into scenes. These scenes may then be rearranged into a different order or merged with scenes from other clips to create a new resource.

However you choose to create and edit your video, you will, of course, need to evidence what you have done.

Apply sound and video effects and transition

You will now need to add all the elements you have been collecting over the past few weeks to your digital showcase. When combining elements, you will need to consider:

- which sound or video effects are applied and when
- what triggers each sound or video effect.

Triggers

Triggers are events that make something else happen. The technical term is 'event-led procedure' (see also Assessment Objective 5, page 147). In a video game, for example, the trigger may be a character entering a room.

In your digital showcase, you may want different sounds to play at different stages or when the user enters different areas of your showcase. A digital showcase about Europe, for example, may have different national anthems playing when different nations are selected. In these cases, the user may not even be aware of the trigger and would, simply, be aware of the music playing. Alternatively, your trigger could require a definite action on the part of the user; the user may need to click on a button to hear more information, for example.

Transitions

Transitions are set animations within software and are usually used to handle the change from one scene to another. You may have come across transitions when working with slide show software, such as Microsoft PowerPoint. This software provides a wide number of transitions, such as Box In, Box Out, or the excellently descriptive Wheels Clockwise, 8 Spokes. These and many more transitions can be used as you change from one slide to another.

Many people do not use transitions when working with slide shows and this is probably because the viewer is comfortable with the format and expects to see quite large changes from one slide to another. However, when working with videos or scenes within a multimedia product, the point of reference is film, and in this

Event-led procedures
These are specific actions that occur because something else (an event) happens. In some cases, this could be something as straightforward as the user clicking on a button. However, it could be something slightly more complicated. Your plan should include a clear indication of how different events may affect other aspects of your multimedia product.

genre the viewer almost subconsciously expects to see a smooth segue from one scene to another. This smooth change is achieved through the use of transitions which smoothly remove the last scene and usher in the next. Transitions are examples of multimedia effects and so should be included in your completed multimedia product.

Investigate copyright of information found

The requirements of this unit are that you must show awareness of copyright in your work. If you capture images from the Internet, do you have permission to use the graphics? Any images you find on the Internet will have been created – either as an original piece of art or as a digital photograph – by someone else. This person will usually be the copyright holder, or will have sold the use of the graphic to the website. Either way, there may be restrictions on how you can use the graphic. Unless you create the graphic yourself, again either as a piece of original art or as a digital photograph, you will need to at least acknowledge the graphic as belonging to someone else.

There are a number of websites that explain the UK copyright laws in some depth. However, before trusting a website, make sure that it is referring to the contents of the Copyright, Designs and Patents Act 1988. Many countries give legal protection to copyright material, but laws differ between countries.

If you do need to trace the copyright owner, the best starting place is to contact the owner of the site or product in which you found the image or other resource you wish to use. This may not always result in an immediate response, unless the owner of the site or publisher is the copyright holder. Where the copyright is held by a third party, the publisher is unlikely to give out contact details. However, it is likely that they would then pass on your request, in which case you may well get a response directly from the copyright owner.

The main exception to this is work that is in the public domain. This is work produced by someone who died more than seventy years ago. Work that is in the public domain is copyright free.

(For more on copyright, see Unit 2: Collaborative Working, page 62.)

Acknowledge sources

The basic principle of acknowledging sources is that any third party should be given enough information so that they may find the resource you have used.

- For resources you have found on the Internet, you will need to give the full web address of the website, as well as any other information on where the resource may be located. You may also consider giving the date on which you accessed the site, especially if you are aware that the website is updated regularly.
- If you are using other sources, such as recorded material, then you would need to firstly comply with any copyright restrictions. Once you had done so, the original source of the clip should then be given.
- Finally, it is good practice to reference any materials you have created yourself. A mention of a clip as being a private recording, for example, would make it clear to anyone checking that the clip to which you are referring is one you created.

Portfolio Activity (AO3)

You should now create the elements you have planned to include in your digital showcase for the Food and Market Group. You will not, at this stage, be combining these to create your digital showcase.

The elements you choose to create will very much depend on your plan. However, you should be aware of the minimum requirements of each level. You must, at least, include text, graphics, animation, sound and audio in your work, as well as providing clear evidence that you have created and edited each of these elements. Remember that it is not sufficient to just create the multimedia product; you must also provide evidence of having completed the creative and preparatory tasks.

Pass – Candidates will provide evidence of creating and editing appropriate graphics, at least one animation and one sound or audio clip. They will acknowledge sources and identify the copyright of some of the components found.

Merit – Candidates will provide evidence of creating and editing a range of approprite graphics, animations and sound clips and at least one video clip. A range of graphic types will be included. They will acknowledge sources and identify the copyright of most of the components found.

Distinction – Candidates provide evidence of creating and editing a range of appropriate graphics, animations and sound clips and at least one video clip. A **wide** range of graphic types will be included. They will acknowledge sources and identify the copyright of the components found. All elements must be of a near-professional standard.

AO4: Optimise multimedia elements

Optimising multimedia elements

Optimising is the process of making your presentation work as efficiently as possible. In effect, this means keeping the overall file size of your multimedia product as small as possible. This is important for two reasons:

- If you are creating a web-based presentation, a large file takes longer to download than a small file. An inefficiently organised presentation will unnecessarily increase the time it will take a user to access your webpage or presentation.
- However large your hard drive or user area, it is a finite resource and it is better not to waste storage space.

There are two ways of optimising.

- Firstly, consider how often you can use an element. The use of common elements where possible, such as a standard Home button, rather than a different Home button for every stage of the animation, will drastically reduce the overall size of the finished product.
- Secondly, make sure that each element you use has as small a file size as possible. This is basically a case of reducing the information needed to create the object.

While the overall concept of optimisation is relatively straightforward, it is necessary to discuss the different techniques available in more depth.

Dimensions

The dimensions of an object are the width and height. When working with graphics or video, the same definitions apply. As was discussed in the section on taking digital photographs in Assessment Objective 3, modern digital cameras allow you to take digital photographs that are far bigger than any monitor. This therefore means that the amount of data held in the file is also far more than is required to create the graphic you need for your digital showcase.

In order to show that you have optimised your work, you should provide evidence that you have taken account of the physical dimensions of your final product when creating any elements. Good evidence for this would be a screenshot of the dimensions information (usually found within the image section of your software).

Compression

Compression may be applied throughout the creative process. If you are creating elements within your multimedia software, many titles will allow you to compress shapes. For vector graphics, this is usually achieved by reducing the complexity of the graphic. This will mean removing some of the curves in the graphic, but this is all very subtle and, if handled with due care and attention, will not reduce the overall quality of the graphic too much. Most software titles that include this facility will give you an opt-out opportunity before you accept the results of this compression technique.

Resolution

You will need to provide evidence of having considered resolution in your work (see Assessment Objective 3, page 138 for more information on resolution). A screenshot of the resolution of any graphics or video clips with an explanation of why this resolution has been chosen would be good evidence that you have taken this into account.

Frame rate

The frame rate refers to how many frames are shown per second. It is generally considered that a frame rate of 12 frames per second is a good working level. This means that for a 5 second clip, you would need to create 60 frames if you were working at this frame rate. Each frame needs to be saved and so, the more frames you have, the greater the file size of the animation which has implications for download speed.

One thing you could consider is trying to reduce the number of frames. This would mean that you need fewer frames per second and, therefore, your animation would have a smaller file size. However, fewer frames per second can reduce the quality of the animation, making the characters' movement appear jerky. A reduction in frame rate from 12 per second to 10 per second would result in a large reduction in the file size, with only a small reduction in quality. You should experiment and come up with a trade off between quality and frame rate with which you are happy.

File formats

Different file formats will deal with graphics in different ways. The first difference of which you need to be aware is that between **vector** and **bitmap** graphics. These are two very different techniques for creating graphics.

You also need to be aware of the difference between file formats. These are the formats you use to save graphics. The two that are most frequently used are .jpg and .bmp. If you are working with bitmap graphics, the general rule is to save your work in .jpg format. This format allows you to compress individual graphics.

Similarly, many multimedia editing software packages will allow you to choose the format in which you publish your final product. Your choice here will depend on how you wish to present your completed product, but it is very much recommended that you at least experiment with the options presented to you by your software and compare the effect of different formats on the final file size.

Export sound and video clips in suitable file formats

The points made above for graphics apply here also. File formats will affect the overall size of your sound or video elements and you need to make a choice about which to use. Also, as with graphics, you need to show why you have reached these decisions. The problem is that while there are many different graphics file types, all supported by different graphics packages, the situation with video files is less clear.

There are, however, a number of commonly used formats. Of these, AVI (Audio Video Interleaved) is used with most windows products and is editable within Windows Movie Maker. As it is a windows product, the format is widely supported. If you use this format, you will end up with a product that is of a relatively high quality, but also has a relatively high file size.

The other highly popular format is the .MOV file format. This is the format used by Quicktime. Quicktime is available for both PCs and Mac machines and produces high quality videos that are relatively low in file size.

Sound may be compressed or uncompressed. WAV files, for example, are not compressed, while MP3 files are compressed. WAV files are therefore bigger than the equivalent MP3 file. However, you should remember that compression is achieved by discarding some of the information held in a file. While this may not have much of an effect when working with graphics files, sound compression can cause a noticeable effect on the quality of your files. However, for your purposes, this may be considered as insignificant when compared to the advantage to be gained by compressing files.

The trade off between file size and quality

One final point to consider before you fly in and reduce the file size of your work, is the effect that this will have on the quality of your completed piece. All digital

> **Vector graphics**
> Vector graphics are made up of geometric shapes such as circles and rectangles, and they are resolution independent. Unlike bitmap graphics, they can be enlarged without loss of resolution.

products are saved as files. The file size of a digital product is directly related to the amount of data that needs to be stored about the product. Some file types are designed to store less data than others. Vector graphics formats, for example, require little information to be stored, yet can create quite complex graphics. However, for all digital products, the ability to reduce the file size once the original element has been created can only be achieved by reducing the amount of data that is held. The unfortunate fact is that if you reduce the file size of a digital element, you are reducing the data that is held in the file. This can only be achieved by reducing the quality of the element, whatever type or format. You should bear this fact in mind when optimising any or all of your elements.

Portfolio Activity (AO4)

Review the elements you have created for the Food and Market Group. You should then optimise the elements so that each element of the product, once optimised, works both effectively and efficiently.

Once you have optimised each of your elements, you should provide clear and valid reasons why you have optimised each element in the manner you have.

Assessment Guidance

Pass – Evidence of some optimisation for most elements will be present.

Merit – Most multimedia elements will be optimised effectively with some appropriate reasons given.

Distinction – All multimedia elements will be optimised effectively with clear and valid reasons given for all decisions.

AO5: Author an interactive multimedia product

Appropriate interactive non-linear multimedia product

This is where you finally put all the elements of your digital showcase together. This will mean bringing all the separate elements into the library as well as setting up all of the actions you have planned to happen. You will need to follow your plan when carrying out your work for this section.

Use a range of multimedia elements

This may seem like a strange task to include, as you have been creating multimedia elements throughout this unit. However, this is a core expectation of Assessment Objective 5. The product you create must be an impressive combination of elements that, when considered together, work to create the effect you have planned. You should aim to include only elements of high quality and the presentation itself must run accurately and present all elements well.

Combining your elements ready for use in the multimedia presentation

The elements you create will need to be included in your completed product. How you achieve this will obviously, depend on your software. However it is likely that you will need to import any materials onto your showcase as assets. Assets are best imported into a central area, which may, for example, be called the library area. The process of importing elements into your library is usually achieved by choosing the import button, which you would expect to find under the file menu, whichever software you are using. Once you have chosen to import your element, it is merely a case of navigating to where the element is stored and then selecting the elements you wish to import.

In many cases, you will be asked to save any project on which you are working when you come to close the software. However, this is not always the case and you should ensure that you save any project on which you are working before you close your work.

Synchronise elements to play at specified intervals

Most multimedia authoring packages will allow you to work with a timeline. We discussed timelines in AO2, but if you need a quick reminder, a timeline is a line that represents the time during which the product plays. The passing of time is represented by the movement along the line from left to right. Different events then occur as time passes along the timeline.

If you have designed an element to play as part of an event-led procedure, then you must ensure that the code for each event is written so that this must occur. If, however, you have written your event to occur at a set time during the performance, for example if you want a video to play automatically after five seconds, you will need to place this within the timeline at the relevant point.

The relevant point on the timeline will depend on the frame rate you have set for your product. If, for example, you have set the frame rate to be 12 frames per second, and you wanted a video to play after five seconds, this video would have to be placed at the point relating to frame 60.

User interaction

You will need to build user interaction into your product. This could be achieved by adding a navigation system, as well as some further interaction such as play buttons.

Navigation system

A suitable navigation system is one that fits in with the general design and style of your product and which directs the user to the precise section of the product that is required. You will therefore need to be accurate in your construction of the product so that your key points are precisely located. How you achieve this will depend on the software you are using. However, the general principal is that you should include key points in your digital showcase to which your navigation system will link.

At the simplest level, you could include a menu-driven navigation system that includes links to different parts of your digital showcase. These could be organised into a block of links that are permanently on-screen, although this may not be as effective as having a menu that only appears when necessary.

A more subtle navigation system might be a drop-down menu that only appears when the user clicks on an icon, or a menu that appears as the product progresses along the timeline. The basic design principle for both of these menus is that they are only on-screen when needed and, therefore, do not detract from the user's experience of the product. An alternative design may include a navigation system that is suitable for the user, either because the language used is descriptive or the menu includes advice and explanation.

We covered more about the design of a navigation system in section 'Structure and navigation' in AO2 on pages 131–132.

You may want to go back to this section to refresh your understanding of the theory and techniques involved with designing a navigation system before you continue with the current section.

Interactive features

As well as a navigation system, you will need to include further interactive features. These may simply be a play button and a stop button, or you could include a range of interactive features, such as drag and drop or forms.

Of the features listed, we have already discussed menus. However, other elements are quite easy to add, with good effect. A start/pause/stop feature allows the user to control how the product plays and can be very effective in allowing the user time to process the information contained in your product. Depending on the software you are using to create your digital showcase, this can be as simple as adding a small piece of script or you may even be lucky enough to find that such buttons come as standard items in a library of standard effects and tools.

Forms allow the user to input data into the product. For example, a form may be included to collect the names and addresses of the users, so that contact may be made later. Alternatively, a form could be used to collect feedback on the product. Either of these options would be appropriate for inclusion in a digital showcase, and there are, of course, many further uses to which you could put such a form.

As with start/pause/stop buttons, you may find that the task of setting up a form within your product is merely a case of using the tools to do so. In which case, such features will be usually found under an insert menu. While the form will need to be well designed and should work as intended, setting up the form may be as easy as clicking a few buttons.

Finally, you may decide to include **drag and drop** features within your product. Most multimedia authoring packages will allow you to create an element that the user is then able to drag to a new location on-screen. This may be as simple as an area of text or a graphic. The complex aspect will be where you set what happens following on from an event; in most software packages, this will require the use of code. However, as with other aspects of this assessment objective, setting up such an event-led procedure will cover other aspects of this qualification as well as the requirement to include a drag and drop element.

Multimedia effects

Alternative pathways

The requirement here is for the user to be provided with **alternative pathways** (the ability to select different routes) through the product, but still be able to view all materials within the product. The alternative to this is to present the viewer with a linear product that shows all materials in a pre-determined, linear fashion. The comparison here is rather like the difference between the way a user may access a novel and a catalogue. Whereas the user would read the novel page by page in order for the story to make sense, a user may flick from one page of a catalogue to another, as each page accessed will make sense, regardless of the order in which it is viewed.

Luckily, you can build in alternative pathways simply by ensuring that your menu system allows the user to move from section to section. In a simple system, this may be to allow the user to always return to the start and from there move out along another pathway. However, such a navigation system would be considered fairly simplistic and, while it may be seen as appropriate, would be unlikely to be considered effective.

A more complex and impressive approach would be to allow access from your current section to all other sections. This may be combined with a menu system that also allows navigation within the current system. Such a system may be achieved easily by a **nested menu**, which is a menu that has submenus that open up when selected. Not only would such a menu allow the freedom of navigation you require, you would also be scoring highly on the appropriate and effective scales!

Portfolio Activity (AO5)

You should combine together the elements you have identified and created for your product. You should include a suitable navigation system, as well as other interactive features, such as buttons to control an embedded video. You should also include a form for users to complete to submit their contact details. Your final structure and layout should fit the plan you created as part of the Portfolio Activity for AO2.

Assessment Guidance

Pass – Candidates will create a multimedia product that combines a range of multimedia elements and offers alternative pathways. The navigation system might be quite simple, for example menu-driven. The product will include hyperlinks and one other interactive feature.

Merit – Candidates will create an appropriate multimedia product that combines a range of multimedia elements effectively and offers alternative pathways. The navigation system will be effective. The product will include some timeline-based events, hyperlinks and more than one other interactive feature.

Distinction – Candidates will create a near-professional quality multimedia product. This will fully demonstrate the effective combination of a range of multimedia elements and will offer alternative pathways. The navigation system will be effective. The product will include a range of timeline-based events, hyperlinks and other interactive features.

AO6: Use the results of testing and feedback to produce the final version

Create test plan and test

Before you publish your completed multimedia product, you must test it to check that it works as intended. This testing should be in two parts. The first should be a series of mechanical tests (sometimes called usability testing) to check that all elements of the product behave correctly (i.e. you should test buttons to make sure that the intended action follows your event), followed by a feedback test from potential users, whom you will ask for their opinion of your work. Once you have completed your testing, you will then need to make any changes you think are justified.

The tasks for this assessment are therefore in three distinct stages:

■ mechanical test on elements
■ gather feedback from prospective users
■ make necessary changes.

Testing the usability of your product

Your usability testing should be in two stages. The first stage is the planning stage and the second is the actual testing stage. The outcome of the planning stage is the test plan, while the outcome of the second stage is the test report.

Creating a test plan

A test plan has three main elements. These are:

■ the element you intend to test
■ how you will test it
■ the expected result.

There are many ways in which you can test an element included in a multimedia product. A button, for example, could be tested to check that the correct event occurred after it had been clicked. However, the button could also be tested to check that the correct 'down' image appeared when the button was depressed or that the button returned to the correct 'up' state. Therefore, it is perfectly possible that parts of your multimedia product could be tested more than once. In fact, with some elements, it is possible that five or more tests could be applied, depending on the complexity and purpose of the element being tested. As a result of this possibility, do not be surprised if your completed test plan includes the same element name in the first column for more than one test.

The second column shows how you will test the element. Many people try to make this too complicated. If you are testing a button by pressing on it, the correct test is: 'I will click on the button with the mouse.'

If you are testing a button, then 'clicking on it' is the starting point for a number of tests. In this case, you would therefore have two cells holding identical text. It is only in the expected result cells that a reader would notice any difference.

The expected result column is where you say what you expect to happen. Again, there is a temptation to overcomplicate this entry. It is perfectly acceptable to state exactly what you expect will happen. A section of the test plan for the button we have discussed throughout this section is shown in Figure 4.5.

What is being tested	How it is being tested	Expected result
The Home button	I will click on it with the mouse	I will be taken back to the Home page
The Home button	I will click on it with the mouse	The Down state button will appear (the button will appear depressed)

Figure 4.5 Section of a test plan

It should be stressed that there are more tests that could be applied to a button! However, it should be clear that the test report is a simple list of what you will be doing to check that the mechanical parts of your project work as intended. The best way to test those parts is to use them in the same way as an everyday user would. If you are testing a button, click on it. If you are opening a section of your product and an animation should run, then the test is to open the section of the product and look to see whether the animation runs.

Below is an example list of tests – if you were to test all of these elements, this would make the basis of a very good test plan:

- links and pathways
- proofreading text
- accurate alignment of elements
- interactive features
- robustness and stability of product in different conditions.

A good test plan will plan to test all elements of a product. Therefore, your document is likely to be quite long. Do not make it complicated at the same time.

Creating a test report

A test report is simply the results of carrying out the test plan. A test report will have two extra columns to a test plan. These are:

- actual result
- action required.

Many people actually create a test plan with all five columns included, but only complete the first three when planning the testing. This document can then be printed and stored. The results of the testing are then added to the remaining two columns to create a test report.

There are two main things to remember about a test report:

- Carry out all planned tests – do not leave blanks.
- Many of your tests will bring the results you expected. Your entry could then either be 'as expected' or could be based on the text you have included in the expected result column. If this is the case, then obviously no action is required. However, if action is required, state what it is.

What is being tested	How it is being tested	Expected result	Actual result	Action required
The Home button	I will click on it with the mouse	I will be taken back to the Home page	I was taken to the second page	Check the ActionScript
The Home button	I will click on it with the mouse	The Down state button will appear (the button will appear depressed)	The Down state button appeared	No action required

Figure 4.6 Results of a test plan

It should be clear to you that your test report will include a lot of repetition. Many of your elements will work as intended and so will require no action. The job of your test report is to show that.

Testing in a range of conditions

If you are targeting a distinction, you will need to test your product in a range of different conditions. These conditions will include testing on a number of computers in addition to the one you used to create the product. The intention here is to prove that your product will work on a range of computers, as it should if it were to be used by many users.

At the same time as checking on different computers, you should try checking your product using a range of different screen resolutions. Screen resolution can be changed using your computer's control panel.

As well as checking your product on a number of computers and resolutions, you should check that your product works from a range of storage media. You could save your work onto a CD-ROM and check that this does not affect the performance. Similarly, you could save it onto an external hard-drive and check that this does not make a difference to the performance of your product.

Review

User testing

As well as the mechanical test, you should test your product to see how well it meets the needs of the intended audience. There are two main areas included in the specification for this unit. The elements included are:

- seek feedback from test users using appropriate methods
- obtain suggested improvements from test users.

The emphasis here is on how potential users regard the product. As you shall see, you do not have to follow the advice. However, if you are targeting a distinction, you need to design and develop appropriate methods to gather feedback and to show clearly how any changes you decide to implement will improve the product. You should also plan this research so that you get a representative sample from a range of different potential users.

Implement changes

You may think that this is the most straightforward part of the whole unit. In some ways it is. For example, you will find things that are wrong with your work as you test it. You should make changes to these elements and then move on. You will also be given advice by your potential users. This advice may be totally useful and relevant and should be followed.

However, there are two issues of which you must be aware. The first is that you will need to make *appropriate* changes. This means that you must be prepared to reject suggested changes that you feel are not appropriate to the product you are creating. This may be because they would create a product that was unsuitable for the target audience or was not fit for purpose.

Secondly, it is likely that you will test your work as you work through it. This will inevitably lead to the identification of errors with your work. However, you may not have created a test plan at this stage, and so you may have a finished and final product that works extremely well before you reach the testing stage.

It is therefore advisable to see the testing document as one that grows alongside the production of your product. As you create an element of the multimedia product, you should stop and develop your test plan for that element at that stage. This has the advantage that you are not creating a potentially huge test plan in one go at the end of your work and, secondly, it means that you gain recognition for the testing and improvements you do as you work through the creation of your product.

Evidence of changes made

You must provide evidence that you have made the changes. This should be in the form of a 'before' screenshot and an 'after' screenshot. These screenshots should show the item on which you have been working. If, for example, you find issues with a piece of ActionScript, then you should show the script before the changes and then once more after the changes have been made.

As well as evidence of change, you will be required to produce evidence of testing. If you have made changes, then the evidence of change, combined with a test report, should be sufficient. However, you may consider including a witness statement from your teacher as further proof that you have tested your product.

Portfolio Activity (AO6)

1   Create full test and feedback plans to test your product. You should then carry out testing of your product. Make any changes to the product that your test plan identifies as being necessary.
2   Review the feedback from potential users and select changes that seem appropriate. Explain why you have chosen each of these changes. Make the changes you have accepted as being appropriate.

Assessment Guidance

Pass – Candidates will provide evidence of testing their product. Candidates seek and obtain feedback from at least one test user. They will suggest possible improvements that could be made to the product. At least one improvement will be incorporated into the final product.

Merit – Candidates will produce a detailed test plan and use it to test their product. They will design a feedback form and obtain feedback from several test users. They will use the results of the testing and feedback to suggest appropriate improvements to the product. Most of the planned improvements will be incorporated into the final product.

Distinction – Candidates will produce a comprehensive test plan and test all aspects of their product in a range of different conditions. They will design an appropriate feedback form and obtain feedback from several test users. They will use the results of the testing and feedback to suggest appropriate improvements to the product. They will fully explain their reasons for the planned improvements. All planned improvements will be incorporated into the final product.

Creating a user guide

A user guide is a document that explains how to use the product you have just created. As a minimum, you should include information on:

- how to install your product
- how to use the product.

If you are targeting a merit, your user guide should include a section on system requirements. If you are targeting a distinction, your user guide should also be of high quality and make good use of graphics to improve the quality of your explanations.

The language of a user guide

A user guide is intended to be a guide for a user. This user is usually assumed to be a non-technical user. This means that the user guide should be a relatively simple document that avoids technical language and does not explain issues in too much depth. In fact, most user guides will avoid the really in-depth issues, as these are more relevant to technical documents.

System requirements

Have you ever bought a piece of software, only to find that when you got it home, you did not have the correct graphics card for the product, or there was insufficient RAM? If this has happened to you, you may have decided to check the system requirements for all purchases, as these are the explanations (usually found on the side of the packaging) that make clear what your computer must include in order for the package to work as intended.

While it is unlikely that your product would need specific graphics cards, you may need to stress that other devices or software are necessary in order for your product to run smoothly.

Writing an effective user guide

Hopefully, you will already have an idea about what could go in the user guide for your multimedia product. You may also have a good idea about the layout and structure of your guide.

Your explanations of each of the areas expected by the exam board must be both accurate and in sufficient depth to explain your point. Rather than writing a user guide from memory, it is a good idea to work through each step you are describing as you write about it. This means that you will not miss any stage and that you can create any relevant screenshots more easily.

Any screenshots you create should be well presented. You should consider exporting these into a graphics package and cropping any unnecessary parts of each screenshot before importing the graphic into your guide. You should remember that extra and maybe irrelevant items in a screenshot may distract the user (such as icons, for example, which should be cropped so that your screenshot shows only the icon to which you are referring). Finally, you should consider using arrows to pick out the important area of any of your more complicated screenshots. Arrows should usually lead from the text to the item being described.

Portfolio Activity (AO7)

Create a user guide for your completed multimedia product. As a minimum, include information on:

- how to use your completed product
- how to install your user guide.

Your section on using the product should cover all aspects, including how to open the product and how to navigate the product.

Pass – Candidates will produce user documentation that includes how to install and use the product.

Merit – Candidates will produce user documentation that includes the system requirements and how to install and use the product.

Distinction – Candidates will produce user documentation that makes good use of graphic images and detailed instructions for use. The guide includes the system requirements and how to install and use the product.

Assessment Guidance

Advanced Spreadsheets

Learning outcomes

By working through this unit you will produce evidence to meet the unit assessment objectives to show that you understand how to:

- design spreadsheets
- create a spreadsheet, according to the design, using advanced spreadsheet features
- use spreadsheets to process numerical data and present required information
- produce user documentation and technical information
- understand and implement spreadsheet testing
- evaluate the spreadsheets.

Introduction

You should read through all the assessment objectives and portfolio activities before you begin producing evidence for this unit. This will ensure that you know what is required to achieve each of the assessment objectives, and what activities you will be required to carry out to do so.

Note that you will be required to produce a test plan and an evaluation of the solution that you provide. It is very important that you consider these factors at the planning stage. This will help you to outline the aims and objectives that you will have to evaluate later in your project. In this unit you will be creating linked spreadsheets. There is data available to help you decide how to lay out the spreadsheets and how they will be linked.

Scenario

A company set up in business three months ago to sell tyres. They do not use spreadsheets to keep track of their sales and income, although they do have supplier details on a spreadsheet file. The company uses two suppliers – Butlers and Youngs.

The company has set out a number of requirements, including the ways in which they would like to be able to search for information and produce invoices.

The lists of products and prices are held in a spreadsheet which has a separate sheet for each supplier. You can access this file on the website at http://www.heinemann.co.uk/Series/Secondary/OCRNationalsICTLevel3/FreeResources/FreeResources.aspx. It is filed under the source documents for Unit 5, file name U5 TYRE-SUPPLIERS.

The company requires records of sales of each product; for example, see Figure 5.1.

Stock Code	PERIOD 4					Total	Cost
	Week 1	Week 2	Week 3	Week 4	Week 5		
AG41165	16	12	16			44	65.00
AG61165	10	12	8			30	98.00
MX165	12	15	14			41	45.00

Figure 5.1 Sample of company records of sales

Figure 5.2 shows the type of data you will require for Periods 1 to 3. Note that Period 3 is last month, Period 2 is the month before, and Period 1 is the month before that.

Manufacturer	Stock Code	PERIOD 1		PERIOD 2		PERIOD 3	
		Price	Sales	Price	Sales	Price	Sales
MICHELIN	AG41165	52.00	36	55.50	60	58.60	60
GT	MX165	36.00	60	38.50	63	40.50	63
PIRELLI	PC165	64.00	50	68.00	88	72.50	88

Figure 5.2 Sample records for supplier – Butlers

Scenario

AO1: Design spreadsheets to meet the needs of an organisation

Designing spreadsheets for a common purpose

Purpose of spreadsheets

A spreadsheet can handle numbers and text; it is capable of recording, displaying, searching and processing data. If you have a number of calculations to make, particularly if they are complicated and complex, using a spreadsheet ensures that the calculations will always be accurate and the results can be relied on to be correct. If you put in the correct data the spreadsheet will provide the correct results. It allows you to perform the same calculation on different data. Once the calculation is set up it is quicker to use than carrying out the calculation manually.

Spreadsheets are extremely useful for modelling to predict effects. For example, if the cost of a product increases, a company might want to identify the mark up they would need to charge to ensure that profits are not affected adversely.

Data presented in a spreadsheet is often easier to understand and clearer, particularly when graphs and charts are used.

The number one rule when designing a spreadsheet is to start with the end in mind. A good spreadsheet should have about 80 per cent planning and 20 per cent implementation. A spreadsheet is about correct information, not incorrect information that looks good.

Audience of spreadsheets

The audience is the person, group or company for whom you are carrying out the work. You will need to consider their abilities and experience.

Those who use the spreadsheet to input the data, operate the macros and print output, rely on you to provide a solution. They see the printed output and use it to make decisions, so it is up to you to organise and present the data they need, when they need it.

User needs and functionality

Evaluation requires the monitoring and gathering of information to make judgements about your project which you then use to make changes and improvements.

The evaluation should be an examination of your work to see that it provides the solution that is required. You should make checks to ensure that it performs as expected and that the company is getting a product on which it can depend. You should look at the purpose, strengths and weaknesses of your spreadsheet.

- The purpose describes the desired outcomes.
- Strengths and weaknesses are points that should be considered when deciding whether your spreadsheet meets the purpose.

What are your aims and objectives?

You have to be clear about what you are trying to achieve and you need to develop specific aims and objectives.

- Your aims should be the delivery of a correctly functioning spreadsheet that meets the requirements. Remember to use language that is helpful and to be clear about your audience.
- Your objectives are the activities you carry out to achieve your aims. Limit the number of objectives, making them focused and appropriate.

Review the aims and objectives – it is important to distinguish clearly between them.

See page 188 about performance indicators, monitoring, evaluation and reporting results.

Spreadsheet layout and formatting

When setting out data, think about the following points. If you use these ideas you will be able to utilise many of the powerful built-in features which often need the data to be laid out in this way.

- Limit the number of workbooks and worksheets – it makes analysing and reporting easier. Place all related raw data on one worksheet in one workbook.
- Apply bold font when entering headings – this will help them to be recognised as headings when you use functions such as Sort.
- Avoid blank rows and columns – many of the built-in features will assume a blank row or column is the end of your data.
- Sort data where possible – many of the Lookup and Reference formulas rely on data being sorted. It also increases the speed of the calculation process.
- If you have to enter names, put the first name in one cell and the surname in the next. If you need to place them into one single cell at a later stage, this can be done very easily.

Lay out your spreadsheet as determined by the needs of the specification. No single design is always right – the size of the spreadsheet, use and frequency of references, complexity of formatting and many other factors must all be considered.

Layout refers to the manner in which spreadsheets are set up and displayed. Formatting refers to the way data is presented.

Spreadsheet layout
While a spreadsheet should be easy to read and follow, this should not be at the expense of efficiency. A common mistake with cell formatting is the changing of alignment of data. By default numbers are right-aligned and text is left-aligned. If you change this you will not be able to tell, at a glance, if the content of a cell is text or numeric – the only exception being headings.

Design sheets that have the appearance of a form or have been customised

A data form is a way for the user to enter data records into a list or table. Forms can also be used to view, change, locate and delete records. You can create a custom data form complete with text boxes, labels and the buttons required to allow any specified activity.

In Microsoft Office 2007 Excel has a feature named Template Wizard. In Excel the Template Wizard, on the Data menu, links cells in a form template to fields in a database so that data entered using a form can be stored automatically. You can use this wizard with any worksheet form that has cells designated for data entry.

From the workbook you create, the wizard creates a template which can be used as the basis for other similar workbooks, and links the cells you specify to fields in a database it creates. When you create a new workbook from the template, enter data in the cells that are linked to the database and save that workbook, Excel creates a new record in the database containing the data you entered in the form.

The Template Wizard creates a template for data entry into a database linked to the template.

1 Select an existing workbook, set up and formatted to allow ease of data entry. The wizard uses the workbook to create the template.
2 Specify the database that you want to link to the template. You can start a new database or use an existing database.
3 In this step, you identify each cell you want to copy data from and the corresponding database field you want the data copied to. The data from each workbook based on the template creates one new record in the database.
4 Select the existing workbooks that contain information you want to copy to the database. Use the Preview area to make sure that the values from the workbooks will be copied to the correct database fields.
5 The new template is ready, and is saved in the Templates folder.

If you are using Microsoft Office 2003 you will need to record a macro which when run, will copy and paste the contents of the form into a list. More information about macros can be found on pages 166–167 of this unit.

You can modify spreadsheets by:

1 Customising toolbars. To alter the way the toolbar is displayed, click Tools, Customise. Figures 5.3 and 5.4 will then be available for you to make the amendments you choose.

Figure 5.3 The Toolbars tab

Figure 5.4 The Options tab

On the Toolbars tab
Make any changes you require.

On the Options tab
Alter how the toolbars are displayed.

2 Introducing a control button to initiate a macro.

To add a control button to initiate a macro

Macros
A macro is a routine, or set of instructions, which allows you to carry out a number of steps automatically and eliminate the need to repeat the steps of common tasks.

a Open the worksheet where you want to add the button.
b Click View, Toolbars, Control Toolbox (Figure 5.5).
c Click the button for the control you want to add.
d On the worksheet, drag the control to the size you want.
e To enter the text you want to appear on the control – right-click on it, point to the name of the object on the shortcut menu, click Edit, enter your choice of text, then press ESC.

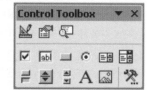

Figure 5.5 The Control Toolbox

f   To set the properties for the control – right-click the control, then Properties.
g   To add macro code right-click the control, then View Code and write the macro code.
h   To quit, click File, Close and Return to Microsoft Excel.
i   To enable the control, click Exit Design Mode on the Control Toolbox.

Calculations required

This is what a spreadsheet is about – formulas and calculations and the results they produce. Excel has over 300 built-in functions.

■ If possible, a formula should refer only to the cells above it. Calculations will then proceed downward from raw data at the top to final calculations at the bottom.
■ If a formula requires a large amount of raw data, move it to a separate worksheet and link the data to the sheet containing the formula.
■ Formulas should be as simple as possible to prevent any unnecessary calculations.

Data entry messages

When creating spreadsheets you can enter your own data entry messages based on the validation that you are introducing.

To specify entries that will be permitted:

1   Select the cell for which you want to specify validation.
2   Click **Data, Validation**, and the **Settings** tab (Figure 5.6).

Use the Allow box to specify the type of validation. You can allow:

■ values from a list – enter values, use a named range of cells, or cell references
■ numbers (whole numbers or decimals) within specified limits
■ dates or times within a timeframe
■ text of a specified length.

You can also calculate what is allowed based on the content of another cell and use a formula to calculate what is allowed.

To display an optional input message:

1   Click the **Input Message** tab (Figure 5.7).
2   Make sure the **Show input message when cell is selected** check box is selected.
3   Enter a title and text for the message.

To specify the response if invalid data is entered:

1   Click the **Error Alert** tab (Figure 5.8).
2   Make sure the **Show error alert after invalid data is entered** check box is selected.
3   Select one of the following options for the **Style** box:

■ click **Stop** to prevent entry of invalid data
■ click **Warning** to display a message that does not prevent entry
■ click **Information** to display an information that does not prevent entry of invalid data.

4   Enter a title and text for the message.

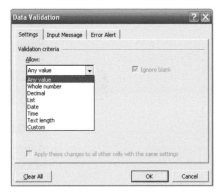

Figure 5.6 Setting data validation

Figure 5.7 Input message data

Figure 5.8 Error alert message

Data validation and associated messages

One problem when using a spreadsheet is keeping the data error-free. Data is often entered incorrectly, but data validation can limit errors by restricting what data can be entered into a data field.

Validation checks can be set on cells and ranges of cells. A range could be an entire column or row, or several columns or rows. The validation rules apply when new data is entered.

See page 168 for Portfolio Activity (AO1) and the Assessment Guidance for AO1.

AO2: Produce the spreadsheets according to the design

Produce spreadsheets in line with user design

Linked spreadsheets

A link is a reference to another spreadsheet or worksheet. In this case, the Cost of the sales item is linked to the price paid in the Supplier file (Figure 5.9).

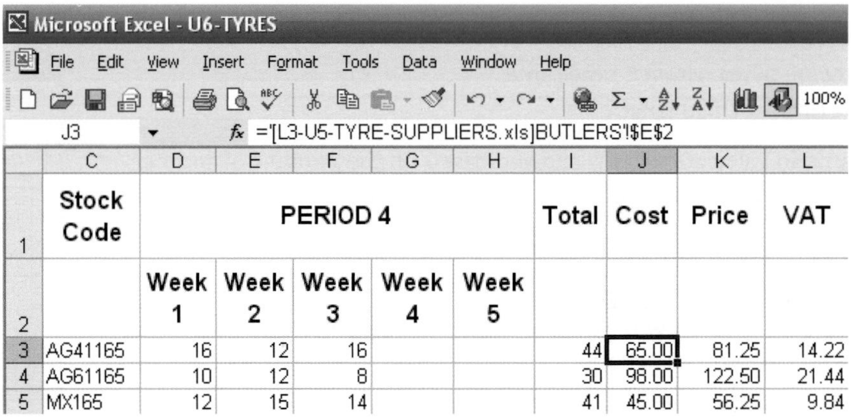

	C	D	E	F	G	H	I	J	K	L
1	Stock Code	PERIOD 4					Total	Cost	Price	VAT
2		Week 1	Week 2	Week 3	Week 4	Week 5				
3	AG41165	16	12	16			44	65.00	81.25	14.22
4	AG61165	10	12	8			30	98.00	122.50	21.44
5	MX165	12	15	14			41	45.00	56.25	9.84

Figure 5.9 Linking spreadsheets

The data in the spreadsheet or worksheet to which the data refers may change and this will make the data in this spreadsheet out of date. By setting up a link this data will automatically update when changes are made to the linked data.

To set up a link go to the cell where you want the link to exist; start with the = sign. The cell reference will be built up on the formula bar as you identify the target cell that holds the data you want to link to.

Linking allows you to use a series of linked sheets without opening all the sheets.

Relative, absolute and mixed cell referencing

- A relative cell reference in a formula describes the relative position of the cell containing the formula and the cell to which it refers. The reference automatically changes if you copy the formula. New formulas use relative references.
- An absolute cell reference in a formula refers to a specific cell only, such as $C$3. The reference remains the same if you copy the formula.
- A mixed reference can have a mixture of absolute and relative cell references. It can have an absolute column and a relative row, or an absolute row and a relative column. The relative reference automatically changes if you copy a formula; the absolute reference does not.

Using relative and absolute cell referencing helps in making your spreadsheet fully adaptable and efficient.

Named cells and cell ranges

Although you can use column and row labels to refer to cells, you can also create names for individual cells, a range of cells, formulas or constant values. When you have named a cell, you can then use the name in formulas. The spreadsheet becomes easier to read and analyse.

Many companies trade with other countries that use different currencies. You may want to incorporate a quick method of identifying the costs in those currencies. To do so you can name cells – in this case it will be for the exchange rates of the US dollar and the Euro.

This is important because the exchange rate varies on a day-to-day basis and you need to keep data up to date. At the time of writing, £1 = US$2 (the exchange rate is 1.9965); £1 = €1.26 (the exchange rate is 1.2594).

Identify the cell you want to name – in this case B2. Go to the name box and enter the name – in this case euro. The same procedure has been used to name cell B1 dollar (Figure 5.11).

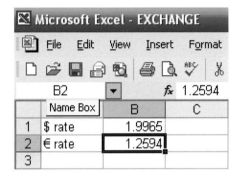

Figure 5.10 Naming cells

	A	B	C
1	$ rate	1.9965	
2	€ rate	1.2594	
3			
4	£	$	€
5	1	2	1
6	10	20	13
7	50	100	63
8	100	200	126
9	500	998	630
10	1000	1,997	1,259
11	10000	19,965	12,594

	A	B	C
1	$ rate	1.9965	
2	€ rate	1.2594	
3			
4	£	$	€
5	1	=A5*dollar	=A5*euro
6	10	=A6*dollar	=A6*euro
7	50	=A7*dollar	=A7*euro
8	100	=A8*dollar	=A8*euro
9	500	=A9*dollar	=A9*euro
10	1000	=A10*dollar	=A10*euro
11	10000	=A11*dollar	=A11*euro

Figure 5.11 Use of named cells

The formulas show that the name has been used to obtain the figures. If you are about to buy products and you have suppliers in both dollar and euro areas, this is a quick way, on a daily basis, of identifying value for money, particularly when figures are high. Simply change the value in the named cells to obtain new figures.

Using names allows easier reference and can make use of relative and absolute cell references clearer.

A range of cell formats including conditional formatting

You can format each cell or range of cells in any chosen format. You can format by row or column (Figure 5.12).

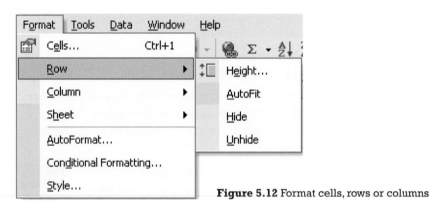

Figure 5.12 Format cells, rows or columns

There are a very large number of ways in which you can format your data. They include:

- changing the alignment of text in cells – for example, the column label is often wider than the data in that column; rather than having wide columns you can rotate text
- adding text formatting such as size and bold
- numeric data – change the appearance of numbers, including dates and times, by determining the alignment, font and font size as well as applying a border, a pattern and applying protection (Figure 5.13)
- changing cell colours – to identify specific data you can apply shading

Conditional formatting
If more than one specified condition is true, only the format of the first true condition is applied, even if more than one condition is true.

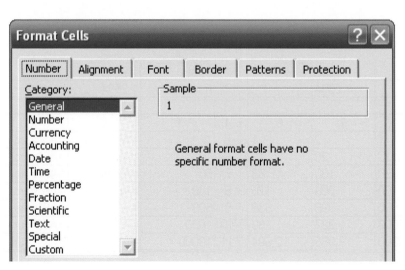

Figure 5.13 Formatting cells

- using the NOW function to add the current date to a spreadsheet
- using conditional formatting, such as cell shading or font colour that is automatically applied, if a specified condition is true
- applying one of the many automatic styles available that combine a number of formatting options, particularly for tables
- using the Style option to set all the options.

Functions to meet requirements

Functions are formulas that have been set up to perform specific calculations. They use specific values (arguments) in a specified order. They can be used for simple or complex calculations.

There are many functions in spreadsheets that you may want to use. They are split into categories, and a few of each category are shown in Figure 5.14.

The structure of a function
The structure of a function begins with an equal sign (=), followed by the function name, an opening parenthesis, the arguments for the function separated by commas, and a closing parenthesis.

Logical	AND	Returns TRUE if all its arguments are TRUE
	FALSE	Returns the logical value FALSE
	IF	Specifies a logical test to perform
	OR	Returns TRUE if any argument is TRUE
Statistical	AVERAGE	Returns the average of its arguments
	COUNT	Counts how many numbers are in the list of arguments
	MAX	Returns the maximum value in a list of arguments
Mathematical	COUNTIF	Counts the number of non-blank cells within a range that meet the given criteria
	SUM	Adds its arguments
Reference	HYPERLINK	Creates a shortcut or jump that opens a document stored on a network server, an Intranet or the Internet
	LOOKUP	Looks up values in a vector or array

Figure 5.14 Functions by category

Nested functions

The IF function tests to see if a certain condition is true or false. If the condition is true, the function will do one thing; if the condition is false, it will do something else.

The IF function is frequently used to check more than one argument, since you may need to use a function as one of the arguments of another function. Nesting IF functions increases the flexibility by increasing the number of possible outcomes.

When a nested function is used as an argument, it must return the same type of value that the argument uses. For example, if the argument returns a TRUE or FALSE value, then the nested function must return a TRUE or FALSE.

A formula can contain up to seven levels of nested functions.

Multi-stage functions

These are functions that have more than one stage. It may be that you have to enter data for a number of different stages and outline parameters. An example of this would be the use of the Solver tool where you have to decide on and enter the adjustable cells, constraints and target cell.

You have a great deal of flexibility in how you choose cells to hold the adjustable cells and constraints, and which formulas and built-in functions you use. Adjustable cells and constraints are usually in groups, so use cell ranges to represent them.

Data validation with customised error messages

You can validate the data to be entered into a cell in any of the following ways:

- allow values from a list
- allow numbers within specified upper and lower limits
- allow dates or times within a time frame or a specific date or time
- allow text of a specified length by entering the minimum, maximum or specific length for the text
- calculate what is allowed based on the content of another cell
- use a formula to calculate what is permitted.

When setting validation criteria you should also specify the error message to be given in the case of an incorrect value.

Macros to operate spreadsheet functions

Macros are routines which allow you to carry out a number of steps at once, usually by pressing a button or specified key.

If you perform a task repeatedly you can automate it with a macro. A macro is a recording of each command and action you perform to complete a task. If a macro is recorded correctly, it will always carry out the same steps in the same order without operator error.

Try this example, which is a heading you want to be available for any spreadsheet you use – the heading should be Arial, size 12, bold and centred. You also want the column to be wide enough to fit the heading. The easiest way to create this macro is to use the macro recorder. Click Tools, Macros, Record New Macro. The Record Macro dialogue box will be displayed (Figure 5.15).

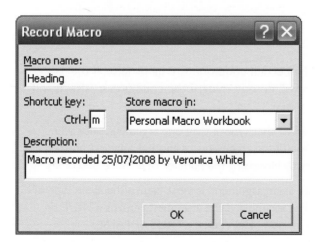

Figure 5.15 Recording a macro

There are four items to be considered.

1 *Macro name* – give your macro a descriptive name, in this case Heading. The first character must be a letter. Others can be letters, numbers, or underscore characters – use the underscore as a word separator since spaces are not allowed.
2 *Shortcut key* – this is optional. Fill in a letter in the available space – use m. This allows you to run the macro by holding down the CTRL key and pressing, in this case, m.
3 *Store macro in* – you can choose between three options (choose option three):
   - the current workbook – the macro will only be available in this file
   - a new workbook – opens a new file and the macro will only be available in this file
   - a personal macro workbook – creates a hidden file which stores your macros and makes them available in all files.
4 *Description* – it is optional to enter a description. There may be text displayed and you can use this or enter your own description.
5 When you have set these options, click OK to start the macro recorder. The Stop Recording toolbar should appear (Figure 5.16).
6 The macro recorder records all keystrokes and clicks of the mouse. To create your macro:
   - go though all the necessary steps manually
   - when finished, click Stop on the Stop Recording toolbar.
7 If you have made any errors, re-record the macro.

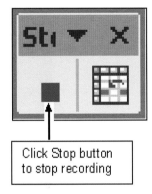

Click Stop button to stop recording

Figure 5.16 Stop Recording toolbar

To run a macro

Go to the cell where you want to run the macro. If you chose a shortcut key when creating the macro, hold down the CTRL key on the keyboard and press the shortcut key – in this case, m.

Alternatively:

1 Click Tools, Macros, Macro to display the Macro dialogue box.
2 Select a macro from the list of those available.
3 Click the Run button.

If you want to run the macro by pressing a keyboard shortcut key, enter a letter in the Shortcut key box. You can use CTRL+ letter (for lowercase letters) or CTRL+SHIFT+ letter (for uppercase letters), where letter is any letter key on the keyboard. The shortcut key letter you use cannot be a number or special character such as @ or #.

Customised menus and toolbars

You can add or remove a button, menu or command on a toolbar. You can create custom toolbars, hide or display toolbars and move toolbars. You can customise the menu bar in the same way that you customise any built-in toolbar.

- A menu is a list of commands. Most are on the menu bar – this is the horizontal bar that contains the names of the menus. Any menu bar can be customised.
- The toolbar is the bar with buttons and options that you use to carry out commands. Any toolbar can be customised.

Customise a toolbar to display items that you use most frequently if they are not on the standard toolbar, or to add the initiation of a macro.

Portfolio Activity (AO1)

The company would like to provide a spreadsheet solution. They need to hold the data showing:

- the current period sales
- the year-to-date figures.

Current period sales

The company needs the sales for the current period, broken down into weeks, for each stock item. They require data on the cost of the tyres from the suppliers, sales for each period for each stock item, and the price at which the company sells the product. The company adds a mark up of 25 per cent to the cost price. VAT is currently charged at 15 per cent. However, as this rate may change it is important that you allow the flexibility to permit any change in this tax.

You should capture the data in such a way that the transfer of the data to the year-to-date sheet is as simple as possible.

Year-to-date figures

The company wants a picture of the sales figures for the year to date. They will update the figures at the end of each period and add the figures for the period that has just finished, so 12 periods (or months) should be displayed. The year-to-date sheet should display:

- the total number of each item sold over the previous periods
- the amount taken in sales for each item for each period
- the total amount taken in sales for each item over all periods
- the total amount taken in sales each period
- the total amount taken in sales over all periods.

The company would like to have the following information, broken down by supplier and by manufacturer. This information will currently be shown from Period 1 to Period 3, but it should always show the data up to the current period, i.e. when the figures are available for Period 4 it should include Period 4; when the figures are available for Period 5 it should include Period 5, and so on:

- the total number of items sold for each period
- the total amount taken in sales for each period
- the increase or decrease in the amount taken in sales for each period
- the increase or decrease in the total amount taken in sales, rounded up to the next whole pound (£).

The company would also like to be able to:

- sort and search the stock items to find the ten items that made the most profit for them in a given period – overall, by supplier and by manufacturer
- sort and search the stock items to find the ten items that made the least amount of profit for them in a given period – overall, by supplier and by manufacturer
- sort and search the stock items to find the top ten bestselling items in a given period – overall, by supplier and by manufacturer
- use the spreadsheets to help them predict future income, particularly with regard to the mark up percentage
- produce charts and graphs for their annual report – for example, to show sales of items during the period, the bestselling products, and to compare sales of items over a given time period by supplier and manufacturer
- see at a glance whether the sales of items have increased or decreased.

Create a design for a spreadsheet that will meet the requirements of the company for the sales and income from tyres. You should provide two worksheets – one showing the data for the year-to-date and the other for the current period figures. The design of the spreadsheets needs to make them easy to use. You should provide simple but effective ways of entering data, including:

- creating sheets that have the appearance of a form
- using data entry forms.

You should include:

- what output information is required
- the data sources
- what numerical processing and modelling needs to be done to get the required output – it should include relative, absolute and mixed cell referencing; named cells, cell ranges and conditional cell formatting; you should include the functions used to meet the company's requirements, and indicate nested and multi-stage functions
- aids that can help with data input or processing
- how the output information needs to be presented
- who is going to use the spreadsheet – and their level of expertise
- information about how the spreadsheets are going to link.

Your design should include the cell formatting you will use, either by annotating your planning sheet or by writing about any features, giving exact details of the cells to which they apply. For example, you should show:

- format of the contents of the cells
- font styles and size to be applied
- text and background colours
- cell borders
- any cells that are to be merged
- direction of any text that is to be rotated.

You should provide users with helpful prompts and identify the data validation and customised error messages. You should indicate your use of customised toolbars and control buttons to initiate macros.

You should identify where you have set up processes such as pivot tables, goal seeking and filtering.

Using the designs you created for Portfolio Activity (AO1), read and complete Portfolio Activity (AO2).

Portfolio Activity (AO2)

1 Use your spreadsheet software to create the sheets you have designed in Portfolio Activity (AO1). Take care to follow your designs in detail, including layout, formulas and formatting.

2 Enter data, including data for Period 4 – the current month.

3 For each formula and macro used, you should briefly describe its purpose. You should explain where data validation has been incorporated and how it has been done. A screenshot of setting up the validation could be provided as evidence. When you transfer your designs onto a spreadsheet, you may find that some of your formulas do not work. If so, make any adjustments that are necessary to ensure that your final spreadsheets work correctly. It is important that you test your sheets, as you can only pass this task if you create working spreadsheets.

4 It is important to evidence the extent to which the spreadsheet meets the intended purpose and where more complex facilities have been incorporated. Check that you have used all of the following, and if necessary, include them in your work:

- relative, absolute and mixed cell referencing
- multi-sheet referencing
- named cells and cell ranges
- a range of cell formats, including conditional formatting
- functions to meet the specific requirements of the company, such as logical (IF, NOT), statistical (COUNTIF, RANK), mathematical (CEILING, FLOOR), reference (LOOKUP, MATCH)
- nested functions
- multi-stage functions
- data validation with customised error messages
- macros to operate spreadsheet functions
- customised menus and toolbars.

The grade you are awarded for this assessment objective will depend on the range of formulas, functions and macros you have used, as well as the customisation you have carried out. When printing, preview pages so that you can set the page orientation, margins and scale to fit the sheets on the page in the best way possible.

Pass – Candidates produce linked spreadsheets that meet the user requirements. The spreadsheets are **mostly** similar to the design and include relative and absolute cell referencing, named cells and cell ranges, different cell formats, functions and macros. Candidates have made **some** attempt to customise menus or toolbars.

Merit – Candidates produce linked spreadsheets that meet the user requirements. The spreadsheets are **similar** to the design and include relative, absolute cell and multiple-sheet referencing, named cells and cell ranges, different cell formats, functions, multi-stage functions, data validation and macros. Candidates have **customised** a menu or toolbar.

Distinction – Candidates produce linked spreadsheets that meet the user requirements. The spreadsheets **exactly match** the design and include relative, absolute cell and multiple-sheet referencing, named cells and cell ranges, different cell formats, functions, nested functions, multi-stage functions, data validation with customised error messages and macros. Candidates have **customised** a menu and a toolbar.

AO3: Use a spreadsheet to process numerical data and present required information

Process numerical data

Pivot tables

A pivot table is used for sorting and summarising data. It combines and compares large amounts of data which it can automatically sort, count and total. It then creates a second table to display the summarised data. After examining the summarised data, you can re-sort it and look at it from a different perspective. Rows and columns can be rotated to see different summaries of the source data.

In a pivot table each column or field in your source data becomes a pivot table field that summarises multiple rows of information.

Create a pivot table report using the PivotTable and PivotChart Wizard

The data before using a pivot table is shown in Figure 5.17. You can produce a pivot table report showing the data in a number of ways.

Manufacturer	Stock Code	Sales	Cost	Price	Profit
BRIDGESTONE	ER305	68	£64.00	£80.00	£1,088.00
BRIDGESTONE	RE205	36	£70.00	£87.50	£630.00
CONTINENTAL	CPC05	68	£91.50	£114.38	£1,555.50
DUNLOP	SP165	50	£67.00	£83.75	£837.50
GT	MX165	60	£36.00	£45.00	£540.00
MICHELIN	ME195	63	£45.50	£56.88	£716.63
PIRELLI	PC165	50	£64.00	£80.00	£800.00
PIRELLI	ZR225	55	£36.00	£45.00	£495.00
TOTALS		450			£6,662.63

Figure 5.17 Data to be used for the pivot table

1 Open the workbook that contains the data that you want to use to create the pivot table, and click a cell in the list.
2 Click the Data menu, then PivotTable and PivotChart Report. In step 1 of the PivotTable and PivotChart Wizard, the wizard helps to create an interactive table that summarises your data in the way that you want. First select the data source.
3 Next select the type of report. Click PivotTable under 'What kind of report do you want to create?' Click Next (Figure 5.18).

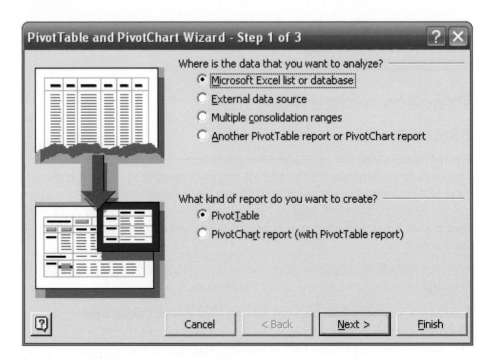

Figure 5.18 Selecting the data source and report type

4 In step 2, you specify the range of data. To enter a range in the box, type a reference or select the range directly on the sheet. Click Next (Figure 5.19).

Figure 5.19 Selecting the data

5 In step 3, specify where the report should be placed. Select New worksheet.
6 Click Finish (Figure 5.20).

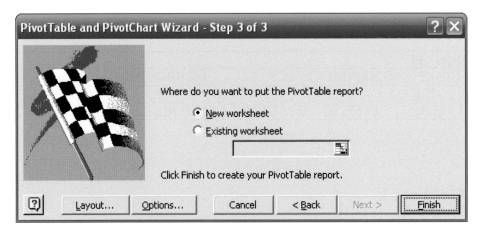

Figure 5.20 Placing the report

To lay out the report on-screen

You are now in a position to lay out the report. You can lay out the report on-screen, and this method is recommended. You will be presented with a screen similar to Figure 5.21.

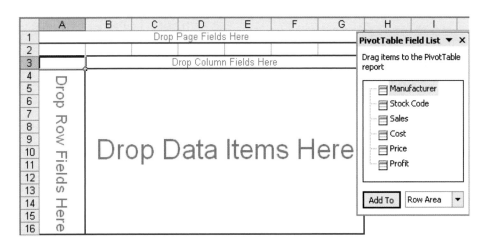

Figure 5.21 Lay out the report

Figure 5.22 PivotTable Field icons

You can drag fields from the PivotTable Field List window and display them in any of these areas: Drop Column Fields Here; Drop Row Fields Here; Drop Data Items Here (only fields displaying icons shown in Figure 5.22 can be dragged to this area).

- ■ If you add more than one data field, you can arrange the field order by right-clicking on the data field, pointing to Order on the shortcut menu, and using the options displayed.
- ■ To rearrange fields, drag them from one area to another.
- ■ To remove a field, drag it out of the PivotTable report.
- ■ To hide the drop area outlines, click a cell outside the PivotTable report.

Following the use of the pivot table function, the data will be displayed in the report showing only those fields you have selected, for example, the Sum of the Sales figures and the Sum of the Profit for each manufacturer (Figure 5.23). You can format the report in any manner you choose.

> **Pivot table report**
> A pivot table report can be customised to focus on specific information. You can also change the layout and format or display more detailed data.

3		Manufacturer ▼						
4	Data ▼	BRIDGESTONE	CONTINENTAL	DUNLOP	GT	MICHELIN	PIRELLI	Grand Total
5	Sum of Sales	104	68	50	60	63	105	450
6	Sum of Profit	£1,718.00	£1,555.50	£837.50	£540.00	£716.63	£1,295.00	£6,662.63

Figure 5.23 Pivot table report

Goal seek

There is a group of commands referred to as what-if analysis tools. Goal seek is one of these commands. Use it when you know the desired result of a single formula but not the input value the formula needs in order to determine the result. The figure is varied in one cell until a formula, dependent on that cell, returns the required result.

Adjust the value of a cell to get a specific result for another cell

You are going to use this function to identify the price an item has to be bought at in order to sell it at £90 (which includes a mark up of 25 per cent). Cost is the buying figure, and Price is the selling figure. The source data is shown in Figure 5.24.

	J	K	L
1		PERIOD 3	
2	Cost	Price	Sales
3			
4	58.60	73.25	60
5	88.40	110.50	52
6	40.50	50.63	63

Figure 5.24 Source data

1 Click Tools, Goal Seek; the Goal Seek dialogue box appears (Figure 5.25).

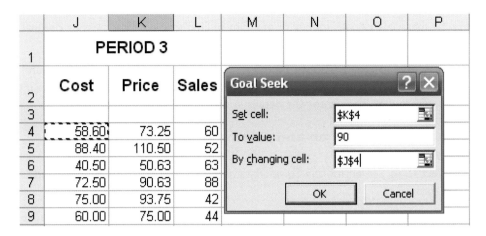

Figure 5.25 Goal Seek dialogue box

2 In the Set cell box, enter the reference for the cell that contains the formula you want to resolve. In this case, it is K4 – the selling price. Note that it is returned as an absolute cell reference.
3 In the To value box, type the result you want – in this case, 90.
4 In the By changing cell box, enter the reference for the cell that contains the value you want to adjust – the Cost price. This cell must be referenced by the formula in the cell you specified in the Set cell box – J4. Again, it is returned as an absolute cell reference. Click OK.
5 The Goal Seek Status box will be displayed (Figure 5.26). Click OK.

	J	K	L	M	N	O	P
		PERIOD 3					
	Cost	Price					
	72.00	90.00	Goal Seek Status				
	88.40	110.50					
	40.50	50.63					
	72.50	90.63					
	75.00	93.75					
	60.00	75.00					

Goal Seeking with Cell K4 found a solution.

Target value: 90
Current value: 90.00

Figure 5.26 Goal Seek Status

The figures on the spreadsheet have been altered. Cost is now £72 as opposed to the original figure.

Modelling of spreadsheet data

Solver is a tool that helps find the best way to allocate resources. The resources may be materials, people, money or anything in limited supply. The best or optimal solution may mean maximising profits or minimising costs.

First you have to create a Solver model – you will have to define the problem and decide which cells on the worksheet represent the adjustable cells, constraints and target cell. You can then enter the details in order to find the solution.

Using Solver to set up and solve a simple optimisation problem

1 Select Tools, Solver and the Solver Parameters dialogue box will be displayed (Figure 5.27).

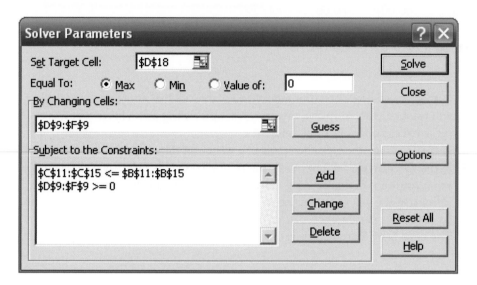

Figure 5.27 Solver Parameters dialogue box

2 In Set Target Cell, enter the target cell reference.
3 In By Changing Cells, enter the cell reference for those cells that are changed until the constraints are satisfied.
4 To add the constraints, click Add and list any restrictions in the problem (Figure 5.28).

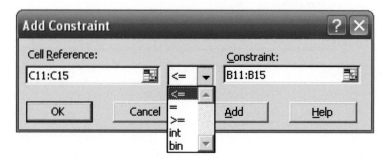

Figure 5.28 Add Constraint dialogue box

5   The Solver Parameters dialogue box should look like Figure 5.27 when all the
    elements are complete. To find the optimal solution click Solve. Solver returns
    the optimal solution.
6   The message 'Solver found a solution' appears in the Solver Results dialogue
    box (Figure 5.29).

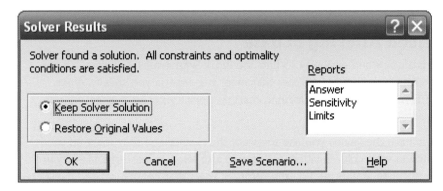

Figure 5.29 Solver Results dialogue box

7   Click Answer in the Reports list box. Click OK to keep the optimal solution
    values. Solver creates another worksheet containing the Answer Report (Figure
    5.30) and inserts it to the left of the problem worksheet in the Excel workbook.
8   The report shows the original and final values of the target cell and the adjustable
    cells, as well as the status of each constraint at the optimal solution. Some of the
    constraints are binding and have a Slack value of 0 – this means that all these
    items were used, but there were 50 units of each of the others remaining.

Microsoft Excel 10.0 Answer Report
Worksheet: [solver try.xls]Sheet1
Report Created: 30/07/2008 19:46:38

Target Cell (Max)

Cell	Name	Original Value	Final Value
$D$18	Total	16000	25000

Adjustable Cells

Cell	Name	Original Value	Final Value
$D$9	No to build Stock car pack	100	200
$E$9	No to build Rally X pack	100	200
$F$9	No to build Off road pack	100	0

Constraints

Cell	Name	Cell Value	Formula	Status	Slack
$C$11	AGILIS 61 No used	400	$C$11<=$B$11	Not Binding	50
$C$12	MAXMILER No used	200	$C$12<=$B$12	Not Binding	50
$C$13	CITNET No used	800	$C$13<=$B$13	Binding	0
$C$14	SPLT30 No used	400	$C$14<=$B$14	Not Binding	50
$C$15	P6000 No used	600	$C$15<=$B$15	Binding	0
$D$9	No to build Stock car pack	200	$D$9>=0	Not Binding	200
$E$9	No to build Rally X pack	200	$E$9>=0	Not Binding	200
$F$9	No to build Off road pack	0	$F$9>=0	Binding	0

Figure 5.30 Solver Answer Report

Use Solver to find an optimal value for a formula in the target cell. It works with a group of cells that are related to the formula. It adjusts the values in the changing cells you specify (called the adjustable cells) to produce the result you specify from the target cell formula. You can apply constraints to the adjustable cells, target cell or other cells related to the target cell to restrict the values.

Advanced filtering of data

Filtering is a quick and easy way to find and work with a subset of data in a list. A filtered list displays only the rows that meet the criteria you specify. When rows are filtered, you can edit, format, chart and print your list subset without rearranging or moving it.

The criteria are the values you use to select the results, and they must be used in conjunction with column labels. You should also leave at least one blank row between the criteria and the list (the series of rows that contain related data). The first row of the list should contain labels for the columns.

There are two commands you can use in Microsoft Excel to filter lists: Auto Filter, which includes filter by selection for simple criteria, and Advanced Filter, for more complex criteria, where you are required to enter criteria you want to filter by in a separate criteria range above the list. A criteria range allows for more complex criteria to be filtered.

To filter using advanced criteria you should insert at least three blank rows above the data you are using. The data must have column labels, and you should have at least one blank row between the criteria and the data. You will enter your criteria in these rows.

To use **multiple conditions in a single column** enter the criteria below each other on separate rows.

Figure 5.31 – This criteria range will show rows that contain MICHELIN, PIRELLI or DUNLOP in the MAKE column.

MAKE
MICHELIN
PIRELLI
DUNLOP

Figure 5.31

To find data that meets **one condition in two or more columns**, enter all the criteria in the same row of the criteria range.

MAKE	CURRENT PRICE
MICHELIN	>60

Figure 5.32

Figure 5.32 – This criteria range will show all rows that contain MICHELIN in the MAKE column and CURRENT PRICE greater than £60.

To find data that meets **either a condition in one column or a condition in another column**, enter the criteria in different rows.

Figure 5.33 – This criteria range will show all rows that contain either PIRELLI in the MAKE column, 165/7OR14 the SIZE column, or a CURRENT PRICE greater than £50.

MAKE	SIZE	CURRENT PRICE
PIRELLI		
	165/70R14	
		> 50

Figure 5.33

To find rows that meet **one of two sets of conditions, where each set includes conditions for more than one column**, enter the criteria in separate rows.

Figure 5.34 – This criteria range will show the rows that contain both MICHELIN in the MAKE column and a CURRENT PRICE greater than £50, as well as the rows for PIRELLI in the MAKE column and a CURRENT PRICE less than £100.

MAKE	CURRENT PRICE
MICHELIN	>50
PIRELLI	<100

Figure 5.34

You can use a calculated value that is **the result of a formula** as your criterion. When you use a formula do not use a column label for a criteria label; either keep the criteria label blank or use a label that is not a column label in the data.

Figure 5.35 – This criteria range will display rows that have a value in a column (column E) greater than the average of all the cells in that column (E5 to E22).

Figure 5.35

Presentation of results

The presentation of information in a spreadsheet is important. You need to consider this from the start in order to produce documents to a professional standard. To present results in appropriate ways, on-screen and on printed hard copy, you need to make suitable use of cell formats and page layout.

Cell formatting

Use formatting to display data in different ways. It makes your work easier to read and you can highlight important data. It also improves the way your work looks and its effectiveness. (See details in AO2, A range of cell formats including conditional formatting, page 164.)

Headers and footers are lines of text that print at the top and bottom of each page. They contain text such as titles, dates and page numbers, and are used to add this information when printing.

To copy formatting from one cell or group of cells to another part of the spreadsheet, use the format painter. It is helpful when extending a spreadsheet to format the new cells to match the original ones.

Set cell width and column height to display all content

You can change the width of a single column or multiple columns. You can choose to fit the contents, specify a width or match another column. You can also change the height of a single row or multiple rows. You can choose to fit the contents or specify a height.

Drawing tools and graphic images

There are a number of drawing tools available to enhance your work. They include:

- Lines
- Arrows
- Rectangles
- Ovals
- Text boxes
- Insert WordArt
- Insert Diagram or Organization Chart
- Insert Clip Art
- Insert Picture From File

- Apply fill color
- Apply line color
- Apply font color
- Apply line style
- Apply dash style
- Apply arrow style
- Apply shadow style
- Apply 3D style.

Graphs and charts

Graphs and charts should be presented with a chart title, axis labels, data labels, axis formats and values, background and gridlines. You should try to use different types of chart, appropriate to the data. Think carefully about the type of chart that will best display the data.

Spreadsheets contain a wide selection of chart types. Using them to display data makes it easier to understand that data – to identify comparisons, patterns and trends that may otherwise be difficult to see.

You can then select the type of graph you want from Standard Types, including Column, Bar, Line, Pie and XY (Scatter) among others. There are also a number of Custom Types including Pie Explosion, Stack of Colours and Tubes.

The quickest and easiest way to create a chart is to use the Chart Wizard. A chart may be placed on its own sheet or be embedded on a worksheet.

On-screen printed hard copy

You must demonstrate that you can print spreadsheets appropriately. Consider the page layout, including margins, headers, footers, page size and page orientation. There are many ways to view a spreadsheet and change how it will appear when printed. Normal view is best for viewing on-screen.

Print preview allows you to see the printed page. You can adjust columns and margins, view headers, footers and print titles. You can change the way your worksheet prints – you can turn gridlines on or off, print a draft copy and change the order in which pages print.

Designate the print area by specifying the area of the spreadsheet that you want to print. Your print options include printing the selection you have identified by highlighting the entire workbook, the sheet that is currently active, or an embedded graph or chart.

Page breaks are based on the paper size, margin settings, scaling options and any manual page breaks you have inserted. You can alter the print settings and use the different views to see the effects before printing.

Alter a number of settings before printing, including the orientation (portrait or landscape). Change the layout to fit the data to the available space, or adjust the margins.

Make the printed image fit the page or paper size by shrinking or expanding the image. You can also alter the paper size, centre the data or control how the pages are numbered. This only alters the printed appearance, not the screen display.

Headers and footers are separate from the data and appear only when you preview or print. Use them to place page numbers, the date, the file name or other text above or below the data on each page. Use the built-in headers or footers or create your own.

You can repeat worksheet data as print titles on every page. You can print row numbers and column letters. Use any combination of headers and footers, repeating labels, and row and column headings. Set a page break to end a page at a particular point and start a new page.

Using the Report Manager you can combine worksheet views. A view is a set of display and print settings that you can name and apply to a workbook. It is then saved with the workbook. You can create more than one view of the same workbook.

Portfolio Activity (AO3)

You will now have to process the data and present your results – there are many ways that this can be done. You must demonstrate good use of numerical processing techniques. Any output, including all graphs and charts, should have a clear purpose.

1 The company would like to see the data in their stock list in order of sales over the last three months, so that they can see the items that have sold the most at the top of the list. This should be carried out by product. Sort the list to show the stock items in the required order and print it out.
2 The company would like to see the impact on income if they change the mark up from 25 per cent to 20 per cent and also 30 per cent. Provide the data in a suitable format.
3 The company would like to know how their prices match those of their competitors. Find comparable prices from at least five competitors for at least six products from each of the suppliers that they currently use.
4 The company would like to produce invoices showing:
   ■ the date
   ■ the customer's name and address

- the make, model, code, size, price, number required and VAT for each item purchased
- the total cost of all the items purchased, the total VAT and the total cost with VAT
- a discount of 10 per cent for all orders with a total value (including VAT) of over £250
- the final total.

The invoice should have space for at least six different items. It will be printed on company headed paper so there is no need to include the company logo or contact details, but leave 5 centimetres blank at the top of the page.

5 Create different types of chart to display the following data for the company:
- the five highest-selling items over the periods for which data is available
- the six lowest-selling items over the periods for which data is available
- how the sales for each manufacturer have changed over the periods for which data is available. You should clearly display how each manufacturer has performed over the periods, and compare the performance of the different manufacturers.

6 There is to be a car event and the organisers have asked the company to supply three types of tyre pack. Each pack is a combination of five different tyres that they have in stock. The tyres are: AGILIS 61, MAXMILER, CITNET, SPLT30 and P6000. The three types of tyre pack are Stock cars, Rally Xs and Off-roads. Figure 5.36 identifies how each pack is made up, and the number of each tyre set in stock.

	Stock car pack	Rally X pack	Off-road pack	In stock
AGILIS 61 set	1	1	0	450
MAXMILER set	1	0	0	250
CITNET set	2	2	1	800
SPLT30 set	1	1	0	450
P6000 set	2	1	1	600

Figure 5.36 Make up of three types of tyre pack

You can only put together a limited number of packs from the tyres in stock. You will have to identify the profit that is made on each pack. You should identify the mix which will maximise profits, given the stock held.

Pass – Candidates use the spreadsheet to process numerical data. The numerical processing is **appropriate** for the user requirements. Candidates print spreadsheets showing all data so that they fit to the page(s), cell contents are visible and headers/footers have been added. Graphs/charts, pivot tables, filtered results and macros are also printed out as appropriate.

Merit – Candidates use the spreadsheet to process numerical data. The numerical processing is appropriate for the user requirements and makes **good use** of functions/formulas. Candidates print spreadsheets showing all data so that they fit to the page(s), cell contents are visible and headers/footers have been added. Graphs/charts, pivot tables, filtered results and macros are also printed out as appropriate. The printouts are **clear** and it is easy to understand the information as it is presented.

Distinction – Candidates use the spreadsheet to process numerical data. The numerical processing is appropriate for the user requirements and makes good use of functions/formulas. The **results** of the analysis are presented in a clear, easy to understand format. Candidates print spreadsheets showing all data so that they correctly fit to the page(s), cell contents are visible and headers/footers have been added. Graphs/charts, pivot tables, filtered results and macros are also printed out as appropriate. The printouts are clear and it is easy to understand the information as it is presented. Headers, footers and titles are appropriate.

AO4: Produce user documentation and technical information

Produce user documentation

A user guide should explain how to use the spreadsheet in terms your user can understand. It should be written in simple language with short sentences. Different users have different requirements, so think about their specific needs, their technical knowledge and how they will use the guide. The users are not usually interested in technical details. Users want to know what the software can do and how to do it – they want to click a button and get a result.

Always use language appropriate to the skill level of your audience. Be consistent in how you address the user and limit the use of technical terms to those they will understand.

What should a user guide include?

A user guide should include a cover page, table of contents and a preface. A preface, or introduction, includes an explanation about how to use the guide. It might include comments about the purpose of the guide, who the guide is for, and reference to other associated documents, such as the technical guide or company guides outlining document conventions, style, and storage.

In the main body of the text, separate the procedures or tasks. This will help the user to find their way through the guide more easily. Procedures help the user to perform specific tasks, such as how to update sales figures.

You should write a list of the major tasks. For each task, give a brief explanation and then write a series of step-by-step instructions that takes the user through it. You may also want to show the user the results of each task. Each task or procedure could form a new chapter or section in the guide.

It is helpful to use a consistent format for each section. For example, you may:

- introduce each section with an overview of the task
- describe the inputs and outputs – what the user must enter into the system and what the system will do as a result
- describe in detail the procedures for accomplishing the tasks.

Use diagrams, screenshots, data entry forms, data output screens and hard copy results to illustrate more complicated procedures.

If there are a large number of definitions, add a glossary. You must help the user to understand your material – do not use jargon. You may want to highlight a glossary term the first time it appears in the text.

A guide longer than about 20 pages should have an index to help users locate specific items. It is very difficult to use large documents effectively without an index.

These points may help in organising and presenting your guide:

- use headings to organise your information
- include section titles and page numbers on every page as a header or footer
- use columns – put headings in the first column and the descriptive text in the next
- help the users by using various formats to identify different types of information; for example, you could identify **input** by using colour, varying the font style with bold or italics, or using icons.

Discuss the requirements with the user during the planning phase – do they already use a specific style that they would like incorporated in your documentation?

Key information to be included in your user guide is:

- how to start the spreadsheet program
- routes through the spreadsheet menus
- instructions about data entry
- advice on how to respond to error messages
- examples of screens, data entry forms, data output screens and hard copy.

Produce a technical guide

A technical guide (or manual) should be an accurate, readable, accessible aid to help users understand the system – remember that they may not be experts. It should be precise and as detailed as possible. Creating quality technical documents is a vital stage in allowing correct usage.

What should a technical guide include?

You should consider all the points you have in the user guide and give details of the:

- hardware and software required
- procedures for opening and configuring the spreadsheet
- numerical processing

- use of macros
- validation and verification procedures
- input and output screens and printed designs.

Avoid making common mistakes when producing technical guides:

- The document should be clear, but never patronising.
- Avoid humour – technical documents are not a form of entertainment; they are read for information.
- Inconsistency – ensure that all the elements are consistent; this applies to tone and layout.
- Errors – by the end you may well be sick of the sight of it. However, what matters is accuracy, so proofread the guide throughout drafting and before it is distributed. Do not rely on spell checkers. If possible, get someone else to read it – they might identify errors you have missed.

Portfolio Activity (AO4)

Produce user documentation that allows a novice user access to various aspects of the spreadsheet, to include:

- a user guide that describes the use of the spreadsheets
- a technical manual containing details of the numerical processing methods, macros and data validation, as well as details of the hardware and other resources required.

Produce a test plan

A number of activities will be carried out during testing, so you need a plan. Your test plan gives details of the process of checking your work to make sure that it meets its requirements and is error-free. Look at each item or test and ask yourself about the requirements.

One of the primary purposes of testing is to detect errors so that they can be corrected. Designing a test forces you to understand the requirements – you may notice activities that are incomplete or incorrect. Testing can identify errors but still leave other critical errors undetected. A test plan must be designed with coverage in mind. If you do not test all of the spreadsheet, you are more likely to allow errors. You should set coverage criteria and evaluate coverage.

It is a good idea to write descriptions before detailing the steps for each test. For each test write one to three sentences. Writing the descriptions also forces you to think more about each test. Make sure to note any requirement problems or questions that you identify.

Each test should be simple enough to clearly succeed or fail. Ideally, the steps of a test are a simple sequence – set up the test situation, test with specific test inputs and verify the accuracy of the outputs.

Selecting test data is as important as defining the steps of the test. You should determine the set of all input values that can be entered for a given input parameter, and define valid and invalid input values.

Your testing should be evaluated in terms of specification coverage, rather than implementation coverage. Testing is more effective if you:

- set specific goals that are appropriate
- ensure good coverage
- prioritise the tasks
- write the tests in detail
- evaluate the tests in terms of the requirements.

Do not worry if you do find errors – the purpose of testing is to find them.

Test No.	Type	Description of test	Input	Expected output	Actual output	Remedial action
1	Data validation	Enter a record	Registration No. Manufacturer Colour Location	The details should be saved as a new record in the Vehicle table		
2			Enter same Registration No. as Test 1	Error message – Registration No. already exists		

Figure 5.37 Sample of a test plan

The testing cycle

Testing should probably begin in the requirements phase, and there is a typical cycle:

- During the design phase, determine which aspects of your design can be tested.
- Determine within which parameters the tests work.
- Produce test scripts to use in testing.
- Test your work based on the plan.
- Report any errors.
- Decide which faults should be treated, fixed or rejected.
- Once a fault has been dealt with, retest.

Portfolio Activity (AO5)

1 Create a test plan and carry out tests on different parts of the spreadsheet. The test plan should include checks that the:
   - spreadsheets meet the original design brief
   - formulas and functions operate as indicated
   - macros operate as indicated
   - validation operates as indicated.

2 If your work does not meet the design brief, or the formulas, functions, macros or validation do not operate as specified, make the appropriate changes and report on your findings.

Evidence for this task will be the electronic file or a printout of the test plan. You do not need to provide screenshots showing the actual tests being carried out, but you should record the results of each test.

Evaluation
Evaluation is the collection and systematic analysis of data.

Before you begin to produce a spreadsheet, you should have evaluated the purpose, strengths and weaknesses of your spreadsheet. Throughout the progress of your work, you should also be using performance indicators, and should be monitoring and evaluating your work. You should also think about how you will report the results of your work. Also refer to User needs and functionality on page 158.

What are your performance indicators?

Performance indicators will help you assess the progress and success of the project. Output indicators help you to assess the work generated by the project.

Once you have set your objectives, you will be able to describe project activities in ways that can be evaluated. You should identify outputs relating to each objective. When this is done, you can decide on indicators for them. Choose the most important and limit their number so that you collect only the information you need most.

Monitoring
Monitoring is the routine and systematic collection of information that will help to answer questions about your project, and using it to report on and evaluate it. You are most likely to need information on your outputs, how your activities are running and progress towards meeting your objectives.

Monitoring

Check on your output and collect information to check on progress. This checking process is known as monitoring.

Collect information about your outputs to identify whether your activities are operating as expected and if there are any unexpected results. When you have collected the information about each of your aims and objectives, you should look back and make judgements about your project.

Evaluation

While monitoring is routine and ongoing, evaluation is an in-depth study, taking place at specific points in the life of the project.

You evaluate, that is, you consider all the information you have collected and make a judgement about your project. Evaluation is about using monitoring and other information you collect to make judgements about your project. Part of this process is making sense of the information you have collected. Take time to consider what the information is telling you.

Reporting the results

How you use the results of your monitoring and evaluation is very important. Think about who will use the results and how that information should be reported. Your users should be taken into account when thinking about how to report.

Portfolio Activity (AO6)

Produce an evaluation report of the effectiveness of your project against the company needs outlined in the scenario and in the design phase of the project. You should:

- carry out any improvements needed for the company
- evaluate the spreadsheets against the company's needs
- ensure that the functionality of the spreadsheets meets the specification.

The evaluation should include a critical analysis of the effectiveness of the solution and you should make suggestions for improvements.

Advanced Databases

Learning outcomes

By working through this unit you will produce evidence to meet the unit assessment objectives to show that you understand how to:

- design a relational database
- create a database according to the design using advanced database features
- interrogate the database
- create a user interface
- produce reports
- produce user documentation and technical information
- understand and implement database testing
- evaluate the database.

Introduction

In this unit you will be creating advanced databases. You should look at the data before you begin your design. You should then decide on the data to be held, how it will be used and how it will be amended. You must decide on the tables you want to create. The data is a starting point – you may add any fields you choose, such as Purchase Date and Selling Date.

Remember, you cannot begin to design your database until you have the full requirements of each assessment objective. You should read through all the assessment objectives and portfolio activities before you begin producing evidence. Note that you will be required to produce a test plan and an evaluation of the solution that you provide. It is very important that you consider these factors at the planning stage. This will help you to outline the aims and objectives that you will have to evaluate later in your project.

Although the elements are assessed in different Assessment Objectives you should create your evidence in the appropriate order – forms, queries and reports are created after the tables, and before the user interface.

You should also be aware that in this practice material that you are asked to provide specific reports. In the assessment material you will decide yourself which tables, queries and reports to create.

Scenario

Private Users is a new company that sells used cars. They also provide after-sales servicing and repairs. They operate at three sites – Disley, Stanton and Denton.

You have been engaged by the company to introduce the use of a database to help them to run the business. They have details of the vehicles for sale and of prospective buyers – people who have made enquiries and are waiting for a particular type of vehicle. The database must be set up to store the vehicle details, and enable the sales staff to search it for specific vehicles and features.

You must produce a complete design for a working relational database that will contain at least three tables and 60 records.

Details of the vehicles for sale and buyers are held in spreadsheets. You can access them on the following website: http://www.heinemann.co.uk/Series/Secondary/OCRNationalsICTLevel3/ FreeResources/FreeResources.aspx. You will need to amend these files to create your database.

File name	Data held
U6 CARS Details of vehicles	Details of vehicles in stock
U6 CUSTOMERS Details of customers	Specific features and locations of stock held
U6 KEY-FEATURES Key features for vehicles	Key features for vehicles

Figure 6.1 Spreadsheet details

The company wants to keep the details of, and search for, customers who buy vehicles, which vehicle they purchased and when it is due for servicing. The company have also asked for the details of the sales staff to be held in the database.

You will need to provide an easy way for the staff to use the database, including the way they search for vehicles, and for vehicles due for servicing, as well as the customer who owns each vehicle.

The sales staff may want to search the database for vehicles by:

- Manufacturer
- Model
- Price range
- Fuel type
- Transmission
- Mileage
- Location
- Body style

Customers may also require specific features such as alloy wheels, air bags, electric windows, or remote central locking. These features will need to form part of the body style table. Staff will need to be able to query and identify these features to meet the needs of the customers.

The company directors will expect management information. This might include, for example, weekly, monthly, and quarterly reports on sales, or stock value showing subtotals for each manufacturer and a grand total. Each sales person gets a commission of 10 per cent of the total price of each car they sell. A report has been requested to show the commissions paid to the staff for each three month period.

You will also need to produce a user guide and a technical manual giving information on the system requirements and how to use the database.

You will also create and implement a test plan. While testing, you should make any necessary changes to ensure that the database meets the specification. The database will need to be evaluated. Before you begin the actual designing of the database you will need to consider the purpose and audience of the database. The purpose and functionality of the database will form the starting points for your evaluation.

Scenario

Design a relational database

Purpose of database

Your database design will be defined by the requirements of the database users. Your database design should provide the users with the functionality that they need. The purpose of the database should be defined at the start of the design process. The purpose is usually provided by the end-user. The end-user will provide details of what they are going to use the database for, what queries they need to run and what output they need. The output may be on-screen or on paper.

While the design is being completed it is very important that the end-user's defined purposes are continually referred to. If they are not, then the database may not meet the end-user's needs.

To be fit for purpose, a database must function correctly – a clear, concise and accurate design will reduce unnecessary risks in a project by providing an outline of how the application should work. Good database planning and careful design saves businesses from wasting time and money on unnecessary errors.

Audience

All software systems have an audience. The audience could be the end-user. But the end-user could also include members of the public or different groups of end-users.

The audience and what they are going to do with the database will have an impact on your design. Again, when you are designing your database you will need to refer to the defined audience to ensure the database is appropriate.

When writing user documentation, you should consider who you are preparing the work for and explain items in terms your users can understand. Use simple, jargon-free language, but explain in detail what the database can do. Think about the users' specific needs and technical knowledge and prepare your work accordingly.

In addition, you should also consider your audience when designing a user interface for your database. You will need to think about how you can make your design user-friendly, how the users are likely to make use of the database, how information should be presented, etc.

Tables

A table is a collection of data about one subject. You should use a separate table for each subject to ensure that you store data only once. This provides a more efficient database and fewer opportunities for input errors.

To create a table for entering your own data, you can:

- Use the Table wizard to choose the fields for your table from a variety of predefined tables such as business contacts, household inventory, or medical records.
- Create a table in Design view, where you can add fields, define how each field appears or handles data, and create a primary key.

- Enter data directly into a blank datasheet. When you save the new datasheet, Microsoft Access will analyse your data and automatically assign the appropriate data type and format for each field.

To create a table from existing data, you can:

- Import or link data from another Access database or data in a variety of file formats from other programs.
- Perform a make-table query to create a table based on data in a current table. For example, you can use make-table queries to archive old records, to make backup copies of your tables, to select a group of records to export to another database, or to use as a basis for reports that display data from a specific time.

More information on tables can be found on page 205.

Data types

Setting the data type for a field means specifying what kind of data it can store. This defines what kind of values you can enter.

Before setting the data type you need to consider:

- how much space you need
- which operations you want to perform
- whether you want to sort
- if you want to use it to group records in queries or reports.

You use the DataType property to specify the type of data stored in a table field. Each field can be of only one data type. The data types available in Access are:

Data type	Use
Text	This is the default in Access. Text or combinations of text and numbers. Numbers that do not require calculations, such as phone numbers. Special characters such as @ and © can also be included.
Memo	Lengthy text or combinations of text and numbers such as notes or descriptions. Special characters such as @ and © can also be included.
Number	Numeric data used in mathematical calculations. Set the FieldSize property to define the specific Number type.
Date/Time	Date and time values for the years 100 to 9999.
Currency	Currency values and numeric data used in calculations. Accurate to 15 digits on the left side of the decimal point and to 4 digits on the right.
AutoNumber	Unique sequential (incrementing by 1) or random numbers automatically inserted when a record is added. AutoNumber fields can not be updated.
Yes/No	Fields that will contain only one of two values. Can be displayed as Yes/No, True/False, On/Off.
OLE Object	An object (such as a spreadsheet, a Word document, graphics or sound) linked to or embedded in a Microsoft Access table.
Hyperlink	Text or combinations of text and numbers stored as text and used as a hyperlink address.

Figure 6.2 The DataType Property

Selecting the data type

Text can store data consisting of either text or numbers. Number can only store numerical data – do not try to store text in Number fields.

You can sum values in Number or Currency fields, but not in Text fields. In a Text field, numbers sort as strings of characters not as numeric values – use a Number or Currency field to sort numbers as numeric values.

Some date formats will not sort correctly if entered in a Text field – use a Date/Time field to ensure accurate sorting for dates.

Storing data with text or combinations of text and numbers

There are two field types for storing data with text or combinations of text and numbers:

- Use Text to store names, addresses and any numbers that do not require calculations, such as phone numbers or postcodes. You can use up to 255 characters, but the default is 50 characters. The Field Size property controls the maximum number of characters that can be entered.
- Use Memo if you need to store more than 255 characters. You can use up to 65,536 characters. If you want to store formatted text or long documents, you should create an OLE Object field instead of a Memo field.

You can sort or group on either type, but only the first 255 characters are used.

Storing data containing numeric values

There are two data types for storing data containing numeric values:

- Use Number if you want to use mathematical calculations (except calculations that involve money or that require a high degree of accuracy). The kind and size of data is controlled by setting the Field Size property.
- Use Currency to prevent rounding off during calculations – it is accurate to 15 digits to the left of the decimal point and 4 digits to the right.

Number and Currency fields provide predefined display formats, or you can create a custom format.

Normalise data

A database is made up of linked tables. Each table needs to have a Primary Key (PK) which is a field in a table that allows the record to be uniquely identified. For example see Figure 6.3 below. The Staff ID can be the PK as the value in each record is different. Surname could not be the PK as there are two people with the surname Smith – this is not unique.

Staff ID	Forename	Surname
1	Monty	Smith
2	Henry	Jones
3	Eric	Smith

Figure 6.3 Primary Key uses a unique identifier

A Foreign Key (FK) is used to create the link between the tables in a database. More information on PK and FK can be found on pages 204–205.

Normalisation
Normalisation is the process of organising data to ensure that it is logically stored. It enables the database to work faster, saves storage and helps protect against corruption.

There are guidelines for normalising databases – referred to as normal forms; they are numbered from 1 to 5. In practice you may see 1NF, 2NF and 3NF. 4NF is used occasionally and 5NF is rarely seen.

Foreign key
A foreign key is a field in a table that matches the primary key column of another table, and can be used to cross-reference tables.

Normalisation ensures that a database is consistent, accurate and reliable. When a database is normalised, data that is duplicated is removed, inconsistencies between data is avoided and it becomes very easy to extract data from the database.

The process of designing a database includes making sure that a table contains only data directly related to the primary key, that each data field contains only one item of data, and that redundant data is eradicated. The data should be structured to remove duplication by specifying and defining tables, keys, attributes and relationships. A poorly designed database may produce poor information, be difficult to use, or fail to work effectively. Applying normalisation helps create efficient systems that produce accurate data and reliable information.

The objectives of normalisation are to:

- arrange data into logical groups, so that each group describes a small part of the whole

- ensure no data is duplicated

- ensure that data can be accessed and manipulated efficiently

- organise the data so that when it is modified any changes made in one place are automatically updated throughout the database.

There are several stages involved in normalisation. These are known as first, second and third form norms. This can also be expresses as 1NF, 2NF, and 3NF.

Before a table gets to 1NF it is in an 'un-normalised' form – UNF or ONF. An example of a table in ONF is shown in Figure 6.4.

Vehicle Registration	Manufacturer	Colour	Sales Price	Employee No	First Name	Last Name	Customer ID	Customer Name	Address	Telephone Number
TW51SST	Range Rover	Blue	£48,000	3	Eric	Smith	249	Henry Jones	Lilac House Puddletown HA27 4NN	07777 666555

Figure 6.4 Flat file to be normalised

First normal form (1NF)

A table is in 1NF if every data value in a field is atomic and each record does not contain repeating data. Atomic means that the data value cannot be broken down any further. The vehicle registration and colour are atomic as they cannot be broken down further. But, the customer name and address fields both hold two, or more, data values. These need to be broken down. Columns are therefore added to the table to make the customer name and address fields atomic, see Figure 6.5.

First Name	Last Name	Address Line 1	Address Line 2	Address Line 3	Postcode
Henry	Jones	Lilac House	Puddletown	-	HA27 4NN

Figure 6.5 Table in 1NF broken down in atomic data

Each row is now uniquely identifiable and each field name is unique. A primary key has been selected – registration number.

Second normal form (2NF)

A table is in 2NF if:

- it is in INF
- all non-key attributes are dependent on the entire PIL (or there are no partial key dependencies).

Second normal form is about removing some of the redundant data.

Vehicle Registration	Manufacturer	Colour	Sales Price	Employee No*	First Name	Last Name	Customer ID*	Customer Name	Address	Telephone Number
TW51SST	Range Rover	Blue	£48,000	3	Eric	Smith	249	Henry Jones	Lilac House Puddletown HA27 4NN	07777 666555

Figure 6.6 Table in 2NF

If we look at the table again we can see whenever Employee No 3 sells a car then his details will appear again. Also every time Customer 249 buys another car all their details will appear. The PK for this table is made up of Vehicle Registration, Employee No and Customer ID.

We need to separate the attributes that depend on the each part of the PK – the partial keys.

If we break the tables into:

- Vehicle
- Sales staff
- Customers

then we have separated the attributes.

Vehicle Registration	Manufacturer	Colour	Sales Price	Feature
TW51SST	Range Rover	Blue	£48,000	1

Figure 6.7 Vehicle attribute

Employee No	First Name	Last Name
3	Eric	Smith

Figure 6.8 Sales staff attribute

Customer ID	First Name	Last Name	Address 1	Address 2	Postcode	Telephone
249	Henry	Jones	Lilac House	Puddletown	HA27 4NN	07777666555

Figure 6.9 Customer attribute

The rule here is that a new table needs to be created for each partial key dependency.

Third normal form (3NF)

A table is in 3NF if it is in 2NF and there is no functional dependency between non-key items. The question that needs to be asked is "Are any of the non-key fields dependant on any other key fields?"

The tables Sale staff attribute (Figure 6.8) and Customer attribute (Figure 6.9) are in 2NF and also 3NF as each non-key field is fully dependent on the PK.

The Vehicle table is not currently in 3NF as the feature information is not dependant on the registration number.

We need to create a feature table.

Feature Code	Description
I	ABS

Figure 6.10 Feature table

The rule here is that a new table needs to be created for each new dependency.

Complete an entity relationship diagram (ERD)

An entity-relationship diagram (ERD) is a tool for planning and designing a database. It shows the logical structure, displaying the relationships of database tables. It is a static picture of the structure as there is no indication of the flow of data, or how data changes. An ERD is particularly useful when used in conjunction with data normalisation. It starts with the entities, whereas data normalisation starts with the attributes, and the two complement each other.

There are many different sets of symbols that can be used to create ERD'S. It does not matter which set you use, what is important is that you are consistent. The set of symbols that will be used in this chapter are discussed below and shown in Figures 6.11, 6.12 and 6.13.

Figure 6.11 One-to-one (1:1)   **Figure 6.12** One-to-many (1:M)   **Figure 6.13** Many-to-many (M:M)

Each entity in the ERD should be linked through relationships.

One to one relationships (1:1)

This shows that only one occurrence of each entity is used by the link entity. For example, one doctor would use one consulting room, as shown in Figure 6.14.

Figure 6.14 One-to-one relationship

One to many relationships (1:M)

This shows that a single occurrence of one entity is linked to more than one occurrence of the linked entity. For example, one doctor would have many appointments, as shown in Figure 6.15.

Figure 6.15 One-to-many relationship

Many to many relationships (M:M)

This shows that many occurrences of one entity are linked to more than one occurrence of the linked entity. These are very common in the real world but when creating an ERD they need to be broken down, or decomposed. For example, many doctors will see many patients, as shown in Figure 6.16.

Figure 6.16 Many-to-many relationship

A link entity is used to decompose the M:M relationship, as shown in Figure 6.17.

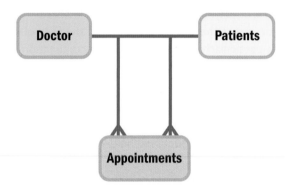

Figure 6.17 Link entity diagram

To clearly and correctly define the relationships between the entities the data must be normalised to 3NF.

To prepare an ERD you must first understand the business processes:

- vehicles are added to the current stock file
- customer details are recorded
- details of each member of the salesforce including cars sold and commission received.

Tips for ERDs

- Make sure that each entity only appears once and has a name
- Check the relationships between entities:
    - Are they necessary?
    - Are there any relationships missing?

At this point you should consider the user requirements – have you included all the attributes in each table to meet all the requirements? For example, in this scenario the management have asked that a report be produced to show the commission earned by each member of sales staff. You need to check that you have included a field/attribute in this table that will enable you to do this.

Data dictionary

A data dictionary stores information about the database organisation and contents, and describes the data objects. It is often described as a database about a database.

Documentation needs to be developed to clarify and support the Entity Relationship Diagram (ERD). The documentation related to an ERD will include entity descriptions, attribute lists and a Data Dictionary.

Each entity in the ERD should have an associated entity description that details the entity name and description, the entity attributes and any relationships/links associated with it.

It is necessary to develop data dictionaries about all the entities being used in a system. It is also possible to hold data about data elements, data structures, data flows, data stores and processes.

A data dictionary may hold the following elements:

- Name
- Description
- Type
- Format
- Values
- Comments
- Security
- Editing

Not all of these elements will be held, only the ones that are appropriate to the entity should be included in the associated data dictionary. It is also possible to define any validation to be applied in the data dictionary.

What is important is that each entity has an associated data dictionary. This means that if there are five entities being used in a system then five data dictionaries should be developed, one for each entity.

An example data dictionary for an entity PRODUCT is given below.

Name	Product		
Description	The table that contains all general information about a product that is delivered and/or sold.		
Relationships			
Related to:	**Type**	**Which end?**	
Delivery	1:Many (1:M)	Many	
Attributes			
Name	**Type/Format**	**Length**	**Key**
Product Number	Text / String	15	Primary Key
Category	Text / String	15	
Description	Text / String	50	
Cost	Currency	10	

Figure 6.18 Data dictionary for an entity PRODUCT

Design a user interface to access all parts of the database

The functionality that an application provides is important, but the way in which it provides it is just as important. Your objective is to design an interface that helps the user to get the most from the system while satisfying their requirements. User interface design is one of the most important components of a successful product – user satisfaction is a critical factor for success.

A good user interface allows people who understand business to use their normal methods to process the data more efficiently and quickly. It should give command of the data, enabling the user to retrieve it, sort it, analyse it, summarise it and report results in moments. It is a good idea to involve users in the design, prototyping and testing.

A good user interface design is important for several reasons. The better an interface is:

- the easier it is to use – increasing employee satisfaction
- the less it will cost to train staff – reducing training costs
- the less help people will need to use it – reducing support costs.

The more intuitive the user interface is, the better the possibility of assisting and increasing productivity.

Design forms for adding and amending data

A form is a graphical user interface (GUI) that simplifies the task of entering information. The main purpose is to allow the user to enter information into one or more tables at one time, the advantage being that the user does not have to open several screens to edit fields in different tables.

You can also use a form to open other forms and reports, or as a custom dialogue box to allow users to enter data and carry out an action based on that input.

Forms can be bound to one or more tables and queries. The source of data for a form is the fields in the underlying tables and queries, but the form does not need to contain all the fields from each of those tables or queries. A bound form stores or retrieves data from its underlying record source. Other information on the form, such as the title, date and page number, is stored in the design. Other items that can be stored in the design include: graphic elements, such as lines and rectangles; an expression to perform a calculation; and descriptive text.

You create a link between a form and its record source by using controls – the most common type used to display and enter data is a text box. Labels display descriptive text.

You also need to consider the design of forms for adding and amending data in your database.

Forms in databases have three purposes:

- *Data entry* – users can insert, update or delete data in a table.
- *Custom information* – users can enter custom information, and based on that information perform a task. For example, you may want to ask a user for parameters such as a range in the selling price before running a report.
- *Navigation* – this provides users with a method of finding the way through their system. For example, you may create a form so that the user can select a form to run a report.

Designs for reports

One of the most common tasks that you perform with your database is to retrieve information. You may want to present this data either on-screen or in a printed report. Whether you are preparing a weekly report for the company or sending details of available products to customers, reports draw attention to your data and make it work for you.

Reports range in complexity from a simple list of available products to meet a customer's requirements, which would probably be viewed on-screen, to a full stock catalogue, which would probably be printed.

Reports can summarise and group data; for example, a sales report might group sales by site, showing subtotals and a grand total. This gives an overview and presents the big picture. This type of report is more likely to be printed, as are invoices, labels and product lists.

Whatever the need, you should design your reports to display accurate, informative and clear information. In reports, overviews and trends are likely to be printed; more detailed, tailored requests are more likely to be viewed on-screen. The type of output you require dictates the way it is displayed.

Data validation

There are many ways to control how users enter data into your database. For example, you can limit the data that a user can enter into a field by defining a rule for that field. A validation rule defines valid input for a field or record in a table, or a control on a form. If the rule is not adhered to, a specified error message is displayed.

Another method of controlling data entry is to create an input mask. An input mask uses display characters (such as parentheses, periods and hyphens) to control how and where data can be entered, the type of data and the amount of data allowed. Set this type of validation by setting properties for fields in tables or by setting properties for controls on forms.

If the data entered into a control on a form is not bound to a field in a table, you should restrict or validate the data entered. Additionally, there are situations where you must use macros to perform more complex validation. For example, you might want to be able to override your validation rule or compare values from different tables.

When considering the design, you should decide whether a field has an appropriate data type – Boolean, Integer, Long, Currency, Single, Double, Date, String or Variant, which is the default.

A field's data type limits and describes the kind of data that can be entered into it. It also determines the actions that can be performed on it and how much memory the data uses. For example, store numbers that will be used in calculations in a Number or Currency field. But code numbers including letters, hyphens, parentheses or other non-numeric characters should be stored in a Text field.

In most cases, it is preferable to define data validation by setting a field's properties in Table Design view. That way, whenever you use that field in a form, the field's validation rule and other properties will apply to data entry performed using the form.

Access Type Name	Database Data Type
Yes/No	Boolean
Currency	Decimal
Number: Double	Double
Autonumber (Long Integer)	Integer
Number (Long Integer)	Integer
Number: Single	Single

Figure 6.19 The most common data types used in Access

Portfolio Activity (AO1)

You must produce a design for a relational database for Private Users. Your design must allow them to use the database to efficiently store and maintain the vehicle details and to target specific vehicles.

You must produce a complete design for a working relational database that will contain at least three tables and 60 records, always remembering who is using the database and why they are using it.

There are some records available for you to examine, so that you appreciate the kind of data that will be held on the database. The files are available at ((website address to come)). You should look at the data before you begin your design. You should then decide on the data to be held, how it will be used, and how it will be added to and amended. You must decide on the tables you want to create.

Make sure that the design allows you to fulfil other assessment objectives such as creating queries and reports. You must be aware of the types of data which are appropriate for the task and methods of data validation that can be used. You should understand the concept of normalisation in a database, as well as the entities and relationships so that you can produce an entity relationship diagram (ERD).

You must produce your design on paper. The ERD can be drawn graphically by hand or by using word-processing, DTP or specialist software such as Microsoft Visio.

The remainder of the design documentation may be produced using word-processing or DTP software. You should provide written details of the purpose of, and audience for, the database, as well as the tables, forms, queries, reports and user interface you intend to use. For example, tables — you should provide written details of: the table structure needed, keys to be used, fields for each table showing the intended field names, data types and field lengths for all fields.

The relationships between the tables will be shown on the ERD, but the validation rules to be used, and input masks for adding and amending data should be in written form. You may include suitable graphics to clarify your documentation.

I   Produce a design for a relational database, to include:
- the purpose of the database
- the audience
- a minimum of three tables
- the completion of an ERD for the database
- normalisation of the data to the third normal form
- a user interface to access all parts of the database
- forms for adding and amending data
- designs for reports both printed and on-screen
- data validation.

The amount of detail in your plans will be important in determining your grade.

Produce a relational database in line with user design

In its simplest form, a database uses tables to organise information. Tables consist of a number of rows (each of which corresponds to a single record) and columns (each of which corresponds to a field in a record). Once you have this basic structure for the database, you can use forms to enter data, queries to interrogate it and reports to display the results of your queries.

Creating a table in Design view

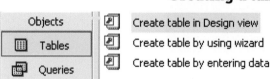

Figure 6.20 Create a table in Design view

1 In the database window, click on the Table tab (Figure 6.20). You can choose to create the table in Design view, by using a wizard or by entering data.
2 Select the Design view option. You can now begin entering your fields (Figure 6.21). Enter the first field name in the Field Name column. Then, in the corresponding Data Type cell, select the appropriate data type.
3 You must select a primary key for each table you create – place the cursor in the designated field and then click on Edit and Primary Key.
4 When you have described all the fields in the table, select View and then Datasheet View. Choose OK to save the new table – it is now ready for data entry.

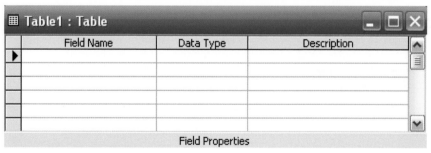

Figure 6.21 Creating fields

Primary keys

Every database table should have one or more columns designated as a primary key. The value this key holds should be unique for each record in the database. For example, assume we have a table called Vehicles that contains information for every vehicle in the company. It is necessary to select an appropriate primary key to uniquely identify each vehicle – a good choice would be to use the registration number.

Once you have decided on a primary key and set it up in the database, it will be enforced by the system. If there is an attempt to insert a record into a table with a primary key that duplicates that of an existing record, it will fail.

To set or change the primary key

1 Open the table in Design view.
2 Select the field you want to define as the primary key.
3 Click the Primary Key icon on the toolbar (Figure 6.22).

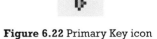

Figure 6.22 Primary Key icon

Most databases can generate primary keys to assign a unique ID to each record in a table. While effective, it is not good design practice, as you then have a field in every record with data that has no other intrinsic value – it is better practice to use that space to store more useful data.

Foreign keys

Foreign keys are used to create relationships or links between tables. Returning to the database for Private Users, if we wanted to add a table containing the details of customers waiting for vehicles of a particular type, this new table might be called Awaiting and would contain information about the vehicles the customer is looking for. We would want to include information about the vehicles, but it would be redundant to have the same information in two tables instead, we could create a relationship between the two tables. The primary key of one table becomes a foreign key in the other table.

For example, in the table Vehicle attribute (Figure 6.7) one of the fields could be Employee No. This could be used to denote, in the final database, which employee sold that vehicle.

The PK of the Sales staff attribute table (Figure 6.8), Employee No, is a foreign key (FK) in the Vehicle table.

Foreign keys do not have to be unique; we will have more than one vehicle in a feature specification. Similarly, there is no requirement for an entry in the Features table to have any corresponding entry in the Vehicles table – it is possible to have a vehicle with none of the listed features.

Linked tables

A table is a collection of data about one topic. Using a separate table for each topic means that you store that data only once – providing a more efficient database and fewer data entry errors.

You can add, delete, rename or customise fields in an existing table. Field properties provide control over how the data in a field is stored, entered or displayed, depending on data type.

A common field links two tables so that the data can be combined for viewing, editing or printing. In one table, the field is a primary key. That same field exists in the related table as a foreign key and identifies how the tables are related.

When you have created your tables, you will need to link them. At this point you could refer to your ERD. You must, however, check all the attributes/fields for each table to ensure they are complete and enable all of the user requirements to be met.

Data validation

You can set field properties that provide control over the values that can be entered into the field:

■ For Number fields, you can choose from a variety of field sizes to control the kind and range of values that can be entered.

AutoNumber
The AutoNumber data type stores a unique number for each record as it is added to a table. There are three types of numbers that can be applied – sequential, random and Replication ID.

- For Text fields, you can set the maximum number of characters that can be entered.
- For all but AutoNumber fields you can require that data be entered in the field.
- For Text, Date/Time and Number fields, you can define an input mask to provide blanks to fill in and you can control what values can be entered in those blanks.
- You can prevent duplicate values from being entered into a field or combination of fields.

Validation rules

Validation rules allow you to define a rule to limit what data can be accepted. They are enforced whenever you add or edit data, whether in table view, a form bound to the table, a query or by importing data. You can define two kinds of validation rules: field validation rules and record validation rules.

- A field validation rule is used to check the value entered into a field as the user leaves the field. For example, you could define ">=10 AND <=100" for a Number field to allow only values from 10 to 100 to be entered.
- Record validation rules control when an entire record can be saved. They can refer to other fields in the same table, making them useful for comparing values in different fields. For example, you could define a rule to ensure that the date an item is ordered is within 30 days of the date the item is required – "[RequiredDate]<=[OrderDate]+30".

When a field or record validation rule is broken, a message informs the user how to correctly enter that data. In most cases, you can verify that data is entered correctly into a control on a form by setting the Validation Rule property for the control, or by setting record or field validation rules in the underlying table to which the control is bound. Macros and event procedures provide additional power and flexibility for more complex validation.

Validate or restrict data in a form

Validation rules allow the database designer more control over what type of information is entered. Although input masks allow you to specify how the data should be entered, they do not allow very much control over exactly what data is entered: with an input mask you could specify that a string of three digits must be entered, but with a validation rule you could specify that the number must be greater than 500 and less than 750.

Character	Meaning
a<b	a must be less than b
a>b	a must be greater than b
a=b	a must be equal to b
a<=b	a must be less than or equal to b
a>=b	a must be greater than or equal to b

Figure 6.23 Validation Rule characters

By validating or restricting data, you can give users immediate feedback about the data just entered and ensure they enter the correct information into a text box or other control.

Creating an input mask

When you design a table in a database and you create a field to hold a certain type of information, you can create an input mask to complement that field. An input mask specifies an exact format for the data to be entered. For example, it would be useful for a field such as the vehicle registration number.

Using an input mask reduces the risk that people will omit information or enter the wrong data. For example, you can create a mask to only permit the number and type of characters found in a registration number.

Character	What it indicates
0	A numeric character between 0 and 9 is required.
#	An entry is optional, but it must be a digit between 0 and 9.
L	An alphabetic character between a and z is required.
?	An entry is optional, but it must be an alphabetic character between a and z.
A	A letter or digit must be entered.
a	An entry is optional, but it must be a letter or digit.
&	Any character must be entered.
\	Causes the character that follows to be displayed on-screen.
9	Entry is optional, but it must be a numeric character.
>	Forces upper case.
<	Forces lower case.

Figure 6.24 Common input mask characters

To create an input mask for a control

1 Open a form in Design view.
2 Select a text box or a combo box, then click Properties to open the property sheet (Figure 6.25).
3 In the Input Mask property box, click the Build button to start the Input Mask Wizard.
4 There are several masks available – choose the one you want.
5 You can customise the mask. Choose the type of character that represents the numbers or letters before they are entered.
6 You have the option to store the other symbols with the data. This is recommended, since it will allow these characters to display in queries and reports.
7 Follow the instructions in the wizard dialogue boxes to set up the mask you require, then click Finish.

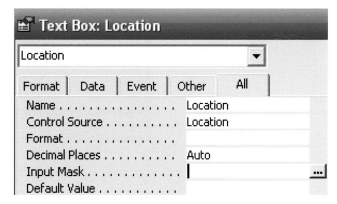

Figure 6.25 Starting the Input Mask wizard

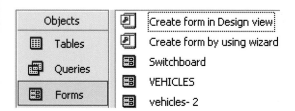

Figure 6.26 Creating a form

Creating a form using the Form Wizard

1 Click on the Forms tab in the database window. Your options are to create a form in Design view or using a wizard (Figure 6.26).
2 Select the Form Wizard option.
3 Select the tables or queries that you want as the table source (Figure 6.27). Remember that if you want to create a form which includes fields from different tables, you must establish a link between the tables.
4 Select the fields you want to include on your form.
5 Click Next.

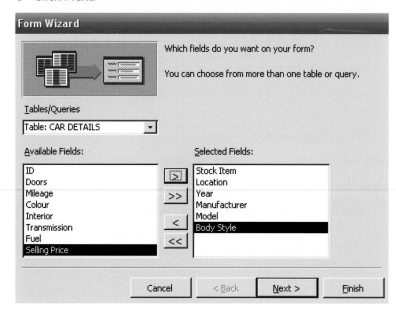

Figure 6.27 Selecting the source data

6 Select the layout (Figure 6.28). Columnar and Tabular are the most commonly used.
7 Click Next.

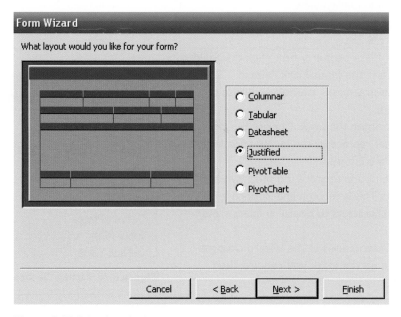

Figure 6.28 Selecting the layout

8 Choose a background style (Figure 6.29). Remember what and who the report is for and select an appropriate layout.
9 Click Next.

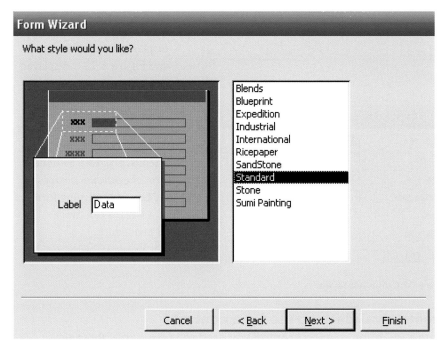

Figure 6.29 Selecting a background style

10 Enter a title for your form (Figure 6.30).
11 Select 'Open the form to view or enter information' option.
12 Click Finish.

Figure 6.30 Selecting a title

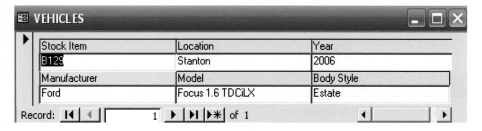

Figure 6.31 Justified layout

Your new form will be displayed on-screen and ready to use. The figures below show different layouts of the same data form – Figure 6.31 is displayed in Justified layout and Figure 6.32 is displayed in Columnar layout.

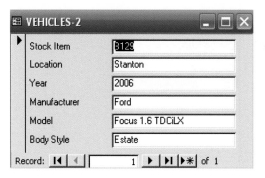

Figure 6.32 Columnar layout

When you create forms in Design view, you can add features such as toggle buttons, drop-down menus, program switches – buttons, checkboxes, images and text boxes. Designing forms without a wizard is a more detailed procedure.

To create a validation rule for a control

To create a validation rule for a control you need to know a little about the Expression Builder (Figure 6.33). It has three sections:

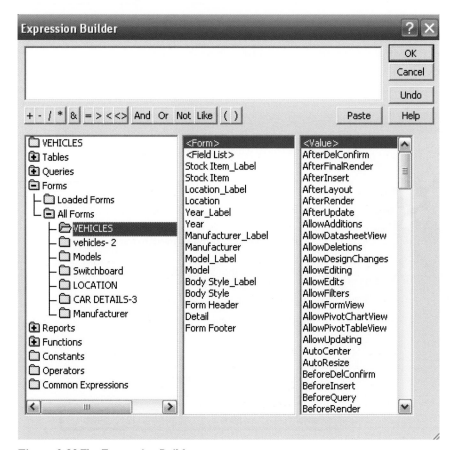

Figure 6.33 The Expression Builder

1 *Expression box* – this is where you build the expression. Use the lower section of the builder to create elements and paste them into the expression box to form an expression or type parts of the expression directly.

2 *Operator buttons*, in the middle section, are for commonly used operators. If you click one of the operator buttons, the Expression Builder inserts the operator at the insertion point in the expression box.

For a complete list of operators you can use in expressions, click the Operators folder in the lower left-hand box and the appropriate operator category in the middle box. The right-hand box lists all operators in the selected category (Figure 6.34).

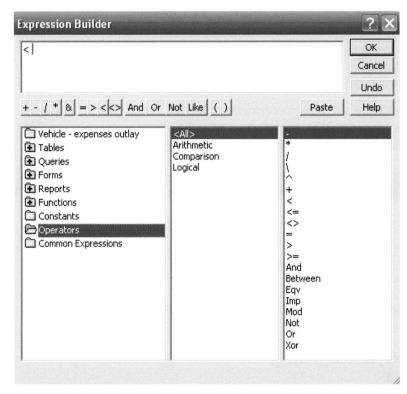

Figure 6.34 The Expression Builder showing operators in the selected category

3 *Expression elements* – in the lower section of the builder are three boxes:
- the left-hand box contains folders that list the table, query, form and report database objects, built-in and user-defined functions, constants, operators and common expressions
- the middle box lists specific elements or categories of elements for the folder selected in the left-hand box, as in the previous example
- the right-hand box lists the values, if any, for the elements you select in the left-hand and middle boxes – as in the previous example. Use a macro or an event procedure for data validation if:
  - your validation rule involves conditions for more than one value verify that any two of three fields are filled in before saving a record
  - you want to display different error messages for different types of errors in the field – if the value entered is greater than the acceptable range, you can display one message; and if it is less than the acceptable range, you can display a different message

- you want the user to be able to override your validation rule – in this case you can display a warning message asking the user to confirm the data
- the validation involves references to controls on other forms or contains a function
- you have a validation rule that you can use for more than one form, and you want the convenience of defining the rule once and then referring to it in each form.

You may need to use sub-forms to create a fully working database. An explanation of how to create sub-forms is given on pages 226–228.

Forms to add, edit and delete records

In your form you can specify whether a user can add, edit or delete a record by opening the form in Design view and double-clicking on the form selector (the box where the rulers meet, in the upper left-hand corner of the form) to open the form's property sheet (Figure 6.35).

- To allow additions, set the Allow Additions property to Yes.
- To allow edits, set the Allow Edits property to Yes.
- To allow deletions, set the Allow Deletions property to Yes.

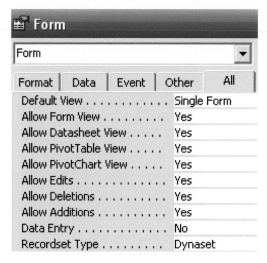

Figure 6.35 Property sheet

Customised error messages

Data can be validated by using a database constraint – a restriction, defined as an expression, placed on a field or table. A violation occurs when a user tries to enter unacceptable data. One of two default error messages is displayed when constraint violations occur. These messages are useful for designers, but they are not user-friendly. When a user encounters a constraint violation, you can display a user-friendly message by using either the validation text extended property or database triggers.

- Extended properties store additional attribute information. You can add validation text in the Properties dialogue box.
- Use database triggers to display a user-friendly message when a user encounters a constraint violation. You can create INSERT and UPDATE triggers on a table that test for the condition and produce an error message.

Portfolio Activity (AO2)

You should now produce the database for Private Users to use. Make sure that your work will provide a user-friendly solution. Follow your design and remember to include data for at least 60 records across the tables.

1 Using the design you have created, produce a relational database. You must add records to each table. The database should include:
- forms to add, edit and delete records
- primary keys
- foreign keys
- linked tables
- at least four data types, such as Boolean, text, number, date
- data validation including input masks
- customised error messages.

The extent to which your database reflects your design work will be important in determining your grade. If you need to deviate from your original plans, there is no need to go back and change your plans, but you need to explain why you have made these changes. You will not be penalised for improving your initial design, provided that you document the reasons.

Use a number of simple and complex queries

You can use queries to view, change and analyse data in different ways and as a source of records for forms and reports. There are several types of query, as shown in Figure 6.36.

Query	Function
Select	Retrieves data from one or more tables and displays the results in a datasheet where you can update the records. Use to group records and calculate sums, counts, averages and other types of total.
Parameter	When run, this type of query displays its own dialogue box prompting you for information, such as criteria for retrieving records or a value you want to insert in a field. You can design the query to prompt for more than one piece of information, such as two prices. They are also useful when employed as the basis for forms and reports – such as a weekly sales report based on a parameter query. When printing the report, a dialogue box is displayed requesting the week.
Crosstab	Use this to calculate and restructure data for analysis. It calculates a sum, average, count or other type of total for data that is grouped by two types of information – one down the left-hand side of the datasheet and another across the top.
Action	This makes changes to or moves many records in just one operation. There are four types: ■ **delete** query deletes a group of records from one or more tables – it deletes entire records, not just selected fields within records ■ **update** query makes global changes to a group of records in one or more tables; for example, you could reduce prices by 5 per cent for a sales promotion ■ **append** query adds a group of records from one or more tables to the end of one or more other tables; use it to add new vehicles ■ **make-table** query creates a new table from all or part of the data in one or more tables. This is useful for creating a table to export to other databases or a history table containing old records.

Figure 6.36 Types of query

Queries can be either simple or complex. They can also be static or dynamic. A simple query is one that searches on one parameter. So for example the database could be searched to find all the Jaguars in stock. A static simple query could be inbuilt into the database but this is not helpful to the users. A dynamic query lets the user specify what they want to search for. A dialogue box is created and takes a value from the user and uses that to search the database.

A complex query means that two or more criteria are searched for. For example a customer wants a **Jaguar and Coupe** or **BMW and convertible**. To create a static query for this you would:

1. Select the Queries tab in the database window. You can create your query in Design view or by using a wizard (Figure 6.37). Both allow you to create the query specifying the input tables or queries, field names, filters, sorting and grouping options.
2. Select the Design view option.
3. In the Show Table dialogue box (Figure 6.38), select the table or query whose fields you want to use. In this case those details are held in two tables. Click Add on each, then Close.

Figure 6.37 Selecting Design view

Figure 6.38 Selecting tables for a query

4. You are now in Design view (Figure 6.39).

Field:	Manufacturer	Body Style	Model	Selling Price	Transmission
Table:	CAR DETAILS	CAR DETAILS	CAR DETAILS	CARS	CAR DETAILS
Sort:	Ascending	Ascending			
Show:	☑	☑	☑	☑	☐
Criteria:	"Jaguar"	"Coupe"			"automatic"
or:	"BMW"	"Convertible"			

Figure 6.39 Selecting tables for a query (Design view)

Select the fields for your query by clicking in the appropriate table and then the appropriate fields. To include all fields from a table, use the asterisk wildcard character (*). The query results automatically include any fields that are added to the underlying table or query after the query is created, and automatically exclude fields that are deleted.

In the above example (Figure 6.39):

- The first field uses the Manufacturer field from the table U6 CARS; there are two criteria, BMW and Jaguar. The items will be presented in ascending alphabetical order – the field will be shown in the query.
- The second field uses the Body Style field from the table U6 CARS; there are two criteria, Coupe and Convertible. The items will be presented in ascending alphabetical order – the field will be shown in the query.
- The third field uses the Model field from the table U6 CARS; no criteria (no sort) – the field will be shown in the query.
- The fourth field uses the Selling Price field from the table U6 CARS; no criteria (no sort) – the field will be shown in the query.
- The fifth field uses the Transmission field from the table U6 CARS; there is only one criterion – automatic. As all the detail will be the same, it does not need to be sorted nor shown in the query.

If you specify a sort order for more than one field, the field furthest to the left is sorted first – so arrange the fields you want to sort from left to right in the design grid.

5   When you have created the criteria, click File, Save. Use a descriptive name for your query (Figure 6.40).

Figure 6.40 Saving your query

6   To run your query and see the results, click the Run button on the toolbar (Figure 6.41).

Figure 6.41 Run button

Calculated fields in complex queries

You can use a query to perform calculations, such as viewing total sales by location, adding two fields together or multiplying a price by a percentage increase. A calculated field is a new field that displays the results of a calculation. It appears with the other fields in the query results, and can also appear in forms and reports based on the query.

You can perform calculations in a query using predefined calculations (including sum, average, count, minimum, and maximum). These are called aggregate functions or totals. They can be used for all records or for groups of records. Select one totals calculation for each field you want to calculate.

If you want to carry out calculations on groups of records you can calculate all types of totals using the Total row in the query design grid. Select the total or aggregate function for the calculation you want to perform on a field.

When you display the results of a calculation in a field, the results are not stored in the underlying table. The calculation is rerun each time you run the query. In this way the results are always based on the most current data in the database.

Creating a calculated field

This simple example shows you how to store the details of a transaction – the cost of a product multiplied by the number sold – but not the result (this is calculated); see Figure 6.42.

▦ BATTERIES : Table			
Manufacturer	Stock Code	Cost	Sales
▶ Varta	A110	67.10	36
Varta	A92	41.00	60
Varta	A75	49.75	60
Varta	A27	55.00	50

Figure 6.42 Creating a calculated field

To perform this calculation you must create a new calculated field by entering an expression in the Field row of an empty column. The expression should consist of a name for the new field followed by a colon then the calculation. The calculation will contain references to other fields as well as the appropriate mathematical operators (+, -, *, /, etc.).

To continue the example, the total value of the sales is calculated by creating the new field in which the cost is multiplied by the sales (Figure 6.43).

Field:	Stock Code	Cost	Sales	Total: [Cost]*[Sales]
Table:	BATTERIES	BATTERIES	BATTERIES	
Sort:				
Show:	☑	☑	☑	☑

Figure 6.43 Creating the new field

Running the query displays the result of the calculation (Figure 6.44).

🖳 Calculated field : Select Query

	Stock Code	Cost	Sales	Total
	A110	67.10	36	£2,415.60
	A92	41.00	60	£2,460.00
	A75	49.75	60	£2,985.00

Figure 6.44 Displaying the results in the new field

The data may not be appropriately formatted, so to format the calculated field as you require:

1 In Design view, right-click on the new column.
2 Select Properties to open the Field Properties dialogue box (Figure 6.45).
3 Select one of the pre-defined formats from the list.
4 Click Close.

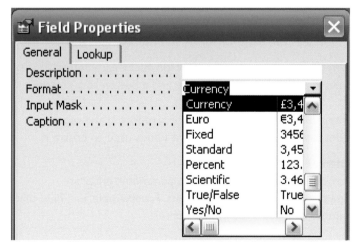

Figure 6.45 The Field Properties dialogue box

Logical and range operators

Operators can compare data to a value, perform calculations, use multiple criteria and combine text fields – known as concatenation. Commonly used types include range (comparison) and logical operators.

Range operators

These compare data to values or other fields. Use them to retrieve data based on how it compares to a value. For example, all vehicles with a selling price equal to or lower than £15,000 – in the query design grid, enter the comparison operator <= before the value in the Criteria cell.

=	equal to
>	greater than
<	less than
>=	greater than or equal to
<=	less than or equal to
<>	not equal to

Figure 6.46 Common range operators

Logical operators

These apply logic to determine whether conditions are true or false – AND, OR, LIKE and NOT. For example, you might retrieve a list of vehicles at a location that are saloon models.

Parameter queries

If you want to repeat a question, but the details – the criteria – are different, use a parameter query. The result always reflects the most up-to-date information because you save the question, not the answer.

In fact, parameter queries can be any sort of query. This is because when you design this type of query you present the user with a dialogue box prompting for the parameter value or values, such as two prices; all records within those prices are then retrieved.

Parameter queries are useful as the basis for forms and reports, and you can also:

- create a custom form or dialogue box to prompt for query parameters, and display the results in a datasheet, for example add a button to a custom dialogue box
- print the criteria entered in a parameter query for a report in the report header, so you can determine from the report the values used to create it.

Using one parameter

In the Criteria cell for the field you want to use as a parameter, enter an expression with a prompt enclosed in square brackets. For example, in a field that displays the current number of miles a car has run, enter:
<[Mileage:]

Using two parameters

In the Criteria cell for each field you want to use as a parameter, type an expression with prompts enclosed in square brackets. For example, in a date field display the prompts "Type the beginning date:" and "Type the ending date:" to specify a range of values:
Between [Type the beginning date:] And [Type the ending date:]

Using parameters with wildcards

In the Criteria cell for each field you want to use as a parameter, type an expression with a prompt enclosed in square brackets. For example, use the LIKE operator and the wildcard symbol * prompt for one or more characters to search for – the records that begin with or contain the characters entered are identified.

In the following example, the first statement searches for words that begin with a specified letter; the second searches for words that contain the specified character:

- **LIKE [Enter the first character to search by:] & "*"**
- **LIKE "*" & [Enter any character to search by:] & "*"**

To create the parameters

1 Enter the text enclosed in square brackets in the Criteria cell (Figure 6.47). The text you enter will appear as the prompt on a dialogue box – you might want it to be in the form of a question to the user.
2 When you run the query, the Enter Parameter Value dialogue box will be displayed at any point where you have entered a parameter in the query field Criteria (Figure 6.48).
3 The user enters a response in the text box and clicks OK to proceed.

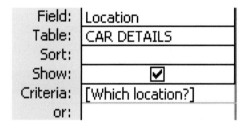

Figure 6.47 Entering the parameter

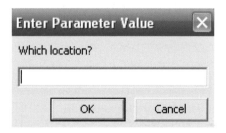

Figure 6.48 Enter Parameter Value dialogue box

In this example the user will be prompted to enter the name of the location when they run the query. The text that the user enters will be used as the criteria for that particular field. If the user enters Stanton, this query would display all the records with the entry Stanton in the Location field.

You can use as many parameters as you want, in as many fields as necessary. The dialogue boxes appear in the same order as they do on the query grid reading from left to right. You normally arrange the fields in the way in which you want to see the results displayed.

Crosstab queries

Use a crosstab query to calculate and restructure data for analysis. It calculates a sum, average, count or other type of total for data that is grouped by two types of information – one down the left-hand side of the datasheet and another across the top. The same information is displayed, but it is grouped both horizontally and vertically so the datasheet is more compact and easier to analyse.

Creating a crosstab query using the wizard

1 Select Queries, New – the New Query dialogue box is displayed (Figure 6.49).

2 Select Crosstab Query Wizard. Click OK.

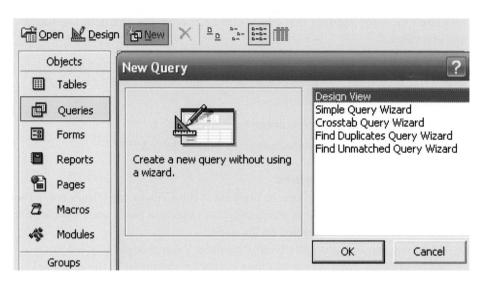

Figure 6.49 Selecting the Crosstab Query Wizard

3 The Crosstab Query Wizard will be displayed (Figure 6.50).

4 Select the table or query containing the fields you require. Click Next.

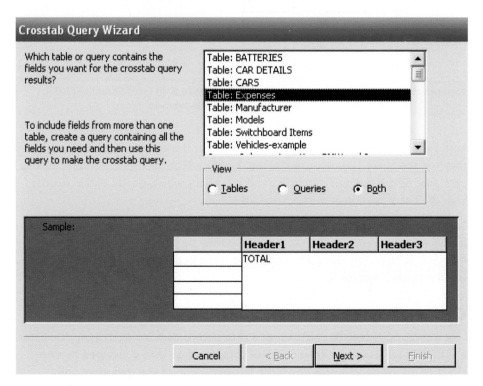

Figure 6.50 Selecting the tables or queries

5 On the next screen (Figure 6.51) select the fields that you want to use as row headings (up to three). Click next.

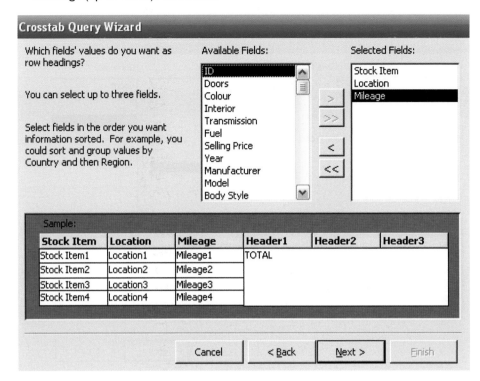

Figure 6.51 Selecting the fields for row headings

6 On the next screen (Figure 6.52) select the field that you want to use as column headings. Click Next.

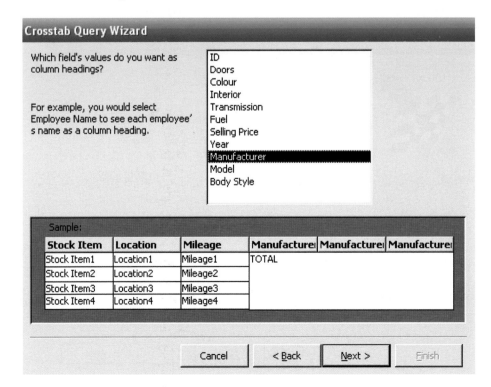

Figure 6.52 Selecting the field for column headings

7 On the next screen (Figure 6.53) select the number you want calculated for each column and row intersection.

8 Tick the 'Yes, include row sums' box. Click Next.

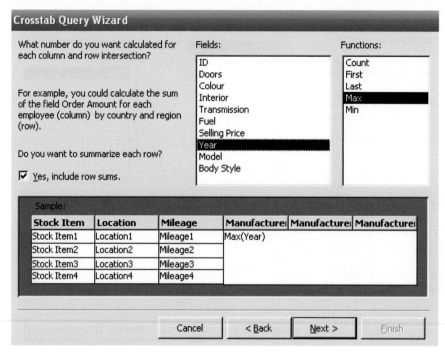

Figure 6.53 Selecting the number required

9 On the next screen (Figure 6.54) enter the name you want for your query.

10 You have the options of viewing the query or modifying the design – select View the query.

11 Click Finish. Your query results will be displayed on-screen.

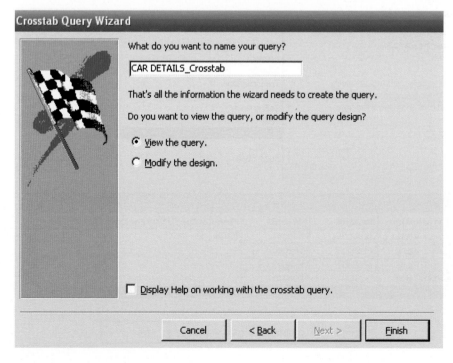

Figure 6.54 Entering the query name

Portfolio Activity (AO3)

Private Users require information in two ways:

a) The staff want to be able to search for customers and vehicles easily. For example, the staff may want to search for:

- vehicles that are between £10,000 and £20,000 and have air bags, anti-lock braking system (ABS) and alloy wheels; they may want the data sorted on the price in ascending or descending order
- a list of vehicles within a price range that are from a specified manufacturer and model, identifying all the additional features of the vehicles.

b) The management wants a report to show the commissions paid to each sales person for a 3 month period. This report needs to be grouped by sales person with an overall total paid in commission.

1 Create the queries that will meet the defined user requirements. (You will need to refer back to the requirements already detailed.) You should also consider the day-to-day usage of the database and create queries to meet these needs.

Before you construct each query, think about what you are going to search for, plan the queries and ensure that you incorporate the correct fields from the correct tables. When you have designed your queries you can create them, but they must incorporate use of:

- fields from at least two tables
- a calculated field in a complex query
- at least three different logical operations such as AND, OR, NOT, LIKE
- at least three different range operators such as <, >, <>, =
- a parameter query
- a crosstab query.

2 Describe the purpose of each of your queries and why it is appropriate.

AO4: Create a user interface

A user interface is the means by which the users interact with the system. The design has an impact on the time and effort required to provide input, interpret the output and learn to use the system. You should provide a solution that can be used efficiently and effectively, for its intended purpose, by its target users.

If you are providing a database solution you will usually only display those items, or objects, that you want the user to access. Allowing users to access tables, queries and reports will give them the ability to alter (whether by mistake or otherwise) the functions you have set up for them.

The design of your interface has the potential to impact on the user in a very positive manner, but it may have a negative impact if it is without clear, defined elements. Aim to deliver solutions that fit your client's needs – tailor frequent actions for experienced users, but cater for inexperienced users too. When preparing the user interface design, consider these points:

- Use appropriate language – use words, phrases and actions familiar to the user, following their environment's conventions and giving information in a logical order.
- Be consistent – users should not have to decide if different words, situations, or actions mean different things:
  - if you can double-click on items in one list to produce an action, you should be able to double-click on items in any other list to produce the same type of response
  - put buttons in the same place on all screens
  - use the same wording in labels and messages
  - use a consistent colour scheme throughout.
- Navigation between items is important – if it is difficult, users will become frustrated. When the flow between screens matches their workflow your application will make sense to the user.
- Navigation within a screen is important – in western societies, we read left to right and top to bottom – if your design follows this pattern users are presented with information in a way that is familiar to them.
- Instructions should be visible or easy to obtain. Describe your messages and labels effectively (the text displayed is the primary source of information) if text is poorly worded then the interface will be perceived poorly by users. Use full words and sentences rather than abbreviations and codes. Messages should be worded positively: imply that the user is in control, and provide insight into how to use the application correctly. Make objects, actions, and options clear: the user should not have to remember information from one part of the system to another.
- Use colour appropriately and sparingly. Some users may be colour blind so you need another method of identifying critical information. You can use colour to provide a common feel throughout, but follow the contrast rule: use dark text on light backgrounds and light text on dark backgrounds to ensure that the screens are readable.
- Align fields effectively: when a screen has more than one editing field, organise them to be both visually appealing and efficient. One clean, efficient method is to left justify edit fields, (make the left-hand side of each line up in a straight line, one above the other), right justify the corresponding labels and place them immediately beside the field. Align data appropriately – it is common practice

is to right align integers, decimal align floating-point numbers, and to left align strings.

- Crowded screens are difficult to understand and therefore difficult to use. Research has shown that the density of the screen should not exceed 40% and density within groups on the screen should not exceed 60%.
- Items that are logically connected should be grouped together (other items should be separated) to accomplish this use white space or boxes.
- Provide help and documentation: it should be easy to use, focused on the user's task, list concrete steps to be carried out, and concise.

Finally, have you accidentally deleted text or a file – were you able to recover or did you have to redo hours of work? Expect users to make mistakes and design the interface to enable recovery. Provide a method for users who select incorrect functions to exit quickly – a good design which prevents errors is better than good error messages. Provide users with a confirmation option before they commit to an action. Express error messages in plain language – identify the problem and suggest a solution. Keep users informed about what is going on – give feedback as quickly as possible.

The interface would usually contain the following basic components:

- Pointer – a symbol used to select objects and commands. Usually, the pointer appears as a small angled arrow.
- Pointing device – a device, such as a mouse or trackball, which enables you to select objects on the screen.
- Icons – small images to represent commands, files, or windows. By moving the pointer to the icon and pressing a mouse button, you can execute a command or convert the icon into a window.
- Desktop – the area on the screen where icons are grouped is often referred to as the desktop because the icons are intended to represent real objects on a real desktop.
- Windows – divide the screen into different areas: run a different program or display a different file in each window. You can move windows, and change their shape and size.
- Menus – most graphical user interfaces let you execute commands by selecting a choice from a menu.

Forms

Customising and creating forms for a table

In Assessment Objective 2: Produce the database according to the design, you went through the process of creating a form (see pages 208–210). You will also find details of what you can do to customise forms under that objective.

Sub-forms

A sub-form is a form that is inserted into another form. The primary form is called the main form, and the form within the form is called the sub-form.

Sub-forms are especially effective when you want to show data from tables or queries with a one-to-many relationship – an association between two tables in which the primary key value of each record in the primary table corresponds to the value in the matching field or fields of many records in the related table.

Main forms and sub-forms
The main form shows data from the one side of the relationship; the sub-form shows data from the many side.

For example, you could create a form with a sub-form to show data from a Manufacturers table and a Models table. The data in the Manufacturers table is the 'one' side of the relationship. The data in the Models table is the 'many' side of the relationship – each manufacturer can have more than one model.

The main form and sub-form in this type of form are linked so that the sub-form displays only records that are related to the current record in the main form. For example, when the main form displays the manufacturer BMW, the sub-form displays only the BMW models.

When you create a sub-form, you can design it to be displayed in any view – Datasheet, Form, PivotTable or PivotChart. You also have the option of setting the default view and disabling one or more views; you can change the view when the main form is displayed in Form view. Sub-forms are not displayed when a main form is opened in PivotTable or PivotChart view.

A main form can have any number of sub-forms if you place each on the main form. You can also nest up to seven levels – that is, you can have a sub-form within a main form, and you can have another sub-form within that sub-form, and so on.

When using a form with a sub-form to enter new records, the new record is saved in the main form when you enter data in the sub-form, thereby ensuring that the records in the 'many' table will have a record in the 'one' table. The main form also automatically saves each record as you add it to the sub-form.

Creating sub-forms based on main forms

Before you can create a sub-form you must ensure that you have defined and set the relationships. You will have defined the relationships when you developed your ERD (AO1) and used these to create your working database (AO3).

To create a form and a sub-form together

1 In the database window, click Forms.
2 Click the New button on the toolbar.
3 In the New Form dialogue box (Figure 6.55), double-click Form Wizard.

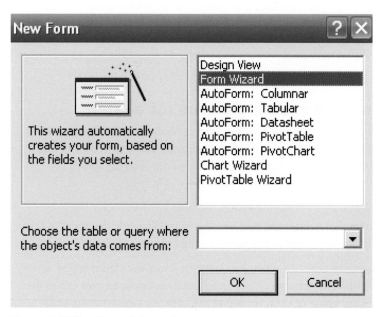

Figure 6.55 New Form dialogue box

4 The Form Wizard will be displayed (Figure 6.56). In the first dialogue box, select a table or query from the list.
5 Double-click the fields you want to include from this table or query.
6 In the same dialogue box, select another table or query from the list.
7 Double-click the fields you want to include from this table or query.

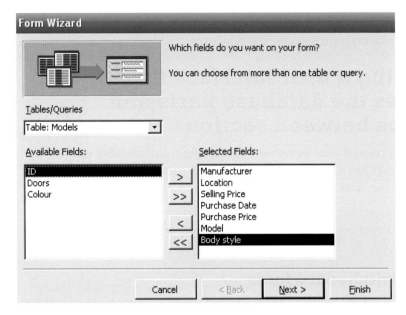

Figure 6.56 Form Wizard

8   When you click Next, if you set up the relationships correctly before starting, the wizard asks which table or query you want to view by (Figure 6.57).
9   In the same dialogue box, select the Form with subform(s) option. Click Next.
10 In the next screen select the layout and click Next.
11 In the next screen select the style and click Next.

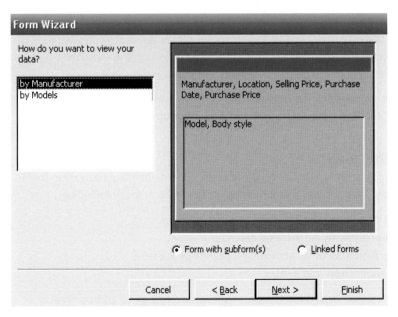

Figure 6.57 Form Wizard options

12 In the next screen enter the titles you want for the form and the sub-form and click Finish.

To create a sub-form and add it to another form

1　Open the form to which you want to add the sub-form in Design view.
2　Make sure the Control Wizard tool in the toolbox is pressed in.
3　Click the sub-form tool in the toolbox.
4　On the form, click where you want to place the sub-form.
5　Follow the directions in the wizard dialogue boxes.
6　When you click Finish, Microsoft Access adds a sub-form control to your form. It also creates a separate form for the sub-form.

Producing a user interface that accesses the database parts and switches between sections

When you have created your forms then you can begin to create the user interface. However, you will also need to consider the reports that will be produced from the database.

You must enable user access to all the defined reports from your user interface. You should read the text relating to AO5: Produce reports before you create your user interface.

Using a switchboard form

A switchboard is a form containing user-defined commands, using either buttons, labels, images or hyperlinks. These invoke actions that will automatically carry out the pre-defined actions you have associated with them, such as opening other forms, running queries or printing reports. A switchboard form allows you to tie together all the objects that you have created for users in a single form, and removes the need for the users to have to navigate from within the database window.

You can use a switchboard form as the interface for your application, employing buttons to replace the need for the user to navigate around the objects. For example, to open a form the user may need to switch to the database window, choose the Forms tab and open the form. However, if using a command on the switchboard interface, the user only has to click one button to carry out the same action.

Switchboard forms contain a limited number of form controls; these include command buttons, labels, object frames and other layout objects such as lines and rectangles.

Command buttons

Command buttons are the simplest type of form control, offering navigation from your switchboard. You can use this functionality to perform tasks including:

- opening and displaying other forms
- opening and previewing or printing reports
- applying filters on a form or activating a search procedure
- quitting the application and exiting.

When creating a switchboard for the first time, a simple way to add command buttons is to use the Command Button Wizard to take you through the steps and create the basic code that will allow you to open one form from another.

Creating a switchboard

You create, customise and delete a switchboard by using the Switchboard Manager. To create a switchboard, first open the database.

1 On the Tools menu, point to Database Utilities, and click Switchboard Manager.
2 The Switchboard Manager dialogue box is displayed (Figure 6.58).
3 Click New.

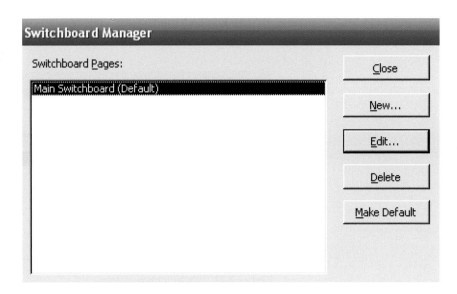

Figure 6.58 Switchboard Manager dialogue box

4 Type the name of the new switchboard in the Create New dialogue box (Figure 6.59) then click OK.

Figure 6.59 Create a new switchboard

5 Microsoft Access adds the switchboard to the Switchboard Pages box.
6 Click on the new switchboard, and then click Edit.
7 The Edit Switchboard Page will be displayed (Figure 6.60). Click New.

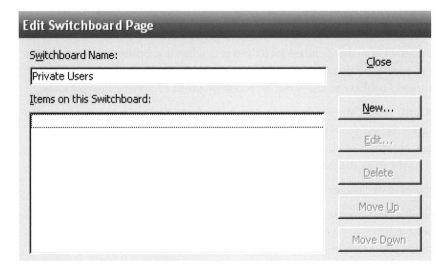

Figure 6.60 Edit Switchboard Page

8   The Edit Switchboard Item dialogue box will be displayed (Figure 6.61).
9   Enter the text for the first switchboard item in the Text box.

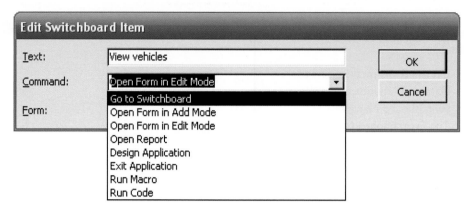

Figure 6.61 Edit Switchboard Item

10 Click a command in the Command box.
11 Depending on which command you click, another box is displayed below.
12 Click an item in this box, if necessary.

For example, enter View vehicles and click Open Form In Edit Mode in the Command box. Click the name of the form you want to open in the Form box then click OK.

Repeat the steps for entering items until you have added all the items to the switchboard. When you have finished creating the switchboard, click Close.

To edit or delete an item, click the item in the Items On This Switchboard box, and then click Edit or Delete. If you want to rearrange items, click an item in the box, and then click Move Up or Move Down.

To make a switchboard open when you open the database, click the switchboard name in the Switchboard Manager dialogue box, and then click Make Default.

Amend the startup options to display the user interface

You can control how the database looks and acts when it is opened by using startup options to specify, for example, what form to display. Alternatively, you can use a macro named AutoExec to carry out an action or series of actions automatically.

When Access opens, the database window is displayed. You probably do not want to give users access to this window, so you can hide it and display a switchboard. To do this, create an unbound form (a splash screen) and use the startup options to open it when the database is started.

Once you have decided on the form design, you can set the startup options:

1   On Tools, select Startup. The Startup options dialogue box is displayed (Figure 6.62).
2   In the Display Form/Page drop-down list, select the form that you want to display whenever the database is opened.

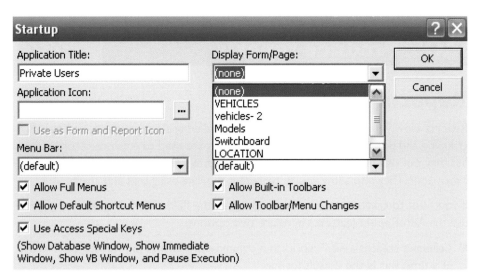

Figure 6.62 Startup options dialogue box

1 Enter the Application Title.
2 Tick the Display Database Window box so that it is hidden (blank).
3 When you have selected all the items you require, click OK.

Portfolio Activity (AO4)

Please complete Portfolio Activity (AO4) after working through AO5.

Produce a customised user interface for the staff at Private Users. Make sure that it reflects the needs of the company and that the layout and style suit the company image. Above all, make it clear and easy for the users.

1 Amend the startup options to display the user interface.
2 Using the database you have created, produce a user interface that will enable the staff to use the database. You should:
 ■ create at least one form for each table
 ■ create a customised form
 ■ create at least one sub-form.

Pass – Candidates produce a user interface that gives access to the main parts of the database. The interface **may** lack structure. They create at least **one** form for each table.

Merit – Candidates produce a user interface that gives access to the main parts of the database. The interface **mostly** matches the design. They create at least one form for each table and a **customised form**.

Distinction – Candidates produce a user interface that accesses **all** parts of the database. The interface **matches** the design. They create at least one form for each table, and a customised form and at least one **sub-form**.

Assessment Guidance

Reports

Reports allow you to analyse data you have collected using calculations, sorting and grouping, and print it in an organised format. They are used to enhance record output, but they can also be used to perform calculations, and sort and summarise grouped information. They also allow you to represent the data using text and charts.

If you want to create a report quickly using all the fields from one table or query, use the AutoReport feature. There are two options:

- *Columnar* creates a new report in a column-type format for viewing one record at a time; this is the default format.
- *Tabular* creates a report where the fields for each record appear on one line with the field labels at the top of the report.

A report is the output – usually a printout – of specified data from your database. Create a report to present the data rather than printing a table or a query result.

Figure 6.63 The New Report dialogue box

To create a report using AutoReport

1 In the database window, click on the Reports tab and then New. The New Report dialogue box is displayed (Figure 6.63).
2 Select AutoReport: Tabular.
3 In the drop-down box at the bottom, select the table or query on which you want to base the report.
4 Click OK.
5 The report will be created and displayed.

You should be aware of the purpose of each section of the report (Figure 6.64).

Section	Purpose
Detail	Used to display records.
Report Header	Used for displaying information that remains the same for every record, such as a title of the report and the date and/or time. The information in this section only appears at the top of the first page.
Report Footer	Used to display information that is the same for every record. The information in this section only appears at the bottom of the last page.
Page Header	Used to display items such as field headings or titles – this information will appear at the top of each page.
Page Footer	Used to display items such as page numbers. This data will appear at the bottom of each page.
Grouped Header/Footer	A special section that can be turned on and off through the Sorting and Grouping dialogue box. It is used to group information related through a one-to-many relationship.

Figure 6.64 Report section functions

Sorting a report on more than one field

You can sort on any field, even if it is not included in the report. When a sort is executed, all of the corresponding field entries for each record are also moved – the entire table, not just the specified field, is reorganised. When you create a report with the Report Wizard you have the option, at step 3 to specify the fields to be used to sort your data, see Figure 6.68 Sorting on page 239.

Grouping a report on more than one field

When you create a report you have the options for sorting (sort data without adding groups) and grouping (group and sort your data). You may want to group data – isolating specific fields in each record and assigning them to categories. For example, you have the names of vehicle models and all of their features; if you want to see all vehicles with automatic transmission, create a group by models in the transmission field.

Customising a report to display grouped and overall summaries

You can sort the data in a report by one or more fields, and you can select ascending or descending order. You can also group by data from one or more fields. Both activities can be carried out using the Report Wizard.

Creating a report with the Report Wizard allows you to customise the report you are creating. There are a number of options, including use of multiple tables and queries, selection of fields to be displayed, the addition of grouping levels, sorting, and selection of layout and style.

Note that under the Available Fields column there are several ways you can choose to bring a field into the Selected Fields column:

- double-click on each field name
- select each field name one at a time, and click on the single arrow button
- if you want ALL of the fields, click on the double arrow button.

If you want most of the fields in the list, click on the double arrow to move them all over. Once they are in the Selected Fields list, either double-click or click on each field name and click on the single arrow pointing to the left to return fields you do not want to the Available Fields list (this may save time).

To create a report to suit your design:

1 In the database window, click Reports then double-click 'Create report by using wizard' (Figure 6.65).

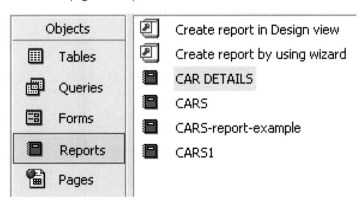

Figure 6.65 Create a report using the wizard

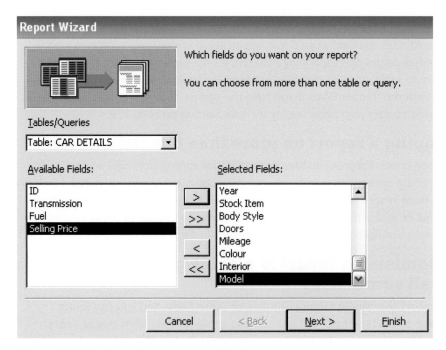

Figure 6.66 Selecting tables, queries and fields

2 Click on the Tables/Queries list, and select the first table or query you want to include in your report (Figure 6.66).
3 Move the fields you require in the report from the Available Fields list to the Selected Fields list.
4 Click Next.
5 Select any fields that you want to group the report on, in the grouping order (Figure 6.67). Choose the grouping level by double-clicking on the field names or using the single arrow. This allows you to display grouped and overall summaries.
6 Click Next.

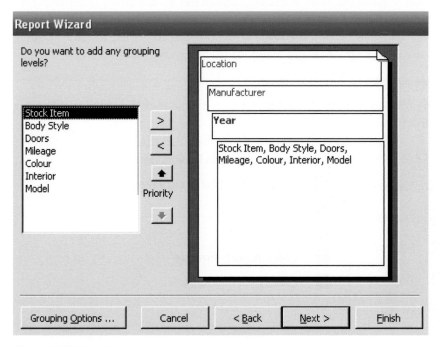

Figure 6.67 Grouping

7 Select any fields that you would like to sort your data on (Figure 6.68).
8 Click Next.

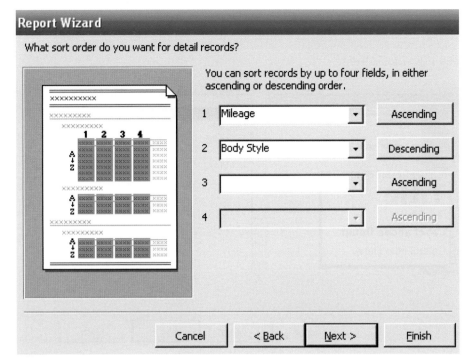

Figure 6.68 Sorting

9 Select the layout option you prefer (Figure 6.69).
10 Ensure that the 'Adjust the field width so all fields fit on a page' option is selected.
11 Select the appropriate Orientation for the report, then click Next.

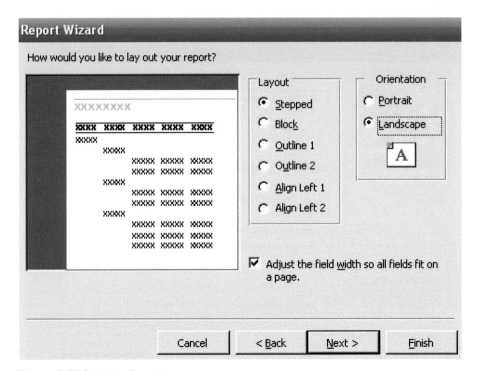

Figure 6.69 Selecting layout

12 Select the style to suit your report (Figure 6.70). Choose from Bold, Casual, Compact, Corporate, Formal and Soft Gray.

13 Click Next.

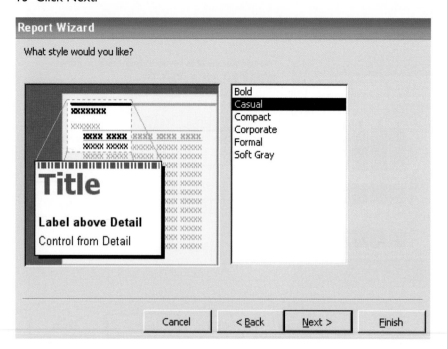

Figure 6.70 Selecting style

14 In the 'What title do you want for your report?' box, enter your choice of title (Figure 6.71). This is the name that will be displayed in the database window. Then click on one of the following options:
   ■ Preview the report (the default)
   ■ Modify the report's design.

15 Click Finish. The report is created and displayed on-screen in the view you chose.

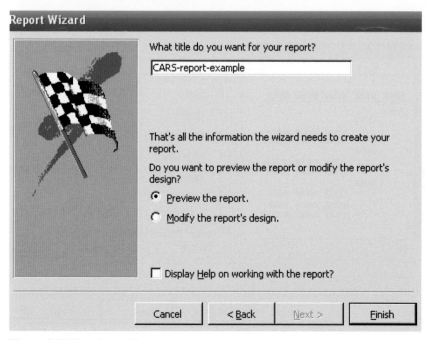

Figure 6.71 Entering a title

You can switch back and forth between Print Preview of the report and Design View. If you want to make changes – such as changing text in labels; deleting, adding, moving or resizing labels or controls; sorting or grouping fields – click the Design View button to edit the report. For example, change sorting and grouping levels:

1 Open the report in Design view. Your report will be displayed something like Figure 6.72.

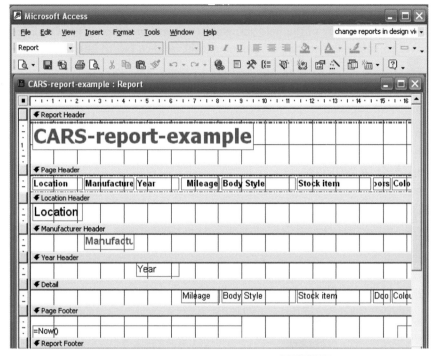

Figure 6.72 Report in Design view

2 Click Sorting And Grouping on the toolbar. **Figure 6.73**

3 The Sorting And Grouping box will be displayed (Figure 6.74).

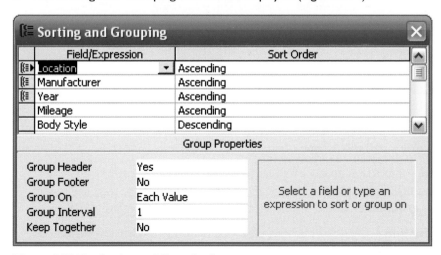

Figure 6.74 The Sorting and Grouping box

To change the sorting or grouping

1 Click the row selector to select the entire row of the field you want to move.
2 Click the selector again, and drag the row to a new location in the list.

To insert a sorting or grouping level

3   Click the row selector of the row above which you want to insert the new field, and then press INSERT.

4   In the Field/Expression column of the blank row, select the field you want to sort on.

When you fill in the Field/Expression column, Microsoft Access sets the Sort Order to Ascending. To change the sort order, select Descending from the Sort Order list.

To delete a sorting or grouping level

1   Click the row selector of the field you want to delete, and then press DELETE.

2   Click Yes to delete the sorting or grouping level, or click No to keep it.

Grouping a report could be used, for example, to group different car manufacturers together. This would mean that all the BMW's, Jaguars, Vauxhalls would be shown together.

Sorting a report could be used to sort on one, or more specified field(s). This could be used, for example, to sort all the customers into alphabetical order, ascending (A-Z) by surname.

Portfolio Activity (AO5)

You need to create the reports for a private user that you have already designed in AO1.

Using these designs, create the reports. You may need to refer to the queries you have already created.

When you are creating your reports you must ensure that:

- each report style is appropriate for the end user
- all data is fully displayed
- the reports match the designs.

You need to produce at least one report for each bullet point below:

- customised
- sorted on more than one field
- grouped and shows overall summaries.

Assessment Guidance

Pass – Candidates produce reports to include at least one customised report and at least one report that is sorted on more than one field. The reports **may not** match the designs.

Merit – Candidates produce reports to include at least one customised report, at least one report that is sorted on more than one field and at least one report that is **grouped** on one or more fields. The reports **mostly** match the designs.

Distinction – Candidates produce reports to include at least one customised report, at least one report that is sorted on more than one field, at least one report that is grouped on one or more fields and at least one report that shows **grouped and overall** summaries. The reports **match** the designs.

Produce user documentation

You should refer to Unit 5: Advanced Spreadsheets, pages 185–86, for guidance on creating a user guide. In addition, the following points may help in organising and presenting your guide:

- Use headings to organise your information.
- Include section titles and page numbers on every page as a header or footer.
- Use columns; put headings in the first column and descriptive text in the next.
- Help the users via different formats to identify different types of information. For example, you could identify input by using colour, varying the font style using bold or italics, or using icons.

These topics should be covered:

- how to start the database
- routes through the menus – how to append, delete and edit records
- examples of screens and data entry forms
- instructions about using the queries and reports that have been pre-set and designed
- advice about how to respond to error messages
- examples of data output screens
- examples of printed reports.

The user guide should not detail how to create queries and reports or how you created these. The user guide simply shows the user how to use them.

Produce a technical guide for the database

A technical guide (or manual) should be an accurate, readable and accessible aid to help users understand the system – remember that they may not be experts. It should be precise and as detailed as possible. Creating quality technical documents is a vital stage in allowing correct usage.

What should a technical guide include?

You should consider all the points you have in the user guide and give details of the following:

- the hardware, software and any other resources required
- procedures for opening and configuring the database
- processing details including queries and reports
- a detailed entity relationship diagram (ERD)
- a detailed data dictionary
- details of validation and verification procedures
- input screens, output screens and printed designs
- all the queries included in the database.

Avoid making common mistakes when producing guides:

- The document should be clear, but never patronising.
- Avoid humour – technical documents are not a form of entertainment; they are read for information.

- Inconsistency – ensure that all the elements are consistent; this applies to tone and layout.
- Errors – by the end you may well be sick of the sight of your guide. However, what matters is accuracy, so proofread the guide throughout drafting and before it is distributed. Do not rely on spell checkers. If possible, get someone else to read it – they might identify errors you have missed.

Portfolio Activity (AO6)

The company is keen to start using the system, but they will require documentation to help the staff while they are becoming familiar with the system. You should produce this user documentation.

1 Produce a user guide, which should allow a user to use various aspects of the database.
2 Produce a technical manual.

The grade you are awarded for this assessment objective will depend on the detail you include in your guides.

AO7: Test the database

Produce a test plan

A number of activities will be carried out during testing, so you need a plan. Your test plan gives details of the process of checking your work to make sure that it meets its requirements and is error free. Look at each item or test and ask yourself about the requirements.

One of the primary purposes of testing is to detect errors so that they can be corrected. Designing a test forces you to understand the requirements; in this way you may notice activities that are incomplete or incorrect. Testing can identify errors but still leave other critical errors undetected. A test plan must be designed with coverage in mind. If you do not test all aspects of the database you are more likely to allow errors. You should set coverage criteria and evaluate coverage.

It is a good idea to write descriptions before detailing the steps for each test. For each test write one to three sentences. Writing the descriptions forces you to think more about each test. Make sure to note any requirement problems or questions that you identify.

Each test should be simple enough to clearly succeed or fail. Ideally, the steps of a test are a simple sequence – set up the test situation, test with specific test inputs and verify the accuracy of the outputs.

Selecting test data is as important as defining the steps of the test. You should determine the set of all input values that can be entered for a given input parameter, and define valid and invalid input values.

Your testing should be evaluated in terms of specification coverage, rather than implementation coverage. Testing is more effective if you:

- set specific goals that are appropriate
- ensure good coverage
- prioritise the tasks
- write the tests in detail
- evaluate the tests in terms of the requirements.

Do not worry if you find errors – the purpose of testing is to find them. Testing should probably begin in the requirements phase, and there is a typical cycle:

- During the design phase, determine which aspects of your design can be tested.
- Determine within which parameters the tests work.
- Produce test scripts to use in testing.
- Test your work based on the plan.
- Report on any errors.
- Decide which faults should be treated, fixed or rejected.
- Once a fault has been dealt with, retest.

Portfolio Activity (AO7)

In order to be able to provide the software to Private Users, you must make sure that it meets their requirements and that it works as intended. You will test your database, but before you do so you need to create a test plan. First, decide how you will test each element and what you expect to happen when the test is carried out.

You may wish to create a backup copy before carrying out the testing to ensure that you have evidence of the improvements made.

1 Produce a test plan covering the following checks:
- Does the database meet the original design brief?
- Does the validation operate as expected?
- Does the user interface operate as specified?
- Do the forms operate as specified?
- Do the queries operate as specified?
- Do the reports operate as specified?
2 Carry out the tests and record each result.
3 If a test identifies any problems, make the changes needed to improve it and report your findings. If you do not identify any problems when testing, record this fact.

Pass – Candidates provide a **basic** test plan that covers **some** of the checks as outlined in the Knowledge, Understanding and Skills.

Merit – Candidates provide a test plan that covers **most** of the checks as outlined in the Knowledge, Understanding and Skills.

Distinction – Candidates provide a test plan that covers most of the checks as outlined in the Knowledge, Understanding and Skills. **Changes are made** as appropriate to the database.

AO8: Evaluate the database

Evaluate the database against user needs (purpose and audience) and data specification

Evaluation
Evaluation is the process of monitoring and gathering other information to make judgements about your project, then using it to make changes and improvements; in other words, the collection and systematic analysis of data.

The evaluation should be an examination of your work to see that it provides the solution that is required. You should make checks to ensure that it performs as expected and that the company is getting a product on which it can depend.

You need to produce an evaluation of your database. This evaluation must consider the purpose and audience that were defined by the user.

You will also need to consider if the defined user requirements have been met. An evaluation should cover each part of the purpose and user requirements with a description relating to whether it has been achieved and how it has been achieved.

Describe improvements needed for the user

Monitoring
Monitoring is the routine and systematic collection of information that will help to answer questions about your project. Use it to report on and evaluate your project. You are most likely to need information on your outputs, how activities are running and progress towards meeting objectives.

All systems can be improved. These improvements should be related to the performance of your database and the user. For example, in the database you have created you may have created static parameter queries based on the defined user requirements. An improvement, related to this, could be to change the static to dynamic queries. The suggested improvements should be relevant to, and useful for the user of your database.

Portfolio Activity (AO8)

Produce an evaluation report of the effectiveness of the database. It should be evaluated against the company needs outlined in the scenario and the functionality you specified in your design. The evaluation should include a critical analysis of the effectiveness of the solution and you should make suggestions for improvements.

1   Evaluate the database against the company's needs.
2   Ensure that the functionality of the database meets the specification.
3   Describe improvements needed for the user.

14 Cartooning and Animation

Learning outcomes

By working through this unit you will produce evidence to meet the unit assessment objectives. This will show that you understand how to:

- investigate the animation industry, its products and technology
- examine the animation and sequencing of a character and its surroundings
- plan the production of a cartoon or animation product
- develop a cartoon or animation character
- create a simple cartoon strip or animated film
- evaluate animation work.

Introduction

Cartooning and animation is a fascinating, exciting and enjoyable area of multimedia. To look at it at a basic level, it is storytelling with the addition of visual elements to enhance the narrative, make it more entertaining and portray the message more clearly.

You may think of cartoons as television programmes like *Tom and Jerry* or *The Simpsons* and animations as animated movies such as *Toy Story* or *Wall-E*. However, their use is much more ubiquitous and they can be found in many places. All computer games use animation, with each element such as characters, vehicles and parts of the environment being animated as separate objects. Advertisements on television also use animation, as do digital billboards such as those in Piccadilly Circus in London. Films also use animation, usually in the form of CGI (computer-generated imagery) where real life is merged with graphics, as in the *Lord of the Rings* series where Gollum was completely made with CGI. In addition, there is animation in places where you may not expect – many kitchen appliances, stereos and other digital appliances have animated displays; for example, a washing machine might use different moving pictures to show which part of the cycle it is currently doing.

Before each animated movie from the Pixar Studio is shown in cinemas, an animated short is shown (http://www.pixar.com/theater/shorts/index.html). This is often to showcase new ideas on which Pixar is working and harks back to earlier cinema where a short cartoon would be shown before the main feature.

A new animation studio, Animagination, is about to release their first animated feature film in cinemas around the world. They have asked you to produce an

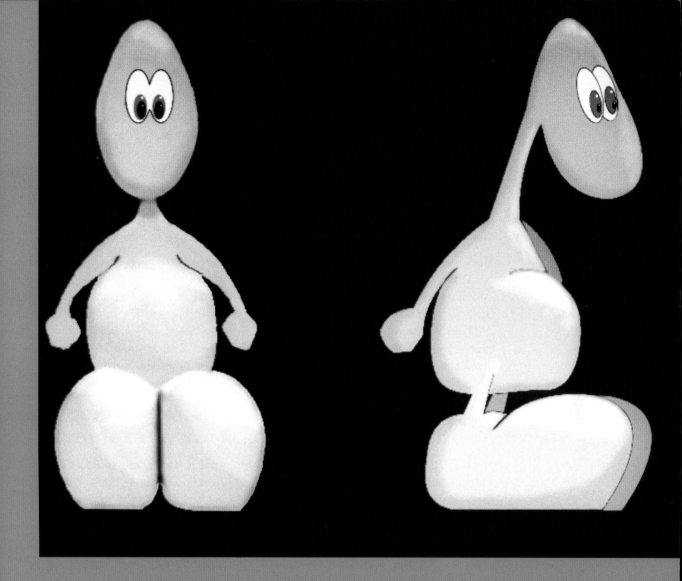

animated short to be shown before the film. They want you to create something which is visually appealing and, more importantly, tells the story of your main character. Your animation must be a minimum of 45 seconds, but can be longer if desired. You must keep accurate logs throughout the whole process, from initial sketches to the finished product. If Animagination likes it, they may even turn your short into their next feature film.

Scenario

Different types of animation

Animation is the translation of images across different dimensions. These are the spatial dimensions where the images can move around the screen and the essential dimension of time, which is the key to animating. By moving images across time, they are no longer still images but, when combined, become animation.

There are essentially two types of animation: 2D and 3D. Two dimensional moves across the X and Y dimensions and is essentially 'flat'. Examples of this include cartoons such as *The Simpsons*, where light and shade might be used but the characters and environments do not appear to have depth. Three dimensional works in three dimensions: X, Y and Z. Films such as *The Incredibles* (2004) use this method and the animation has a higher level of realism. However, 3D animation is more complicated to create and produce, and therefore takes more time and money.

Studios and their creations: well-known animated films and cartoon characters

The first 'animation' has been dated as 5200 years old; it is a painting of a goat on a bowl which, when spun, appears to be leaping. Animation became popular in the early 1800s when machines such as zoetropes could be spun and the images inside would appear to move. With the invention of film, many people began to create animations, one of the first being *Humorous Phases of Funny Faces* in 1906, where line drawings of faces morphed into new faces.

The early days of animation

The first animated popular character was Felix the Cat, who debuted in 1919 and was the creation of animator Otto Messmer. The last Felix cartoon was released in 1928 when the first Mickey Mouse cartoon was published. Created by chief animator Ub Iwerks for the Walt Disney Studio, Mickey Mouse has become a hugely popular character worldwide and is one of the most instantly recognisable brands. Three Mickey Mouse cartoons were released, but with the advent of the 'talkies' they were redrawn and re-released with new soundtracks added, including music and speech. *Steamboat Willie* (1928) became the precursor for modern day animated films.

Other popular cartoon characters developed in the 1930s included Betty Boop, Popeye and Superman, all by the Fleischer studio.

The Warner Bros Studio began in the early 1930s, and created the two series *Looney Tunes* and *Merrie Melodies*. It recruited two great animators: Tex Avery and Chuck Jones. During this period up to the 1950s, the characters of Daffy Duck, Bugs Bunny, Elmer Fudd, the Pink Panther, Road Runner and Wile E Coyote, Tweety Bird and Porky Pig were created. The studio's irreverent, zany style of animation is still seen as innovative and can be best seen in the cartoons *What's Opera Doc?* (1957) and *Duck Amuck* (1953).

The partnership of William Hanna and Joseph Barbera began in the late 1930s and they released their first cartoon in 1940 about a cat and mouse, for which they won an Oscar. They went on to make over 100 cartoons starring these characters, whom they named Tom and Jerry, and won many more Oscars. Other characters developed by Hanna–Barbera Productions include Huckleberry Hound, the Flintstones, Yogi Bear, the Jetsons, Scooby-Doo and the Smurfs.

The beginning of animated movies

The Walt Disney Studio, always innovative, continued to be pioneering as more and more studios began to develop cartoons. In 1937 they released their first full-length animated feature film, *Snow White and the Seven Dwarfs*. Although there had been two earlier attempts at animated feature films by other studios, this was the first to be commercially successful. During the four years it took to make, with a cost of $1.5 million, the papers nicknamed it 'Disney's Folly'. However, Disney had the last laugh when the film grossed $8 million and became the most successful film release of that year.

Disney continued to release animated feature films, including *Pinocchio* in 1940, *Dumbo* in 1941 and *Bambi* in 1942. However, it was their other release in 1940 which is seen as hugely ground-breaking: *Fantasia*. This film was highly experimental and involved seven animations set to classical music, including Mickey Mouse in *The Sorcerer's Apprentice*. *Fantasia* cost nearly four times as much as a live action film of the time, but it was too much before its time and was not a huge commercial success like *Snow White*. However, this was one of the turning points in animation history, and when *Fantasia/2000* was released on 1 January 2000, the film finally received the popular acclaim it deserved.

As animation became a popular and recognised method, more studios grew up and an increasing number of cartoons were released. During this time Disney not only continued releasing animated feature films, such as *Cinderella* (1950), *Lady and the Tramp* (1955) and *Sleeping Beauty* (1959), but also produced live action films. A notable example is *Mary Poppins* (1964) which includes a scene during the song 'Supercalifragilisticexpialidocious' where actors interact with animated characters. This would be later developed in the 1988 release *Who Framed Roger Rabbit*, as the whole movie is about 'toons' interacting with real people.

Modern animation

During the 1970s and 1980s a huge number of cartoons were created, becoming popular on Saturday morning television. These included *Teenage Mutant Ninja Turtles*, *Thundercats*, *The Care Bears*, *Dungeons and Dragons*, *My Little Pony*, *He-Man and the Masters of the Universe*, *She-Ra: Princess of Power* and *Transformers*. Similar cartoons which are currently produced include *SpongeBob SquarePants* and *Avatar: The Last Airbender*. However, although cartoons of this sort for young audiences remain very popular, they are not produced in the quantity that was seen in the 1980s.

Cartoons are now not only focusing on younger audiences, but are also being created for a more general audience or even adults only. *The Simpsons*, created by Matt Groening, is the longest-running television cartoon series, beginning in 1989; new episodes are still being released. Groening is also responsible for the series *Futurama*, a science-fiction animated series. Animations created for an older market include Trey Parker and Matt Stone's *South Park*, Seth MacFarlane's *Family Guy* and *American Dad*, and Mike Judge's and Greg Daniels' *King of the Hill*. Judge and Daniels were also responsible for the earlier *Beavis and Butthead* animation shorts on MTV.

Claymation

An area which should also be included in animation is claymation. The method has been used in television cartoons including *Pingu* and *Bob the Builder*, and in feature films such as the *Wallace and Gromit* films by Nick Park's Aardman Animations, and Tim Burton's *The Nightmare Before Christmas* (1993).

Anime

Animation in Japan has always been a popular art form. In contrast to Western audiences, who until recently considered animation to be solely for younger audiences, anime has always been created for a more general or adult audience. Starting with the popular *Astro Boy* television series in 1963, Japanese studios have produced a huge number of animation shorts, cartoons and feature films. A classic anime feature film which was released in Japan in 1988, called *Akira*, was influential in introducing Western audiences to anime when it was released in the UK and USA in the early 1990s. Since that point, anime has found a place in the Western market. A studio of significance is Studio Ghibli, which has produced some of the most renowned anime movies, including *Spirited Away* and *Princess Mononoke*.

Print cartoonists

Two print cartoonists who should also be considered are Carl Giles and Charles Schultz. Giles is the creator of a series of cartoons in the *Daily Express* featuring a family based around the matriarchal figure Grandma. Charles Schultz is the creator of the *Peanuts* cartoon series which has appeared in a number of newspapers; the central character Snoopy has become a major star in Western culture. Neither has the luxury of storytelling through movement and yet their main characters have become iconic.

Animation technology and software developments

Animation works in frames; each frame has a different image and playing them together at speed creates the illusion of movement. In traditional, hand-drawn animation each frame was drawn individually on a cel (an abbreviation of celluloid). Early animation would just play one cel after another on a film strip, whereas later animators would overlay cels to create an impression of depth, with each cel having an element of the scenery and characters.

Limited animation

Limited animation is a method of animation that became popular for cartoons which needed to be produced every week. This is where similar scenes or scenery are used again and again to reduce the amount of work needed to be done by the animators. For example, in *The Flintstones*, Fred could be running along a street and he may pass a house and a tree, then the same house and the same tree. The story is still being conveyed because it shows he is running a long way, but the same background cels are being reused.

Rotoscoping

Rotoscoping is where live actors perform and then animation is drawn over the top of them. The method was invented by Max Fleischer in 1915 and was used for the characters Betty Boop and Superman. Disney used the technique in *Snow White and the Seven Dwarfs*, *Cinderella* and in subsequent films. Rotoscoping is becoming even more popular as CGI techniques improve and has been used to create ultra-realistic films such as *The Polar Express* (2004) and *Beowulf* (2007).

Computer-generated imagery

Over the years, digital animation techniques have developed and they continue to produce increasingly more realistic animations. CGI (computer-generated imagery) and special effects allow films to go beyond the limits of real life and take actors and audiences to fantasy lands such as Mordor in *The Lord of the Rings* trilogy (2001–2003). It can also be used to create new characters such as the tentacled Davy Jones in *Pirates of the Caribbean* (2003). Also, quantity can be created in crowd scenes or for armies. This was famously used in the film *Gladiator* (2000) in the fighting arena, where a crowd of 2000 extras was turned into 35,000.

To create three-dimensional animation, a structure known as a wire-frame is created and a texture is wrapped around it to form the whole object or character. The more lines the wire structure has, the more variations are available for movement.

Stop motion animation involves a still camera taking single frame images and between each shot the image in front of it is moved. Types of stop motion include claymation and using cut-outs such as those used in early *South Park* cartoons.

Software tools

There are a huge variety of animation tools available at a wide variety of levels and prices.

- At the top end are professional-quality programmes such as 3D Studio Max and Maya, which are used in animated films and video games. They are expensive but produce extremely high-quality images and have an extensive range of tools.
- Other software is made for smaller studios, hobbyists and education, such as Caligari trueSpace. Blender is a free animation package released under the GNU general public licence.
- Adobe Flash is a very popular package and, unlike the others, is primarily for 2D animation. It is a good learning tool with a straightforward user interface and is also used to develop professional 2D animations and games which are often published on the Internet.

Portfolio Activity (AO1)

Animagination has asked to see your research to gauge your initial inspiration. This should be provided in writing to them with accompanying images to illustrate your points. You may wish to give examples in electronic form to show the animation.

1 Select at least five animators, either from those discussed or others of note. Research them and describe their history, including the studios for which they worked, the characters and animations they have made and the techniques they have used.
2 Describe the works of two print cartoonists and how their creations could influence your animation, even though produced in a different medium.
3 Choose at least four methods of animation and describe in detail how each works. Give at least one example of their use.
4 Describe software which is available to animators. Name at least three products and describe their purpose and uses, and how they are different from other packages.

Principles of movement and timing, including acceleration and fairings

Movement and timing are the essential components of animation. Both must be in harmony for them to have an effect on the audience and to convey the message or story.

There are 12 principles of animation which were developed by the animators at Disney Studios in the 1930s who were pioneers of animation techniques. These 12 principles which are still true of all animations are described below.

1: Squash and stretch

As an object moves, depending on the material from which it is made, it will not retain its shape but squash and stretch, especially if it comes into contact with another object. This is best demonstrated with a bouncing ball. If you draw a circle and a line for the ground and animate it so it moves up and down, it may be bouncing but it will not look realistic. Now try squashing it when it hits the ground and stretching it when it bounces back up. This gives it a much more realistic effect as the bounce has an effect on the ball. This effect should be used regularly in animation, especially for the movement of a character.

2: Anticipation

When something moves, generally it does not just start, but there are smaller movements that run up to the bigger movement. For example, a dancer making a jump does not just take off from the ground, but may lean backwards and swing their arms in preparation for the movement. This anticipation of the main movement will give a more realistic effect and also prepare the audience to anticipate the big move.

3: Staging

This is like the staging in a theatre. The characters, props and background should be synchronised so they are not competing or conflicting and should, moment by moment, progress and develop the story. Consider the placing of objects and characters and the pose of the characters themselves.

4: Straight ahead and pose to pose animation

These are the two methods of producing a sequence of frames.

- Straight ahead refers to the animator creating each frame in their real order. This can make the action dynamic and exciting, but there can also be problems in retaining proportions and realism.
- Pose to pose involves creating the main frames in a sequence then filling the intervals in later. This can give the animation less fluidity but, on the other hand, ensures that the key points of the sequence are drawn correctly.

Frames
Every animation consists of a series of images. If using celluloid film, these would be cels. In digital animation, each image is a frame. When the frames are played at speed, the animation appears, like in a flipbook.

Most animation will use a combination of both methods, especially with computer animation which can automatically fill in the intervals in pose to pose (although often an animator will want something more specific than what the computer will produce). These are known as tweens and will animate between two specified points.

5: Follow through and overlapping action

These refer to the fact that when something stops or changes direction, part of the object will continue moving. For example, if a character is running, if they stop sharp, their hair, clothes and some body parts will still keep moving from the momentum. If they change direction, these things will still move in the original direction for a split second before they catch up to the new course. The timing of these effects is crucial; too short or too long and they may become unrealistic or seem like a parody.

6: Slow-out and slow-in

These are also known as fairings or ease. Slowing down the animation or speeding it up can have different effects. For example, a character who is running may have a slow-in as he builds up speed, then the animation becomes extremely fast to show he is sprinting. In traditional animation this involved drawing more frames for the slower sequences and fewer frames for the fast ones.

In an animation package like Adobe Flash, tweens can have different eases, either slower or faster, and this will alter the number of frames that are drawn accordingly. This can further be demonstrated with the bouncing ball example (see page 255). As well as the stretch and squash, if the downward animation is faster than the upward animation, it can be shown that gravity is also having an effect on the ball and the resulting animation becomes increasingly realistic.

7: Arcs

Human and animal movements generally operate in arcs, rather than straight lines. For example, the swing of an arm or leg or the turn of a head all follow arcs and this can be replicated in animation for more realistic movement.

8: Secondary action

Movement of one part of an object is generally not in isolation but will have secondary associated actions. For example, if a character turns their head, their hair will also move. Consider a character walking: the primary movement will be the legs, but also the hands may swing, the head may turn and their clothes may flap behind them in the wind.

9: Timing

Timing in animation is crucial and there are two parts to it: physical movement and storytelling. In terms of physical movement, if a character jumps but they stay off the ground for too long, this will seem unrealistic. However, there is also the timing in terms of storytelling to consider. If a joke is cracked, comic timing is needed in order to make it work. If other emotions are being expressed, the timings should be considered to convey these properly. For example, if a character has just been told some bad news, you might hold the image a little longer for the news to sink in before moving on to the next sequence.

10: Exaggeration

Exaggeration in this sense is not necessarily creating something which is wild and outlandish, unless that is the desired effect. A perfect imitation of real life may seem a little staid, whereas a small amount of exaggeration can give it more vigour and interest.

11: Solid drawing

This refers to an animator understanding the principles of good drawing, even if with modern programs they do not carry out much drawing themselves. Composition, weight, balance, volume, light and shade give an animator a useful level of knowledge which can be applied to animations.

12: Appeal

Just as actors have charisma, animated characters should have appeal. This does not mean that the character should be cute or attractive, but there should be something which causes the audience to have an interest in the character and want to find out more.

Storyboards, bar sheets and log sheets

While you are planning the style of your animation, you should think about timing – how long each scene or segment will be and where timing should be used for effect. You may find that starting to create a storyboard, bar sheet and log sheet for your animation helps you to develop your concept. You can find further information on these techniques in AO3 (pages 258–260).

Portfolio Activity (AO2)

Animagination wants to make sure they have employed the best person for the job so they have asked you to describe your thoughts on animation and examples which have motivated you.

For each of the 12 principles of animation described above, explain what it means and find an example to demonstrate it. Include a screenshot and annotate it to explain how it works and the effect it produces.

Pass – Candidates demonstrate a **basic** understanding of the principles of character animation. They discuss movement and timing and how to apply them to storyboards, bar sheets and log sheets.

Merit – Candidates demonstrate a **sound** understanding of the principles of character animation. They **clearly** discuss movement and timing and how to accurately apply them to storyboards, bar sheets and log sheets.

Distinction – Candidates demonstrate a **comprehensive** understanding of the principles of character animation. They discuss **thoroughly** movement and timing and demonstrate a detailed knowledge of storyboards, bar sheet and log sheet production.

Assessment Guidance

Planning an animation

The first step in creating an animation is deciding what you will make – getting that first idea which will then be translated into a full animation. It may be that the character is designed first and the story fitted around them, or a specific genre might be desired or a certain location. Perhaps the story will have a moral or message which is to be conveyed, or perhaps it will tap into the trends of the day.

Aim

What is the purpose of the animation? Is it to entertain or is there a more serious reason for its creation? Is it advertising or promoting something or is it a piece of artistic expression? Deciding on and defining the aim of the animation gives it a focus which needs to be fulfilled by the final product.

Audience

The target market needs to be decided upon as this will set certain limits and lend certain freedoms. For example, an adult audience could allow a more hard-hitting story to be told, whereas a younger audience can permit more flights of fancy. Although an animation may be for everyone, you should aim towards a certain sector of the public. This could be defined by age, gender, interest or another attribute.

Initial ideas

Under no circumstances leave home without a notebook and a pencil, as you never know when you will get ideas. Initial ideas are generally rough sketches and notes jotted down as thoughts appear, and need to be captured before they are forgotten.

Once the initial ideas are on paper, they can then be fleshed out into fuller forms. For example, you could walk down the street and see an enthusiastic dog taking its owner for a walk, of which you make a note. Later, you could start to sketch the dog more fully and think of what mischief he can get into, thereby forming the bare bones of the storyline.

Characters and storyline

It may be that you have produced several initial ideas. Now is the time to choose one and develop it further. The character should acquire a personality. Are they nice or nasty? What are they trying to achieve? These things can be shown very quickly, which is especially important in an animated short. The character could be portrayed through their clothes, their posture or the environment around them when they are on screen. For example, in traditional cartoons, to quickly portray good and evil, the 'goodies' appear in bright colours and are introduced in locations where the sun is shining, whereas the 'baddies' appear in blacks, greys and browns and their surroundings are cold, wet or dark, often with lightning.

The storyline should also be developed and you should know where it is going. A typical story has a beginning, middle and end, although they do not necessarily have to come in that order. However, there must be a starting point and a finishing point, with events in the middle which make the audience want to keep watching and find out what happens. Some sort of conflict or problem should occur and be resolved or solved by the end.

Let's take our dog taking its owner for a walk as an example. The start would set up the scene: it's a sunny day, the owner is admiring the view, the dog is bounding along with a mischievous glint in its eye. Then the purpose of the dog could be revealed: an ice cream truck drives past and the dog begins to chase after it. The conflict is the will and strength of the dog versus the owner trying to keep the dog under control. The resolution could be that the dog escapes and reaches the ice cream truck, only to find that it needs its owner to buy an ice cream, and the owner does because he loves his dog.

Type of animation

The choice of the type of animation to be used could be crucial to whether the plan needs to be changed, as some types will have limitations which others do not. For example, a 2D animation program will not easily allow the audience to see all around an object and it would be time-consuming to draw it from each angle. Claymation is very difficult to make as realistic as digital animation. The choice might also depend on the budget of the studio, the expertise of the animator and the time available to complete the product.

Design documents

When animating it is important to first of all design what you will create and then keep these documents up to date as you progress through the project. Animation cannot be created on the fly, as proportions will be lost and the narrative of the story will not be as effective.

Produce a storyboard

Once the initial ideas and sketches have been made, a storyboard is the first port of call to put down ideas in the order in which they will appear in the animation. Generally, the first storyboard will have the key moments of the sequences drawn, while a later storyboard will have more detail.

Storyboard

A storyboard is a series of boxes, often six per page if using A4, and in each box a frame from the animation is drawn. These drawings could be very rough or in detail, depending on the art skills of the designer and the development stage of the idea; they could even be photographs if this is an appropriate method. Each box should be numbered in order and underneath there should be comments. These comments can include the characters and objects involved, the action which will take place, the effects to be used and any dialogue, sound effects or music to be played. They should also describe or explain any transitions between sequences, for example whether the action just moves straight to a different place or whether there is a moment of black in between.

Bar sheets

A bar sheet is very similar to a storyboard but also adds the number of frames for each image. This usually means that a bar sheet is drawn in more detail than a storyboard. The purpose of a bar sheet is to show the sequence and how it relates to the timing of the animation.

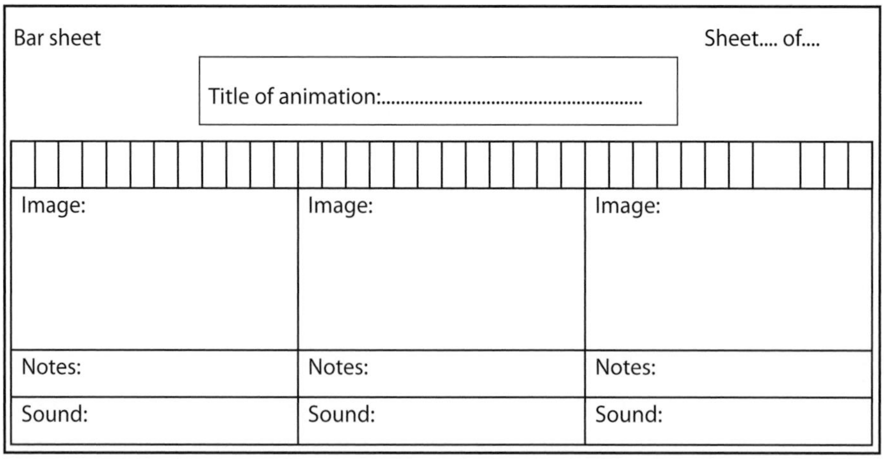

Bar sheet		Sheet.... of....
Title of animation:...		
Image:	Image:	Image:
Notes:	Notes:	Notes:
Sound:	Sound:	Sound:

Figure 14.1 Example of a bar sheet

In the example above, the bar sheet has twelve frames per image. This would be useful to show animations run at 12 frames per second or a multiple of 12. The sheet can be altered to show different numbers of frames per image.

Log sheets

Log sheets take the planning of the timing in the animation one step further and indicate at what point in real time each frame takes place. For example, in a quick sequence each frame may take a quarter of a second, so that four frames occur during the first second, whereas an image which is held still on screen may last for several seconds.

Frame	Real time	Layer	Assets	Actions	Sounds	Notes
1	00:00					
2						
3						
4						
5						
6						
7						
8						
9						
10						
11						
12						
13						
14						
15						
16						
17						

Title of animation:..

Figure 14.2 Example of a log sheet

Portfolio Activity (AO2/3)

Animagination is happy with what you have shown them so far and is ready for you to start designing your short animation.

1 Define, in writing, the aim and audience of your animation.
2 Sketch the initial ideas for your character and any other significant characters, objects or environments. These could be created by hand or on computer.
3 Draw your main character in more detail and annotate it to explain each part.
4 Write your storyline in detail.
5 Decide on the type of animation and explain your choice.
6 Create a detailed storyboard for your animation with very clear notes for each image describing:
   - content of the animation
   - text
   - images
   - sound
   - video
   - timing
   - transitions
   - effects.
7 Create detailed bar sheets for your animation with very clear notes.
8 Create detailed log sheets for your animation with very clear notes.

AO4: Develop a cartoon or animation character

Physicality

Deciding on the physical characteristics of a character can be difficult, as they need to fulfil a wide range of criteria. Primarily a character should be original and should not closely resemble any existing character. There also needs to be enough scope in the character to have different poses and expressions. This is increasingly difficult, although not impossible, when using animals or robots as characters.

It is vital that your characters maintain the interest of the audience and convey the right emotion to them. The audience should be able to empathise with the protagonist and get behind them, willing them on to succeed. They should also be able to recognise the antagonist and other supporting characters, who should not look too similar so they are identifiable.

The way characters look is hugely varied, more so than in live action as the only limit on animated character is imagination. Some characters are very 'cartoony', such as those in *The Incredibles* (2004) where proportion is used to give an instant impression of the character. Mr Incredible is hugely muscular, although his legs are very much out of proportion, showing that he has great physical strength but perhaps not much speed.

Just as when they meet people in real life, audiences make judgements based on appearance and body language. Animators can use this tendency to quickly convey to the audience the traits of the character.

Personality

The most typical way to convey personality in a character is by facial expression. Standard facial expressions include happy, sad and angry, but consider other emotional reactions such as surprise, terror, grief, eagerness or mistrust.

Figure 14.3 The expression used can give more meaning to dialogue

Usually animators will design the original face with a basic expression – the one in which their face naturally falls. They will then redraw the face many times, each with a different expression. In computer animation, this becomes much simpler as the basic head shape can be copied and only the expression needs to be redrawn. As the animation is created, these different heads can be used when needed. A similar method is used in claymation, where many heads with different expressions are made.

Not only does the storyline for the animation need to be written, but it is also helpful to write a character outline for the protagonist. This will outline their back story (where they have come from), their current situation (the conflict or problem) and their personal journey. Will they change in some way by the end of the animation? Will they change their ways, or will they just become happy or sad because of the outcome?

Portfolio Activity (AO4)

Animagination is very character orientated and would like to see the main character that you have created and are developing.

1   Show an initial basic sketch of your main character. This can be hand-drawn or a digital image.
2   Show at least two developmental digital images of your main character. Annotate each to show what has been changed and any future alterations you plan to make.
3   Show a final digital image of your character. Annotate it to explain your reasoning for each part of your design.
4   Show at least five facial expressions for your character demonstrating diverse emotions.
5   Write a description of your character in words. Describe their:
   - physical features
   - personality.

   For each attribute of your character explain how your design demonstrates this.

Assessment Guidance

Pass – The candidate develops, at a **simple** level, a new cartoon character from initial sketches through to finished drawings. The character functions at a **low level** of personality but may lack attention to fine detail. Candidates are able to develop a character at a **basic** level and are able to place the character in a **simple** narrative.

Merit – The candidate designs a **new** cartoon/animation character from initial sketches through to finished drawings. They show a **well-developed** sense of style and characterisation. The character functions at an **effective** level making it believable to the viewer. The candidate shows **good** knowledge of the features that make up a cartoon/animation character, ranging from the concept and development of a character through to placing that character within a story.

Distinction – The candidate designs a **new** animation/cartoon character from initial sketches through to finished drawings. They show a level of **professionalism** in the development process. The progression from initial sketches through character development to final drawings displays a **well-rounded** character that displays a range of expression and emotion. The candidate has a **detailed** appreciation of the sum parts of a cartoon or animation character and has described the character's elemental make up in a detailed manner.

AO5: Use tools and features to create a simple cartoon strip or animated film

Keep records of the production

Throughout the production it is important to keep all documents up to date, including storyboards, bar sheets and log sheets. There will be changes as the animation is made, but if the documents are updated when these changes occur, the animator can keep track of alterations and ensure there are no problems such as continuity errors throughout the animation. Additionally, if the animator is working in a team, all team members will be referring to the same documents and they can take on board changes as and when they occur.

Tools and features

Physical hand drawing skills

Although computer packages do provide the facilities to create all the graphics for the animation digitally, a lot of artists still prefer to create the elements for their animations by hand. These can be scanned into the computer and then, if desired, can be traced over in a graphics package or straight into the animation package.

Graphics library

There are also graphics libraries from which images can be obtained. For example, if trees are needed for the background, there is no point drawing them all from scratch if they already exist somewhere else. There are stock image libraries such as GettyImages or Stock.XCHNG which provide images, mostly photographic. Some can be obtained for free – these are classed as royalty free. Others are available to subscribers for a fee. In the animation industry, copyright is an issue which is fiercely guarded, so when using non-original images, make sure you have the right to use them.

Animation software tools

The following tools are generally available in most animation programs.

Tool	Use
Pencil	Allows freehand drawing with a thin line
Brush	Allows painting with a brush with definable thickness
Line	Draws a straight line
Shape	Draws rectangles, ovals or other predefined shapes
Text	Adds text
Fill	Fills an object with colour (all outer lines must fully join)
Erase	Rubs out an area to the background colour, whether that has been set to transparent, white or a colour
Pen	Draws precise lines and either straight or flowing curves
Eyedropper	Selects a colour currently on the screen and puts it into the palette to be used
Selection	Selects an area of the image, either a circle, square or lasso which can be any size or shape area; the selected area can then be altered, copied or affected in some way
Transform	Alters the image by stretching it, skewing it or modifying it in some other way

Figure 14.4 Commonly used animation software tools

Layers

Layers are separate elements of an image which can be laid over each other.

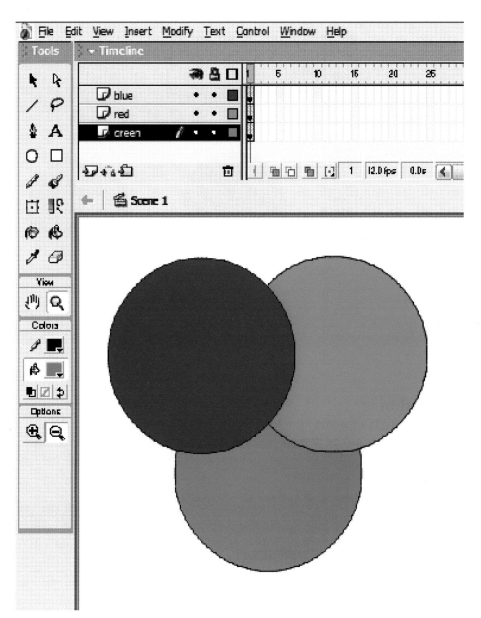

Figure 14.5 Layers can overlap to create a composite image

Timeline and frames

A timeline is a visual representation of the sequence of events. It is broken into frames, and keyframes are those on which an action occurs.

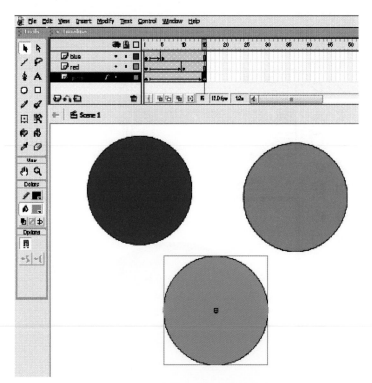

Figure 14.6
Keyframes
on a timeline
with tweens

Onion skin

Onion skinning is a method in which previous frames are shown transparently so that future frames can be drawn correctly. This can ensure that each object and character drawing remains in proportion. It also allows straight ahead animation to be carried out with fewer errors.

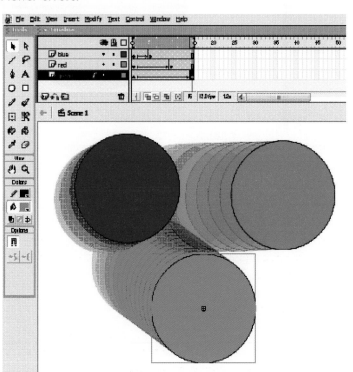

Figure 14.7
Onion skinning
shows previous
frames
transparently

Portfolio Activity (AO5)

Animagination has approved all of your designs and you are now ready to create your animation. Make sure you do it to the best of your ability and ensure the final product is as flawless as possible.

1. Make your animation. As you do so, update copies of your storyboard, bar sheets and log sheets to reflect any changes you make (do not alter the originals in your design documents).
2. Keep a production diary as you create your animation. Use annotated screenshots to show the variety of tools you have used (at least five). Explain any changes you make to your original design and explain your reasons. It should be added to each time you work on your animation.
3. Once the animation is completed, test it thoroughly and make refinements as required.

AO6: Evaluate the animation work

Evaluation

An evaluation of the completed product and the process through which it went to reach its final form is important so that you, as an animator, can learn, develop and improve. You should see the evaluation as an opportunity to highlight the things which are good about your animation, but also those which did not turn out the way you intended and to explain why that is the case.

Technical quality

The first area to look at is the technical quality of the animation. Is it well made? Are timings used appropriately? Is the movement suitable for the character? Have the principles of animation been applied?

Creative quality

This refers to the storyline and character. Can the audience believe in the character? Will they find watching the animation interesting? Does it fulfil the original aim which you outlined at the beginning, perhaps conveying a particular message?

Appeal to target audience

Having defined a target audience at the beginning, is the product still suitable and appropriate for this group of people? Will they want to watch the animation?

Software and techniques used

Has full use been made of the tools available in the software? Was it the right choice of animation method for this product?

Compare with professional animations

Having completed your animation it is useful to compare it with professional animations which already exist. You should choose the comparison wisely – there is no point comparing a 3D animation of aliens in space with an episode of *The Simpsons* as the dissimilarities are too vast. Try to find a similar character or style of animation with which to compare your work. You may find some suitable animations on the Internet, for example at www.homestarrunner.com and www.weebls-stuff.com.

Peer feedback

Show your animation to other students in your class and ask them for their opinions. This should help you shape your own evaluation and you may find that they have different opinions from yourself. This is because you are very close to the work and have seen it from the initial ideas stage right to the final product. By obtaining opinions from those who have only seen the final product, you get a more true overall opinion of the product, as an audience will only ever see the final product, not the work that has gone on before.

Suggest improvements

Finally, suggest some improvements to both your final product and the process through which it was created. Could the timings be more accurate? Could you have used sound more appropriately? Could the storyline have more structure? Perhaps you could manage your time better.

Portfolio Activity (AO6)

Now your animation is complete, Animagination would like you to screen it for them to ensure it is suitable to be shown in front of their feature film in cinemas.

1 Screen your animation for your peers and others. Obtain feedback from your audience in terms of the storyline, characters and quality of the animation.
2 Evaluate your animation in terms of:
   a) technical quality
   b) creative quality
   c) appeal to target audience (referring back to your design)
   d) software and techniques used.
   For each part of your evaluation, refer to the feedback which you obtained from your audience and give your own opinion.
3 Select a suitable existing animation and compare your work with it. Do so in terms of the style of animation used, the main character and the storyline. Comment on the similarities and differences. You may also wish to say whether your animation is at or near professional standard.
4 Suggest at least five improvements you could have made to your animation. Explain what effects these would have on the final product.
5 Suggest at least three improvements you could have made to the process of creating your animation. Explain what effects these would have on the project and on the final product.

Assessment Guidance

Pass – Candidates produce a **basic** evaluation. It focuses on the end product. Feedback is sought and recorded. **Some** improvements are identified.

Merit – Candidates produce a **detailed** evaluation. It covers the end product, the processes involved and the technical aspects of the finished product. Feedback is sought and recorded. Some **valid** improvements are suggested.

Distinction – Candidates produce a **comprehensive** evaluation. It covers the end product, the processes involved and the creative and technical aspects of the finished product. Feedback is sought and recorded. A **range** of valid improvements are suggested, along with detailed notes on how they could be implemented.

Learning outcomes

By working through this unit you will produce evidence to meet the unit assessment objectives. This will show that you understand how to:

■ demonstrate an understanding of programming principles and analyse game-specific code examples

■ describe professional programming languages and development tools and entry level systems for hobbyists

■ demonstrate an understanding of games programming practice and specialist areas

■ describe the principles and practice of game prototyping and small-scale development using authoring tools, game authoring systems and games modifications

■ specify and plan a simple game demonstration using a game authoring system or simple programming language

■ produce a simple working game demonstration, using a game authoring system or basic programming language.

Introduction

There are a number of different software applications referred to in this unit. It is not necessary to use any or all of them, but the more experience you gain, the wider your breadth of knowledge. Projects can be created in a general programming or scripting language, or a game-specific language or environment. It is not necessary to use professional level tools and DarkBasic and BlitzBasic would be suitable.

Programming is a fundamental part of all games. It is the element that ties together all the artwork, storyline, dialogue, inputs and outputs.

Think about a simple game like *Tetris*. The programmer will need to have created code to randomly select a new piece, tell it how to move down the screen, how to rotate as a result of a keypress, drop faster when required, land when it touches the other pieces, know when a line has been created, add points to the score total, and numerous other actions. The computer does not know how to do any of these things until the programmer tells it using code. Now consider a modern computer game, and the role of the programmer and the scale of their importance become clear. Players may comment on the graphics, the sound and other aspects of the game, but rarely on the programming. If it has been programmed well, it should be invisible – it is only when there are bugs that it becomes noticeable for the wrong reasons.

HIGH SCORE
460   1240

You have been employed by a new independent studio which is looking to break into the casual games market. Casual games are those which are relatively simple to play and do not require time commitment, unlike larger games. This market has become increasingly popular due to the introduction of Nintendo DS, Wii and Xbox Live Marketplace. Casual games on the Internet, such as Flash games, have always been popular. Even the free games which are bundled with the Windows operating systems are popular, *Minesweeper* having become quite iconic in status.

The studio is planning to hire more programmers as they expand and would like many of these to be recent university graduates. These graduate programmers may have the talent but be lacking in experience. The studio has asked you to compile a handbook on the fundamentals of games programming which will help them when they start work at the studio.

Once the handbook is complete, they would like you to start work on their first game which will go on the market. They are aiming to release it on the Internet, with a view to selling the rights to Nintendo, Sony or Microsoft in the future.

Key principles of the game include:

- it must be easy to play, requiring few instructions
- it will have quite simple graphics
- it will be challenging to the player and not require a great deal of time to complete.

Comparable games include *Snake*, *Zookeeper* and *Pacman*.

Scenario

Generalised programming

There are numerous programming languages available, each with their own words, syntax, style and purpose, but they all share certain principles. This means that when you have learned one programming language, it is easier to learn more.

Process analysis, including inputs and outputs

All programs are written to do something. Their purpose may be to perform a calculation or to run a computer game, but all programs will perform a task, also known as a process.

All programs take the following structure.

Figure 16.1 All programs use input → process → output

The input includes user controls such as keyboard, mouse, game controller, voice and so on. It will also include data from the user, computer or other programs.

The output may be on-screen, printed or in another form such as sound from speakers. An output could also be an event on-screen such as a character moving.

The process is the programmed code which understands the input and produces the output.

Figure 16.2 Using the controller affects the character on-screen

Data structures

Programs need to store data at some time during the execution of processes. Data is held in variables which are named containers for each piece of data. For example, if the game starts by asking for the player's name, the variable may be called PlayerName and contain the value 'Simon'. This would then be stored and could be used throughout the game: 'Would you like to save your game, Simon?'

Each variable must be given a name so it can be referred to again and again throughout the program. It should be something that is recognisable because what 'variable1' is, for example, would soon be forgotten in a substantial piece of code. Variable names cannot be the same as code words such as 'print' or 'run' (depending on the language being used); they must start with a letter and should not contain spaces.

Algorithms

Every program is made up of sets of algorithms. These are the individual chunks of code which each carry out a process. When the algorithms are combined the whole game is formed.

A common algorithm in games creation is a 'game loop'. This is code which controls the actions that are carried out when there is no input from the user. Ordinary programs like a word processor will not do anything when there is no user input; they will just wait for the next command. However, a game must keep running constantly, therefore a game loop runs constantly in the background of a game and is established when there is a pause in the input. This could just be to keep the environment active, such as a waterfall that keeps flowing or trees that keep rustling in the wind; some involve the character making a reminder movement to the user. This could be humorous, such as the character scratching themselves, or an appropriate movement for the character, such as swinging their sword as though practising. These movements not only remind the player that the character is waiting but also send out the message that the game has not crashed and is still running, even though the player is not currently making an input.

Control structures

Programs, especially computer games, are usually not linear; they are not carried out sequentially but jump around the code as different parts are needed. It is not always possible to predict what the user will do, therefore good programming allows the user the freedom to do what they like and the code will react appropriately. For example, the game might expect the player to drive the car down the road during the race. The player, however, might choose to turn the car round and go the wrong way, or drive off the road and into a field. The code needs to be flexible to allow these things to happen, even if simply to tell the player that they have gone the wrong way. Not only should the code allow this movement to other parts of the code, it should also allow smooth transition back to where the player was before, for example back on the road driving in the right direction.

Control structures are essentially the navigation system in the code that allow different sections to be called on when necessary. This is often done by having a core section of code which runs in a linear fashion throughout and holding each activity in functions which are separate and can be called upon at any time.

The structure of games

The structure of games can be very important and determine how a programmer will approach the construction of their code.

Linear games follow a written storyline and are fairly restrictive to the player. They may give the player some freedom over movement, but will not let them progress without having completed a previous part. This is often done with levels, but modern games are demonstrating a linear structure without using levelling.

Sandbox games are defined as open-ended, although this can take several forms. Usually this means that a player can roam around the environment and choose which tasks and missions they will carry out and in which order. Games which are close to true sandbox allow the player a huge amount of freedom. For example, in *Dead Rising* almost any object can be picked up and used as a weapon. However, also in that game the storyline is quite linear as certain parts will only be opened up once a player has completed particular parts of the game.

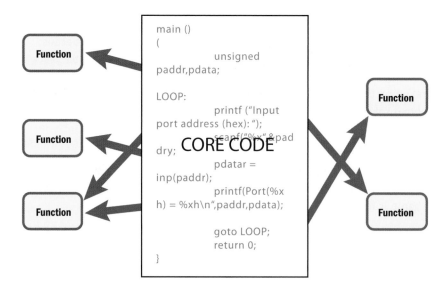

Figure 16.3 The code will call in functions which can be used over and over again

Good programming practice

It is important to write your code in a manner that will easily be understood by you and others, especially if working in a team of programmers. Your aim should be to write as little code as possible to perform the desired function. This makes the whole program simpler and, therefore, easier to read through when debugging it later.

Programs use variables to store data and each one can be given a name. These should be sensible names which you will be able to recognise later. If you call your variables a, b, c or number1, number2, number3 when creating a substantial program, you are very likely to forget what each variable name refers to.

All sizeable programming languages use conditional and reiterating code such as IFs and loops. These can be embedded into each other and can get quite complex. If each one is indented to a different point from the left margin, it is much simpler to identify which segment of code performs which action.

It is also good practice to include comments in your code, and this facility is provided in programming languages. Comments are entries into the code which are ignored when the code is run and, therefore, notes can be added to explain the code or remind the programmer of the functionality of each part.

Portfolio Activity (AO1)

For your handbook, explain the fundamental principles of programming.

1 Explain the following areas:
   a) process analysis, including inputs and outputs
   b) data structures
   c) algorithms
   d) control structures
   e) good programming practice.

2 For each area, give a range of examples from existing games.

3 Obtain the code for a simple game and annotate it to explain the processes which are occurring.

Pass – Candidates demonstrate a **basic** understanding of programming principles. They use **limited** game-specific examples.

Merit – Candidates demonstrate a **detailed** understanding of programming principles. They **analyse** a simple game sequence and **describe** the underlying programming processes which make it work. They use a **range** of game-specific examples.

Distinction – Candidates demonstrate an **in-depth** understanding and practical knowledge of programming principles and practice. They **analyse** events and processes from existing games with comprehensive clarity. They use a **wide range** of game-specific examples.

AO2: Describe professional programming languages and development tools, and entry level systems for hobbyists

Professional languages

There are hundreds of programming languages available for use, but only a handful will be able to provide the huge range of functionality required to create sizeable computer games. Of these, only a few are used professionally. This is based on their flexibility, use and reliability.

When there is a limited amount of programming languages in use, it means that those in the industry only need to know a few. For example, it would not be unusual for a games programmer to be fluent in only one or two languages but be highly proficient in these; comparable to a web designer who may be able to use seven or more.

High- and low-level languages

Programming language generally falls into two categories: high-level and low-level, although recently there has been a trend in creating very high-level languages (VHLL).

- High-level languages are very similar to English and relatively straightforward to learn because of this.
- Low-level languages are, in contrast, very close to 'computer language'.

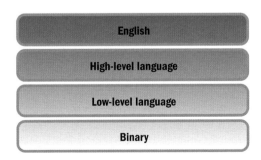

Figure 16.4 Low- and high-level languages

High-level languages

C was created in 1972. It has been a very influential programming language and has become the base of many other languages, including C++ and Java. C++, developed in 1979 and in full release by 1983, was designed as a general purpose language, but is often regarded as crucial to games programming and underpins a large proportion of modern games. Java was released in 1995 and is considered a more stable language than C++. Although heavily influenced by C++, Java is not particularly suitable for console programming.

'Hello World' is a classic introductory program which is often the first piece of code taught to novice programmers. The purpose is to display the phrase 'Hello World' on-screen.

```
C:                        C++:                      Java:
#include <stdio.          #include                  class HelloWorld {
h>                        <iostream.h>              public static void
main()                    main()                    main
{printf ("Hello           {cout << "Hello           (String args[]) {
World!\n");}              World!";}                 System.out.
                                                    print("Hello
                                                    World");
                                                    }
                                                    }
```

Figure 16.5 The 'Hello World' program in C, C++ and Java

Graphic API

A graphic API (application programming interface) is a transparent layer of code which allows other code or hardware to connect and use its facilities. (For more information on graphic APIs, see Unit 18: Computer Games Technology, page 322.) In terms of programming, graphic APIs are considered to be high level and could, for example, be used to run a routine to access a user's graphics processor.

Low-level languages

Assembly Language is generally regarded as the lowest-level programming language, meaning that the wording is less like English but does execute more quickly. It 'speaks' directly to the CPU, which means it is executed faster but is much more unwieldy and cumbersome to use to program. There are different types of assembly language for different types of processors, but all are similar in that they use short mnemonics as instructions.

Most games are created in high-level languages but low-level languages are still very useful. For example, when programming a flight simulator which needs precise and exact measurements and responses, a high-level language might give a slight delay as the code is compiled and executed, whereas because the low-level language 'speaks' directly to the CPU, this delay is eliminated. Also, these languages are used in the equipment itself, such as games consoles and mobile phones where commands are hard-coded directly into the components.

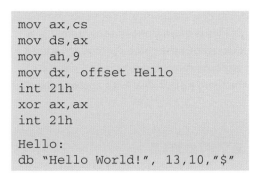

```
mov ax,cs
mov ds,ax
mov ah,9
mov dx, offset Hello
int 21h
xor ax,ax
int 21h

Hello:
db "Hello World!", 13,10,"$"
```

Figure 16.6 The 'Hello World' program in Assembly Language

High-level	Low-level
Similar to English	Less similar to English
Easier to learn	More difficult to learn
Takes time to compile or interpret to be run	Can be compiled or interpreted very quickly to be run
Creates a relatively large file	Creates a relatively small file
Includes C, C++, Java	Includes Assembly Language

Figure 16.7 Comparison of high- and low-level languages

Compilers and interpreters
Code has to be converted into a form the computer will understand before it is run e.g. from English to binary. A compiler will convert all the code before it executes. An interpreter will convert one line at a time as it executes.

Development tools

As well as pure coding, which is generally written manually, there are several tools available to help with the development of computer games. These are generally not made by external software houses such as Adobe, but by studios and teams in the games industry. As a consequence, the tools are very specific to games development and are often named after the game on which they are based, such as *Unreal* or *Half-Life*. The purpose of the development tools is to make tedious, monotonous, time-consuming jobs much simpler and faster, so developers can concentrate on the more important parts of the game. A tool which does this is TreeGenerator which, as its name suggests, creates many trees for scenery which would otherwise take several hours.

Level editors

The purpose of level editors is to provide all the tools needed to create fully operational levels, including environments, environmental controls, object control and, essentially, an engine to allow all parts of the game to function. All that needs to be added are the assets such as characters, objects and, if designed, a skin to change the look of the environment. The issue is that level editors do restrict the individuality of the game somewhat. For example, using the Quake engine will create other FPS (first person shooter) games.

3D-modelling systems and graphics editors

Most modern games employ three-dimensional environments, and these not only have to be created graphically but also need to be programmed. Graphic APIs are programmed to be able to access the graphics hardware on the computer or console. Rendering is the process of translating a model into a complete asset and applying texture, lighting and other effects. This is often done in programming, as these are factors which need to change throughout the game. As modern games improve in graphics quality, these effects become more important and difficult; recent games now have one person on the team just to deal with applying dynamic lighting to all assets in the game.

Simpler integrated systems

In addition to professional programming languages, there are also simpler systems available which will provide a similar level of functionality, although a lesser amount of control and flexibility is the price of the simplicity. These systems often come with their own programming environment which allows less complex development. They are mostly used by hobbyist games developers or to train games programmers in colleges and universities.

Two popular integrated systems are DarkBasic and BlitzBasic. DarkBasic is published by The GameCreators and BlitzBasic by Blitz Research Ltd. They are based on the BASIC programming language, which also underpins Visual Basic, and are therefore relatively straightforward to learn and good for beginners. DarkBasic is released alongside several other packages which can add on to a game created in that language, such as graphics and sound, but is available for Windows only. BlitzBasic is a cross-platform system which includes Apple and Linux. They are very similar in price and often choice between them is based on personal preference.

Find out more about DarkBasic at www.thegamecreators.com and about BlitzBasic at www.blitzbasic.com.

Portfolio Activity (AO2)

For your handbook, describe and compare programming languages and tools.

1 Describe the difference between high-level and low-level programming languages, giving examples and reasons for use.
2 Describe, in detail, two high-level programming languages and create a small code example of each to compare.
3 Describe, in detail, two low-level programming languages and create a small code example of each to compare.
4 Compare the languages used by hobbyists and those used professionally in the games industry. Identify the strengths and weaknesses of both.
5 Describe a range of development tools, including level editors, 3D modelling systems and graphics editors, giving examples. Compare those used by hobbyists and those used professionally in the games industry.

Pass – Candidates produce evidence of their **basic** knowledge of programming languages and tools used in computer game programming. Their descriptions **may not** be fully accurate.

Merit – Candidates **describe** and **discuss** professional games programming practice, demonstrating knowledge of the programming languages and toolsets used at professional and hobbyist level. Candidates demonstrate a **good** understanding of the difference between high- and low-level languages and their relationship and deployment in games programming.

Distinction – Candidates describe and discuss professional games programming practice, demonstrating an **in-depth** knowledge of the programming languages and toolsets used at professional and hobbyist level. Candidates demonstrate a **comprehensive** understanding of the difference between high- and low-level languages and where each is best deployed. They will **compare** and **contrast** different hobbyist and semi-professional languages and **analyse** the strengths and weaknesses of each.

AO3: Demonstrate an understanding of games programming practice and specialist areas

Programming as a part of the games development process

During the design phase, programmers need to be included to ensure that what is being planned is feasible in terms of coding. If an idea will be impossible to code, it can be altered at design, before it goes too far though the development process.

Once the design phase is completed, all teams in the games studio begin the production process during which the game is created. The programming team is somewhat restricted, however, as they need to wait for assets from the other teams to incorporate into the program.

While the assets are being created, the programmers are able to spend time building the infrastructure for the game, or adapting it if using an existing engine. They may also use 'fake assets' as placeholders which will mimic the real assets until they are available or until drafts are available. For example, if they know a character will be 300 pixels by 100 pixels, then can use an appropriate shape to represent the character until the real one is completed.

At the testing phase, the programmer should again be involved as they will be able to debug the program, especially if they have clear feedback from testers or focus groups.

Assets
Assets are all the elements which are used to create a game, including graphics, animation, sound, video and anything else which is to be incorporated into the program.

Specialist game programming areas

As games development is a highly complex process, very often developers will specialise in one or two areas. This can allow a team to be built with the specialism needed.

Graphics

Once the graphical assets have been created, they are passed over to the programming team who will bring them to life. Three dimensional models will be rendered to add texture and lighting. Graphic APIs are created to allow the game to make use of the technology in the graphics card of the computer or console. The art team usually includes animators who will allow characters to perform their basic functions, for example walk, run, pick up, crouch, jump and so on. The programmers will need to put these movements into the environment and coordinate them. For example, when the character walks, make them traverse through the environment; when they run, create the effect that they are moving through the environment even faster.

Artificial intelligence (AI)

AI is where the software controls sentient beings. These are often other characters known as non-player characters (NPCs). These could be enemies or helper characters.

Programming is key to creating AI and uses logic to do so. Logic involves the computer making deductions from the data being inputted. Early computer games had NPCs which would have a set pattern of moves, such as the ghosts in *Pacman*. As games became bigger, a simulated form of AI became popular, but it was just that NPCs had a larger range of patterns and could to some extent choose the pattern based on the player's moves, such as in *Magic Pockets* on Atari and Amiga.

Modern games, which have a massively increased amount of code controlling them, have true AI. This is done with complex logic. NPC movements react to player actions. In addition, they are beginning to be able to truly think for themselves. For example, in *F.E.A.R.*, enemies can distribute themselves around the environment and ambush or flank a player; in *Gears of War 2,* the Locust Horde are able to swarm like a well-trained army, each with its own control and awareness of environment and other NPCs, allowing more enemies to be in the game and making the games themselves more challenging and exciting.

Physics

Physics is a hugely important area of computer game programming. Early games had very simple physics, if any, but a great many modern games aim towards greater realism, and physics is crucial to this.

The area that is mostly thought about in physics is gravity. This not only holds the character to the ground, preventing them from floating away, but also has an effect on their movement, especially jumping. This is also an area which can be altered to distort reality, such as in *Crackdown* where gravity in jumping is lessened so the player feels as though they have the super-human ability to jump extremely high.

Ragdoll physics is where the bone structure of a body is accurately represented. For example, if a human character falls, they will not fall as one solid lump, but the body will crumple as it would do in real life, adding realism to the game.

A fairly early experiment in this field can be found at http://secretexit.com/games/stairdismount; the aim of *Stair Dismount* is to cause maximum damage to the character. This program has won awards for its innovation and is still under development to improve the underlying programming. An extension from this which is being developed in games like *Grand Theft Auto* is that a human character will fall in the correct way depending on how and where they have been hurt. For example, a person who is shot in the leg will fall differently from a character that has been stabbed in the back.

Audio

Sound in a game is vitally important in creating the immersive atmosphere. Try playing a game with the sound on mute – it is quite disorientating and certainly would not encourage continued interest in the game. Programming sound involves two disciplines: sound effects and music. Both must be activated at the appropriate moments to create atmosphere or help tell the story. For example, as a character is moving down a dark alley, eerie music could be played with a rising volume to increase the tension. As this is reactive to when the player moves down the alley, it is dependent on the programming as to when it is played. In addition, there could be the footsteps of the main character as they walk down this dark alley, echoing in the still night; if the character stops, the footsteps sound effect also needs to stop.

Game play and scripting

At the design stage of games development the script will be written. If the game is linear, such as *Halo*, then this will be fairly strict and programmers must ensure it is followed. Linear games can allow programmers and level designers to create a difficulty curve which can keep players interested for longer. At first, as the player is getting used to the game and controls, it is relatively easy. As players move through the game it gets progressively harder, but generally your character will get progressively more powerful as well.

A game that does this well is *Castlevania*. Although it seems that you are playing in one huge environment, sections of the castle are not available to you until your character is ready to tackle them. This game does not involve traditional levels, therefore the player does not specifically realise they are progressing up the difficulty curve, but it is there, encouraging the player to continue playing.

More complex games are those which are sandbox, such as *Grand Theft Auto*, where players can go anywhere and attempt tasks in any order. The definition of sandbox is having an open-ended game where the player defines the storyline. However, there are different levels of openness. For example, there is a storyline in *Grand Theft Auto* which is actually played in order, but the player can choose whether to follow it or detour to perform other tasks.

Games are aiming to obtain true sandbox, but there will always be the limitation of practicalities, in that everything needs to be programmed. A truly sandbox game could be programmed forever, so a balance needs to be found.

Middleware

Middleware sits between the hardware and the software. For example, if the hardware is a console and the software a game, the middleware is the programming which runs the console. In computer gaming, middleware is the operating system. Often coded in low-level languages, this allows the game to take full advantage of the high-end games technology available, in terms of processing power, memory, graphics and audio.

Graphical user interface (GUI)

The GUI is what the player sees on-screen. The majority of games use a heads-up display (HUD) to show up-to-date information about the character, for example lives, health (HP), magic power (MP), maps or radars and objects held by the character. There might also be different types of sights used for different situations, for example cross hairs might be used for certain weapons. Deciding what is included on the HUD to give as much information as possible without crowding the player's screen can be difficult, as can deciding on the symbols which will represent each part. In addition, the programmer must consider how the player will control the character. For example, will this be via computer and mouse/keyboard or via a console and use a controller? Which buttons will correspond to different actions?

Tools development

When creating a game, programmers may also be developing tools. These might be to help the team create parts of the game more easily or quickly, or for users to edit the game after it is released. These latter tools are often used for mods, which can modify the game. Tools development could be as simple as creating user-defined maps or as complex as using the game engine to create whole new environments.

Portfolio Activity (AO3)

For your handbook, select three specialist game programming areas and describe them in detail.

For each chosen area:

- describe its role in computer games
- explain its place in the computer games development process
- illustrate its function in the overall completed game
- give more than one example of its use in current game titles.

Game development systems

Game development systems are tools which provide an environment for programmers to build games. Their aim is to simplify and support the programming process to make it more efficient. This could include colour-coding the language so different parts are easy to identify, such as instruction words, variables and strings.

Most systems are focused on the programming aspect of the development, but some are designed as a 'one-stop-shop' for games creation, especially for hobbyists. In these cases there are also tools for working with the graphical and 3D modelling aspects of the game.

Portfolio Activity

Carry out research into existing game development systems.

1. As a class, divide into four or eight groups. Give each group a number from one to four.
2. Each group has 15 minutes to research the topic corresponding to their number and make some notes.
   - One – Virtools
   - Two – Connitec 3D Gamestudio
   - Three – Auran Jet
   - Four – Quest 3D
3. Once the 15 minutes are up, each group should stand at the front of the class and explain their research to the others, who take notes.
4. After the groups have shared their research, all students will have a set of starter notes as a basis for the research part of the Portfolio Activity at the end of this section (page 284).

Modifications (mods)

Mods are changes which are made to computer games. Mods are made by the general public or a developer, and have become popular through the Internet. It is increasingly common for games to be released with modding tools.

Mods can be partial conversions, such as the creation of new levels or environments within a game. For example, in *Halo 3*, the Forge tool enables players to insert and remove game objects such as weapons and adjust the environment of the levels. Mods can also be full conversions where the whole game is changed, as is possible with the Quake Engine.

Mods can encourage players to continue playing a game even after it has been completed and can produce new depths to the original storyline and concept. Alternatively, a whole new game can arise from mods. The Quake Engine is a very popular modding tool; from mods built using it, *Half-Life* was created and has become a very successful series in its own right. Similarly, the Unreal engine has been used to create other full games such as *Gears of War, Bioshock* and the *Rainbow Six* series.

By using existing engines, mods can allow hobbyists and smaller studios to create more intricate and complex games, as the development tools are already made for them. This saves them having to develop the game from scratch, for which they might not have the time, money or expertise.

Mods, however, have also caused controversy. An example of this is the Hot Coffee mod made for *Grand Theft Auto: San Andreas,* which allowed players to access a minigame within the full game which had been completely disabled for its worldwide release. The minigame that was unlocked with the mod allowed more sexually explicit content to be available. The mod caused outrage and controversy, resulting in the game being re-rated from Mature to Adults Only by the ESRB, some stores refusing to sell it and Rockstar being faced with legal action.

Portfolio Activity

Carry out research into existing mods.

1 As a class, divide into three or six groups and give each group a number from one to three.
2 Each group has 15 minutes to research the topic corresponding to their number and make some notes.
   - One – Quake
   - Two – Half-Life
   - Three – Unreal
3 Once the 15 minutes are up, each group should stand at the front of the class and explain their research to the others, who take notes.
4 After the groups have shared their research, all students will have a set of starter notes as a basis for the research part of Portfolio Activity (AO4) below.

Portfolio Activity (AO4)

For your handbook, demonstrate prototyping and small-scale development.

1 Select a game development system or game modification system with which to create examples.
2 Create at least five programs using this platform or system to solve programming problems. These should demonstrate a wide range of skills, including conditions and loops. Each should require some form of input and produce on-screen output. They should be focused in game programming rather than general programming.
3 Evaluate your chosen platform or system, explaining its strengths and weaknesses and identifying possible improvements.

Prototyping
Prototyping is the process of making a small version of a game or part of a game in order to test it to make sure that it works. This is similar to an architect making a model of a building in order to check that it is sound and to test it against various weather conditions. Prototyping is essential when trying something new and innovative.

Pass – Candidates follow **simple** tutorial-led procedures using a game development tool or game modification system, showing that they are aware of the toolset and its **basic** methods and techniques. They **may** struggle when it comes to solving problems which do not have template solutions. They **may** require a fair amount of assistance.

Merit – Candidates develop a **basic** competence in the chosen game authoring or game modification tool to be able to go beyond tutorial level and start to **develop** their own content, with some assistance. They show a **good** understanding of the principles and procedures used by the given system. They **list** the main strengths and weaknesses of the authoring system or game modification tool.

Distinction – Candidates develop **competence** in the chosen game authoring platform or game modification system and are able to **create** and **solve** programming tasks and problems using these tools, requiring little to no assistance. They also are able to **critically analyse** the strengths and weaknesses of the authoring system or game modification tool and **suggest** improvements in its design.

AO5: Specify and plan a simple game demonstration using a game authoring system or simple programming language

Plan the project

When carrying out a project of any size, it is essential to plan the whole process properly and clearly before beginning. Planning can be done in the following stages.

- Identify the overall aim – what will the final product be? How will you know when it is finished? When is the final deadline?
- Break the whole project down into a series of tasks and allocate a timescale to each task.
- Divide each task into a series of steps which will lead up to the completion of the task. Allocate a timescale to each step, making sure to stay within the time allocated for that specific task.
- Decide what resources will be needed for each task, including, if applicable, human resources.
- Review the allocated times and add contingency time in case there is a problem.
- Review the plan and make sure it is realistic. If you have prior commitments, make sure that they are taken into account.

Specify functionality

Games can be broken down into a series of functions or processes, each with a certain desired outcome. There are several methods which can be used to design these, including top-down design, bottom-up design and pseudocode.

Top-down design and bottom-up design

These methods allow the functionality of the game to be explained in diagrammatic form. In top-down design, the whole system is broken down into subsets and then broken down further and further until the core tasks are revealed. In bottom-up design, core functions are considered and then connected to form a whole.

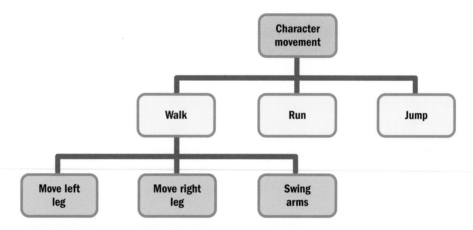

Figure 16.8 A flowchart diagram shows the core functions

Pseudocode

Pseudocode is also known as structured English. It is language which is halfway between English and code. It allows the bare bones of the code to be written without having to worry about correct wording and syntax constraints. An example of pseudocode is shown in Figure 16.9.

```
//For character to walk
Load sprite
Loop
      Move left leg
      Swing right arm
      Move character forward one pace in environment
      Move right leg
      Swing left arm
      Move character forward one pace in environment
Until user stops input or character meets an object
```

Figure 16.9 Pseudocode uses a mixture of code and English

Paper design

A paper design can be used to simulate the game in very basic terms before beginning to create a prototype. The aim is to identify any major flaws in the idea in a practical sense or any problems which may occur and which designers need to be aware of.

Flowchart

It is useful to be able to see a visual representation of the design. A flowchart is a diagram which essentially shows the code processes in pictures. This can then be referred to while programming to ensure that it is correct. A flowchart is often created very large and pinned to the wall of the studio so that people can easily refer to it.

There are four shapes used in a standard flowchart – oval, diamond, rectangle and square, although there are methods of flowcharting with many more available symbols.

Figure 16.10 Start/end indicators

Figure 16.11 Input or output

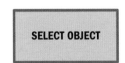

Figure 16.12 Process

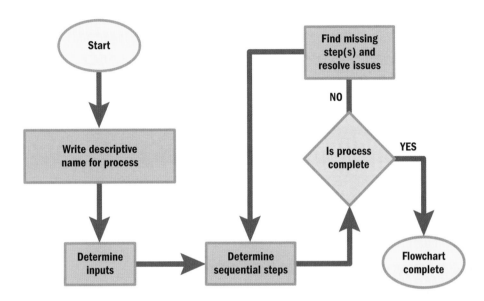

Figure 16.14 Arrows are used to connect each of the symbols together

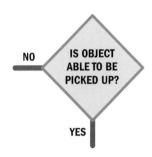

Figure 16.13 Decision (the Yes/No branches can come from any of the four points)

Portfolio Activity (AO5)

Design a simple casual game as described in the Scenario on page 271.

1 Create a project plan outlining the steps that need to be taken in the project and an estimated timescale.
2 Specify the functionality of the game using recognised design techniques.
3 Plan the game using a paper design.
4 Create flowcharts for the critical algorithms of the game.

Pass – Candidates specify and plan a **simple** game demo to a basic level, outlining functionality without any particular level of detail or depth. **Basic** flowcharting skills are demonstrated.

Merit – Candidates **efficiently** analyse and plan their own game demo using paper design and flowcharting techniques. The specification will be **feasible** and **well thought through**.

Distinction – Candidates demonstrate a **thorough** understanding of the game development process and an **understanding** of the production procedures used in the modern game development environment. They **effectively** analyse and plan their own game demo. Flowcharting skills, algorithmic analysis and application of control structures are used to a **very high** standard.

AO6: Produce a simple working game demonstration using a game authoring system or basic programming language

Review design and flowchart

A good designer will create a clear design which can easily be followed and is thorough and detailed. They will also review their design before beginning to create the program. This will prevent any ambiguity and help to avoid a number of problems occurring.

Acquire assets

Assets are any elements which are used in the program; these include graphics, animation, sound, video and anything else which is to be incorporated into the game. In a games development studio, assets would be created by other teams and the programmers would receive them completed to be included in the game. This means that the different teams need to work closely together in order for these elements to be compatible.

Build and implement

The implementation of the program is the stage where it is written and run. Throughout the process of building the game, the programmer should constantly be running the code to ensure each part works. If all of the code is written and then run at the end to test it, not only could there be numerous bugs but it will be much more difficult to identify in which area of the code the problems are located.

Test, tune and debug

Testing is a vital stage of development and should never be omitted or rushed. If a game is released with major or numerous bugs, it will not be successful. There have been various games which should have been successful but, due to code which had not been properly and thoroughly debugged, the games flopped and some studios went bankrupt in the process. There is always the temptation to hurry testing as it can be tedious and monotonous, and there is also the desire to see the game finished, but a good programmer should never give in to these temptations and should continue testing until they can honestly say that the code is the best it can be. With a well-planned project, there should be plenty of time for this stage to take place.

When testing, it is useful to create a plan so that the tests are organised. This will ensure that you do not repeat any tests and that, crucially, nothing is omitted.

Test number	Position in game	Test element	Expected result	Actual result	Success or failure	Action to be taken
1	Level 1: in-game screen	Press left cursor key	Spaceship moves left	Spaceship moves right	Failure	Function: Ship_move Line 27 – change RIGHT to LEFT
2	Level 1: in-game screen	Press space bar	Spaceship fires (graphic appears and disappears)	Fire graphic appears and disappears	Success	None

Figure 16.15 A test plan such as this could be used to test a program

Document the program

Documenting the code once it is complete is always done, no matter the size of the game or the studio. This is a stage which must be completed even when prototyping. The purpose is that, should you return to the code later, perhaps to adapt it for a different game or if someone else in your team wants to use it, then the documentation will clearly explain to them how it works without their needing to spend hours poring over it in an attempt to understand it.

Documentation should have two parts:

- First, there should be an explanation of each section of the code. This could be a description of each function, what it does, how it works and from where it is called.
- Second, a printout of the code should always be included. This should have either annotations written onto the printout or comments within the code, explaining each part. Additionally, if numerous variables have been used, there should also be a list of them with their names and purposes stated.

Portfolio Activity (AO6)

Use your game design to build a working model for demonstration. The game should be small and simple enough that the whole program can be created; however, if necessary create a prototype of essential functionality. The demonstration should be sufficient for someone who has not seen the game or the designs previously to understand it.

1 Review your design and make any amendments required.
2 Acquire your assets, including backgrounds, characters and objects. You may also include sound.
3 Create your game.
4 Test your program to ensure it functions correctly. Also ensure it is robust and will withstand user activity, whether expected or unusual.
5 Debug your program based on testing and provide evidence of this process. This could be a testing log with changes recorded.
6 Document your program to explain how it functions. Include a printout of code either annotated or including detailed comments within the code.
7 Pitch your game idea to a panel, using your working model as part of the demonstration.

Pass – Candidates are able to construct the initial workings of a game demo; however, it **may not** necessarily run with the desired or predicted functionality. Candidates may require **some** assistance and guidance either with their programming or use of a game development system. Candidates provide evidence of **some** testing. They **may not** provide evidence of debugging some errors. Some **limited** documentation is provided. The finished demo **may not** reflect their plans.

Merit – The final game demo project will be **mostly robust**, but not all the specified functionality will have been successfully implemented. Candidates require **minimum** assistance with either programming or when using a game development system. Candidates provide evidence of testing **most of** the main areas of the program. They **may** provide evidence of debugging some errors. The documentation is **thorough** and of a consistent quality. The finished demo **will reflect** their plans.

Distinction – Candidates **effectively** build and implement their final game demo to a good standard, resulting in a smooth-running and robust build demonstrating competence in game play programming and execution. Candidates require **little or no** assistance with either programming or when using a game development system. Candidates provide evidence of testing **most** of the main areas of the program. They also provide **evidence** of debugging some errors. **All** programming will be thoroughly documented. The finished demo **will match** their plans.

Computer Games Production

Learning outcomes

By working through this unit you will produce evidence to meet the unit assessment objectives to show that you understand how to:

■ describe the functions of a computer games development team

■ define the role of the producer within the development team

■ investigate the stages of games development

■ develop an understanding of the role of the publisher in game development

■ create a production plan for the development of a computer game title.

Introduction

The UK games industry is expanding at a tremendous rate; it is currently worth over £2 billion and rising all the time. Although this market is dominated by large development companies such as Rockstar (*Grand Theft Auto*) and Rare (*Viva Piñata*), there is an opportunity for small independent games companies to be born and grow in this fertile ground.

In the earlier years of gaming, it was quite possible for one teenager sitting in their bedroom with a Spectrum ZX or an Atari ST to be able to develop their own games. This was in the days before the Internet and it was more difficult to share programs. Software would be released as 'public domain', which would allow people to copy it and share it between friends; also, it could be released for free with disks on the front of magazines.

As games have become more advanced in terms of quality and quantity, it is no longer realistic to produce a game single-handedly. A team of people is required. For example, for *Halo 3* over 120 developers worked for three years to create this hugely successful game – and that doesn't include the 820,000 gamers who tested the beta version of the game.

Scenario

Independent UK games companies are taking advantage of the buoyant market and also a liking for smaller games, with Flash games being popular on the Internet and console facilities such as Nintendo DS minigames and Xbox Arcade.

As an entrepreneur, you have seen a gap in the games market and have decided to set up your own independent computer games studio. You will need to consider the

people you will need in your team and how to plan the creation of a full game, from initial concept to publishing it for people to play. You will be aiming to create large-scale games for console.

In setting up a games design studio, you need to consider several questions:

- Who will work with you to produce games that are good enough to be successful?
- Where will you be located?
- What sort of games will you make and for which platform?
- Why are you doing this? For example, is your primary aim to make a huge profit or to make games that fewer people play but are more passionate about?

Scenario

Portfolio Activity

1 Brainstorm ideas for:
   - the name of your company
   - the game you will produce (a title and a very brief outline idea).

2 Write an introduction for your portfolio, explaining your task and these initial ideas.

These elements are not assessed so do not spend too much time on them, but you will need them to be able to carry out the other portfolio activities in this unit.

AO1: Describe the functions of a computer games development team

Games development teams

As modern games have become more complex, the number of people creating them has had to increase. Either a team is a company in itself or one of several teams working for a larger company. For example, Team 17 is a single studio of one team, whereas Rockstar have development teams all over the world.

In a development team, each person has a role and is part of a functional area or department. Each department will have someone in command, a senior member or leader, who then reports to the producer (see pages 293–294). Above the producer there may be one owner-manager of the company or a senior management team.

Market research

Market research
The purpose of market research is to identify the needs of the potential market audience. By understanding the market needs, games developers will have a better chance of making a game which will sell once it is made and will fill a gap in the market, rather than one which is too similar to games that already exist.

The purpose of a market research team is to investigate how the public would react to a certain product. You may have been stopped in the high street by a person with a clipboard wanting to ask you a few questions – these are market researchers wanting to find out the public's opinions. There are other ways to carry out market research, including investigating products available in stores already or finding statistics such as sales figures.

It may be that the team has already thought of an initial concept for the game. If so, market research will investigate the public's potential interest in this type of game and what else is similar on the market. If they do not have an idea, market research can analyse the current marketplace to see what is popular to help generate ideas.

Market researchers will continue to work throughout the project, testing changes and new ideas on the public. They are also often involved in the planning of the marketing strategy to advertise and promote the game.

Design

Design
At the design stage the aim is to create a plan which could be followed by all members of the team. This means it has to be highly detailed and cover all aspects from art to programming. Any professional joining the team should be able to follow the design and create exactly what was envisioned.

The design department is responsible for developing the initial concept into an outline which the other departments can use to create the game. They will plan the project in terms of time, budget and resources. They are responsible for the overall viability of the project before production starts.

The design will often include sketches of characters and environments, written storylines and scripts, storyboards of animation sequences, level designs and plans for the gameplay and online multiplayer features.

Design is a vitally important stage as, if this is not correct, a lot of time and money can be wasted only to discover that the initial idea was no good in the first place. Games have been cancelled after they have been made because the original idea was deficient, with studios losing a lot of money and some smaller companies being closed because of this.

290   OCR National ICT Level 3

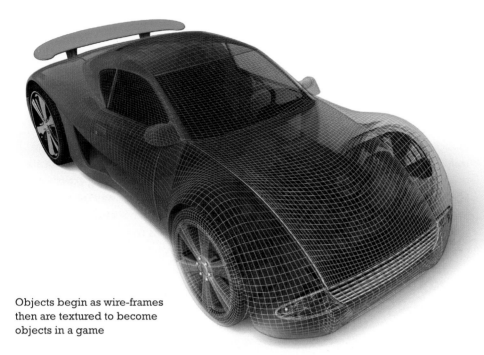

Objects begin as wire-frames then are textured to become objects in a game

Art and animation

Art and animation are usually a large team which encompass several diverse areas, including hand-drawn art, digital graphics, 2D animation and 3D animation. To see an artist at work creating a variety of artwork for animation please refer to page 293.

The initial drawings are always done by hand by concept artists and then will be created as 2D digital graphics, which are then rendered into 3D models. A rigger will apply textures to the model. For example, a character rigger may apply the textures of the clothing to the figure. This 3D shape can then be animated – for example, a character could be made to walk, run, jump, crouch, etc. Each of these processes is often done by different people in the department, which is also divided into at least three sections: characters, environment and user interface (UI).

Once the characters and environment are created and animated separately, cinematic artists put them together, taking into consideration the cinematic effect of aspects such as camera angles and lighting effects. It is customary on a large production that one person will be in charge of one thing. For example, one 3D modeller might be in charge of creating just the pickup objects in the game; another animator might solely be in charge of the introduction menu.

Programming

The programming department provides the code which makes the game work. Usually there will be a core bank of programmers who create the majority of the software, but there may also be specialist programmers within that department in the areas of:

- physics – creating realistic gravity and movement
- artificial intelligence (AI) – controlling the non-player characters (NPCs), which are controlled by the computer rather than the player
- user interface (UI) – designing the heads-up display (HUD) and menu interfaces
- online and multiplayer
- console – creating the console-specific code, such as for Xbox, PlayStation, Wii, DS or PSP.

Art and Animation
This is considered a separate task from design as it is quite specific in terms of its aims. This section of pre-production is where all the visual elements are planned. These are generally drawn by hand and, as a three-dimensional graphic is being designed, views from several angles are sketched. Notes are also added so that when they are to be created into digital graphics all thoughts can be incorporated.

Programming
Programming is the piece which supports all the others and ties together disparate graphics, animation and other elements into a whole. It controls the events in the game and allows interactivity for the player.

Audio

The audio department is responsible for all the sound in the game, which includes music, voices and sound effects. The audio is crucial for making a game completely immersive and believable. Try playing a game with the sound turned off and you will see it becomes an entirely different and remote experience.

Voice actors may be hired to speak for the characters or narrate cut-scenes. Musicians may be brought in to record the music and could range from rock bands to full orchestras. For the sound effects, although some are created digitally, a lot are made by Foley artists – sound effects specialists who create noises using actual items. For example, in the production of *Gears of War*, an actual chainsaw was recorded to create the specific sound effect to ensure maximum realism in the game. Gamers who play a lot of first person shooters (FPS) want their guns to sound realistic and can tell the difference if a studio has taken shortcuts in this department.

Production

Production is where all the separate parts are brought together and integrated to make a whole game. The people in this department need special skills, as they need to be able to communicate with different people in the team to bring together their elements of the game, for example the artists and the programmers.

Testing

Testing is often the last stage of development, although if a problem is found the game may need to go back through the stages to correct it.

Testing can be done by individuals or focus groups, all of whom play the game and then give feedback on their experience. They could be looking for bugs in the game, in which case they may be asked to play a certain scene over and over in an attempt to find problems, or they may be asked to give their opinions, in which case they will play the game normally. Testers can be in-house and part of the team, or they can be hired just for the time needed to test. Sometimes studios will invite people involved in game websites and forums or university game courses to test. When *Halo 3* was ready to be tested, Bungie released a beta version (see Beta build, page 298) with the game *Crackdown*, which increased the sales of *Crackdown*, increased the hype of *Halo 3* and also allowed Bungie to have hundreds of thousands of testers working for them free of charge.

Portfolio Activity (AO1)

For your games development studio, decide who you are going to recruit for your company. Remember that you are aiming to take the game from the initial concept stage right through to publishing. Consider all the stages of the process.

1   Draw an organisation structure for your studio. You should have at least one person for each department, although some may need more. State their job titles.
2   For each different role in your organisation structure, write a job description, including what the role involves and what skills will be needed. (You do not need to describe the producer's role as this will be covered in the next section.)

Pass – Candidates describe in **broad** terms **some** of the key game development team roles, but **not necessarily** with any depth of understanding. Some **limited** examples are given.

Merit – Candidates give **detailed** descriptions of **most** of the key game development team roles, showing some depth of understanding. A **range** of examples are given.

Distinction – Candidates give **comprehensive** descriptions of **all** the key game development team roles, including the differences between individual levels and job titles. A **wide range** of examples are given.

AO2: Define the role of the producer within the development team

The producer's role

The producer (also known as project manager) is the person who sees the project as one whole venture, rather than the individual segments on which the other team members may be focused. It is their responsibility to ensure that the game is delivered on time, on budget and of high quality. They oversee all the departments and can work with each one when necessary. The lead members of each department report to them and keep them updated on progress. They also communicate with senior management, publishers, investors and other stakeholders to ensure they are kept informed of progress. Modern companies typically have an internal producer as part of their team, but very small companies may use an external producer who is actually part of the publishing company (see page 300). All games design companies are different and therefore the role of the producer varies but their core tasks and responsibilities are generally similar.

Scheduling

The producer is responsible for planning the timing of the project. They will estimate the overall time and also the time of each phase within that. As some projects can last two or three years, this is a big undertaking requiring a lot of strategy and pragmatism. In addition, contingency plans need to be created in case something goes awry, for example if a key employee is ill or a deadline is missed.

Budgeting

Ensuring large projects run to budget is a difficult task and one that is often reported in the media when it fails. The producer must look at the purchase of equipment, renting of studios, employees' wages, purchasing of resources and employing of external people such as musicians. Scheduling and budgeting are closely linked, as if the project goes over schedule, usually it will result in higher spending. Similarly, if the project goes over budget, it may need to be completed in a shorter time in order to still be affordable for the company.

Formulating technical and creative strategy

In games development teams, there is often a perceptible divide between the artists working on the creative side and the programmers on the technical side. The producer must bridge this gap and ensure that both teams work in harmony and can be the communicator between the two. They must ensure that both teams are progressing at the same rate and in the same direction, and they have charge of the overall strategy to accomplish this.

Devising work pipelines and procedures

The producer will ensure that the work is done on time and in the most efficient manner. They will decide the breakdown of tasks and allocate these to different teams, and then monitor the progress to ensure that each task is advancing in the right direction and in good time. Some tasks can only be started after others are complete, and it is up to the producer to manage this dependency, to ensure that there are no bottlenecks and no team delays another. They will also ensure that milestones are met and provide quality control to ensure that work is completed on time and to a high standard.

Managing human resources and studio resources

Often games development teams are not large enough to warrant employing a dedicated human resources manager and, therefore, the producer also takes on this role. They deal with hiring and firing employees and managing any complaints or issues the team members might encounter. They keep employee records and manage sick days, holidays and any other parts of employment such as benefits or expenses.

They are also in charge of purchasing for the studio. This can include equipment, furniture, stationery and any other products that may be required during the making of the game. They may be required to hire recording studios for the audio department or locations for the art department to research.

Facilitating team communications

The producer is key in ensuring that all departments have clear and candid communication. Although there may be competition between them, the producer ensures that this does not turn into opposition, as ultimately they are all working together towards the same goal.

Portfolio Activity (AO2)

For your games development studio, consider the person you will hire as your producer. This will be one of the most important people in your team and could determine the success or failure of the project. Consider carefully their role within the team and the type of personality and skills they will need to possess.

1   Write a job description for your producer, including what the role involves and what skills they will need, including technical, creative and personal.
2   Explain how the producer will interact with the rest of your team and what their responsibilities will be.
3   Describe the difference between internal and external producers and the differences in their roles and responsibilities, giving examples of existing companies to reinforce your comparison.
4   Consider a large, commercial company and describe how the producer's role would be different compared with your company.

Pass – Candidates **list** a producer's (or project manager's) responsibilities without necessarily covering any detail or depth of the different components of their job.

Merit – Candidates show a **good** awareness of the producer's roles and responsibilities in game development. They **list** the qualities and skills that a producer needs in order to do the job effectively.

Distinction – Candidates show a **comprehensive** awareness of the producer's roles and responsibilities within game development. They **describe** the qualities and skills that a producer needs in order to do the job effectively. They **highlight differences** that may exist from one company to another, giving examples.

AO3: Investigate the stages of games development

Typical project stages

In order to manage a games development project effectively, it is divided into stages, with specific tasks occurring at each stage. If a problem occurs it is possible to go back to a previous stage, but you must then work through each stage again. For example, if in testing it is found that an extra map is needed, the team can go back to the designers who will draft a map, then the artists and programmers will create it, then it will need to be tested again.

Pre-production

The first stage of the project is to produce the idea for the game, make sure it is viable and design it. Deciding on the initial concept is crucial, as the wrong choice could lead to months or years of work on a product which will not sell. Sometimes this phase can be almost as long as the production phase, but can run alongside the production and testing of previous projects.

Initial concept

This is the very first stage of production and is where the initial idea for the game is generated. It may be that the team has an idea for a character or a world or a storyline, or they may just know they want to create a racing game or a sports game. Ideas are thrashed around, rough sketches are drawn and research is carried out. The result of this phase should be a solid idea that is agreed can be taken forward into implementation.

This phase can sometimes take weeks, sometimes months, but it is important to spend as much time as necessary getting this right, as once it goes into the next stage it becomes more time-consuming and costly to stop and start again. The crux of the idea may be a flash of inspiration while sitting in the bath, but this stage also involves putting meat on the bones and expanding the original thought into a full game concept.

In the initial concept stage, it may be that a few members of the team are involved, especially in a new company which may decide to come up with the idea before hiring the right people to take on the task. For example, for a racing game they may wish to employ people with racing game experience. For established teams, it could be that this phase is carried out by the whole team so that everyone's view is heard and big problems with production can be eliminated immediately. For example, if a suggestion is made and it is impossible to program, the programmers are there to indicate this before the idea gets into the design stage and it becomes more difficult to backtrack. In this way, the whole team gains ownership of the idea and becomes more dedicated to the process.

Game design

Pre-production is the design stage of the process. The concept, which has been produced in the first phase, is passed over to the designers, who now have the task of making these quite rough ideas viable and achievable.

The schedule and budgeting will be organised to make sure they are both realistic. Concept art will be created by the designers – this is usually hand-drawn images of characters, environments and any other aspects of the game, which can be passed to the artists to be created digitally. Storyboards will be created to show the progress through the game and the specifics of areas such as cut-scenes. The full storyline of the game will be planned out; this even applies to games which may not seem to have a storyline such as racing, sports and puzzle games, but they are still thought through precisely from beginning to end. All aspects of the game are designed in meticulous detail, ready to be passed over to the other departments. It is essential that all plans are clear and can be understood by other people in the team.

Production planning

Once the game has been designed thoroughly, the plans can be distributed to the various departments to be created. Each team can establish their own ways of working, procedures and schedules for the tasks for which they are responsible, as long as they work towards the overall goal and deadline. Each will define their own milestones to work towards and how to assess their progress and output (see Assessment Objective 5, page 305).

Tools development

There are two main types of tools used in games development. Firstly, there are graphics, animation and programming environments. These are usually off-the-shelf software, for example 3D modellers like Maya and 3D Studio Max are standard programs which can be used by anyone.

Secondly, there are the game-specific tools. This type of tool usually consists of a game engine, which is the core software that runs all the parts of the game. An example is the Unreal engine, which was first created for the game *Unreal* in 1998. Since then the engine, has been continually updated and has been used to create very popular games, including *Gears of War*, *Tom Clancy's Rainbow Six* and *Bioshock*. Engines are bespoke software and can be altered to suit the game being created or can be created from scratch by the studio, perhaps if they are aiming to create a type of gaming which has not yet been attempted.

Programming

The programmers will decide which is the best language to use for the creation of the game. Popular languages for games include C++, Java and DarkBasic.

Pre-production
Pre-production encompasses all the design elements of the project and runs from the thinking of the initial concept through to the completion of the design, ready to be created.

Prototypes

A prototype is a small trial version of a larger product. Just like an architect might make a small version of a building before making the real thing, games developers will make mini versions of parts of the game to test whether they will work. For example, in a game where the player is controlling a flying vehicle, they might build a prototype of just the undercarriage of the vehicle to simulate just the take-off. They may then build several prototypes to test different methods of taking off.

Prototypes can be used to investigate whether a routine will work without risking time and, therefore, money on building the full system only to find that it does not work. Developers may also use prototypes to put certain parts of the game into the testing stage more quickly in order to gain potential audience feedback. For example, they may build a demo version of a level and ask a focus group to play it. They are then able to incorporate testing feedback while they are still building the game, which is cheaper and easier than trying to make all changes at the end and can save them wasting time on elements the target audience may not like.

Art development

Each visual element of the game is hand-drawn as concept art, usually in the design phase. From this the artists can create a digital 2D representation which is then converted into a 3D model and animated. For instance, a road vehicle would be drawn by hand, then on computer in 2D. It would then be wire-framed into a 3D model. Textures are wrapped onto the wire-frame to simulate the bodywork, windows, tyres, etc. The 3D model is then animated to be able to move forward, turn left, turn right and make other moves, but also more unusual moves like what would happen to the vehicle if it were to crash into a variety of things such as trees and buildings. Remember that each tiny bit of what you see on-screen has to be designed, drawn, rendered and visualised; if you are playing a racing game, each tree that you zoom past probably took at least three people to create.

Level design

An important aspect of games is the design of the levels. Whether these are alien planets, football stadiums or the streets of London, each one needs to be planned thoroughly. The development team may choose to create these from scratch or use a tool to support their creation. For example, for games created with the Unreal engine, the UnrealEd tool can be used as a level editor.

Prototype production

Localisation plan

Games can be made specifically for one platform, but are often made cross-platform, meaning they will work on PC and several consoles such as Xbox, PlayStation and Wii. A localisation plan maps out how the game will be ported to the different systems.

Also, games can be sold all around the world, but changes need to be made to make them appropriate. This includes translation into a different language, which may involve, at a simple level, subtitles and, at a more advanced level, a new script, new voice actor recordings and possibly even changing the lip synching of the characters. In some cases some larger design elements need to be altered to suit different cultural audiences. For example, in Germany the public display of a swastika is illegal, except for scholarly reasons; as computer games are considered to be entertainment, they do not fall under this exemption. As a result of this, games set in the Second World War such as *Call of Duty* and *Medal of Honour* have had to change their graphics to remove swastikas. The localisation plan outlines how these changes will be made.

Alpha and beta builds

Testing, tuning, debugging

A crucial part of the process is testing to ensure that all parts of the game work. Testing leads to making amendments to the game. Usually this will involve fine-tuning the game and debugging the code, but occasionally can result in rehashing whole sections of the game and even postponing the final release date. Early stages of testing are to ensure the bulk of the game works and the audience like it, whereas later stages are to polish it to a release version, in essence quality control. If a game is released with flaws it can sometimes lead to the game being a flop. This will lose money for the studio and could make them bankrupt.

Pre-alpha build

Testing at the pre-alpha stage is when an element is trialled even though it is not complete. This could be for a prototype before it continues to be created fully. Testing is often kept in-house at this point to keep the game concept secret from competitors.

Alpha build

An alpha build of the game is a nearly complete version of either a section of the game or the whole game. It is usually used for internal testing only, as it still has a number of known and unknown flaws. However, some companies choose to try to push their deadlines forward by releasing an alpha build for public testing and eliminating a beta testing phase. Although this might reduce the testing phases and therefore time, it can run the risk of gaining a poor public image or not being tested thoroughly enough and being released with bugs and faults.

Beta build

Once the alpha build has been tested in-house and appropriate changes made, the game is then put out as a beta release. This is the full game which is near total completion and the aim of the testers is to find any final bugs which can be removed. A closed beta build is released to a select group of people who are invited to test the game, sometimes signing confidentiality contracts so they do not speak about the content of the game until its general release. An open release is when the beta version is released to a wide community of people, such as those who use a specific game website or forum. An example of this is the fourth edition of *Shadowrun*, for which the developers changed the style from role-playing game (RPG) to more FPS. To allow them to test the game and also gain public opinion about the change, Xbox 360 users could sign up on Microsoft's website to test the beta release of the game.

If necessary, a game can also go through delta and gamma builds if more testing is needed after changes are made.

Gold master

When the game is as complete as possible, it is considered to be a gold master and ready to go on general release. Occasionally, if a team is running out of time, they might release a game too early as it still has problems. However, as this only reduces sales and damages the company's reputation, most companies find it better to delay the release than to release an incomplete game.

Portfolio Activity (AO3)

The plan will be submitted as part of your proposal to the publishers. As you are producing for console, these will be Nintendo, Sony and Microsoft. This will hopefully allow you to release your game exclusively for a specific console or across all three. Your plan needs to be realistic so that you gain that elusive console publication deal – too short and the publishers will be sceptical of your ability to deliver on it; too long and they may think your idea will be out of date by the time you complete the project. Remember the team you defined in the portfolio activity for Assessment Objective 1 (page 296) and utilise your team appropriately.

1. Create a mind map for the different activities involved in the creation of your game.
2. On a sheet of A4, write these headings in three columns: pre-production, production, testing. Under each heading, write the activities involved. Number each activity in the order in which they should take place – you should notice that some happen concurrently.
3. For each activity, write a description of what happens during that stage. Use a range of examples of real world companies to highlight your points.
4. Draw a diagram to show the whole process of the creation of the game, from initial concept to release. Use boxes and arrows to show how activities are related. (You may use a critical path diagram if you wish, but it is not compulsory.) Mark which activities are dependent on others.
5. Describe variations which could occur to your plan if you were producing different types of games (for example, different genre, different platform, different audience, etc.). Use a range of real world examples to support your points.
6. Describe contingency plans for five events which could cause a problem with your plan.
7. (Optional) If you have not included prototyping in your plan, describe this practice.

Testing
Testing completes the process of developing the game before it goes to be manufactured and published. At this stage the opinions of the potential target audience can be gained, the programming can be debugged and the whole game can be tweaked and fine-tuned.

Assessment Guidance

Pass – Candidates identify the **main** stages of game development and show an understanding of the **basic** logical order of production, but deeper understanding of causal relationships may be lacking. There may be some gaps in the understanding of underlying concepts.

Merit – Candidates identify **all** the stages of game development and show a **thorough** understanding of the order of production. Dependencies and relationships between the stages are briefly **explained** and **analysed**. **Some** examples from their research will be used.

Distinction – Candidates exhibit an **in-depth** knowledge of the game development process and can **accurately map** the stages of game production, even indicating likely **variations** to the stages with different types of title development. Dependencies and relationships are briefly explained and analysed. **Many** examples from their research will be used.

AO4: Develop an understanding of the role of the publisher in game development

The publisher's role

The publisher can be internal or external to the game development studio. In larger studios they may be internal as they will publish their own games. In this case they will finance and distribute their own projects. Money from previous successful games can be reinvested into new projects. In smaller studios, it is usual to use an external publisher, who will provide finance for the project but will also demand returns and possibly want a say in the game content. Sometimes the publisher can be the console organisation. For example, Microsoft may publish a game but they may demand that the game is only made for the Xbox 360.

Financing

An external publisher provides the finance for the game but will demand a percentage in return from the profits made once it is released. This gives the publisher a stake in the project and they may wish to have a say in the production process. They also have the right to refuse to publish the game at the end of the process if they are not happy with it, and the studio can decide to make changes or find a different publisher.

Commissioning

The publisher may be the initial instigator of the project by commissioning the project. For example, Nintendo may have an idea for a new DS game and they may commission a games development studio to create it. Alternatively, a studio may come up with the idea themselves and pitch it to the publisher in the hope that they will agree to fund the project.

Strategic management

Strategic management is a continual process in a business and involves looking for opportunities in the market, setting and progressing towards organisation objectives, managing finances and dealing with competitors. A publisher will be able to decide on the best time to release a game by looking at the release of competitors' games and the cultural market. For example, if a competitor is releasing a war game which is very similar to the one their studio is developing, they might try to push the studio to ensure theirs is the first to be released. Similarly, a game set on sandy beaches in the sunshine might sell better if released in the summer rather than for the Christmas market.

Marketing

Advertising and promotion can be crucial to the success or failure of a game. There is an impression in the industry that consumers will often go for the game that is publicised most fiercely and for which much hype has been generated. The publisher will organise the advertising, including billboards, television and radio ads and posters. They will also organise promotion, including sending advance copies to games magazines and television shows for them to review.

Distribution

The publisher will organise the distribution of the game. This is from the point the game becomes a gold master, through manufacture of the actual disks (or suitable media) to them being delivered to stores in the high street or e-Commerce websites.

Portfolio Activity (AO4)

For your games development studio, consider how you will publish your game. You have put your proposal forward to the console manufacturers to allow your game to be released on their machines, but you may wish to publish the game through a different publishing house. You need to investigate what will be the best deal for your game and your studio.

1 Research five existing publishers. Try to have a mix of console-specific (e.g. Sony) and independent publishers (e.g. Activision).
2 Referring to your research, describe the role of a publisher. Compare internal and external publishers.
3 Explain what your company would do about publishing and why.

AO5: Create a production plan for the development of a computer game title

Project management and planning skills

It is important when carrying out large projects that they are planned thoroughly in terms of time, budget and resources. All the people involved need to have a clear idea of what has been done, what is being done and the overall aim of the project.

Analysing a project into component tasks

To understand the project clearly, it can be broken into stages, and each of those should be divided into individual tasks. Not only does this allow for better planning, it also sets achievable goals. It may be difficult to work towards a target that is a year away, but carrying out a single part that can be completed in a few weeks allows for a sense of achievement and progress which can be felt by the whole team. Each project is divided into pre-production, production and post-production or testing (see page 295–298), and each of these is broken in several separate tasks.

Scheduling

In order to meet the final deadline, all the small parts of the project need to be scheduled. However, there also needs to be unallocated time to allow for slippages in the schedule. If something goes amiss during the project, such as a part takes longer to complete than planned, there is a technology failure or an employee is ill at a critical moment, there needs to be contingency in order to absorb these problems so the project can still be delivered on time. It is also useful to be able to show which tasks are dependent on each other and which will be carried out in simultaneously.

Budgeting and resource allocation

Money is a key factor in ventures, and bringing a project in on budget is a mark of success in project management. Other resources also need to be allocated. These include items such as computers, furniture and stationery, all of which need to be costed, purchased and allocated to a department or individual. Employees themselves can be considered to be resources as well and each task needs to have at least one person responsible for its completion. Even the studio in which the team is working is a resource.

As the project progresses, certain stages may take longer than anticipated or there may be unforeseen problems. In this situation, the studio needs to decide whether to move the deadline back, to later in the year; sometimes projects can delay by more than a year. This could have implications, as the release date will have been carefully selected with consideration of competitors' products, market attitude and seasonal factors. Alternatively, the studio could decide to bring in extra developers to speed up that stage or rectify a problem and still bring the game in on time. This option, however, can be extremely expensive, as freelance designers, programmers and other skilled people are generally much more expensive than those who are employed for the whole project. The studio, therefore, has to decide what is more important – bringing the game out on time or spending more money than expected. For some it may be that no more money is available, or that other stages, such as advertising, have to be done more cheaply in order to pay for the extra staff.

Grand Theft Auto IV was delayed by a whole year, allegedly due to problems with the multiplayer aspect of the game. However, this changed release date did not affect their sales and it has become the biggest-selling entertainment product of all time, outselling *Halo 3*'s $125 million on the first day of release by making $310 million in its first 24 hours.

Project management tools and techniques

There are numerous tools and techniques available for project management. By using recognised techniques, everyone in the team can understand the project documentation as can anyone who enters the team after the planning stage.

Risk analysis

In every project there is an element of risk and it is best to be prepared rather than burying your head in the sand. Different stages of the project may be more risky than others, and the overall level of risk is dependent on the project being produced. For example, a large scale FPS which is released for Xbox near to the time of release of *Gears Of War 2* is more risky than a small-scale game which will not result in the studio going bankrupt if the game flops. Along with identifying the risks, planners should also decide on contingency plans in case the risks do actually cause the problems which have been anticipated. Obviously there are always unforeseen obstructions which can hinder a project, but a risk analysis will reduce as many of these as possible.

Critical path analysis

A project is broken into several tasks, each of which has a specific duration. Some of these tasks may only be able to start once other tasks have been started or completed; this is called dependency. A critical path will identify the order of tasks, the dependency and the direction. The aim is to find the most direct route through the project and, therefore, discover the sequence which produces the shortest possible overall time for the project.

Critical paths are normally displayed in a diagram consisting of numbered circles representing each task and arrows showing direction. These are annotated with times. More complex critical path analyses will show longest times, shortest times and prioritisation.

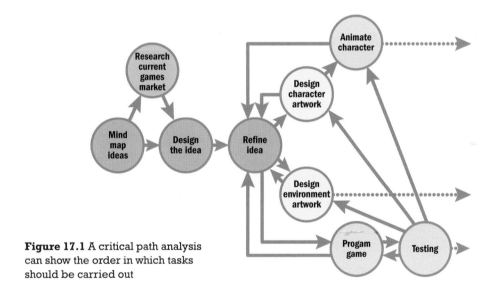

Figure 17.1 A critical path analysis can show the order in which tasks should be carried out

The first task is mind mapping all ideas. Once this process is started and focus begins to narrow, perhaps to a particular genre, market research can be carried out simultaneously. Only after these two stages are completed can the idea be designed, because it is dependent on those two tasks. Once the design is complete it can be refined and this becomes a cyclical process. Character and environment artwork can be done concurrently, as can programming, with each developer able to return to refining the original design as new ideas occur or problems are encountered. The testing of the programming is done as each routine is written. It would only be as all these parts are completed that they would be brought together and the whole game would begin to take shape and it would be tested as a whole.

Reporting structure

The reporting structure generally covers two areas: documentation of the planning and how that documentation is cascaded through the company. The planning may be meticulous, but if it is not clearly documented then it cannot be followed, especially for projects which will last several months or even years. Once documented, the planning should be shared with everyone in the company. This is not only so they can understand and follow it, but also so they feel ownership of the project and become more committed. This is especially important in games development studios, as they are relatively small teams and so each and every member must be devoted to the project, especially when nearing the deadline.

Project management software

There is much software available for project management. Microsoft Project is part of the Office suite and is an excellent program, especially for those who have not used this type of tool previously. It will allow a user to create Gantt charts and critical path diagrams to manage and analyse the project effectively. Team members can be allocated responsibility for tasks and resources can be assigned. There are also features to manage the project's finances and ensure the project stays within budget. In addition, 'what-if' scenarios can be modelled to see what would happen if certain circumstances were to occur, allowing different solutions to problems to be tested.

Portfolio Activity (AO5)

Using your project plans from Assessment Objective 3 (page 303), refine your plans using project management software. For your proposals to the console manufacturers and publishers, you need to be able to prove that your plans are robust and that you can guarantee that you can meet your deadline with a quality product. They are investing a lot of money in your studio, so they need to be able to depend on you.

1 Create your project plan using project management software.
2 Analyse your plan and make refinements (show both your original and refined versions).
3 Prove your plan is robust by testing it against possible slippages and pitfalls which could occur.
4 For the distinction criteria, demonstrate your project problem-solving skills:
    a) Identify at least five problems which could occur during your project and suggest how these might be overcome. Try to identify problems which are difficult to solve.
    b) To demonstrate your problem-solving skills, suggest at least one solution for the following project problems:
        ■ During the planning stage, the whole team have discussed many game ideas and have now settled on two from which they need to pick just one, as they can only finance the development of one idea. One is a large-scale FPS game targeted at the 18 years+ market. The other is a large-scale strategy game targeted at the younger market and hoping for a 3+ rating. The team is split over which game should be developed, with arguments on both sides saying that there is opportunity in the

market for each. Both games would cost a similar amount to develop and take two years before being ready to be released.

- The team have decided which game they will produce and have begun production. The team is relatively small – less than 50 people – which means that every person is allocated a specific area of the game to develop and there is no overlap. A member of the Art team becomes ill and it looks like it could be several weeks before they are able to return to work. The studio pay her sick leave and they do not want to lose her from the team as she is very talented, but now they are one person down. This means they either need to find another way to get the work done or wait for her to return, which will make that section of the project last longer.

- The Programming team are well underway with the core coding of the game but suddenly realise they have a problem. The unique selling point of this game is that it will have a new way of controlling the character and the programmers are having problems in making this work the way they wanted. This means that the hours needed to complete this stage have increased dramatically; more people will be required to work on this stage or it will be necessary to shift the games deadline back. The programmers could change their idea to use something more traditional which is tried and tested, but this may have an effect on the sales of the game.

- The studio is using an external publisher to market and distribute their game. The publisher had agreed to the project during the planning stage. The game is now at testing and the publisher has decided that perhaps this game would not sit well with other titles they have released and is thinking of pulling out.

- The game is ready for release. The marketing has been done; there is good interest being shown in the game; the disks, artwork and game cases are in manufacture. A week before the actual release date, a rival company releases a game which is very similar.

Pass – The production plan is complete for **the most part**, with **simple** project management techniques successfully applied to the basic scenario. More advanced tools and analysis may be omitted. In presentation, when tested against different scenarios and slippages, candidates have **developed awareness** of the issues but may not have developed sufficient techniques in order to accommodate them within their production plans.

Merit – The production plan is **well developed**, with **good** application of the project management tools and techniques applied. The plan proves to be **robust** when tested against various possible scenarios and slippages.

Distinction – The production plan is **detailed** and **comprehensive**, with **extremely thorough** application of project management tools. The plan proves to be **extremely robust** when tested against possible slippages and project pitfalls. Candidates **demonstrate** that they have developed an almost instinctive flair for project problem solving.

18 Computer Games Technology

Learning outcomes

By working through this unit you will produce evidence to meet the unit assessment objectives to show that you understand how to:

- compare and contrast major console platforms
- analyse games-related PC technologies
- compare and contrast hand-held and mobile devices
- describe game development tools and technologies
- explore current technical challenges for computer games
- investigate and describe future developments.

Introduction

Game development studios have a wide range of options when it comes to selecting the platform on which they will release their game.

They could release specifically to one platform. For example, they may be commissioned by Nintendo to make a game solely for the Nintendo Wii. This has the advantage of being exclusive to one manufacturer, which will put their resources behind its marketing and the developers can focus on making full use of that console's specific technology. However, it also limits the potential number of customers, as only those with the correct platform will buy it. Occasionally, a game is so good that releasing it on only one platform actually increases the sales of that console, for example for *Halo 2* and *Halo 3* (Xbox and Xbox 360), the *Grand Theft Auto* series (when it was released on Playstation systems a year before all others) and *Dr Kawashima's Brain Training* (Nintendo DS).

The game could be distributed just on a PC. This has the advantage that PCs are more prevalent than consoles; in the UK alone more than 70 per cent of the population owns a home computer. In addition, the Internet can be utilised as either a method for distribution or to provide a huge global multiplayer capability. Games such as *World of Warcraft* have taken advantage of this and this game has over 10 million subscribed players worldwide, each paying for the initial cost of the game (and addition packs) and a monthly subscription fee.

Often games will be released on a console and the same company's hand-held device at the same time. For example, Nintendo may release a game on the Wii and the DS simultaneously; Sony may release a game on the Playstation as well as the PSP.

This allows for the manufacturer to still retain exclusivity of the game but widens the market to owners of either platform. The disadvantage is that the game needs to translate well between each format, as what works well on a console with a big screen and a complex controller may not port well to a hand-held with a small screen and simpler buttons, and vice versa.

Independent studios have the option of releasing games across platforms. They may choose PC and a console, or two consoles, or all consoles and hand-helds. This maximises the potential buying market but can also cause problems when attempting to translate the game across so many platforms. Also, the studio needs to be confident in its game as this can be a costly approach; they may need to pay a royalty fee in order to use a specific manufacturer's technology to allow the game to work on their system. Unlike most royalty fees, which are paid out of profits made, royalty fees in the games industry are generally paid as the game goes into manufacture, therefore passing the risk onto the studio.

Scenario

You have been employed by a leading independent games studio to research the market for the game they are developing. They would like you to advise them on the different consoles and hand-helds currently available and inform them of the latest PC technology. As they are still in the design phase of the project, they would like you also to research current games development tools and technological and creative challenges in creating modern games. Finally, they would like you to advise them about possible future developments in gaming; as the project is likely to take at least two years, they would like to be aware of potential opportunities so they can make the most of them and gain advantages by incorporating them into their product quickly.

Introduction: a brief history of consoles

Consoles are built solely as machines on which to play games, although modern consoles are now able to perform other tasks such as global communication and media storage and presentation, for example of photographs and movies.

The first computer games were made in the 1950s, although there are a lot of arguments over who created the first game. Early games were monochrome (black and white) and relatively simple. *Tennis For Two*, which later became *Pong*, involves a bat at either side of the screen and hitting a dot (ball) across a line (net). Compared with the games of today, this may seem quite boring; however, it had all the elements of a modern game and proved to be very addictive and highly successful.

Over the next 30 years, the market was flooded with ever-increasing technology; each new release saw something innovative added. Score tables, sound, multiplayer – all features that we take for granted today – had to be invented and improved. This period saw some classic names in gaming emerge: Spectrum, Commodore, Atari, Amiga.

The early 1980s saw the explosion of interest in gaming with the release of the Nintendo Entertainment System and the Sega Master System. Home gaming overtook the previously popular arcades, which went out of fashion. With the introduction of these consoles, and the marketing wars which accompanied them bringing the prices down, home gaming became affordable and desirable. This was the period in which you did not play games; you 'played on the Nintendo'.

Sixth-generation consoles

At the turn of the twenty-first century, sixth generation consoles were released, also known as 128-bit. These formed the basis of modern consoles and provided the link to earlier technologies.

Dreamcast
The Sega Dreamcast, although not known at the time, was to be Sega's last foray into the field of consoles. Sega have since moved wholly into the software market, becoming an independent third-party publisher (see Unit 17: Computer Games Production, page 300). The Dreamcast, being the first sixth-generation console released, was hailed as being a huge shift in technology.

Playstation 2
However, before the Dreamcast could take hold of the market, in 1999 the Sony Playstation 2 was announced. With the original Playstation having been such a runaway success, this console was highly anticipated and popularity was inevitable on its release a year later. Even though the Playstation 3 has since been released, Playstation 2 continues to be prevalent in households, with many preferring to stick with their PS2 rather than pay the quite expensive price tag to upgrade.

GameCube and GameCube online
In late 2001, Nintendo released GameCube, a sixth-generation console targeted towards 'family-friendly' gaming. GameCube was popular with young gamers, but this market represents a small proportion of gamers and sales were not as high as

expected. Another factor in this was that an online facility, the new technology of the day, was not supported and promoted as much as its competitors. As GameCube's sales could not compete with the Playstation 2's, game publishers decided to release for the Playstation 2 rather than spend time porting games to the GameCube, which would be likely to provide fewer sales for them. Nintendo went back to the drawing board and, after a few years of intense development, came back to the market with the Wii (see page 311), targeting the same market as they had with the GameCube but now it was the right place and the right time. Nintendo has since conquered their desired market share, now being a serious seventh-generation contender.

Xbox

The other console which was released in late 2001 was to have a very shaky start but was eventually to become a console strong enough to rival Sony. Xbox was the first ever console release by Microsoft and was a result of the threat of consoles to the sale of PCs. Being the last sixth-generation console to be released, Xbox had a hard time finding its position in the market. The release price was higher than that of the Sony Playstation, which was now lower than its original price had been two years previously on its release, and the GameCube and Dreamcast were lower-priced consoles anyway. After just over a month on sale, Microsoft lowered the price of Xbox by nearly one-third for all units across the world. At this point the Xbox looked doomed to be relegated to the annals of console history, but it was the games that saved it. *Halo: Combat Evolved* was a release title for the console and later *Halo 2* became the biggest-selling media product ever, outstripping books and films in the first 24 hours of release. Consoles were purchased just to be able to play these exclusive games.

Xbox Live

When Xbox Live was launched in 2002, it took advantage of the widespread adoption of home broadband, which had not existed when the Sega Dreamcast had attempted the same thing. Although the Xbox always appeared to be hanging onto its market position alongside Playstation 2 by a thin thread, on the release of the Xbox 360 it strongly established its position in the market and became a true contender to the crown of console with the largest market share.

Seventh-generation consoles

We are now in the seventh generation of consoles and games. The PC is a powerful system capable of playing games; some PCs are even dedicated to that task. The three console giants, Microsoft Xbox 360, Sony PlayStation 3 and Nintendo Wii, are developing bigger and better games and technology in order to be at the front of the market.

The hardware cycle and future consoles

A generation is defined by a significant shift in technology which makes previous versions obsolete. In general, the leading console manufacturers of the time will release next-generation consoles within months of each other.

The hardware cycle of a new console or device begins when the previous one is released. The manufacturers will immediately start assessing its sales and whether there are any problems. Comments from users are assessed and these feed into ideas for the next product. From this point new features are included, prototypes are built and tested, and the next console is eventually put into production. This whole cycle can take years.

Seventh-generation consoles
Seventh-generation consoles were released between 2005 and 2007 and included Sony Playstation 3, Nintendo Wii and Microsoft Xbox 360. These are the three consoles which are currently available, although eighth-generation consoles are already in the pipeline as companies are constantly trying to improve on their own technology and outdo their competitors. Getting to the market first can play a huge role in the success of a console.

Current games consoles, including online connectivity for consoles

Game exclusivity
Exclusivity of a game to a single console is used as an important unique selling point for both the game and the console. On its release in 2007, *Halo 3* prompted many people to buy an Xbox 360 on which it was exclusively released. Sales of the 360 rose at that time beyond the normal sales of the console. This meant that once these people owned an Xbox 360, they would begin to buy other titles for that console, and Microsoft and Xbox game publishers benefited from this increased market.

Xbox 360

The Xbox 360 was released by Microsoft in November 2005, their second dedicated games machine. This was the first seventh-generation console to be released and it is believed that this early infiltration into the market secured a higher number of buyers than it would have had there been competition. There was a rush to have the latest technology and the Xbox 360 delivered on expectations. With a 3.2 GHz tri-core processor, custom graphics cards which can produce 9 billion pixels per second and multi-channel surround-sound audio output, the technology inside the console is on a scale never previously seen. On an interface level, there is a new, easier-to-use navigation system, and capability for wireless controllers is built into the console (which had only previously been achieved with a bulky dongle). There are interchangeable features such as the hard drive and face plate. It also plays CDs, MP3s and DVDs. An HD DVD drive is also available as an add-on for an extra cost, Microsoft deciding to go with the HD technology as opposed to Sony (see page 320) who opted for Blu-Ray.

Xbox Live

The 360 is able to be connected to Xbox Live through an Internet connection and allows for online gaming and communication, for a subscription fee. This had been available for the original Xbox but was greatly upgraded for the release for the 360. Xbox Live gives users access to downloadable content such as extra levels and game demos, communication through headsets and the ability to play multiplayer with gamers around the world. Unlike original Xbox games, all 360s have Xbox Live features.

Microsoft also set up a way of measuring a player's performance against others across all games by introducing achievement points. Every Xbox game has a certain number of achievement points (usually 1000 for full titles) which can be collected throughout the game for fulfilling certain tasks. These might include completing all the levels, collecting all instances of a certain object or doing unusual things such as completing a level without firing a weapon. Along with each player's gamertag (their identifying nickname), their achievement points are displayed. This is a way to compare and compete without having to play the same games.

The game series that Xbox is most famous for is *Halo*, the record-breaking trilogy in which

Xbox 360 was the first seventh-generation console released

each instalment has topped its own remarkable records. Not only did each game sell more than any other game at their time of release, but also more than any other media release ever, including music, books and movies. The movie *Spiderman 3* grossed $59.8 million on its opening day, whereas in the first 24 hours, sales of *Halo 2* reached a staggering $125 million. *Halo 3*, released in September 2007, outstripped that with $170 million in the same time period. Other key 360 releases have included *Gears of War*, *Bioshock* and *Viva Piñata*.

The console also allows original Xbox games to be played, although some do lose quality due to the emulation process, but this made the purchase of the new console a less risky prospect for those who owned an Xbox and several games already.

There have been technical issues with the Xbox 360. In February 2007 the BBC consumer show *Watchdog* ran an article explaining how they had received nearly 250 complaints saying that Xbox 360s had broken just when they were only a month or two out of the one-year manufacturer's warranty. The consoles had stopped working, displaying the infamous 'ring of death' – instead of the ring of green light on the front of the Xbox, they displayed a ring of red, indicating a 'general hardware failure'. As a result of these issues, Microsoft extended the manufacturer's warranty to three years for general hardware failures and made modifications to the console's design.

Wii

Of the three current major console manufacturers, Nintendo has the longest history, having produced consoles since the 1970s. The Wii was released in November 2006, just in time for the Christmas season and caused chaos in shops when stocks quickly flew out of the door, some stores selling all their newly shipped consoles in the first hour of trading. Due to high demand and low supply, the hype which surrounded them increased as they became the coolest present for children that Christmas.

Shigeru Miyamoto, the Senior Managing Director of Nintendo, stated in 2007 that, in a games console, power is not everything; that too many powerful consoles cannot coexist. The Wii is significantly less powerful than its competitors but compensates for that with a completely revolutionary controller system. The Wii is unlike any controller ever seen for a games console. It is rectangular, like a television remote control, and has a strap attached which goes over the wrist for safety. A Sensor Bar plugs into the Wii console and this allows the controller to be wireless, using infra-red and Bluetooth signals. The Sensor Bar can detect whatever movement is being made by the Wii Remote. This includes 3D positioning, 180-degree movement, speed (acceleration and deceleration) and the angle at which it is being held. It includes a directional pad and buttons to allow for a wide range of input options. It also provides rumble feedback, which is a vibration in the controller.

Due to the innovative control method, new games have had to be created, although the Wii is backward compatible and able to play Nintendo GameCube games. Releases such as *Wii Sports*, *Mario Party* and *Legend of Zelda: Twilight Princess* have made full use of the pioneering technology and produced a gaming experience which cannot be found elsewhere.

Cross-platform games

A lot of games are released cross-platform to maximise the potential market. However, there are a number of challenges in porting a game to different consoles, especially with the current three on the market. The major difference is the way the games are controlled. Xbox 360 has a standard controller, PS3 has a standard controller with added motion sensing and the Wii controller is completely original. Trying to have the same game controlled in these three ways is a challenge to designers. There is also the challenge that the Wii is specifically targeted to a different market from the 360 and the PS3, which has resulted in many games being ported between those two consoles, but not as many also being available on the Wii.

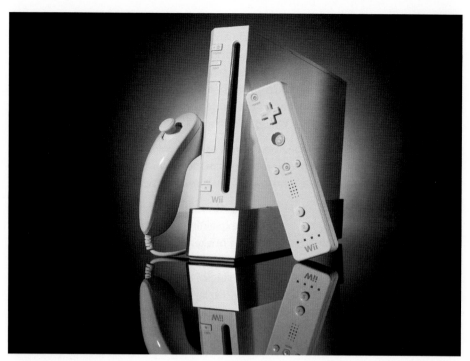

The Wii is one of the most revolutionary, exciting console developments in recent years

Online connectivity

The Wii is capable of going online and users can create their own Mii, a visual cartoon representation of themselves for use in multiplayer games (which can also be used offline). Nintendo do not charge for use of their online services, which include communication, Internet browsing, multiplayer game facilities and Virtual Console – this has proved incredibly popular, as users can purchase and download games, including classic games from defunct systems such as the SNES (Super Nintendo Entertainment System) or Commodore 64.

There have been criticisms of the Wii. The majority stem from the risk in using the controller. There have been several news reports of gamers, or those around them, being injured or items in the home (including televisions) being damaged by over-enthusiastic movement. There were some reports of the safety wrist strap breaking during play and, a month after the console's release, Nintendo announced it would replace any broken wrist straps for free and that the design had been modified so the wrist straps were now safer.

Playstation 3

The Playstation 3 is the third version of this console made by Sony. It was released in Japan and the USA in November 2006, but the European release was delayed until March 2007. However, when it was released its technology proved significant competition for the Xbox 360. Although they have very similar specifications, the Playstation 3 just has the edge in terms of processing power and graphics capabilities. The controller incorporates both the traditional layout of a console controller and the innovative positioning concept of the Wii by using Sixaxis technology which includes motion sensors in the controller. This means that not only does a player have a directional pad, two thumbsticks, four buttons and four triggers, but also the movement of the controller itself will influence the character's or vehicle's movement on-screen.

Similarly to the Xbox 360, the Playstation was marketed as a games console and media centre and it comes with an inbuilt Blu-Ray DVD drive (unlike the 360 where the HD DVD drive has to be purchased separately). Sony opted for Blu-Ray and Microsoft went for HD and, with most film studios and manufacturers now saying they will only produce Blu-Ray disks and players, the battle appears to have been won and Sony is the victor.

Playstation Network

In terms of online accessibility, the Playstation Network is different from Xbox Live in that it is a free service, rather than a subscription, although some games charge for downloadable content or access to multiplayer facilities. However, Sony also has Playstation Home, where users create an avatar version of themselves which 'lives' in a Second Life-type experience. They live in an apartment which they can furnish, and they can also buy clothes, pets and other items for this virtual existence.

Significant game titles for the Playstation 3 include *Project Gotham Racing*, *God of War* and the *Metal Gear Solid* series. The console is capable of backward compatibility with PS1 and PS2 games, but there have been problems reported, with some games not playing as they should, for example with no sound.

An issue for consumers about the Playstation 3 was the price. The Xbox 360's original selling price on release in the UK was around £300 for a Premium system, the Wii's was merely £150, whereas the Playstation 3's was nearer £400. Also at the PS3's time of release, the other two consoles had already started lowering their prices, as happens with all technology.

Backward compatibility
Producing backward compatibility is a difficult issue for console manufacturers. Firstly there are the technical issues which need to be overcome. Can they make the new and improved hardware read and run the original games? In some cases it can be a challenge just getting the old game media, such as cartridges, to fit into the new console. Secondly, there is the consideration that allowing gamers to play their old games may prevent them from buying as many new titles as they may have done without that facility. Thirdly, there will be inevitable loss of quality, as the older games were not designed to perform on higher-specification machines. The manufacturers need to decide whether to release the old games to play at their original quality or to upgrade them to nearer the quality of which the new console is capable. Often manufacturers will release modern versions of the popular old games, such as *Tekken*, to overcome these issues.

The PS3 has the most powerful graphics and sounds capabilities of all three consoles on the market

Portfolio Activity (AO1)

Advise the independent games studio about the current major consoles. With them still being in the design phase of their new game, they have the opportunity to choose for which platform they will design and this decision will affect the way the game is made.

1 Describe the Xbox 360, including hardware, games, features, online facilities and gaming experience.
2 Describe the Wii, including hardware, games, features, online facilities and gaming experience.
3 Describe the Playstation 3, including hardware, games, features, online facilities and gaming experience.
4 Compare and contrast these three consoles, suggesting who each point may benefit or impede.
5 Suggest which console(s) the studio may wish to publish with, justifying your advice.
6 Research the history of games and give descriptions of consoles created from the first to the sixth generation to demonstrate your understanding of how we have reached the point we are at today.
7 Discuss where technology has diverged to produce new products.

More information can be obtained from the official websites of each console.

Assessment Guidance

Pass – Candidates list **some** of the major console platforms. They compare at least **two** of these, identifying the essential and more straightforward differences between the consoles. They **may not** understand the underlying technical divergences. They **may not** use the correct terminology at all times.

Merit – Candidates identify **all** the major console platforms. They compare at least **three** of these, identifying and comparing a **range** of differences between the consoles. They show **some** understanding of the underlying technical divergences. They **use** the correct terminology most of the time.

Distinction – Candidates identify **all** the major console platforms. They compare and **contrast** at least **three** of these, identifying and comparing a **wide range** of differences between the consoles. They compare and contrast features and any advantages of them to a **high level** of detail. They show a **near-expert** understanding of the underlying technical divergences. They **always use** the correct terminology.

Games as a driver of PC technology advances

Games have always been a driver of advances in PC technology. As computer games have become more demanding, the manufacturers have had to create machines at affordable prices to provide what the market is demanding. Often games studios will create games that are more advanced than the technology widely available. This can occur because studios will start development on a game two or three years before it is due to be released and, therefore, often need to guess what advancements will be in place at that time. They need to have a good awareness of the direction of the market but can sometimes overestimate the position they will have reached by that point. For example, a few PC games were released needing Direct X10, which was only available with the Microsoft Vista operating system, and they were on the market before Vista had been adopted by many PC users. PCs that are designed for gaming are often the most expensive on the market due to their higher processing power, memory, graphics and sound. The high expectations of the large market of PC gamers mean that consumers can drive demand for better, faster machines.

3D graphics card features, manufacturers and specifications

One of the most important pieces of hardware in a gaming PC is the graphics card, as it has to be capable of rendering high-quality images, and quickly. Often they will have their own processor on the card, known as the graphics processing unit (GPU). Graphics cards are used to connect to the PCI slots on the motherboard. For a short period AGP (Accelerated Graphics Port) slots became popular which provided a dedicated graphics interface to the motherboard. Modern motherboards now use PCI Express slots and graphics cards are designed to interface with those slots.

Due to the power of this processor, a fan or other cooling method is also often incorporated to prevent the card from overheating. The card may contain a number of ports for connecting display units, including HD-15, the standard monitor port, S-Video, which allows connection to televisions, and HDMI, which is the high-definition multimedia interface.

It is possible to have multiple graphics cards running simultaneously and this can produce incredible results, but also staggeringly high price tags.

There are currently two leading manufacturers of high-level graphics cards for gaming PCs:

- NVIDIA, who provide the graphics processor for the Playstation 3
- AMD (incorporating ATI), who provide graphics processors for Xbox 360 and the Wii.

Both provide products for the development industry as well as business and home use.

Sound cards

After graphics, the area of hardware which is also very competitive is sound cards. Basic sound can be provided by in-built cards on the motherboard, but for gaming PCs a separate card is needed, usually using a PCI Express slot on the motherboard.

Sound cards need to be capable of converting digital sound to analogue for output through speakers or headphones, and most will convert the other way for input from microphones as well. Some will also provide MIDI interface or similar for use with musical instruments such as keyboards. The quality of the digital to analogue conversion is called the sample rate, and the higher the sample rate, the clearer the sound and the closer to 'real' sound, be it speech, sound effects or music.

There are several brands of sound card available, but some of the major manufacturers include SoundBlaster and Creative.

Processor speeds, memory, hard disk capacity, screen resolution

A gaming PC will need more than just a graphics card – processor speeds for gaming need to be higher than normal. Unlike other software and media-like programs and films, games have to be processed constantly while they are running. It is preferable to have a dual-core or tri-core processor which can run two or three processes simultaneously.

The memory needs of a gaming PC are high; modern games can consume 1GB or more of RAM during play, temporarily storing all non-graphic data. Often RAM of this size will also have its own cooling system.

Hard disk capacity is a consideration for gaming, as it needs to be large enough to store the game software and be used as virtual memory during play. However, of bigger significance is the speed at which the data is accessed from the hard drive, measured in hertz (Hz, MHz, GHz).

Resolution on a display device is the measure of how many pixels it is able to hold, measured by the number in the width multiplied by the number in the height. The current standard for monitors is 1024 x 768, although the user can change to suit their preference. Also, with the introduction of widescreen monitors, new measurements of 1280 x 800 and 1440 x 900 are becoming common. Display units are also measured by their frame rate – the number of whole-screen images they can display per second (the lower the number, the slower the ability to change the images on-screen). Games often run at 30 frames per second (fps), although they are being released with the capacity for higher fps. Even if a graphics card processes at a higher rate, the actual image output is limited by the capabilities of the display device. It is becoming popular to use high-definition televisions rather than monitors to allow for more powerful output which can cope with the graphics card's intensity.

There are also gamers who make non-standard adaptations to their gaming PCs such as water-cooling the PC and overclocking, to force more power out of the components. It is useful to be aware of these practices, but they can be highly dangerous, sometimes resulting in overheating and destroyed cards and chips, fires or explosions. They also invalidate any warranty or insurance applicable on a machine.

Controllers, peripherals and input devices

PC games are often controlled by mouse and keyboard. There are specialist versions of these devices which can include extra buttons or quick keys; some include programmable buttons and keys. Other controllers can be connected, including game pads (like those on consoles), joysticks and steering wheels.

Other peripherals which can be used include headsets with microphones, speakers and sometimes printers, which allow reports from within the game to be printed automatically for the player to read.

Gaming PC cases are usually visually more appealing than those of standard PCs, often with perspex panels so the components inside can be seen (to show off expensive modules and as some have LEDs and coloured cables).

Networked and online connectivity

With the increasing adoption of broadband, online gaming is becoming possible for more players. Games such as *World of Warcraft* and *EverQuest* can be purchased as normal in shops and then played online for a subscription fee. Others are available to download online, such as *MapleStory*, which is free, or *EVE Online*, to which players subscribe for a fee.

Second Life, the virtual world where 'players' can create an avatar version of themselves, also has a crossover to the gaming world. Unlike traditional games where there are limits, *Second Life* will allow virtually anything, including the creation of new environments, new characters, new objects and just about any other part of the world. If it can be coded, it can be added to *Second Life*. Although there are game elements which are missing, such as goals, storyline, good versus evil conflict, etc., 'players' can create these elements in *Second Life* and build games within the environment. Some are saying it is gaming without boundaries and an exciting possibility; others are saying it is not true gaming and is more like children making up games in the school yard that exist and are then discarded.

Portfolio Activity (AO2)

1   Advise the independent games studio about current PC technology. Just as you have advised them about consoles, PC is also a major platform which they could consider, and they need to understand the platform and current trends in technology.
2   Describe how the PC gaming experience is different from the console gaming experience. Identify specific games to highlight your points.
3   Choose five different modern gaming PCs currently available on the market and explain the technical specifications. Compare these three PCs in terms of how their features affect performance and experience.
4   Describe how games have pushed the development of technology, identifying specific features which affect game performance. Identify two specific games to highlight your points.

Pass – Candidates reproduce information provided about the evolution of PC technologies with **reasonable accuracy** and to a **basic** level of detail. They demonstrate an understanding of simple PC specifications and their relative implications on gaming capabilities of the machine. They **may not use** the correct terminology at all times.

Merit – Candidates explain **in some depth** the development of different aspects of home PC technology. These explanations are **accurate** and **detailed**. They demonstrate how this has been reflected in PC games releases. They **use** the correct terminology **most** of the time.

Distinction – Candidates **explain** and **decipher** all relevant PC technical specifications. These explanations are **comprehensive** and **accurate** throughout. They **fully understand** their evolution and development and have detailed awareness of which features and specs will have affected game performance. They **always use** the correct terminology.

AO3: Compare and contrast hand-held and mobile devices

Current hand-held devices

Hand-held gaming devices are single unit consoles which include a screen, controls, speakers and usually a headphone port. Comparing them to standard consoles, they are completely portable, run on batteries (for modern hand-helds, usually rechargeable batteries) and are small and light. However, they are unable to have the same power that standard consoles have, as the technology has to be shrunk to the size of the case.

A brief history of hand-held consoles

The first hand-held gaming device was released in 1979, called the Microvision. Due to a tiny screen and only 13 available games, it did not become as popular as had been hoped. Other hand-held devices were developed but the LCD screens and keypad technology were not of sufficient quality to withstand use on a portable device and were generally too fragile.

Atari Lynx and Game Boy

In 1989 two hand-held devices were released, creating a viable market and competition. The Atari Lynx featured a relatively large colour screen and modern-looking casing. The Nintendo Game Boy had quite a small screen that was monochrome. However, the Game Boy had two tricks up its sleeve. Firstly, the screen was not backlit, which meant that it did not use huge battery power, resulting in longer playing time. Secondly, Nintendo knew they needed a killer application (commonly shortened to 'killer app') to give the Game Boy the edge over the Lynx, so it came bundled with a game which was relatively unknown in the West at that time: *Tetris*. The popularity of *Tetris* exploded and the Game Boy became the market leader. With the addition of iconic *Mario*, the popularity of the Game Boy obliterated all other competitors.

Game Gear

In 1990 Sega released the Game Gear, which was their attempt to conquer the hand-held market. The Game Gear had a colour screen and was essentially a portable Sega Master System. Although it managed a longer battery life than its predecessors with backlit screens, it could not compete with the low power of the monochrome Game Boy screen. Also, the colour screen made the Game Gear a more expensive device, and for many gamers their standard consoles were their expensive purchase; the hand-held was an add-on and they were not willing to pay the high price tag. Many gamers were already loyal to the Game Boy and the Game Gear's later release could not pierce the market as they had hoped.

The Game Boy casing was altered, being offered in several different colours and becoming slightly smaller for the Game Boy Pocket and Game Boy Light. However, the actual technology was not changed until 1998 when the Game Boy Colour was released. Finally, this was a Game Boy with a colour screen without losing too much battery life. This version also had double the processor speed, four times the memory and infra-red communication.

Game Boy Advance

In 2001 the Game Boy Advance was a significant change to the design of the Game Boy. The controls were moved from underneath the screen to either side, allowing for a smaller unit with easier-to-use controls. The Game Boy Advance SP can be clearly seen as the forerunner of the DS, having a flip-up lid with the screen on the top part and the controls on the bottom part.

Nintendo DS

The Nintendo Game Boy was originally very bulky and had a black-and-white screen with very low resolution by modern standards. From that point there have been a number of versions of it, including Game Boy Advance SP which had flip-case design, colour screen and quality sound output. From this Nintendo developed a new line of hand-held called Nintendo DS, the latest release being Nintendo DS Lite, which is a smaller version of the original, released in 2006.

The DS is innovative in that it has two screens, one normal and one touch screen which can be used with the stylus that is attached. It also has wifi connectivity which can be used to play wirelessly with other gamers in close proximity and also, through a router, with DS gamers all over the world. McDonalds have signed a deal with Nintendo in the US to provide DS wifi hotspots in their restaurants across the country, allowing a customer to eat and play their DS globally. Wifi is becoming available in more and more places across the UK and it is foreseen in the next ten years that it could be available everywhere in the country.

A huge array of games has been produced for the DS and it is proving to be a very popular device. In the same way as the Wii, it is inviting new audiences to try gaming, including young children, families and older people, creating a wider target market for Nintendo.

The Nintendo DS uses innovative technology to attract users who would not normally buy a games device

Sony PSP

The Playstation Portable (PSP) was released in the UK in 2005. It has one screen but this is very large and produces extremely high-quality graphics. Also innovative is its use of an optical disk as its storage medium, unheard of in hand-held gaming devices. In 2007 the Slim and Lite version was released which was smaller in size and less heavy, and sales subsequently increased. The PSP has exceptional processing power for this type of device, which is put to full use in games with high-quality graphics, sound and game play.

Current mobile devices

Modern mobile phones are also able to play games. They often come with a few standard games and more can be purchased and downloaded onto the phone. Developing games for mobiles is a specialised field as there is limited display and processing power. Some phones are being created specifically with playing games at the fore.

The Nokia N-Gage was released in 2003 as a gaming phone and Nokia has now announced they are releasing an N-Gage application for smartphones to enhance their gaming capability. There are also portals available, such as Vodafone Live, allowing more multimedia facilities.

With the advent of third-generation (3G) mobile phones, the potential for mobile gaming has increased. Popular games include classics such as *Tetris*, versions of console games such as *Metal Gear Solid Mobile* and made-for-mobile games such as *Treasure Arm*.

Portfolio Activity (AO3)

Advise the independent games studio about the current major hand-held and mobile devices. Although they may choose to develop their game for one of the consoles, there is always the option of releasing a version for hand-held. Alternatively, they could develop straight to hand-held, as this is an area which is growing at a tremendous rate at the moment. A complementary version for mobile phones could also increase the popularity and distribution of the game.

1   Describe the most popular hand-held devices currently available, including hardware, games, features, online facilities and gaming experience.
2   Compare and contrast two of these devices, suggesting who each point may benefit and impede.
3   Suggest which device(s) the studio may wish to publish with, justifying your advice.
4   Research mobile devices and describe the market for these, discussing developments in this field (including future ones), features and gaming experience and popularity.

Pass – Candidates list **some** of the major hand-held/mobile devices. They compare at least **two** of these, identifying the essential and **more straightforward** differences between the devices. They **may not use** the correct terminology at all times.

Merit – Candidates identify **all** the major hand-held/mobile devices. They compare at least **two** of these, identifying and comparing a **range** of differences between the devices. They **discuss** and **compare** a range of products and titles for these devices. They use the correct terminology **most of the time**.

Distinction – Candidates identify **all** the major hand-held/mobile devices. They compare and **contrast** at least **two** of these, identifying and comparing a **wide range** of differences between the devices. They can compare and contrast features and any advantages of them to a **high level** of detail. They demonstrate a **near-expert** understanding of mobile platforms. They discuss and compare a **wide range** of products and titles for these devices. They use the correct terminology **all** of the time.

AO4: Describe game development tools and technologies

Art and animation

There are several tasks involved in the area of art and animation in games development. These can be anything from 2D graphics to 3D modelling to cinematic animation involving lighting and special effects. Often studios will use off-the-shelf packages, as there are many good ones on the market which will perform the tasks needed.

Professional 3D-modelling and animation packages

In games, characters, vehicles and objects have to be created in three dimensions so they can be treated as 'real' entities. They will need to move realistically, interact with and be affected by other things on-screen, and be able to be viewed from all angles.

3D-modelling packages create objects from geometric shapes known as polygons which are all connected together to create the illusion of 3D. The more polygons on the object, the smoother the appearance of the object; however, the higher the number of polygons (or polygon count), the more processing power it takes to render the object by the processor.

Models are usually generated using four windows simultaneously, each one showing a different angle or view of the object. For example, they could show the wire-frame model of the object in one window and the front, side and back with textures in the other three. The object will be able to be rotated and zoomed into and out of so the designer can see all aspects of the model and edit accordingly. Popular 3D-modelling software includes 3DS Max, Blender and Maya.

Level-editing and world-building toolkits

There is specific software available to create levels and worlds. Some will allow the generation of brand new environments. This is especially useful if the designers want to try something completely new and different. Others will allow worlds and levels to be built using an engine or other game as a foundation. Valve Software's Hammer Editor uses the Source engine to allow designers to create worlds using that engine as a basis, giving them a lot of freedom for creativity without having to be concerned with the underlying base of the game system.

Other editors are available within games, such as the Forge map editor in *Halo 3*, allowing players to create their own maps; however, they are restricted to the *Halo* world.

Software development

The opposite side of the coin to art and animation is programming. Each is as important as the other when creating a game.

High- and low-level programming languages

Computers, at the very lowest level, 'talk' in 1s and 0s which represent pulses of electricity moving through the circuits of the motherboard. These 1s and 0s are called binary and have to be converted in order for human users to understand them. There are different stages that can be gone through in order to convert the binary.

Low-level programming is done with languages which are relatively close to binary and need less conversion in order to be understood. Languages like these can be hard to understand by the user but are more quickly processed by the computer, as there is less interpretation and compiling required when running the program. Low-level languages include Machine Code and Assembly Language.

High-level languages are closer to human language and are, therefore, easier to understand and learn. However, large amounts of code can take time to be interpreted and compiled to be run by the computer. The majority of languages are high level and those used in games development include C++, Java and DarkBasic.

DirectX, Open GL and Graphic APIs

DirectX is a group of APIs created by Microsoft. Previously they were all separate, with names such as Direct 3D and DirectMusic; DirectX is the assimilation of all these separate programmes into one entity. DirectX 10 is the latest release. However, it will only function on Windows Vista, so a large proportion of users are still using DirectX 9.

OpenGL stands for Open Graphics Library and is created by Silicon Graphics. It was originated before and competes with DirectX. As a cross-platform tool it incorporates more than 250 separate files which will run a wide variety of functions, from simply drawing lines to rendering 3D objects.

Middleware and tools

Middleware in games development is a tool which is created to make the production of games more efficient. It is like a ruler, which was invented to draw straight lines and is 'in the middle' between the paper and user. For example, SpeedTree will create realistic trees for an environment in a game, created to make this time-consuming process faster and therefore allowing designers more time to work on other parts of the game. In contrast, middleware such as Emergent's Gamebryo provides tools for developers to create the foundation of a game or a prototype without having to begin from scratch.

Portfolio Activity (AO4)

Advise the independent games studio about current game development tools and technologies. At the design stage, they are able to incorporate this new expertise into their game. If it was left any later it would be difficult to append to the project and it would look like an add-on rather than an integrated feature that had been planned from the beginning.

1 Select five current art and animation packages and explain their features, advantages and disadvantages. Compare their main attributes and give examples.
2 Select five current software development tools and explain their features, advantages and disadvantages. Compare their main attributes and give examples.

AO5: Explore current technical challenges for computer games

Physics and dynamics

Physics and dynamics (the effects of forces on objects) are of serious consideration in games, even ones which take place in fantasy worlds and on distant planets. Gravity is the crucial one and is needed to keep the character from floating away from the ground and also to allow for realistic walking, running and jumping. Other elements to be considered include light, sound, heat and other forces. Even the wind rustling the trees by the side of the road needs to be considered to give the player a more immersive experience.

Improvements in the movement of a character, especially when they fall, have produced a method called ragdoll physics. Previously, characters would just fall to the ground as a single entity, whereas ragdoll physics considered the movement of the body, including how the bone structure allows the limbs to move, therefore creating a more realistic movement. This is a field which is still being heavily developed.

The main challenge of physics and dynamics is replicating reality. Natural forces such as gravity are always difficult to imitate by digital means. Also, if the game environment is alien, how can realistic dynamics be used while creating a believable alien world?

Artificial intelligence (AI)

AI is used in games for non-player characters (NPCs) – all the characters that are controlled by the computer rather than the player. These can include members of the protagonist's team, the antagonist and their team, and incidental characters who are moving around the environment.

Early games used simulated AI, where NPCs would have a set number of movements which would be random, but not true AI as they never thought for themselves. Modern games use a great deal of AI and each NPC can have its own programming routines, allowing it to move wherever it wants within the environment and react to the player's actions.

F.E.A.R. (released in 2005) has been hailed as having extremely good AI NPCs. They have a wide variety of behaviours, including ducking to travel through small passageways, jumping through windows, climbing ladders and pushing objects over. They can also team together against the protagonist.

The main challenge of AI is always the desire to have more and more automated NPCs. The aim is to have enemies who truly think for themselves, so that the game becomes as challenging as playing another human being. It is incredibly difficult to create true AI, and so far only simulated intelligence has been developed. This takes many hours and metres of lines of code. However, more independent AI gravitates towards the long-standing fear that AI computers will become too clever and too 'human'.

Advanced character animation

Players have an expectation that with each game release the quality of character animation will improve. It is notoriously difficult to create an animated human that looks realistic, mostly because this is trying to create something organic with digital methods.

Technology used in animated movies is improving; however, games developers have two added problems. Firstly, unlike movie makers who can draft in as much technology as required and only have to render it once, game developers have to have characters which can be processed using the console or PC technology available and rendered 'on the fly' during the game. Secondly, whereas movie characters will always perform the same actions, game characters could make many movements, including combination of actions, some of which the developers themselves may not have envisioned.

Motion capture

The development of motion capture has been hugely beneficial to the world of animation in creating more realistic characters. Actors wear sensors and make the desired movements against a plain screen, usually green or blue. Their movements are captured by a computer which then interprets them into code, which can be applied to the characters in the game.

Terrains and landscapes

Modern games have massive environments and these are becoming increasingly realistic. A method which is becoming popular is to use real photographs of a location or aerial photographs of the Earth, which are then mapped onto the structure of the environment. The structure is a mesh known as a wire-frame and is built in three dimensions. The images are applied to the wire-frame in polygons, which are usually triangles, meaning they are able to be manipulated to fit the structure. The higher the number of polygons, the higher the level of detail but also the more processing power required.

The main challenge of terrains and landscapes is choosing a balance between high-quality textures and processing power. As the landscape is the environment and essentially the backdrop of the action, there would be a disparity if all the processing power went on the environment rather than the characters and objects.

Dynamic lighting

Early games generally used a single light source, always from the same angle, as the ability to shade was only available during design. Modern games have the capability to change the lighting during gameplay. For example, a character walks through the lobby of a brightly lit hotel, leaves by the door and walks down a street-lit road, the lights of passing cars glaring as they pass. Each instance of that short journey involves the changing of light and shadows, and modern games have the facility for them to be calculated dynamically as the game progresses. This means that the lighting and related shadows and shading alter as the player moves the character and other objects, therefore creating a more realistic experience.

The main challenge of dynamic lighting is keeping the effect consistent through the whole game and being able to handle the different amount of effects needed throughout the game. For example, when a character moves down a dark street with street lamps, lights from windows, the moon and car headlights driving past, all light sources need to be taken into account during each moment of that game. Even just a second of dynamic lighting can be very complex. In addition, if dynamic lighting is automated, the darker sections of the game could result in a scene being too dark. This was a criticism of *Gears of War* and, with better graphics and animation, has been rectified for *Gears of War 2*, along with clearer, better-defined lines and edges.

MMOs (massively multiplayer online games)

An MMO is a game which takes place across the Internet, involving high numbers of players and very large worlds with a huge array and variety of characters. MMOs are often RPGs (role-playing games) such as *World of Warcraft* or RTSs (real-time strategy games) such as *Ballerium*.

The Uncanny Valley
The main challenge of advanced character animation is the Uncanny Valley. This is the theory that animation which is too realistic falls in an area of perception known as the Uncanny Valley, where the human brain cannot decide whether it is real or not. This gives the viewer a range of symptoms from being unnerved to feeling ill, headaches and dizziness. It has been said that the motion capture, animated movie *The Polar Express* (2004) was unsuccessful at the box office due to the extreme realism of the film. Games, having an added interactive element, may fall more deeply into the Uncanny Valley and it is yet to be seen if it will actually reduce sales of games if their graphics are too realistic.

MMOs are not developed very often, as it is a difficult market to break into due to the strong leaders who have large shares of the audience. Attracting players to a new game is tricky, as the essence of an MMO is that there will be other people with which to play.

The main challenge of MMOs is providing the service. MMOs require large servers able to distribute the games and essentially be the machines that run the games. A typical server can hold about 10,000 character accounts, with about half of them active simultaneously. If the server fails, those 10,000 people will not be able to play the game. If they have paid for the game and then for subscription, they expect the game to be available at all times. Therefore, the MMO provider needs to have replicated servers, which then doubles the costs of maintenance. If you consider that *World of Warcraft* has around 10 million subscribers, the difficulty of providing the online service becomes evident.

Portfolio Activity (AO5)

Advise the independent studio about technical challenges in games development. By understanding the current field, the studio would be able to develop a contemporary, modern game. They may wish to devise a new take on one of the areas. For example, *Gears of War 2* has a completely new AI system that has never been attempted before. Because of this new feature, they may attract more gamers to buy the game who want to try fighting more intelligent enemies. Although these areas are challenges and often difficult to cultivate, they can be the unique selling point of the resulting game.

1 Research three specialist areas.
2 Explain these specialist areas in your own words and analyse the related technical and creative challenges. Use examples from your research to back up your points.

AO6: Investigate and describe future developments

Possible future developments

The field of games is one of the most exciting because it is developing and changing so quickly. Unlike a lot of areas of ICT which have reached a level of stability, all parts of games, gaming and games development are still growing. This means there is the potential for individuals to have completely new ideas and be the first to create something in this field.

The popularity of games is growing exponentially, with more and more people discovering an interest and passion for games all the time. A game now will reach a much larger, international audience and games developers can bring enjoyment to many people.

Console manufacturers, games developers and others involved in the games industry are notoriously secretive about new projects being developed until they are almost ready for announcement and release – and even then sometimes games and products can be cancelled at the last minute. All employees working in the industry generally have to sign a non-disclosure agreement (NDA) which forbids them legally from revealing any of their company's secrets.

Hardware developments

Gaming hardware is constantly being improved, with more processing power, graphics capabilities, sound quality and memory capacity.

New input methods are being developed to make the gaming experience more immersive, such as being able to control the character by body movements with sensors pads or clothing like gloves.

Virtual reality (VR) has always been talked about as the zenith of gaming experience, as portrayed in many movies and television shows. There have been attempts at creating it in the past, but with results which have not become popular. It is something which is becoming more of a reality as technology advances, although whether we will ever reach the point of it becoming the standard of gaming is yet to be seen.

Software developments

The aim of software development is usually to reach a new level of realism or immersion. As processing power and memory increase, enhanced art and animation are able to be created. This allows images and movement to be more realistic.

With the development of artificial intelligence, NPC characters are becoming cleverer. It is predicted that this AI will continue to offer more and more realistic opponents who can think almost like a human.

New technologies

It is becoming popular to connect the Xbox 360 to a Windows PC, which is easily possible as both are Microsoft products. XNA is a set of tools which allows games to be built for Xbox and tested through this connectivity. Where hobbyists had been frowned upon by console manufacturers in the past, Microsoft are positively encouraging homebrew games. They run competitions to find newly developed XNA games and release them on Xbox Live Arcade. This is not only evidence of the future of homebrew games and hobbyists being accepted, it also signals the integration of consoles with other media equipment such as PCs, MP3 players, microphones, webcams and other USB devices. In this way the console becomes the central element to a whole integrated media system. It may be that in the future the console is the integral part for controlling a house, including the lighting, temperature and other devices.

New places and ways to play

There are more places, such as cafés, trains and some whole cities, which offer free wifi connections, which users with laptops or other portable devices could use for gaming.

Virtual communities

With increased broadband speed and availability, it is progressively more possible to build virtual communities with boosted numbers of participants. Virtual worlds such as *Second Life* have created a new environment for gaming. In these, players can take on a whole new character and personality. This could be considered a game in itself, though within *Second Life* games can also be played.

Portfolio Activity (AO6)

Advise the independent games studio about possible future developments. Games can often take several years to develop and studios need to be aware of possible future developments so they can take advantage of them in their designs. For example, if they know a new piece of hardware is being developed, they can contact the company constructing it and request to produce the launch game for the new hardware. If the new development is in an original way to play, the studio should try to integrate that into their design, even if they can only start building that section halfway through the project. When the original Xbox games were being released, only some were capable of being played online on Xbox Live. As this technology became more popular, games which had not considered this new technology generally sold less than others which had. The studio will need to future-proof their game so it is cutting edge and modern, even on its release two or three years in the future.

1 Research possible future developments in game development.
2 Give at least one possible future development for each of these areas.
   - hardware
   - software
   - new technologies
   - new places and ways to play
   - virtual communities.

   Describe how it may come about, what effect it may have on the industry and justify why you think it may realistically happen.
3 For each development, describe the advantages and disadvantages to the industry as a whole, developers, gamers and anyone else involved.

20 Web Authoring

Learning outcomes

By working through this unit you will produce evidence to meet the unit assessment objectives to show that you understand how to:

- understand how website accessibility affects a website
- analyse existing websites to help your website design
- effectively plan the creation of a website that is fit for purpose
- build a website you have designed
- test a website you have created
- upload the website to the Internet
- evaluate a website you have created.

Introduction

The Internet is a valuable tool and is now integral to everyday life. Not only does it allow communication, sharing of information and distribution of entertainment, it has also become an integral part of business.

An organisation that does not operate online at some level is seen as old-fashioned and can be quickly outpaced by their competitors. The Internet allows businesses to trade 24/7 and reach a global audience, opening up a huge marketplace that had previously been difficult to reach. Communication through email can be instant and documents, such as invoices and receipts, can be shared without the need for postage. Businesses can order stock online, and systems can even be automated to reorder automatically when they reach a certain level, meaning no human interaction is required to ensure a business is fully stocked.

It was once thought that only tangible products could be sold over the Internet, but the services industry is getting a foothold in e-Commerce and it is proving to be very successful.

There are, of course, down sides to e-Commerce. These include the loss of social interaction between customers and the business staff, so it can become a much more clinical, isolated experience. Also, customers have to wait for products to be delivered to them rather than take them home immediately after purchase, as in a traditional shop. It can also be more difficult to return an item to an online business, and items like clothes cannot be tried on.

Overall, the advantages outweigh the disadvantages of e-Commerce, which is why it is growing in popularity.

The Tourist Information in your area advertises events and activities in your local district. They currently have no website, but realise that if they are going to encourage more people to be interested in the events and activities, they will need to get online. They have employed you as a freelance web developer to help them gain a presence on the Internet.

Firstly, they need you to provide them with information about current web practices so they can decide what features they will want to be incorporated into their website. Then they have asked you to design, build, test and evaluate a website for them. They have decided at this point they are not ready to sell online, but would like the best website possible to advertise and promote their products.

They require a website of at least ten pages which should include a homepage, product pages, customer account pages, special offers, a page about the company and a contact page. Other appropriate pages can also be incorporated.

Introduction

The aim of most websites is to get their message to the greatest number of people possible. This is especially important for a business that is advertising or selling products or services.

When designing a website, users with disabilities should be taken into consideration and efforts should be made to allow them easy access to all parts of the website.

Factors affecting web accessibility

People with disabilities

The types of disabilities that could affect users' experiences of a website include those listed below.

Factor	Description
Visual	Visual disabilities include blindness, partial blindness, colour blindness and the inability to differentiate between colours with low contrast. This could affect the user's ability to read text on a page or see optical elements such as images.
Auditory	This includes varying levels of deafness. If information is given aurally, or video is used, it may not be heard or heard clearly.
Physical	This could affect a user's use of the mouse or keyboard, for example their ability to click on small areas of the page.
Cognitive	This includes issues involving understanding and can affect a person's ability to read and understand the words or follow a complex navigation system. Navigation that is not uniform across pages, or has a confusing array of unnecessary options, can make a website difficult to use.

Figure 20.1 Disabilities affecting web accessibility

People may have disabilities from birth or an early age, or their abilities may become impaired due to age. Web developers should consider the very valuable older audience.

Social factors

There are sociological factors which can affect the accessibility of websites.

Language barriers can be a huge issue. English is the predominant language of the Internet. Although English is not the most-spoken language in the world, it was the main language of the country that instigated the Internet – the USA. Web languages and scripts such as html are English-based. Users who do not speak English are excluded from a lot of sites if they are not offered in other languages. Furthermore, those who speak minimal English or have English as an additional language may not understand slang or jargon on a website. This can be prohibitive to older people or, if the subject is technical, those who are not literate in that subject.

It is becoming more popular to offer websites in several languages. If this is not possible, web developers should make sure that text is written clearly using straightforward language. It must be remembered that a website is available to a global audience.

Legal and policy factors

In 1995 the Disability Discrimination Act was introduced. This stated that all websites must be accessible to people with disabilities by October 1999. It is therefore now a legal requirement to consider and provide accessibility for websites created and hosted in the UK. As more and more websites have adopted this approach, it is spreading further than the UK as websites hosted in other countries realise that to compete they must also address accessibility to increase their population of available users.

In the USA, the Rehabilitation Act was amended in 1998 to include the requirement that all electronic and information technology be made accessible to those with disabilities. This pattern is being replicated around the world, either through being enforced by law or by market pressure to keep up with competitors.

Technical factors

Not all users have the same level of access to technology. There are still a number of areas in the UK that cannot get broadband, meaning they can only get a 56 Kbps connection. This is reflected across the world; there are areas that have no access at all, but also many that have low-speed connections. Websites with lots of images, or that require a high bandwidth for animations, film or other data, can be unusable by people with low-speed connections.

Another technical issue involves users' choice of browser – although this should not exclude them from using a website. There are many browsers available (including Internet Explorer, Firefox, Opera and Safari) and each browser interprets the code behind websites slightly differently. Also, some users may have older versions of browsers that may not cope as well with modern elements such as interactivity and multimedia. A developer should endeavour to have a website that will operate correctly in different browsers.

Systems for web accessibility

There are many methods available to provide accessibility to a website. Some of the main methods are described below.

Alt tags

Although known as 'tags', alt tags are actually parameters of the <img> tag which will insert an image into a webpage. The alt tag is given words or a phrase and this will show up as a yellow tool tip when the user hovers over the image on the page. If a user has sight problems and is using a screen reader to read webpages to them, the screen reader will read the alt tag so the user knows what the image is and their understanding of the content is not hindered. In addition, for a user with a low-power computer who may be viewing the page without pictures, the alt tag will be displayed as text so the user can know what image would have been displayed there.

Alternative content

Alternative content is a facility which can be built into a website for users with a computer which will not play Flash animations or execute scripts. This may be a choice due to their computer or it could be that they do not wish to allow websites to download executable material onto their machine. Alternative content is where the user is presented with a different version of the site without losing any of the actual information which is to be conveyed. To provide this, many sites have a button offering a link to the different pages. However, it is becoming more popular not to interrupt the user's browsing by making them choose, but to identify whether they have Flash or scripting enabled and automatically navigate them to the alternative content. This means the user may not be aware that they are having a different experience from other users.

Dynamic styles

Dynamic styles allow a user to choose how they wish to view a particular site. The website will be shown initially in the standard view and then options will be available to the user to change certain design features. These can include the colour of the background, the size of the text, the removal of images or animation, and other styles which may make it easier for the user to access the actual content of the site.

Portfolio Activity (AO1)

Tourist Information has asked you to produce a short presentation about accessibility issues that can be delivered to all the employees in the local council, including the local MP. They would like you to suggest which of these issues may affect their website.

1 Research factors which affect accessibility of websites and analyse at least ten existing websites, looking for examples of good and bad practice. Make notes as you research to help you create your presentation.
2 Create a presentation that explains at least three factors that affect the accessibility of websites. For each:
   - describe how the factor has an effect on users (this might be more than one effect)
   - explain the systems that could help accessibility by overcoming the effect(s) of this factor and how they operate
   - give at least three examples of existing websites to reinforce your points
   - suggest how this factor might be overcome on their website.

Reviewing existing websites

Obtaining ideas

By looking at websites which already exist, a developer can gain a better idea of what is popular and can also use this research to design something entirely different and new. They can obtain ideas in terms of layout, multimedia and interactivity.

When researching existing sites, it is important not only to look at websites similar to the one being created, but also at those which are entirely different, as ideas from those sites may be incorporated into it. Areas such as e-Commerce, advertising, educational and informative sites are useful to look at, even if these are not the topics to be covered on the website being designed.

Design and layout

Ideas for design and layout could be obtained from this type of research and also the inspiration to do something wholly unique. A developer cannot know that something is distinctive unless they have checked what is currently available.

There are fashions and fads in web design, just as in clothing. A few years ago the fashion was for sites with black backgrounds and all-singing-all-dancing Flash animations. Currently, white backgrounds are in vogue with a standard styling of buttons across the top or down the side. Although a developer should review existing websites at the beginning of the project for ideas, they should also maintain an interest in other websites and, if they notice the trends changing, try to be ahead of the game by redesigning theirs as soon as possible, or perhaps even attempting to start a new trend themselves.

Use of multimedia features

As technology improves, users are becoming increasingly able to access multimedia features, and this is extremely noticeable when researching those currently available on the web. Once broadband began to become available in an increasing number of homes, websites with video content started to emerge. Now video is seen as quite a standard addition to a site. For example, play.com will allow a user to watch a trailer of a movie before choosing to purchase it, which is a fairly recent development. Increasingly, multimedia is being included in sites, and streaming is beginning to be used regularly as users' computers and Internet connections allow for it. By examining what other sites are using, a developer can gain ideas and see the popularity of the multimedia elements being used by other sites.

Use of interactive features

Webpages can no longer be just static and give information if they wish to be popular. Interactivity must be present in order to allow users to have an effect on the site, tailor their experience to their own needs and want to return to the site after their initial visit.

By researching other websites it can be seen how other sites are implementing these features. This can be as simple as the BBC homepage, which allows you to select your location (which it will remember each time you visit) and give you local information such as weather and news. The BBC's GCSE Bitesize section allows users to play games and take quizzes.

Use of features to aid website accessibility

As discussed in the previous section (page 333–334), there are many different ways to make a website more accessible to its users. A developer can get many ideas from other websites as to how they have implemented these features. These could include an intuitive navigation system, ways of using images and multimedia, and offering an enjoyable experience to those who may not be viewing a website in the standard way, such as using a screen reader or a simplified version of the site. From research a developer should notice that it is no longer acceptable to attach an accessible section to the main site; it must be integrated into the design from the beginning.

Portfolio Activity (AO2)

Tourist Information has asked for your advice in deciding on the design of the website. Produce a short report on a variety of features which could be included, justifying their inclusion.

1 Research at least five features of websites and analyse at least three existing websites for each, looking for examples of good and bad practice. Evaluate (using bullet points) their positive and negative characteristics.
2 Of these three websites, identify which features may be useful for your website and which may not. Make notes as you research to help you create your report.
3 Research at least four systems for accessibility and analyse at least one existing website for each, looking for examples of good practice. Identify which you could use in your website. Make notes as you research to help you create your report.
4 Create a short report that explains at least five features that have provided you with ideas for your website. For each:
   ■ describe the feature, how it works and the effect it has on the user
   ■ give at least three examples of good and bad practice on existing websites
   ■ explain why you think it should be included in your website.
5 In your report, explain in detail at least four systems for accessibility in websites, using examples of existing websites. Identify at least one of these methods that you will use in your website.

Planning a website

The design stage of creating a website should be done carefully, ensuring that the idea has been completely thought through and that the documentation is clear, especially if there will be a team of developers creating it.

Action plan

An action plan is designed to plan out the whole project from start to finish with timescales ensuring that the whole product is delivered completed and on time. The whole project should be broken into phases and each of these into individual tasks; each task should be measurable so it is clear when each has been completed. Start dates and end dates should be allocated to each task, and you should consider which tasks are dependent on other tasks.

Contingency time should also be included so that if something unexpected happens during the project, there is time that can be used to catch up or do extra tasks. In this way the whole product can still be delivered by the deadline.

Purpose and target audience

The website being created should have a clear purpose. It may be that it is to entertain or advertise or sell a product, but it should be a palpable objective. A website is not developed and put on the web for no reason – if time is spent on it, there must be a good reason for doing so. Often a website will have a main function, but may also have several additional purposes that are not core to its development.

Understanding the target audience of your website will dictate some of the design choices. A website that is made for an older audience would be very different from one designed for children. A target audience should never be 'everyone', as that is not targeted and it would be impossible to make a website that suits everyone.

Site plan

A site plan defines the pages that will be in the website and how they will be connected together. This plan should always fit on one sheet of paper so that it can be easily referenced, whether that is A4 or a poster-sized sheet to be put on the wall. The names or contents of each webpage are written into boxes, and lines or arrows connect these together. It may also have information of how the connection is made, for example text hyperlink, graphic or button, although this is optional. The site map is often drawn in a hierarchy style, working down from the homepage, even if the style is more matrix (see Storyboard on page 339).

Dependencies
Tasks which are dependent are those that cannot be enacted until another is complete. For example, images cannot be added to a website until they have been created. Also, it may be best to ensure that the layout and styles of the site are correct on the homepage before replicating them onto the other pages.

Target audience
The target audience should be a group of people who the website is mostly intended for, but this does not exclude other users.

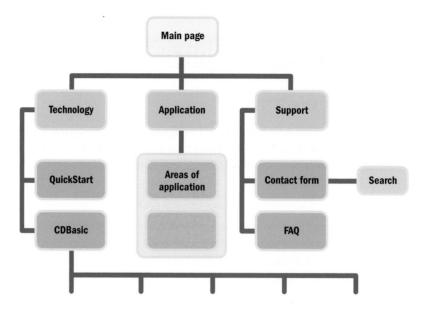

Figure 20.2 A site map not only helps the design of the site, but can also be included in the actual site to help users navigate the pages

Page plans

Once the pages in the site map have been decided, each page can be individually designed. There should be one page plan for each page in a website, even if the designs are very similar.

How to draw a page plan

The layout of the elements on the page should be drawn within a rectangle on the page. These could be just boxes representing parts of the page, such as text or images, with a short description of what will be placed there. Each element should be marked on. Text should be annotated to show the font, size, alignment, colour and any other important information. Images should state what the image will be or suggest the type of image that could be used. Hyperlinks should be annotated to explain where they link to. Outside the rectangle, there should be more information about the page, such as the file name under which it will be saved (see File names on page 342–343 for information on file name conventions), the title of the page and any meta tags that will be used.

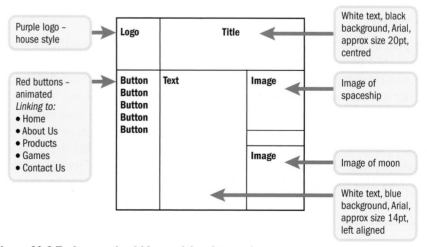

Figure 20.3 Each page should be useful and engaging

Storyboard

The storyboard will bring together the elements of the site plan and the page plans. It shows the realistic method of connecting the pages together. There are three main styles of storyboard for websites: linear, hierarchical and matrix.

Linear

The linear structure is similar to the way a standard PowerPoint presentation is organised, where each page follows another. This is quite a limiting structure as it forces the user to view the pages in a certain order.

Figure 20.4 Linear structure for a storyboard

Hierarchical

The hierarchical structure provides more freedom of movement to the user, but it is still somewhat restricted, as at the end of a branch a user would need to come all the way back up to traverse another branch,

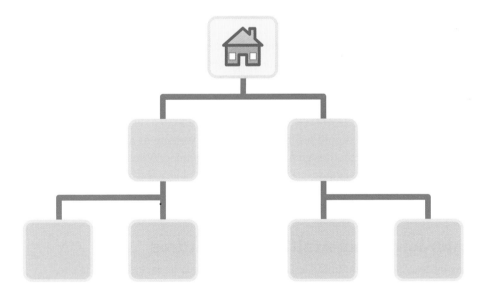

Figure 20.5 Hierarchical structure for a storyboard

Matrix

The matrix structure provides the most freedom to the user, as they can access any page from every page. This means they can go wherever they want throughout the site. This is the most modern style and is currently the most popular.

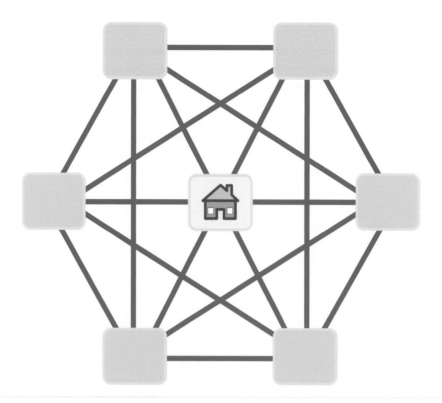

Figure 20.6 Matrix structure for a storyboard

There is also the option of mixing the styles together. For example, a website may have an introduction page which has a linear connection to the homepage from which it is a matrix structure.

Features to enhance accessibility

Accessibility features should not be bolted onto a website as an afterthought but should be integral to the design from the very beginning. When creating the design there should be a detailed description of the accessibility features which will be included and how they will assist users in using the site. Any features in the design should also be included in the page and site plans.

Interactive and multimedia features

Any interactive and multimedia features which are to be included in the site should be designed separately and included in the overall design. The format these outlines will take depends on the type of feature being used. For example, scripting may be written in pseudocode with a clear explanation alongside of the purpose of the script. Flash animations may be storyboarded.

When creating designs for these features, the developer must also consider how they will be integrated into the site, as they should provide a seamless transition rather than be appended awkwardly.

Meta tags

Meta tags are keywords which are placed in the <head> section of a website and are invisible to the user. However, they are used by search engines to ensure the site is correctly listed in their databases. Most search engines use automated bots called 'spiders' which trawl the Internet and record the details of each new or changed site they encounter. They will read meta tags and use them for that site's entry into the searching engine database, otherwise they will read the content of the page and take a best guess. It is good practice to use clear meta tags which are unambiguous in meaning. It can also be useful to use words which are unusual and relate to the site, as there is a chance the site will be more highly listed in a search if those unusual words are used. For more information on meta tags see Unit 21: Hosting and Managing Websites, page 370.

Portfolio Activity (AO3)

Tourist Information now has a good idea of the features of websites and accessibility issues. They have asked you to draw up a design for their website. The site should contain at least ten pages and the pages should follow a house style, incorporating a logo. It should look professional and promote the region well. All design documents should form a single pitch that can be presented to the panel from the local council, including the MP, for their approval.

1. Create an action plan listing separate tasks to be carried out throughout the project. This should start at the point where the design is approved by the owner-manager and finish at the end of the evaluation. Include estimated start and finish times for each task.
2. Write a proposal for the website clearly declaring the purpose and target audience. This should explain clearly to the owner-manager how the website will increase their sales and the different type of customers their website may attract.
3. Design a site plan showing the entire site's webpages and navigation between them. This should be on a single page.
4. Draw page plans for each webpage showing the layout of the page and the features that will be contained. Indicate file names, page titles, meta tags, colours, fonts, possible images and the pages to which hyperlinks connect. Remember to develop a house style and ensure each page follows it.
5. Create a storyboard to show the navigation system of the website and how the pages will interconnect.
6. Explain at least five features you will use on your website to increase accessibility and how this will improve the site.
7. Collect relevant material for the website and indicate where this has been obtained. This could include components you have created yourself or sourced from elsewhere. For each element which has been obtained from another source, explain how copyright affects your use of it.

Pass – Candidates produce a **brief** plan of the website they intend to build. This will include details of purpose and target audience. They list **a feature** that they will use to help website accessibility. They produce **a list** of tasks to be carried out, mind maps and **simple** page plans for the website, including **possible use** of links.

Merit – Candidates produce a **detailed** proposal for the website they intend to build; this will include purpose and target audience details. They provide a **clear** explanation for the inclusion of at least **two** features that will help website accessibility. They produce an **action plan** that has **some** details completed, e.g. task details and expected start/finish dates. **Detailed** page plans will be created as well as a site plan and identification of all links.

Distinction – Candidates produce a **comprehensive** proposal for the website they intend to build. This will include purpose and target audience. They provide a **detailed** explanation for the inclusion of at least **three** features that will help website accessibility. They produce a **detailed** action plan that shows **all** tasks to be completed, dates and actions. **Thorough** page plans will be created as well as a detailed site plan. **All** links and objects to be linked will be clearly shown. These plans will **all** be accurate.

AO4: Implement a website

Set up a suitable directory structure for the website

Folders and file structure

Before beginning to build a website, it is important to have the right file structure in place. All the website files should be held in one folder. This is because when you come to upload the website onto a web server, it is easier to move one whole folder than to try to locate individual files. Also, if files are moved after the website is built, hyperlinks will be broken and the navigation system will not work.

Within the website folder, there should be other folders for different elements on the site. An important folder that is found in most websites is an Images folder, which holds all the graphics, buttons and other visual components. If necessary, there may be folders for sound, video and other elements. Each of these could be built into subdirectories for sites with numerous multimedia files. The more folders used, the more organised the website and the easier it will be for a specific file to be found during the design. These folders will make it easier to find components during the building of the website, especially for those that are used on several pages, such as the logo, which might appear on each page.

File names

Website file names need to follow more rules than other files such as documents and spreadsheets. This is because website files are interpreted by web development software and browsers that expect them to follow strict naming conventions. File names should not contain spaces or any punctuation, except for a hyphen (-) or underscore (_). They should always be kept as short as possible. A file name cannot be changed once hyperlinks have been made as this will cause the links to break and no longer work.

Keep copies of work on a suitable backup device

When starting to build a website, save a blank webpage before starting work on it, and save regularly to avoid losing work. It is good practice to save the homepage as 'index' as most web servers will be set up to initiate the index page as the homepage. Make sure there is a backup system in place to protect the files in case they are lost or damaged. This could be as simple as taking a second copy of all the files onto a USB memory stick at the end of each working session, possibly overwriting it each time. Alternatively, if working on a network, there may be a more complex, automated backup system onto tape run by network administrators. Even if there is a backup system in place, it is always best to back up the files individually as well.

Create a website that is fit for purpose

Produce a template and a website that adhere to a chosen house style

When it comes to building the website, the designs you created for Assessment Objective 3 should be used. If your designs have been created thoroughly and clearly, they should make the building of the website an easier and more straightforward process.

By creating a template, a developer can ensure that all of the pages follow the same house style. In this way the site as a whole feels more like one entity rather than a bunch of pages which happen to be on the same subject.

A template can be created in most web development software and will look very similar to the page plan from the design, with areas blocked out for text, images and so on (see page 338).

Use a range of targets

Hyperlinks can be targeted to send the loading page to different places. 'Self' will load the new page into the current browser window; 'Blank' will open the page into a new window.

Use cascading style sheets

In the web design industry, cascading style sheets (CSS) are used to define the styling of the webpages. Rather than including all the layout, formatting and content in the html of the page, the CSS will hold all formatting and often also layout, and the webpage itself will only hold the actual content. If the formatting is included throughout the html, and a style has to be changed, for example the colour of all the text, the developer would have to search through and find all instances of that tag, which would be very time-consuming and result in inconsistencies. If CSS is used, the developer will only need to make one change, and all content which uses that style throughout the whole website will automatically change.

Text

Text on a website is known as copy and can be typed directly in or imported from another location.

The formatting of the text should ensure that the text is easily readable; legibility can be affected by the choice of font style, size and colour. Bold, italics and underlining can be used for emphasis when necessary.

It is best to use as few different font styles as possible – generally no more than two on a page. For example, Arial, 16, red and Times New Roman, 12, blue and Comic Sans, 20, black would make for very confusing appearance and reduce the professionalism of the site. The styling of the font should remain consistent throughout the site and follow the defined house style.

Text can be aligned to the page: left, centred and right. It can also be aligned vertically to top, middle or bottom. However, for more consistent alignment of text, it is better to use a table for layout.

The language of the copy should also be considered carefully and you should use unambiguous wording wherever possible. Remember to proofread your text so your website looks professional.

Tables

Tables can ensure a more consistent layout of text and visual elements. Widths and heights of columns and rows can be set by specific measurements or by percentages of the browser window. The choice is whether the table structure should remain fixed or be adjusted dependent on the size of the user's screen and browser window.

Images

When including images in a website, the file format should be considered. Formats such as jpg and png files are popular for high-quality images, whereas gif and bmp are good for simpler images as they have smaller file sizes. This is mainly because they reduce the number of colours used in the image, therefore compressing the file.

It is best to make any alterations to images before they are inserted into the website. If an image is put into a website and then made smaller by resizing, a browser will read the file at its original size then make it appear smaller. This will delay the loading of a page – perhaps by as much as a couple of seconds (a long time in terms of web design). Therefore, images should be made to the correct size and then inserted into the webpage.

Rollovers

Navigation on a website is made through hyperlinks. These could be text, images or buttons, and any of these could be rollovers. A rollover is a link that has several states: one where it is unaffected, one where the mouse cursor is over it (known as hover), one where it is clicked (known as active) and one where the link has been visited and then the user has returned to that page (known as visited).

Create a range of internal and external hyperlinks

Links can be 'internal', where pages are linked to other pages within the website, or 'external', where the hyperlinks connect to other websites. To connect to an external website, the link should be to the address of the website and start with the protocol such as http://.

Once a link is clicked, the default is for the page to be loaded into the same browser window as the one being used. This can be changed by adding a target to the link. For example, if the page is to be opened in a new window, the target can be set to 'blank'. This target should be used sparingly as it can annoy users if all links open in different windows. In addition, those with different browser security settings or pop-up filters may not allow this action to happen.

Relative and absolute links

Links can be made to be relative or absolute.

■ Relative links are the easiest to make and are often the default type created in web design environments. The link will take the format of the smallest possible file location. For example, if the page to be linked to is in the same folder as the page from which the link originates, only the page's name will be included in the link, for example <a href="home.htm">link</a>.

■ Alternatively, an absolute link can be made. This is where the full path is used, for example <a href="file:///D:/My Documents/MyWebsite/home.htm">link </a>. This can be useful if the location of the originating page is changed, since the link will not break.

Multimedia and interactive elements

When including multimedia and interactive elements on a website, these should be seamlessly integrated, not bolted on as an afterthought. In the design it should have been decided where these will be placed and how they will be accessed. The aim is to give the user a continuous experience which will encourage them to stay and return again later.

Multimedia elements can include sound, video and animations. When using these it should be remembered that not all computers and Internet connections are capable of handling this data and, therefore, they should be allowed to be optional, even if as standard they are included. It should also be noted that the use of sound should be quite sparing, as many users may find it annoying and will navigate away from the site to get away from the sound. Make sure the sound is appropriate.

Interactivity should not require a user to read instructions and should be intuitive. Modern users of technology want to be able to immediately use a system, and being halted to read instructions may encourage them to navigate away from the site. Having said that, instructions may be necessary for users who are less familiar with the technology and should be available for their access if desired.

Features to enhance the site's accessibility

The accessibility features will have been planned in the design and it should have been ensured that they are integrated cleanly into the overall experience. When it comes to implementation, it is important to ensure that the accessibility is available on all the pages of the site, not just the homepage or the main pages. Alt tags on images should be on every image used on every page. If there are options to alter the styling of the site, such as the size of the text, users should be able to choose once and then their preferences applied to all pages, rather than having to select their preferences on all pages which are visited.

Portfolio Activity (AO4)

The council has approved your design proposal and you can now build the website. Use your designs to guide you. Once it is complete you can demonstrate your whole website to them.

1 Set up a new folder for the website and create suitable sub-folders within this. Ensure all your files remain within this website folder, otherwise you will have problems when you come to upload your website. Also make sure you make regular backups.

2 Create a template for the webpages using CSS. This will ensure your whole site uses the same house style throughout.

3 Using the template, build the website, which should contain at least ten pages.

4 Proofread your website and correct any errors found.

Assessment Guidance

Pass – Candidates implement a **basic** directory structure for the website. Candidates show **basic** competence in producing a website of at least ten pages containing text, images and additional components, using a **basic** template they have created themselves. There **may be** errors in the text, but meaning will be clear. The images and components must be suitable for purpose. A method of navigation to all pages is evident. They include **one** feature that they will use to help website accessibility. Webpages are printed from a web browser, **some** content may be missing.

Merit – Candidates implement a **sound** directory structure for the website. Candidates produce a website of at least ten pages containing text with appropriate styles applied for headings and body text, images and a range of additional components, using either a template they have made or CSS. Meaning will be **clear** but there **may be some** errors. The images and components must be suitable for purpose. A **good** method of navigation to all pages is evident. They include **two** features that they will use to help website accessibility. Webpages are printed from a web browser. **All** content is shown.

Distinction – Candidates implement a **good** directory structure for the website. Candidates produce a **high-quality** website of at least ten pages using CSS. The website includes a **range** of additional components and interactive elements. Meaning will be **clear** and there will be **minimal** textual errors. A **good range** of suitable images and components will be evident. Image optimisation will be evidenced in the form of a screenshot which clearly shows that image size has been altered for all files used. A **good method** of navigation to all pages is evident. They include **three** features that they will use to help website accessibility. Webpages are printed from a web browser. **Whole** pages will be displayed.

AO5: Test a website

Once a website has been completely built, it should be tested thoroughly to ensure there are no errors. A website that does not work correctly can alienate users and they will navigate away from the website and not use it again. Users may become frustrated or confused and not have a pleasant experience of using the site; this could even turn them against an entire business. A bad website can have such a dramatic effect on an organisation that it can, in extreme cases, make them bankrupt.

Creating a test plan

A test plan is usually in tabular form with several columns (see Unit 4: Creating a Digital Showcase, pages 150–152). First it should identify the elements on the site that are to be tested, such as the Home button on the Products page. It should be very specific as to which page and which exact component is being tested. It should then specify how it will be tested, for example a single left-click. Next it should state what is expected to happen.

This is the first part of the test plan and should be completed before moving on to the other columns. Once this is done, the next columns should state what actually happened when the test was carried out and whether the test was a success or a failure. If the expected result and the actual result match, then it was a success. If they do not, it was a failure. The final part of the test plan should be a reference to screenshots which provide evidence of the test being carried out.

Many elements of the website should be tested to make sure that the website works effectively. These include testing of the following:

- each of the hyperlinks to ensure they navigate to the correct page
- each image to ensure they load fully on the page and in the correct place
- the text to ensure it is readable and there are no spelling or grammar errors
- any interactive features to ensure they work correctly
- any multimedia features to ensure they load properly and function as expected
- accessibility features, such as alt tags, show up as planned
- that house style has been followed on each page
- that each page loads correctly in different browsers.

For any test that has resulted in a fail, you should endeavour to repair the problem. The website should be as close to perfect as possible before it is uploaded onto a web server and made accessible to the public.

As well as testing the technical aspects of the site, it is important also to test that it is appropriate and attractive to the target audience. This is often done by inviting members of the target audience to become a focus group and to view the site before its launch. They will give feedback on areas such as the content, the design and the navigation system. They will be able to identify if it is suitable, easy to use and fulfils their needs, as representatives of those who you would wish to visit and use the site once it has gone live.

Portfolio Activity (AO5)

Now your website is complete, you need to test it and make sure there are no bugs remaining. If Tourist Information goes live with a faulty website, it could turn visitors away and damage the area's reputation. Tourists may think that if they cannot put effort into their website, then they may not put effort into their region.

1 Create your own test plan. This will need to include the part you are testing and how you are testing it; what you expect to happen; what actually happened; and a reference to a screenshot.

2 Fill in the first part of your test plan, declaring what you will test, how you will test it and what you expect to happen. Your testing should be comprehensive and cover all aspects of each page.

3 Test your website using your test plan and complete what actually happened. Remember to take screenshots of each test and reference them from your test plan.

4 For the tests that failed, show how you have corrected these problems. For each one, explain what the problem was and how you fixed it. Provide evidence with before and after screenshots, annotated code and/or annotated screenshots.

Assessment Guidance

Pass – Candidates **create** a test plan/table covering all pages in the site and carry out **some** tests.

Merit – Candidates test their website using a **detailed** test table. The tests cover **all** the main areas of their website and all tests are appropriate. Candidates test every page and provide annotated code or screenshots highlighting before and after changes where appropriate.

Distinction – Candidates test their website using a testing table. The tests are **appropriate** and **comprehensive** and will cover all areas of their website. The test table indicates action that is required to solve any problems. Candidates test every page and provide annotated code or screenshots highlighting before and after changes where appropriate.

Uploading a website

In order for the public to access the website, it needs to be uploaded onto a web server from where it can be accessed. This process is known as 'going live'.

Prototype testing

Often in web design a prototype is created and tested before the actual site is produced. A prototype is a small version of the site or part of the site, just as an architect would model a new building and check to see whether it was resilient to all weather types.

Prototype testing will often be used when the website has something unusual on it, for example a new payment system, method of navigation or numerous interactive features. It will first be tested to ensure it works correctly, then the testing will involve using it incorrectly to see if there are any bugs. Any errors that are discovered can then be rectified when building the full version.

A website on the Internet needs to be hosted on a web server. This can be done by the owner of the website, but for larger websites with more visitors it may be better to use professional hosting services. They will provide a web server, ensure the software is up to date and the uptime is the best possible. They may also provide visitor statistics in order to improve the site, for example that the majority of visitors reach the site by typing a certain word into a certain search engine, or that their visitors are mostly from Europe.

Domain name registering

A domain name is the core part of a URL. For example, in www.ebay.co.uk, 'ebay' is the domain name. A website could go live without a domain name, but users would only be able to access the site by the server's IP address. A domain provides a name for the website which can help identify it and be easier for the users to remember. For more information on domain names, see Unit 21: Hosting and Managing Websites, page 358.

A website on the Internet needs to be hosted on a web server. This can be done by the owner of the website, but for larger websites with more visitors it may be better to use professional hosting services. They will provide a web server, ensure that the software is up to date and the uptime of the website is the best is can be. They may also provide visitor statistics in order to improve the website. For example the statistics may be able to show the website owner that the majority of visitors reach the website by typing a certain word into a particular search engine, or that their visitors are mostly from Europe.

File and folder names and organisation

This was covered earlier in this section; see pages 342–343.

File Transfer Protocol (FTP)

FTP is the method used to upload webpages and associated files onto a web server. By using this protocol, both the developer's workstation and the web server can communicate and the files will be understood on both sides. For more information on FTP see Unit 21: Hosting and Managing Websites, pages 361–362.

Portfolio Activity (AO6)

Tourist Information has asked you to help them upload the website onto the Internet. Without this crucial step, the website would not be 'live' and they would not be able to use it to attract customers. They also want you to put together a leaflet which they can distribute to council employees, so that everyone has a better understanding of the uploading process.

1 Research at least three ways of hosting the website and add this information to your leaflet. One could be hosting the website themselves; the others should be real world hosts. Explain the facilities that each provides and the benefits available if Tourist Information chooses to use each one. Make a recommendation as to which ISP they should use and explain why.
2 Explain what a domain name is and why it is important to choose an appropriate one. Suggest a domain name for Tourist Information's website and explain your reasoning behind your choice.
3 Demonstrate how you have uploaded their website to a web server and explain the process through which you went.
4 Explain how the choice of host will affect the users of the site.

AO7: Evaluation of own website

Evaluate your website

The final stage of a project, whether it has been successful or otherwise, is to evaluate what happened. Every opportunity should be taken for learning from what you have done and identifying how you can improve in the future.

There are two elements to evaluation: assessing the product that has been made and analysing your own performance. Improvements should be suggested in light of the weaker points that are identified, and could be proposed for future enhancements or if you were to carry out a similar project again.

Suitability for purpose and audience

The purpose and target audience are defined in the design, and this is an opportunity to explain how the website is suitable for both. The questions that you could ask yourself include:

- Does your website fulfil the purpose you defined in your design?
- Is it appropriate for your target audience?
- Do you think it would attract that audience and why?

Content

The content includes the copy (text), images, multimedia features, interactive features and any other elements that are included in the page. However, it usually excludes hyperlinks, as these are considered in usability. Questions that you could ask yourself include:

- Does the website give the information the target audience needs?
- Is it presented clearly and attractively?
- Is it easily found and ordered well?
- Is it interesting?

Readability

The readability of the site is important, as websites are usually created to convey information. For a business website this is especially crucial, as they need to ensure that descriptions of products and services are clear to potential customers, to encourage them to purchase them. Entertainment sites also need to be easy to read. For example, on a game website the players will need to read the instructions before playing. Possible questions for this topic include:

- Have you chosen a legible font?
- Is the font size easy to read?
- Do the colours of the font and background contrast well so the text is clear?
- Has appropriate language been used, without slang or jargon?
- Has the text been proofread and corrected thoroughly?

Usability

Usability is the measure of the ease of use of a product. For a website, this is mostly concerned with the navigation system. Each page should be intuitive to use and the navigation from page to page should be obvious.

If a user cannot find a hyperlink they need or the information they were looking for, there is a good chance they will navigate away from the site and look for it elsewhere. With the wealth of alternative pages and competitors' websites available, it is very important for a website to keep a user once they have arrived at a site. The questions that could be asked include:

- Is the navigation clear?
- Would a novice user be able to get around the site easily?
- Is the design intuitive?
- Is the site designed so it is suitable for both a new visitor to the site and one who visits regularly?
- Is the website compatible with more than one browser?

Accessibility

As discussed on page 332–334, accessibility can increase the number of users visiting and staying on a website. Evaluating this area can identify elements which can be improved or extra features which can be added to maximise the audience of the site. Questions that could be asked include:

- How have you made the website more accessible?
- Could this attract more people to the website?
- Is the website suitable for all users, including those with disabilities?

Obtaining the opinion of potential users

By asking members of the target audience for their opinions of the website, you can evaluate the site using other peoples' views. This can be useful as:

- it gives a different perspective from your own – this is especially useful if you have been working on the site for a long time
- you can see how people of different levels of ICT and Internet experience use the site
- you can gauge the reaction of potential customers by asking members of the target audience to analyse it.

To obtain the opinions of potential users, you could ask them to write a few comments about their experience of the website or to fill in a short questionnaire. It is most useful to invite people who are part of the target audience to try it. For example, if it is a site for teenagers, there is not much point asking people over 50 years old to test it. In addition, it is valuable to gain the opinions of people with different experience of using the Internet, including those with minimal online experience and those who are very experienced.

Own strengths and weaknesses

By identifying areas where you performed strongly and those where you could have improved, you are demonstrating that you can self-evaluate; that you can look at what you did and identify where you could have done better. By doing this you are going through the process of self-improvement, which will make you a better practitioner.

Self-evaluation is especially useful if you are going to carry out a similar website project in the future, as you will be able to learn from your mistakes now. If you are not going to make a website again, you can still learn from self-evaluation because all projects have the same essential ingredients, such as design, time management, organisation, following a brief and so on.

When you look at areas where you could have done better, remember that the purpose of identifying weaknesses is not to condemn yourself, but to think about how you can improve in the future and become better.

You may wish to ask yourself:

- Have I understood the needs of the target audience?
- Is my website different from others out there?
- Have I included features in my website that would engage users and encourage them to return?
- Did I organise my time appropriately and meet all my deadlines?
- Could I have worked more efficiently?
- Do I need to learn more skills in web design?
- Have I carried out this project to the best of my abilities?

Identify areas for improvement

This is the point where you take the areas you have identified as weak and explain how you would improve them. This shows that, as well as recognising elements of yourself and your skills that are inadequate or just satisfactory, you can learn from the project and aim to improve yourself to be the best you can be.

Portfolio Activity (AO7)

The final task Tourist Information would like you to do is to evaluate the project. This will form part of the documentation for the website and will be useful if they wish to make any changes in the future. They would also like to know honestly how successful the project has been.

1. Provide a thorough evaluation of your website project, identifying good and bad points. Critically assess your website on the following topics, using several screenshots from your website to exemplify each one:
   - suitability for purpose and audience
   - content
   - readability
   - usability
   - accessibility.

2. Analyse your own strengths and weaknesses in building your website. Comment on areas where you think you performed strongly and areas where you feel you could have done better. Scrutinise your performance at each stage (design, implementation, testing) and explain how you think you performed.

3. Obtain the opinion of potential users of the website. Try to gain the opinions of a variety of people with different experience of using the Internet. With reference to these opinions, discuss the good and bad points of your website and your performance.

4. Identify areas for improvement as follows:
   - *For your website* – this should take into account the areas you have already discussed which you considered weak and also anything you would like to have done had you had more time or experience.
   - *In your performance* – consider each stage of the process (design, implementation, testing) and suggest how these could have been improved in terms of your execution. Reflect on your organisation and time management, your application of new skills and balance of technical and creative abilities.
   - *Based on your user feedback* – discuss the areas which the potential customers identified as weak and explain how you could improve these in the future.

Pass – Candidates produce a **brief** evaluation of their work. This covers: suitability of the website for purpose and audience (as identified by the candidate) and readability of the website; candidates will support their comments with examples taken from their website. They give **limited** examples of their own strengths and weaknesses.

Merit – Candidates produce a **detailed** evaluation of their work. This covers: suitability of the website for purpose and audience (as identified by the candidate), readability and usability; candidates will support their comments with examples taken from their website. They give **detailed** examples of their own strengths and weaknesses.

Distinction – Candidates produce an **extensive** evaluation of their work. This covers: suitability of the website for purpose and audience (as identified by the candidate), readability, usability and accessibility; candidates will support their comments with examples taken from their website. They give **thorough** examples of their own strengths and weaknesses.

21 Hosting and Managing Websites

Learning outcomes

By working through this unit you will produce evidence to meet the unit assessment objectives to show that you understand how to:

- specify website hosting requirements
- upload a website and test all features
- implement server-side scripts
- promote a website
- maintain a website
- monitor usage and performance.

Introduction

Once a website has been created, it needs to be uploaded onto a web server in order for it to be accessed by the public. This process is known as 'going live'. It can be quite a risky moment, as weeks or months of work are being tested by the general public. If there are any technical or information problems, they will become evident very quickly and could damage the reputation of the website owner. If a user visits the site for the first time and it does not work – perhaps because a link is broken or the pages take too long to load – they may never visit it again. The developer must make certain that the whole website is tested thoroughly and there are no errors anywhere in any of the pages.

Going live is not the end of the process. A site needs to be monitored to see how much it is being used and how well it is performing. If the site is getting a huge number of visitors, it may be that the site needs to be uploaded with a different host so that more people can visit it without the speed of the pages being affected.

A website that has taken time and money to create may get fewer visits than was hoped. A site can be promoted to increase its popularity. Websites can be visited in two ways: the exact address being typed in or being found through a search engine. To increase the number of people typing in the address, the URL should be used wherever possible. For example, a business could use it on all their stationery, in their poster adverts and anywhere the company's name is mentioned. To be found in a search engine, the site needs to be listed, and a developer can increase the site's chance of being listed by a process called search engine optimisation.

In addition, websites require maintenance – adding new content and encouraging users to keep visiting the site regularly. Website designs go in and out of fashion quite quickly; therefore, a redesign of the site will be needed at some point. This can either be done with a complete overhaul, or each part can be tweaked or added to. The latter method can have much less of an impact on users, as a redesign can sometimes make the site confusing for those familiar with using it in a certain way.

Having created a website for Tourist Information in Unit 20: Web Authoring, you should now upload your website. They will need your help in understanding the website hosts available and choosing which they should use. In addition, they were so impressed with your original website that they have asked you to add some extra features that could provide more interactivity for the user. They would also like you to explain how they can promote the site and carry out maintenance of the site.

Produce a specification of requirements

Before choosing a website host, it is useful to decide what features will be needed. There is no point in paying for advanced services if you do not need them, such as a large amount of space that will not be used, or bandwidth that exceeds the amount of traffic you will be attracting.

Web hosting

For a website to be available on the Internet, the pages need to be hosted on a web server. From here the users will obtain the pages using the URLs and download them onto their computers to view. Hosts can also offer added benefits such as traffic monitoring and technical support.

Most web hosting is done for a fee and this would certainly be the case for any professional websites. Some amateur websites use free web hosting from websites such as Angelfire. Although these hosts will offer space for free and often free email and tools to help build the site, they have the caveat that the URL will start with their domain name so it can be quite long. They will also place adverts on the hosted site.

Domain names

A domain name is the main part of a website address. For example, in the address www.google.co.uk, the domain name is 'google'. The 'co.uk' section is the top-level domain (TLD) name, often referred to as the suffix.

When choosing a domain name, it should be something that can be used to promote the site in a good light. This should include being memorable, easy to spell and easy to say. A good example of this is iwantoneofthose.com, which defied the theory at the time that a domain name should be short. It is memorable, spelt easily and can be said out loud to tell others about the site, as word of mouth can be a very valuable advertising tool.

It may be necessary to choose a range of domain names that would be suitable for the site in case your first choice is no longer available. Each domain name can only be used once. If there is a specific name that the site must use, it might be possible to buy the domain name from the current owner. There have been cases in the last few years where domain names of celebrity names have been purchased and then the celebrities have been charged exorbitant prices to buy them for themselves. Domain names need to be purchased for use, but the price can range from a few pounds to millions, depending on the name.

Disk space

The web server needs to have enough disk space to hold all of the files of the website. Each webpage will have quite a small file size because the content is not embedded into the page but linked. Therefore, all of the files for the images, videos, sound and all other elements need to be uploaded to the web server as well – and these can be large. Therefore, the host server needs to have space for all of these files. Furthermore, the more space that is needed, the more expensive the hosting.

Monthly traffic

When paying for hosting, the expected traffic of the site needs to be estimated so that the correct bandwidth can be purchased. If the site is going to be very popular and used for downloading files, then a great deal of bandwidth will be needed, as the host needs to provide the connection for the users to access the content of the site. However, if a large volume of users is not expected, it would be a waste to purchase hosting with a high bandwidth.

FTP access

Most hosting will allow FTP access to the website owner so they can upload files for the website directly onto their area of the host web server. FTP stands for File Transfer Protocol and is the method of moving website files onto a web server to allow them to be distributed live on the Internet.

Some hosts, however, provide a more user-friendly browser-based method of FTP access for uploading files onto the server. It may cost a little more for this service, but some users prefer this method of website maintenance.

The level of FTP access can vary between hosts, with the more expensive giving the website owner the most control over their access and files.

Log files and usage reports

When running a website it is useful to be able to see how many visits it is receiving and how well it is performing. The web host can provide these reports for the owner at a range of levels for a range of prices: the more information that is provided about usage and performance, the more expensive the hosting service.

Obviously, the cheapest option is to have no usage reports. From there, it can range from raw data where just the daily, weekly and monthly figures are provided, right up to the hosts providing graphs and tables of information and even some analysis of the data. Based on these reports, the owner can make decisions about whether to advertise the website more or purchase more space and bandwidth if it is proving to be popular. Without this data, the owner is largely unaware of the true usage and performance of the site.

Hit counters on the homepage are seen as amateurish, especially on business websites; this can be a reason for potential customers not to trust the site. They also have a reputation for unreliability as they can be manipulated into showing more hits than have actually occurred. (For more on hit counters, see Assessment Objective 6, page 376.)

Platform specification

The support that is needed for a site depends on the content of the site. If the website is quite basic, the server will only need to support html and maybe CSS, which is done by all hosts. Further to this, a server may also support client-side scripting languages such as JavaScript and VBScript, server-side languages such as ASP and PHP, and database facilities such as SQL.

The more languages and facilities that are supported, the more expensive the hosting. Also, the more uncommon the service needed, the higher the price for supporting it; for example, if unusual languages have been used.

Technical support

Some web hosting companies not only provide the hardware and software for a website to be uploaded and distributed, they also offer support in uploading and maintaining the website. This can be useful for website owners who are not experienced in this area. However, the more support that is provided, the more expensive the service.

Additional features

Other features can be purchased as part of the website hosting package.

- The host can provide security features, such as anti-virus software with updates, firewalls and other features to keep a website safe from hackers and viruses.
- They can also offer a backup service that can be at different levels of regularity, for example weekly or daily or, for extremely important data, hourly.
- New features that have recently become common on websites can also be supported by certain hosts, such as streaming – this is very heavy usage in terms of bandwidth and can therefore be a costly addition. However, it can be worth the expense if it draws in a larger audience.

Portfolio Activity (AO1)

Tourist Information has asked you to investigate current website hosting packages and suggest which they should use, as well as an appropriate domain name. Once you finish working with them, they are considering employing an ICT graduate to maintain the website but they do not know how much website experience this person will have. Therefore, they need a host who offers some level of technical support.

1 Select two commercial website hosting providers and compare the services they provide, including the scripting language(s) they support.
2 Recommend which should be used for Tourist Information's website and justify your selection. Include printouts of the webpages for the package you have chosen.
3 Suggest an available domain name and suffix which would be appropriate for the website.

Pass – Candidates identify an appropriate and available domain name for their website. Candidates **identify one** suitable website hosting package and describe the main features in **basic** terms.

Merit – Candidates identify an appropriate and available domain name and **domain suffix** for their website. Candidates **identify two** alternative website hosting packages. They **justify** their choice with a **clear** explanation of the main features, including the scripting language(s) supported.

Distinction – Candidates identify an appropriate and available domain name and **domain suffix** for their website. Candidates **compare two** alternative website hosting packages. They **fully justify** their choice with a **clear** explanation of the main features, including the scripting language(s) supported.

AO2: Upload a website and test all its features

Upload files to a web server

By uploading files onto a web server the website is essentially 'going live' and becoming available to the general public. This is done through a protocol, called FTP, which was devised so files could be transferred to a web server and distributed.

There are three main methods of using FTP to upload files to a web server:

- command line
- software
- browser.

Command line

This method uses the core of the operating system, so on a Windows-based machine that would be DOS. Once the command line is accessed, the web server can be accessed through its IP address, and the FTP command can be used to transfer the files to the host. Unlike the other two methods, this is not user-friendly and does take some knowledge of commands, but it can be the fastest. A lot of web developers prefer this method because of its simplicity and the fact that it can be done any time, anywhere.

Software

There is dedicated software available which will just perform FTP, such as CuteFTP. In addition, some web development software provides FTP services, for example Adobe Dreamweaver, so that the files can be uploaded to the web server while still inside the program.

Browser

Most browsers allow FTP to be done straight through them. This is usually by typing into the address bar: ftp:// and then the IP address of the web server.

For each method of FTP it is essential to know the domain name and IP address of the web server. Also, there will be a username and password needed to access the files. If the server is owned, then this will be the administrator login. If it is a hosting service, one will have been provided to access that specific part of the server.

Folder management, file extensions and using appropriate naming conventions

All the files for a website should be contained in their own folder, and within that follow a naming convention. This makes the uploading process much easier. For more information, see Unit 20: Web Authoring, page 342–343.

Testing pages, resources and hyperlinks

Once a page has been uploaded, it cannot be taken for granted that the whole site will work, even if it has been thoroughly tested while offline. It may be that a page or image has not been moved over to the web server correctly, or that a file name has been accidentally changed in the process, which would prevent it loading and perhaps break a hyperlink.

To be completely thorough, all the tests that were performed offline should also be carried out now the website is online. This testing should be performed as soon as it is uploaded, as this is the point it is 'live', and if any errors are present they should be corrected as soon as possible. If a big problem occurs, the website should be taken back down again – sometimes it is better to have no site than a bad site.

For more information and practical methods for testing websites, see Unit 20: Web Authoring, page 347.

Portfolio Activity (AO2)

Tourist Information has agreed for you to upload the site and make it 'live'. This means that it will become available on the Internet for the public to access.

1 Organise all of your website files into appropriate folders with appropriate file names.
2 Upload the website onto a web server.
3 Thoroughly test the website to ensure all pages have been uploaded and they are all working correctly. This includes checking that all components load in the correct places and that the hyperlinks all work.

Pass – Candidates upload their website to a web server. Candidates provide **basic** evidence of testing that all pages, resources and hyperlinks operate correctly. Candidates **may not** use appropriate file naming conventions.

Merit – Candidates upload their website to a web server. Candidates provide **detailed** evidence of testing and ensure that all pages, resources and hyperlinks operate correctly. Candidates **use** appropriate file naming conventions.

Distinction – Candidates upload their website to a web server. Candidates provide **comprehensive** evidence of testing and ensure that all pages, resources and hyperlinks operate correctly. Candidates **organise** files in a folder hierarchy and **use** appropriate file and folder naming conventions.

AO3: Implement server-side scripts and outline the relevant legal considerations

Design and build interactive features using server-side scripts

Interactive features can give users a much more fulfilling, exciting experience on a website and can encourage them to return again and again – an important goal for websites. These can be made with client-side scripts or server-side scripts. The difference between these two types of scripts is where they are processed. Client-side scripts are downloaded with the webpage and executed on the user's computer, using their machine to process the code instructions. Server-side scripting is executed on the web server.

Client-side script processed

Server-side script processed

Webpage is downloaded
- all intact client-side script
- results of server-side script

User

Web server

Figure 21.1 Server-side scripts are processed in the server; client-side scripts are processed on the user's computer

Client-side scripting

Client-side scripting includes languages such as JavaScript and VBScript; it is often used to make interactive elements. The processing power of the user's computer is used instead of the web server, meaning that the server can be kept free to process other elements of the website. However, the results of these scripts can be quite temporary and insubstantial, as they are just stored on the user's computer and generally not sent back for storage on the web server.

In addition, there are security implications with client-side scripting, for both sides. The user gives permission for the script to be downloaded onto their machine and executed; this could be malicious code such as a virus. Also, if more important data was to be processed on the user's machine, there is the chance it could be stolen by the user, as it would be on their computer.

Script can be embedded within the main language of a webpage, such as within the html. Alternatively they can be separate and placed within <script> tags in the <head> which allows the script to be loaded into the computer's memory, ready to run, while the page is loading, which allows it to be executed more efficiently.

Example of Javascript within html	Example of Javascript in <head>

``
<html>
<head>
</head>
 	
<body>
<script>
age=16;
document.write("My age is:");
document.write(age);
</script>
</body>
</html>
``
	``
	<html>
	<head>
	<script>
	mobile = 1
	chocolates = 2
	sunglasses = 3
	product=prompt("Please enter search product","")
	if (product=="mobile phone")
	        {document.write("Item found. Catalogue number" + mobile)}
	        else
	        if (product=="chocolates")
	                {document.write("Item found. Catalogue number" + chocolates)}
	                else
	                {document.write("Item found. Catalogue number" + sunglasses)}
	</script>
	</head>
	<body>
	</body>
	</html>
	``

Figure 21.2 Comparing Javascript within html and in <head>

Server-side scripting

Server-side scripting languages include ASP, PHP and JSP. Server-side scripting is also used to make interactive elements, but is able to do more because they are being executed on the web server.

The biggest difference between client-side scripting and server-side scripting is that server-side scripts are able to write to and read from files on the server, allowing them to use databases. They allow websites to change from delivering information in quite a standard way to enabling users to interact with the information. Server-side scripts are crucial for e-Commerce – a database could hold product information that users can browse through, or user accounts to allow users to log into the site and perform actions such as personalising their view of the site or receiving specific information. A good example of this is Amazon, where suggestions for other products you may want to purchase are provided.

Server-side scripting can be embedded in the webpage code but is usually written in a separate file and called from the webpage. This separate file uses a different extension, for example for ASP it uses the .asp extension and for PHP it uses the .php extension; or .phpx to specify the version of PHP e.g. .php4.

Example of PHP within html	Example of PHP in a separate file

```\n<table>\n<tr>\n<td>Name</td><td>Days</td>\n</tr>\n<?php\n for($i=0; $i<12; $i++) {\n?>\n<tr>\n<td>\n<?php\n echo($names[$i])\n?>\n</td>\n<td>\n<?php\n echo($days[$i])\n?>\n</td>\n</tr>\n<?php\n }\n?>\n</table>\n```	In web page:
	`<?php include("myscript.php"); ?>`
	
	In myscript.php:
	``\n<?php\nfor($i=0; $i<12; $i++) {\necho($names[$i].)\n
	\necho($days[$i])\n
	\n}\n?>\n```

Figure 21.3 Comparing PHP within html and in a separate file

Form elements

Feedback forms are very common elements of websites and are used to get information from a user. This may be to gather users' opinions about the quality and performance of the website, or it could allow the user to ask for more information on an aspect of the site, such as a product that has been displayed.

All forms have certain elements in common, as shown in Figure 21.4.

Figure 21.4 Forms provide interaction to gain information from the user

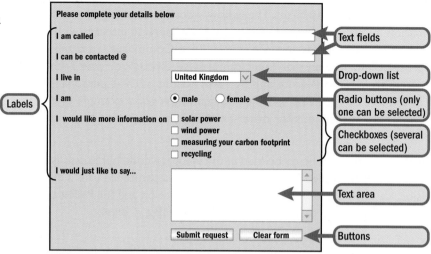

Below is the Javascript which would create the above form. Notice how the script for a form sits within HTML.

```
<form method="POST" action="mailto:me@address.com">
<table border="0">
  <tr>
  <td>I am called</td><td><input type="text" name="name"></td>
  </tr>
  <tr>
  <td>I can be contacted @</td><td><input type="text" name="email"></td>
  </tr>
  <tr>
  <td>I live in </font><td><td><select name="location"><option value="UK">United Kingdom</option></select></td>
  </tr>
  <tr>
  <td>I am</td>
  <td><input type="radio" name="gender" value="male" checked>male
      <input type="radio" name="gender" value="female">female</td>
  </tr>
  <tr>
  <td>I would like more information on</td>
  <td><input type="checkbox" name="info_topic1" value="ON">solar power
      <input type="checkbox" name="info_topic2" value="ON">wind power
      <input type="checkbox" name="info_topic3" value="ON">measuring your carbon footprint
      <input type="checkbox" name="info_topic4" value="ON">recycling</td>
  </tr>
  <tr>
  <td>I would just like to say...</td><td><textarea name="comment"></textarea></td>
  </tr>
  <tr>
  <td></td>
  <td><input type="submit" value="Submit request" name="submit">
      <input type="reset" value="Clear form" name="reset"></td>
  </tr>
</table>
```

Figure 21.5 Javascript for creating the form in Figure 21.4

CGI programming

Common gateway interface (CGI) refers to server-side scripting that allows execution on the web server and for data to be transferred and manipulated. Server-side languages include those listed in the table below.

Language	Description
ASP/ASP.NET (Active Server Pages)	Developed by Microsoft, ASP was originally intended to be an extra of IIS (Internet Information Services) but has become a standard part of Windows Server operating systems. ASP.NET is the latest release of the language using the .NET Framework. ASP is able to connect to Access databases and is designed to work with VBScript.
PHP (originally Personal Home Page, but later changed to Hypertext Preprocessor)	Created by Rasmus Lerdorf in 1995, PHP was released as free software and open source. It is very popular owing to its flexibility and ability to work with most servers and scripts. It can be linked with most database systems and is commonly used with SQL.
JSP (JavaServer Pages)	JSP was originally developed by Sun Microsystems and is based on the Java programming language. It is now maintained and developed by a community of several groups working to improve JSP and some versions are released under a free, open source licence. The script dynamically reacts to user requests and creates XML as needed. It is built into servlets, which can be thought of as mini-programs that are executed on the web server.

Figure 21.6 Server-side languages

As server-side scripting allows the code to connect with storage media, there is a choice of methods of recording the data. It could be executed directly into the browser so it is displayed on-screen and not saved, or it could be saved to a file or a database. If saving to a file, a CSV file (comma-separated values; a text file with each element of data separated by a comma) can easily be read into other files such as databases or spreadsheets. For the databases, SQL (Structured Query Language) is usually used with most types of databases to locate the appropriate position in the database for the data to be stored. It works in the other direction as well, in that files and database can be read and the data used in the webpage.

Outline the relevant legislation

It is important for web developers to have a good understanding of legislation that affects their activities so they can ensure they do not break the law. Few laws are international and it can be unclear which country's laws apply to some websites. For example, sometimes the website owner may be in one country, the web developer in another and the web server itself in another country entirely – the question is always which country's law is applicable. If a website is found to be breaking the law, the authorities may consider it to be primarily the website owner's responsibility, but they can also prosecute the web developer.

In terms of UK law, there are several acts that are applicable specifically to websites. There are also acts that apply generally to all published material, such as the Obscene Publications Act 1959, and selling, such as the Trade Descriptions Act 1968.

Data Protection Act 1998

If a website is collecting and storing information about members of the public, it must be registered with the Information Commissioner and the type of data it is holding and why must be declared. Once registered, the website owner has a responsibility to keep this data under the regulations specified in the Act, such as keeping it safe and only taking relevant information. (For more on the Data Protection Act, see Unit 3: Problem Solving, pages 92–93.)

Computer Misuse Act 1990

This Act was designed to protect computer systems from hackers and viruses and is applicable to websites. If a website is used to spread a virus, the owner can be prosecuted. In addition, if a website is a victim of hacking or viruses, the owner can gain legal protection under this Act. (See also Unit 1: Digital Business Communication, page 49.)

The Privacy and Electronic Communications (EC Directive) Regulations 2003

These regulations were devised to ensure that websites use opt in rather than opt out. This refers to the area, usually at the end of registration forms, where the user is asked if they would like to receive extra information such as a newsletter or offers from third parties. Early practice was to phrase these questions in a complex way so that it was unclear what effect ticking the box would have, such as 'Untick the box if you do not wish to avoid receiving the newsletter'. More recent practice was to have a clearer statement but to have the box ticked by default so the user would have to physically untick the box to opt out of the service. The regulations now state that a user should have to opt in to the service and that the questions should be worded clearly.

Testing and troubleshooting

All scripts which have been implemented in the website also have to be thoroughly tested. This should involve entering correct and incorrect data, as well as making unexpected actions such as clicking outside a prompt window, with the aim of finding any bugs which can then be fixed before the pages with the script are uploaded and made live. (For more information and practical methods for testing, see Unit 20: Web Authoring, page 347.)

Portfolio Activity (AO3)

The Tourist Information website is becoming more popular and they have asked you to implement some more features on the website. To do so you will need to build the features locally and test them, then upload them onto the web server. This way the public will not see unfinished components.

1 Design a website feature which will capture feedback from visitors. This should include an adapted site plan showing how the new feature will fit into the whole site, a page plan and an outline of how the feature will work.
2 Explain in detail any legal constraints applicable to the feature.
3 Using a server-side script, build the feature.
4 Thoroughly test the feature to ensure it works correctly.
5 Add the feature to the uploaded website and check that it functions as expected.
6 For merit and distinction, design, build, test and upload two more features using a server-side script.

Assessment Guidance

Pass – Candidates produce a **basic** design plan for a website feature that will capture feedback from visitors. They outline **briefly** the appropriate legal considerations. Candidates implement the feature using server-side scripting, capturing user feedback in an email, file or database, and provide evidence of testing. There is **some** acknowledgement of information sources used.

Merit – Candidates produce a **detailed** design plan for a website feature that will capture feedback from visitors. They outline **clearly** the impact of appropriate legal considerations. Candidates **fully** implement the feature using server-side scripting, capturing user feedback in a file or database. They provide **detailed** evidence of testing. Candidates **implement** at least **two** additional server-side scripts, produce an accurate summary of how they function and clearly acknowledge the information sources used.

Distinction – Candidates produce a **comprehensive** design plan for a website feature that will capture feedback from visitors. They outline **in full** the impact of appropriate legal considerations. Candidates **fully** implement the feature using server-side scripting, capturing user feedback in a file or database. They provide **comprehensive** evidence of testing. Candidates **implement** at least **two** additional server-side scripts, produce an accurate and concise summary of how they function and clearly acknowledge the information sources used. At least **one** script should be original or significantly customised.

AO4: Promote a website

Promotion methods

A website needs to be promoted if it is to be noticed among the hundreds of millions of other websites available on the Internet. For a business website, it is good practice to ensure that the URL is included on all stationery and adverts, including print, radio and television.

There are also online methods of advertising. Banner adverts can be used on other websites; these are usually horizontal bars across the top or bottom of the page or vertical down either side. There are also more 'in your face' adverts, including Flash animations, which can appear as a floating layer across the middle of a webpage or as a pop-up. These latter types are falling out of popularity as users find them more irritating than enticing and they give the company a bad reputation for bothering people.

A common method of promoting a site, and one that is free to a point, is to attempt to get the best listing of the website on search engines. By using well-thought out meta tags, titles and alt tags, search engines can list the site appropriately. There are options to pay for an even better listing as well, if that is desired for the website.

Identify keywords

When selecting the keywords and other descriptors of the webpage, you should ensure that they are accurate about the content of the webpage. It is also an option to try to use a few more unusual words in the hope that searches containing unusual words will result in the site being listed higher in the search. This is because there may be fewer pages using that word as a keyword.

Basic webpage optimisation techniques

Meta tags

Meta tags are always put in the <head> section of the webpage code and apply to only that webpage. There are several forms of meta tag that can be used; one or more – or all – can be used if desired. These are a rare type of html tags; they do not have a close tag.

Type	Example	Description
Meta keyword tag	<meta name="keywords" content="fruit, bananas, apples, pears, tangerines, lychees, papaya, exotic">	These are key terms that describe the content of the page. Try to think of words that may be used in a search for the site.
Meta description tag	<meta name="description" content="High-quality fruit from a leading UK grower">	This is a one-sentence description of the page. This could form the description of the page if it were found in a search.
Title tag	<title>Sunshine Fruit: grown in the UK</title>	Title tags are also placed in the <head> section. They are not only used by search engines but are also shown in the browser and the taskbar in the browser listing.
Alt tag	<img src="watermelon.jpg" alt="juicy watermelon">	Alt tags are used as part of the img tags for images. Although it is common to call them tags, they are in fact attributes of the img tag. They show up as a tool tip when the cursor is hovering over the image in a browser. Also, for partially sighted and blind users, screen readers will read the alt tag so they know what image is being used.

Figure 21.7 Forms of meta tags

Keywords in the body text

If there are no meta tags, keywords or alt tags, a search engine will take a best guess at the content of the webpage based on the actual words on the page. This will work from the top of the page downwards, meaning that it is advisable to have the most important information at the top of the page, such as clear titles and headings. The search engine will attempt to read the actual content on the site rather than the tags; however, this process is automated so poor coding can lead to inadequate listings.

Directories

The majority of modern search engines use automated bots to look at webpages and make entries in the search engine database of new or modified pages. However, there are still some that use directories. It is worth being listed in these as well, as this will maximise the potential number of visitors – some users may not use other search engines such as Google.

A directory search engine, such as Yahoo!, has websites listed under specific topics. To be listed, a website has to register and select which category they are to be listed under. Unlike other search engines where a website will be listed under a best guess, the website owner can select the topic under which they are to be catalogued. A user can select the categories they wish to search under, moving down through the groups until they find the category they seek. For example, Yell.com is the online version of the Yellow Pages telephone directory. This site allows users to search based on a keyword, company or location, and will look through its directory of UK telephone numbers and addresses.

Figure 21.8 The homepage of Yell.com (November 2008)

'Paid for' and reciprocal links

If websites want to guarantee a higher listing, they can pay the search engine. If a user enters a search term that matches one of these paid for listings, the website will appear at the top of the search, usually with an indication that it has been paid for. In Google, they are listed on the right of the screen as sponsored links, or highlighted as the first result.

Another way a site can be found is by being listed on another related site. Usually this arrangement is made by both sites linking to each other. For example, Sunshine Fruits could have a link to an organic farming website and vice versa. Traffic from both sites may also visit the partner site.

Portfolio Activity (AO4)

The Tourist Information website is proving to be very popular, but they believe they can reach more people with better promotion. At the moment they are using their web address on all their business stationery, and they would like you to use the Internet to promote the website as well.

1 For at least five of the webpages in the Tourist Information website, suggest a range of keywords and phrases for each. Justify each word and provide evidence to support your choice.
2 Using these keywords and phrases, optimise the pages for search engines. Print and annotate your source code.
3 Explain in detail other methods which could be used to generate Internet traffic to the website. Use examples of existing websites to highlight these methods.

Assessment Guidance

Pass – Candidates identify **some** keywords or key phrases for search engine optimisation, with **little** or **no** supporting evidence. Candidates show **basic** evidence of optimising at least **one** page of their website for their chosen keywords. Candidates provide a **basic** description of methods for generating traffic to their website, supported with **few** or **no** examples.

Merit – Candidates identify **many** appropriate keywords and key phrases for search engine optimisation, with **some** supporting evidence. Candidates show **detailed** evidence of optimising at least **three** pages of their website using **appropriate** keywords based upon the content of the page. Candidates provide a **detailed** description of **appropriate** methods for traffic generation to their website, supported with **appropriate** examples.

Distinction – Candidates identify the **most effective** keywords and key phrases for search engine optimisation, with **justification** and supporting evidence. Candidates show **comprehensive** evidence of optimising at least **five** pages of their website using **effective** keywords based upon the content of the page. Candidates provide a **comprehensive** description of **effective** methods for traffic generation to their website, supported with a variety of **well-chosen** examples.

Produce a maintenance guide for users

The web developer who originally designed and created the website is rarely the person who maintains the site. This job is either passed over to the owners or to a business that specialises in maintenance. Even if the development and maintenance are to be done by the same web company, the different tasks are generally performed by different teams. Therefore, creating documentation for the site is essential. It must be clearly understood by others who have knowledge of web development but not of this specific site.

Site map

A site map is a diagram of how all of the webpages interconnect. It should be on one page, whether that be A4 or poster-sized. This can be quite a complex diagram, especially as websites can have hundreds, even thousands of pages, but if some hyperlinks break it means it is easier to repair them. (See Unit 20: Web Authoring, page 337, for further information.)

Editing a page

Each developer has their own style of creating a page and the person maintaining the site needs to be aware of this method so that they can work on it. There will be general guidelines that can be followed. For example, there may be a standard way of including alt tags, such as using 'an image of' before the image content is described, or the page titles may all start with the company name and a colon before the subject of the page. Often this is defined in the website's house style, but if not, it is best to sustain the standardisation across the whole site.

File- and folder-naming conventions

There may also be a naming convention for files and folders that needs to be understood to find and save documents. For example, all images may start with 'img_' so they can be easily identified. For a site with hundreds of pages and even more images, it is a very good idea to ensure the naming rule is followed, otherwise it will make the maintenance of the site a much more difficult and time-consuming task. (For more information on file- and folder-naming conventions, see Unit 20: Web Authoring, page 342–343.)

Uploading

This part of the documentation will give the details of the web server, including its IP address and log on account. The receipt for the purchase of the domain name (and often also an ownership certificate for UK domain names) is usually included, as this will need to be renewed regularly – probably every year.

This section is the main reason that this documentation should stay confidential within the organisation and limited to a small number of people, so that as few people as possible know how to access the web server.

Undertake quality assurance

The person responsible for the maintenance is also responsible for ensuring that the quality of the website is maintained so that users' expectations of the site are fulfilled. The quality of new content, whether a paragraph of information, a new image or a full page, should always be assessed.

Spelling and grammar checks

When adding new copy, it should be checked thoroughly for spelling and grammar mistakes. If you are not confident that you can identify your errors, you should ask someone else with good language skills to proofread it for you.

Hyperlinks

All hyperlinks should be tested, including the internal links to the other pages and files in the site and external links that will take the user to other websites. These should not only be checked when adding new links, but regularly throughout the maintenance to ensure they have not broken. An external hyperlink could break if the other website (or webpage) is moved, renamed or removed. For internal links, the creation of other pages and folders could possibly have an effect on existing links. This is especially true if relative links have been used, whereas absolute links are much more robust and less likely to break (see Unit 20: Web Authoring, page 345).

Image features

When adding new images, the quality of the graphics should be considered. Most of the time, images should not be stretched or squashed horizontally or vertically, and the aspect ratio of the image should be maintained during resizing. The resolution of the image should also be taken into account. The resolution refers to the number of pixels contained in an image (width by height, e.g. 100 x 200). The higher the number of pixels, the better the quality of the image will be. This is most important on bitmap images as it will restrict the amount the image can be stretched; if it is enlarged too much, the image will begin to pixellate. This is the point where the pixels become visible as large blocks of colour, as the quality of the image can no longer be retained. Pixellated images can make a website look amateurish and are best avoided at all cost.

Consistent styles

A good website should follow a house style that defines the layout of each page, the fonts used and their styling, including size, colour and so on. The use of consistent images, such as logos and any other elements, on each page adds a recognisable brand to the website. New content should follow the house style to maintain the uniformity of the site.

Cross-browser testing

As each browser reads the code behind webpages differently, each new page and any new elements on existing pages should be tested to ensure they work on different browsers. If there are browsers on which the page does not work, a proportion of potential visitors could be alienated, which could reduce the amount of people seeing the site.

Accessibility

New content and pages should be considered for accessibility, such as adding alt tags onto new images so they can be read by screen readers and those with non-graphical browsers. By taking accessibility issues into account, the website has the potential to gain more visitors than if it did not.

Validation

Webpages are written using languages; like English, they are prone to changes over time. You would not say, 'I do believe that thou speakest well', as that style has fallen out of fashion; you are more likely to say 'I believe you speak well.' Similarly, certain tags, words and syntax in many languages and scripts (e.g. html) have fallen out of use and become redundant, although in some instances they are still used. Programming languages evolve faster than spoken languages, so validation (checking all code against the latest standard to highlight any parts that need to be changed and updated) is an important process. The W3C sets the standard for valid webpages and provides validators on their website where code can be checked to ensure it conforms to their standards.

Word Wide Web Consortium
The Word Wide Web Consortium (W3C) provides guidelines on web language usage and tools to easily validate webpages. It will check mark-up languages such as html and XML, CSS and even locate broken links, which makes the quality assurance process a lot easier. The director of the W3C is Tim Berners-Lee, who is credited with inventing the World Wide Web by conceiving of hypertext and hyperlinks. The W3C is an international organisation and is well respected by web developers globally; it is the closest thing to standardisation of the Internet.

Portfolio Activity (AO5)

As your contract with Tourist Information is coming to an end, they are thinking about how the website will be maintained. They have just employed a recent ICT graduate who will be responsible for maintaining the website. They have asked you to produce user documentation to ensure that the site continues to run successfully.

1 Produce thorough documentation for the Tourist Information website, including:
  - a site map
  - the site's folders and file names
  - evidence of elements which have been edited since uploading and an explanation of why these changes were needed
  - evidence of quality assurance, including corrections which have been made.
2 Write a user manual for editing and uploading pages of the website.

Tools to monitor usage

Monitoring a website is a difficult task, but there is a huge range of tools available to help in this process. They provide different levels of support and information, ranging in price dependent on the amount of data collected and whether analysis is carried out.

Raw log files

Most usage monitoring software will produce, at their lowest level, raw usage files. These will generally be long lists of statistics. If the tool does not provide analysis, then the website owner will need to wade through this data to analyse it themselves.

Log file analysis programs

Most modern tools will provide a level of analysis of the raw usage data. This can range from a simple graph or pie chart to a complete breakdown of usage at different times of the day, in different countries, via different browsers and all sorts of other statistics. From this analysis the website owner can make decisions about the website in terms of providing a better service for the current visitors and attracting more.

Hit counters

The most basic monitoring tool is a hit counter. These are counters that can be placed on a webpage and that add one each time the page is visited. They are often freely available, but they can look amateurish. Also, if the hit counter number is low, this does not reflect well on the site. This method is unusual as it shows the visitors the usage data. There is also the added issue that the data displayed is quite easily faked or artificially inflated.

Analysis of usage and performance monitoring

Hits and page views

A hit is one visit to a page. Counting hits, however, can give slightly skewed results as the same person could visit a page several times in one time period. Therefore, unique visitors are also recorded. This is based on the IP addresses of individual machines, which is also flawed if more than one person uses the same machine, but it is more accurate than counting hits.

In addition, the views of particular pages can be recorded, as different pages have different levels of popularity. For example, you would expect the most visited page to be the homepage; if it is not, perhaps users are getting in through certain search terms and changes to the meta tags may be needed.

Unique visitors, popular pages, days, time of day and session duration

Not only can the number of visits to each individual page be recorded, but also when they are visited, for how long and by whom (usually divided into countries). For example, it may be discovered that the page of the site where products can be bought is accessed the most by visitors from the USA at noon local time and they stay for an average of 15 minutes. This could be compared with the logs of purchases made at that time, and it could be deduced that users in the USA are logging on during their lunch breaks to purchase items. Thus special offers at that time could entice more people to make more purchases. It could also highlight that users in other parts of the world are not accessing the site as much and, therefore, more advertising could be provided in those areas.

Browser and operating systems

Often the analysis will also show which makes and models of browsers are being used. This data should be understood alongside the popularity of current browsers. For example, if it is found that more users are accessing the site with Internet Explorer, this is not a huge revelation as it is the most popular browser currently in use. However, if it is found that a relatively large number of people are accessing the site with older browsers, then the website owner can ensure that their content is fully understandable by those older browsers and, therefore, take advantage of this population of users.

Referring sites and failed and broken links

Analysis can also show from where users have accessed the site. This might include from search engines, referrals from other sites, via advertising banners or by typing straight into the address bar. From this it can be determined where more advertising could be used. For example, if the banner adverts are not proving to be popular, perhaps they are not worth the expense and more attention should be paid to other ways of informing the public of the website's existence.

High-quality analysis tools will also identify broken links and highlight them for the website owner to locate and repair them. This is especially useful, as broken links are one of the main reasons why users will navigate away from a site.

Portfolio Activity (AO6)

As a final task, Tourist Information has asked you to explain how analysing the usage and performance of the website can help them improve the website.

1   Describe in detail how the website could be monitored for usage and performance.
2   Identify how the results of this monitoring could be used to improve the website.

Pass – Candidates provide a **simple** description of how they would monitor website usage and performance.

Merit – Candidates provide a **clear** description of how they would monitor website usage and performance.

Distinction – Candidates provide a **detailed** description of how they would monitor website usage and performance. They **identify** how they could use the results of analysis reports to improve their website.

Assessment Guidance

By working through this unit you will produce evidence to meet the unit assessment objectives to show that you understand:

- the history of the Internet
- the reasons for the growth of the Internet
- the current features of the Internet and how to use them
- the moral, ethical, social and commercial implications of the Internet
- future developments of the Internet.

Introduction

The Internet has only been around in a form we would recognise for a couple of decades, yet it pervades daily life and has become an essential tool which most of us cannot live without. It provides us with information and communication, allows social and business connections to be made, and is something on which most of us rely.

The Internet can be seen as a force for good or evil, and indeed it can be both. The Internet is unpredictable – at times unstable and wholly uncontrollable. There is no enveloping organisation which manages it, no controlling body which states what the Internet should do or what should be allowed to be added and removed. The Internet is an organic being, living through the millions of people who inhabit this virtual landscape.

Scenario

During this unit you will create materials which could be given to ICT pupils in a school to help them learn more about this fascinating area of study. For each activity you will first carry out some research. This could be on the Internet or it could include magazines and books. All your research should be printed or photocopied and kept in a research folder. At the back of your research folder include a sheet of paper entitled Bibliography; here you should make a note of each of the sources you used, as follows:

- for websites, make a note of the URL, the title of the website and the date you accessed it
- for books, note the author, title, publisher and date of publication

- for magazines, note the title of the magazine, the title and author of the article, the publisher and the date of publication.

Once the research for the activity is complete, you will be asked to use this information to create something for the ICT pupils in the school. You should strive to ensure that the product you create is suitable for these younger pupils, especially when discussing the moral and ethical issues surrounding the Internet. You should also make it as interesting and well presented as you are able. Use as many examples from your research as possible to back up the statements you make in the product.

Scenario

Significant events in the development of the Internet

Since its early days, the Internet has developed at an extraordinary rate and has gone through many rationales for existing. Even though the Internet is an unpredictable, revolutionary entity, one thing can be certain – it will continue to grow and take on many different purposes and forms in the future.

1969 – ARPANET (Advanced Research Projects Agency Network)

ARPANET is considered to be the beginnings of the Internet. It was created by DARPA (Defense Advanced Research Project Agency) in the United States. As with a lot of new technology, it was developed for military purposes, although it was initially a research project. The aim was to allow different bases to be able to share information, and this was tested with three terminals in three universities. Although there had been other networking projects, ARPANET was a circuit-switched network, working the same way as the telephone networks .

1971 – Email

Having developed a method of connecting computers together across a distance, the next step was communicating. The first message was sent across ARPANET at 10:30 p.m. on 29 October 1969. The concept of email was developed, and in 1971 Ray Tomlinson instigated the use of the @ symbol in addresses for senders and receivers. The successful implementation of email secured the successful development of ARPANET.

International packet-switched service, 1978

The first packet-switched network, like ARPANET, was created in 1978. It was a collaboration between Western Union (a US communications company), Tymnet (a US-based data communications organisation) and the Post Office in the UK. This system was successful – the IPSS network grew within Europe and the United States and spread to Australia, Hong Kong and Canada.

1970s – Newsgroups, bulletin boards

During the 1970s, a system called Usenet developed, utilising the current network technology of the time. This allowed users to post messages to newsgroups which could be read by all registered members of that newsgroup. This system was decentralised, meaning that it was spread across several computers and not owned by any one person or company. This was possible, as the Internet, in its initial stages at this point in time, still had relatively few users compared to today's numbers.

From Usenet developed bulletin boards as the size of the Internet network grew. These are hosted on specific computers and controlled by an owner. As they were on dedicated servers, more facilities were available. These have become forums on the modern Internet.

The birth of the Internet
The Internet began as a military network called ARPANET in 1969. Email was made available two years later and seven years after that packet switching was developed, which forms the basis of the modern Internet.

Packet switching
This is a type of network where messages are split into 'chunks' before they are sent and reassembled by the receiver.

1983 – TCP/IP protocol, National Science Foundation (NSF)

On 1 January 1983, all parts of ARPANET and connected networks were officially converted using the TCP/IP protocol, meaning that every part of the network could use the same method of communicating and data transfer at a fundamental level.

In the mid-eighties, the National Science Foundation created their own network similar to ARPANET for the purposes of education and research, called NSFnet. By the end of that decade the two networks had merged. The result was a stronger backbone, meaning this super-network could continue to grow with robust foundations.

1984 – Domain name addressing system

Originally, users of ARPANET would contact other members of the network using telephone numbers. They would dial into an individual computer and that would be the network they could access. With the growth of the Internet, there needed to be a better way of locating sites. Domain names are unique names which use human language rather than computer language. URLs start with www and end in an extension such as .com or .co.uk, and the domain name is the part between these. For example, in www.google.com, google is the domain name.

1980s – Increasing number of hosts

In 1984, the number of hosts on the Internet reached 1000. Three years later, in 1987, it had exceeded 10,000. One year on and the figure had reached 60,000, and in 1989 it reached 100,000. It would only be another three years before the number topped 1 million. The figure is now well over 500 million.

1990 – First commercial dial-up

Although modems connected to telephone lines had been used from the times of the Internet's inception, it was only in late 1990 that dial-up modems became widely available to the public, with an online speed of 9600 bps, compared to the 56 Kbps which became the standard in 1998. The current speeds available through broadband are anything from 1Mbps upwards to 50Mbps and even faster. In Japan speeds of up to 100Mbps are currently possible.

1990 – Search engines

The first search engine was created in 1990 by an American university student. Called Archie, its aim was to archive and be able to search for information over the Internet. At its highest point it reportedly held 150 gigabytes of indexing data, which for the time was a huge amount. Compare this with Google, which can process around 20,000 terabytes of data every day.

1991 – World Wide Web

The first real webpage was published on the Internet in 1991. Prior to this Tim Berners-Lee and Robert Cailliau, working with CERN, created the feature that allowed this to happen: hypertext and hyperlinks. Tim Berners-Lee is often credited with being the inventor of the World Wide Web.

1993 – First widely used browser (Mosaic)

Mosaic was the first graphical web browser which became popular for use across the Internet. It was released in 1993 and was officially discontinued in 1997. Prior to this the software used to view content on the Internet was purely text-based.

1996 – Word 'Internet' in daily use

It became noticed in 1996 that the word 'Internet' was in daily use in the news, the media and society. The word had become part of the national consciousness and almost everyone knew what the term meant and understood what the Internet was.

1997 – 10 million users

In 1997 the Internet reached 10 million users. Considering this was less than 30 years after the conception of this amazing network, it represents a startling rate of take-up. The exponential rate at which the Internet is still being integrated into societies around the world is astounding.

2000 – Dotcom bubble burst

With the rise of the popularity of the Internet and the introduction of e-Commerce, many companies and individuals jumped on the bandwagon and a huge assortment of websites were set up offering products and services. Some of these businesses were massively successful; some made millions in a few months. This rate of business was simply not sustainable and in 2000 the dotcom bubble burst, meaning that a lot of people in these short-term, high-profit companies lost a lot of money as their businesses collapsed. Since that point the world of e-Commerce has settled and is now a realistic business opportunity, considered to be parallel with traditional selling methods.

Recent trends

Other areas which are becoming popular include the following:

- webcasting (transmitting audio and video over the Internet)
- blogs (online journals)
- Voice over Internet Protocol (allowing telephony over the Internet).

New technologies are still continuing to be developed and the Internet's capabilities, functions and purpose will continue to change and challenge us.

The growth of the Internet

At the beginning of the 1980s, there were approximately 1000 hosts on the Internet. By the end of the 1980s, there were over 1 million. The figure is currently over 500 million and still rising.

In 1997 the figure of 10 million users on the Internet was reached. Today there are over 1.5 billion users, which is around one-sixth of the world's total population.

Portfolio Activity (AO1)

Create a timeline for use in an ICT classroom in a school. Make sure it is legible and suitable for the pupils to use. Ensure all your facts are correct by carrying out thorough research.

1 Research the significant events in the history of the Internet and keep a detailed bibliography.
2 Create a timeline of key events in the history of the Internet which would be suitable to be put up on the wall of an ICT classroom in a school.
   - For each point on your timeline, add some text to describe the event.
   - With the description of the event, add how this event affected the Internet and, briefly, how it also affected society.

Pass – Candidates research and outline **briefly some** of the significant events in the development of the Internet.

Merit – Candidates research and outline **clearly many** of the significant events in the development of the Internet.

Distinction – Candidates research and outline **in full most** of the significant events in the development of the Internet.

AO2: Discuss reasons for the growth of the Internet

Drivers for continued development

The Internet is still growing and, because it is in the ownership of the public rather than one overarching organisation, it will continue to evolve.

Technological

Advances in technology have encouraged progression of the Internet and have sometimes been a driver of development. The advent of broadband has allowed communications to be faster, which has facilitated the transfer of larger files such as sound and video. This ability marked the beginning of the modern era of sites such as YouTube and iTunes.

In addition, improvements in computer hardware have supported this development, including the ability for computer and servers to process data faster and for memory to store increasingly larger amounts of information.

Academic

From the early days of the Internet, academia has been a force in development. The first three terminals of ARPANET were based in universities and the first messages between them were sent by a student supervised by his professor.

The Internet is still a huge area for research, and this opportunity is being taken by students and research departments all over the world. A good proportion of people who have been successful on the Internet began their preparation while in education. For example, Larry Page and Sergey Brin, co-founders of Google, met at Stanford University and began creating one of the world's most important contemporary organisations.

Social

The Internet is not just a technological concern, but is at its heart a social utility. The communication aspect of the Internet is key to its survival, as humans naturally strive to find new and better ways to correspond and interact with others. This has become even more important with people often living further away from their friends and families in modern times. In order for them to communicate better, the Internet has provided methods from the simple, short text-based messages of early email to modern web conferencing.

Political

The Internet is not regulated or governed by any one body. This has proved to be a problem when trying to prosecute people over content being distributed. For example, if a web designer is based in the UK, but the site's web server is in America and their data is held on a server in Japan, which country's law does the website fall under? Web designers who want to create sites with salacious content such as pornography or provide illegal MP3 downloads take advantage of this ambiguity by choosing countries with more liberal laws.

The debate over whether the Internet should be regulated continues without resolution. And every time this is discussed, the key question remains of who would actually do it. Each country has different laws regarding the content of the web, from complete freedom to very strict limitations, as in China.

Commercial

The Internet has provided a unique opportunity for businesses to reach new markets and new potential profits. E-Commerce allows companies to be available 24/7, operate across the globe and provide exclusive services such as the ability to search through product ranges easily. Businesses will always be a motivation for change, as they are always looking for new opportunities. When e-Commerce began it was mostly focused on selling products, and it was thought that it would not be possible to sell services over the Internet. However, services are now becoming popular on the Internet, such as online banking, dating and television, with services such as BBC iPlayer and ITV Catch Up.

Portfolio Activity (AO2)

Carry out a debate about the growth of the Internet which would be suitable for the pupils in a school to educate them about both sides of the situation. One side should examine how the Internet has advantaged society and the individual, and the other side should look at how it has hindered or damaged society and the individual.

1 Research reasons for the growth of the Internet and keep a detailed bibliography.
2 Prepare notes about reasons for the growth of the Internet, including relevant examples.
3 Carry out a debate of these topics, making points and arguments and backing them up with examples. Make sure you make in-depth points and back them up with examples. Your teacher can film this debate and/or complete a detailed witness statement as evidence.

Pass – Candidates make a **basic** contribution to a discussion on the reasons for the development of the Internet. Their contribution is **limited**, uses **few** examples and shows a **limited** understanding.

Merit – Candidates make a **detailed** contribution to a discussion on the reasons for the development of the Internet. Their contribution is **appropriate**, uses a **range** of examples and shows **some** understanding.

Distinction – Candidates make a **comprehensive** contribute to a discussion on the reasons for the development of the Internet. Their contribution is **in-depth**, uses a **variety** of **well-chosen** examples and shows a **thorough** understanding.

AO3: Use current features of the Internet

Current features of the Internet

The Internet is always changing; new features are being developed while others are becoming unpopular.

Search engines

There are many search engines available currently, including Google, Ask Jeeves and Yahoo! They have become so pervasive that the verb 'to google' has entered the English language.

Share information

The Internet is a fantastic method of sharing information – it can make information sharing instantaneous. Files can be transferred through email, online facilities such as yousendit.com and uploaded onto web servers through the File Transfer Protocol (FTP).

Social networking

Social networking sites build online communities of many people. Popular sites include MySpace, Facebook and Bebo. For these, each person can create a profile about themselves and link to others as 'friends'. Friends can then chat, blog and share files such as home movies.

Second Life is another phenomenon – a virtual world on which users can actually create a second personality. (See also Unit 18: Computer Games Technology, page 317.)

Collect appropriate information in suitable file formats

Information on the Internet is available in many file formats. Mostly it is text that is directly on the webpages and is normal text which can be copied into documents.

Other text may be distributed as PDF files. These were created by Adobe as documents which can be read by Adobe Reader, available free as a download from the Adobe website, and remain 'locked' unless a copy of Adobe Acrobat is purchased. The aim was to have a file format which was readable by several platforms, including Unix and Apple Macintosh. PDF files are useful to use if the content is to be used in another form, as the original cannot be edited.

Other types of documents can be uploaded to and, therefore, downloaded from the Internet. These include Microsoft Office documents such as Word documents and Excel spreadsheets.

Graphics can be obtained in many different file formats such as bitmap, gif, jpg and many others. Animations saved as gifs can be obtained as well; however, animations made in Flash are 'locked' and cannot be taken from the Internet.

Other types of files can be obtained from the Internet, such as music files, podcasts, animations, games, applications and many others.

Link information

The essence of the Internet is that content is hyperlinked together, which allows a user to move from page to page, investigating different copy and images. A user should not just look at the content on the page accessed directly, but also consider the sites to which it is linked, as generally this will lead to more information being found.

User interaction

A key feature of the Internet is allowing users to communicate and interact. This could be asynchronous, such as email or forums where sender and receiver do not need to be in the same place at the same time. There are also synchronous methods, such as webcasting, chat rooms and instant messaging.

Business transactions

E-Commerce has become hugely popular and is realistically rivalling traditional stores. Businesses can opt to have both traditional stores and an e-Commerce site, known as 'bricks and clicks' or 'clicks and mortar'. Alternatively, they could just operate an e-Commerce site such as Amazon and Dell.

Remote access

As the Internet is all-pervading, remote access is a feature which can be used. This can generally take two forms: for installation and to take control for support. It is cheaper for companies to install software for businesses with remote access rather than sending an engineer. Access is granted by the business to their network and the software is then installed. This can be cheaper and easier, but it can be risky as, if something goes wrong, there is no engineer on site to fix the problem. It also gives a third party access to a business's network, which is always uncertain. For support, a company can take control of a computer to show a user how to do something or to fix an error. For example, a company like AOL can give support by discussion in a private chatroom or on the telephone and also by using remote access to demonstrate on-screen what should be done to resolve the issue.

Portfolio Activity (AO3)

Using screenshots, use the following Internet features and write instructions which could be given to ICT pupils in a school to help them use these features. Make sure that the instructions are clear and could easily be followed by the pupils.

1 Demonstrate full use of a search engine, including Boolean searches and using advanced search tools. Search for information for the topics for the next activity (page 396) and keep a detailed bibliography. Ensure all files obtained are in a suitable format.
2 Use four other Internet features and provide evidence of use. Ensure any files obtained are in a suitable format and that they are appropriate and useful.
3 Demonstrate how a business transaction could be carried out to purchase this textbook online.
4 Carry out a web conference where each person can hear and see the other(s). Use the conference to discuss what you have learned so far in this unit.
5 Transfer your instructions, either by FTP or an online facility such as yousendit.com, to someone to proofread them.

Assessment Guidance

Pass – Candidates provide evidence of using at least **three** features of the Internet, including using advanced features to search for complex information and collecting appropriate information in suitable file formats. Their evidence shows **competence** in use of the features.

Merit – Candidates provide evidence of using at least **four** features of the Internet, including using advanced features to search for complex information and collecting appropriate information in suitable file formats. Their evidence shows **appropriate** use and **competence** in use of the features.

Distinction – Candidates provide evidence of using at least **five** features of the Internet, including using advanced features to search for complex information and collecting appropriate information in suitable file formats. Their evidence shows **appropriate** use and **good competence** in use of the features.

AO4: Investigate the moral/ethical, social and commercial implications of the Internet, including security issues and protection methods and present the findings

Moral and ethical issues

As well as providing tools to assist society, the Internet also harbours websites which are considered to debase society and the individuals who use them.

Pornography

Pornography similar to that found in top-shelf magazines is available on the Internet, but there are also sites which are much more unsavoury and some which are illegal and disturbing. There have been many news reports about people being arrested for accessing child pornography online.

Violence

Some people take advantage of the anonymity the Internet provides and take on personas, some of whom can be verbally unpleasant to other users. Also, services such as YouTube allow users to upload videos they have made. This has attracted some taking and sharing of alarming home movies. These have included dangerous Jackass-style stunts and 'happy slapping', where teenagers have violently attacked unsuspecting members of the public.

Chatrooms

Chatrooms allow users to communicate with other people by typing messages to each other. The risk is that it is impossible to know if the people involved in the chat are actually who they say they are. A teenager could think they are chatting to another teenager, when the person could actually be an adult masquerading as a young person. This could progress to the teenager agreeing to meet them, which is hugely dangerous.

Gaming/gambling

The Internet has provided a forum for people to play games with a wide community of people and there is the risk that this becomes addictive. Furthermore, some games which are rated as appropriate for young people to play may become highly unsuitable once other players are involved, which is reflected in new warnings on games.

Online gambling means that it is now easier to pour money into betting, casinos and amusements such as bingo. As the money is treated virtually, rather than handing over actual notes, it is easier for players not to see it as real losses and can encourage them to spend more. This gambling can be done from the comfort of their own homes, meaning it may be harder to stop if it reaches the level of addiction and they are losing vast amounts of money. There have been reports of people getting into hundreds of thousands of pounds of debt due to online gambling.

Social implications

With the Internet pervading society internationally, issues have arisen which affect the huge amount of users all around the globe.

Dominance of the English language

On the Internet, English is the dominant language. This is because the Internet was developed in the USA and the UK and so English has become the language of online communication. This could cause other users who do not speak English to be excluded, which is in opposition to the Internet's principle of globalisation.

Blurring of national boundaries and changes in the social order

The Internet is an international phenomenon which is having an effect on people all over the world. There can be an alienation of those who do not have access to the Internet or are not Internet-literate. This could be in terms of people and countries which cannot take advantage of cheaper, faster business and tapping into the global marketplace.

There are also issues surrounding the different access rights. For example, users in China have limitations on the content the government will allow to be shown. For instance, if 'Tiananmen Square' is typed into www.google.com, it shows the famous incident where a protestor stood in front of Chinese tanks, whereas the same search in www.google.cn will only show picturesque images of Tiananmen Square.

Changes to employment patterns and working practices

The Internet allows businesses to run 24/7. This can be an advantage for companies and consumers; however, it can have an adverse affect on employees. If a company moves from a traditional store to being solely online, it might mean lower outgoing costs but result in employees losing their jobs. The Internet also permits employees to keep working even when at home, as they can stay in communication with the office and access their data on that network from home, meaning that working hours can extend into the evenings and weekends.

Business in general has become faster due to the Internet, with instant communication via email and computers speeding up processes, which has in turn increased the level of stress in business.

Increased addiction

There are increased opportunities for addictions to be nurtured on the Internet and it is possible for people to be addicted to the Internet itself. There have been cases of users being addicted to eBay, chatrooms and other features that were not available before the proliferation of the Internet.

Commercial concerns

E-Commerce has revolutionised the world of business and has also raised a number of issues.

One crucial issue is security. Is it safe to enter bank details over the Internet? Once they are inputted, can the company be trusted to keep them safe? In the early days of e-Commerce, there was a worry that if a customer paid via credit card then the company would then use those details to spend the customer's money, essentially identity theft. E-Commerce is now more trusted in that sense, but there is still much concern over the security on the business's servers and whether the data will be safe from hackers.

Also, consumers are worried about data tracking. Amazon provides a service in which they suggest other products based on previous purchases. This can be helpful, but if it was to be done on a bigger scale, perhaps across companies, then some consumers may think that this is an infringement of privacy.

Other issues arising from e-Commerce include that, when buying online, a customer cannot be sure of the quality of the product that is delivered and descriptions may be deceptive. Products cannot be tested and clothes cannot be tried on before purchase, unlike shopping in traditional stores. Delivery relies on the postal service and items are not available immediately.

Security risks

When using the Internet there are several security risks, which users should be aware of so that they can protect against them. (All of the security risks summarised below are covered in more depth in Unit 1: Digital Business Communication, pages 47–52.)

Viruses and malware

Virus is a catch-all term which encompasses Trojans, viruses and worms. These are malicious programs which can cause a nuisance, damage equipment or even steal data, such as credit card details which have been entered into e-Commerce sites. Malware can include spyware which obtains information from a user's computer without permission and adware which displays unwanted advertising, sometimes based on information on a user's computer or their activity. Special software, similar to anti-virus software or as an add-on, can be used to protect against or remove it if necessary.

Hackers

Hackers are people who will attempt to access computer systems for which they do not have permission. They can get in through back doors which have been left open in computer systems, and the Internet has allowed this practice to become more prevalent. Hackers can simply cause a disruption or may be more malevolent and steal data, such as financial data of individuals or business data of companies.

Identity theft

Identity theft is a crime which is increasing in prevalence. This is when someone steals the personal details of another person and pretends to be them, doing things like opening bank accounts and spending on credit cards as that other person. When the thief runs up massive debts, it is the person whose details were stolen who is then held accountable.

Email attachments

Email attachments can be quite dangerous as they can contain viruses. It is the most common way for viruses to spread. Emails can also be spam, which is a form of digital junk mail. These are not only a nuisance and may contain malicious software, but may also tempt receivers into replying, which can then have disastrous consequences; for example, tricking people into sending personal or banking details, thereby allowing others to steal their identity and obtain credit cards or mortgages in their name.

Protection techniques

Being aware of security risks is half the battle; to win the war it is important to know how to protect your equipment and data. (All of the protection techniques summarised below are covered in more depth in Unit 1: Digital Business Communication, page 55.)

Firewalls: software and hardware

A firewall is a piece of software which will defend a computer system from unwanted entry, especially by hackers. It will watch for data flowing in and out of the computer and only allow that which it knows is safe to have access.

Anti-virus software

Anti-virus software will scan a computer for viruses, worms, Trojans, spyware and other malicious software. Scans can be run automatically or when directed by the user. It is important to update anti-virus software regularly so it has the latest virus details and protection. This could be a minimum of every week or, for computers and servers with valuable data, every day or even every hour.

Code of practice

By having a set code of practice, a business can guard against behaviour which can be risky on a network. This could include rules such as:

- using a strong password (of over eight characters, including letters, numbers and punctuation, and upper and lower case letters)
- everyone changing their password every three months
- not opening emails which are not from a recognised sender, since these may be spam or contain viruses.

By everyone following good practices, the risks can be reduced.

Encryption

When data is transferred over a network, especially wirelessly, there is a risk that it can fall into the wrong hands. Encryption is a way of encoding the data so that if it does fall into the wrong hands it cannot be read by that person, or at least it would take a long time to crack the code. Encryption is based on prime numbers; the higher the prime number, the harder the encryption algorithm will be to break.

Secure payment systems

With the advent of e-Commerce, customers needed to be reassured that their payments would be secure. Several methods have been introduced in order to provide that security. These include the following:

- SSL – secure sockets layer, which provides high-level encryption across a network
- HTTPS – secure http, which provides encryption and authentication across a network
- electronic cheques – a digital version of cheques which can be used on the Internet (whereas ordinary cheques can only be used in a paper version)
- PayPal, NoChex – businesses which provide a mechanism for online payments
- CV2 – an extra security number on the reverse of credit and debit cards which provides an extra piece of data that can be verified when paying online
- prepay cards – these are similar to debit cards but can be loaded with a specific amount of money then used for purchases. This means that if the details are stolen, only the money loaded onto that card can be accessed.

Portfolio Activity (AO4)

Create a presentation and leaflet which could explain to ICT pupils in a school the issues involved in using the Internet. Make sure they are both accurate and interesting.

- Consider a teacher who might give the presentation and what would be required in the content and design.
- The leaflet must be appropriate for pupils' use and clear in terms of content and design. Pupils should be able to refer to it without any other materials or guidance and it would give them thorough and exact information.

1 Research the areas of moral/ethical, social and commercial issues, security risks, on the Internet and keep a detailed bibliography.
2 Create a presentation about two moral/ethical, two social and two commercial issues, and two security risks on the Internet. Include supporting examples.
3 Research security issues involved with the Internet and keep a detailed bibliography.
4 Create a leaflet describing most of the security issues involved with the Internet. Half the leaflet should describe the security risks and the other half should explain the protection methods available.

Assessment Guidance

Pass – Candidates provide a presentation that includes at least **one** implication from each of moral/ethical, social and commercial aspects. The presentation is supported with **few** examples. They provide a description of the security risks inherent in the use of the Internet. They identify **some** of the available protection methods.

Merit – Candidates provide a presentation that includes at least **two** implications from each of moral/ethical, social and commercial aspects. The presentation is **detailed** and is supported with **appropriate** examples. They provide **detailed** descriptions of most of the security risks inherent in the use of the Internet. They **clearly** identify **some** of the available protection methods.

Distinction – Candidates provide a presentation that includes at least **two** implications from each of moral/ethical, social and commercial aspects. The presentation is **comprehensive** and is supported with a **variety** of **well-chosen** examples. They provide **comprehensive** descriptions of most of the current security risks inherent in the use of the Internet. They **thoroughly** identify many of the available protection methods.

Global Environment for Networking Investigations (GENI) initiative

GENI is a research programme run by the National Science Foundation (NSF), which was significant in the early development of the Internet (see Assessment Objective 1, page 381). Its aim is to resolve current problems in distributed networking, of which the Internet is an integral element. They are building their own version of the Internet on which to test and experiment so that they can try revolutionary ideas which have not been considered or tested previously. Experiments of this size and complexity require the backing of large research organisations such as the NSF to make them possible.

Pervasive and wireless networking

Originally the Internet was restricted to access from terminals and, therefore, the user had to be physically sitting at a computer to access the network. Nowadays the Internet can be accessed by more devices and in an increasing number of places. It is available on laptops, mobile phones, Internet street kiosks and even hand-held games consoles such as the Sony PSP or Nintendo DS. There is increasing wifi availability in cafés and trains, and some towns are providing access in metropolitan areas. Pervasive networking is the objective of providing Internet access anywhere and everywhere, in an increasing range of places and methods.

A sensor network is one which can be used to monitor an environment and adjust it accordingly. For example, it could be used to assess the temperature of rooms in a house and regulate each room accordingly. It could also monitor light, sound, motion and a whole range of other factors. These types of networks are already used in the healthcare industry, the military and traffic control, and have many more exciting potential uses. The Internet allows such networks to expand across huge areas and could link several locations. Systems such as these could possibly allow people to control things in their homes remotely through the Internet and wireless networking.

Advanced security

Security is always going to be one of the biggest issues with the Internet and is something which many companies are striving to improve. When it was originally created as ARPANET, it was not dreamt that it would be available to such a massive number of people or that it would be used for commercial purposes. Therefore, security features are tacked on rather than built in as a fundamental part of the system.

A key feature of Microsoft's latest operating system, Vista, is improved security on the Internet. A system called Secure Electronic Transaction (SET) is being developed by banks to make digital money dealings safer.

One area which is popular in the theory of future protection is using biometric data, which includes a person's fingerprints, irises, voice and DNA. This is something which has been a feature of science fiction for years and, even though it is beginning to become a reality, it is still an area which is vehemently disputed. We know for sure that biometric data will indeed identify an individual, but can that data be replicated or kept completely secure? Terminal Five at Heathrow, which opened for operation on 27 March 2008, has a system for fingerprinting all passengers. ID cards, which have been proposed by the UK government, may contain several items of biometric data.

Non-computer sources

The Internet is beginning to be used for systems which are not computer-based but provide foundations for them to function. Global positioning systems (GPS) can locate a specific point in the world (depending on the coverage of the particular system). This has been used in a variety of systems, from automotive navigation systems and mobile phones to military systems.

Radio-Frequency Identification (RFID) is mostly used in commerce to ensure the security of products in stores. Each product is given a tag with a frequency and at the exits of the shop are RFID readers, usually as columns between which customers must walk. As the item is purchased, the cashier will deactivate the RFID tag. Items which pass between the readers which are not deactivated, and therefore not purchased, will set off an alarm. RFID can be used in other areas, such as passport control, transportation payments (e.g. tolls and congestion charges) and animal identification.

Internet telephone

Voice over Internet Protocol (VoIP) is a protocol which allows communication over the Internet (see also Unit 2: Collaborative Working, page 170). One method which is being developed and is beginning to be popular is making telephone calls over the Internet. This is starting to be as easy as making a normal telephone call. Originally this was difficult, expensive and depended on the recipient also having VoIP (which then was unlikely), but as technology has developed, it is becoming a real possibility for replacing the ordinary landline phone.

Portfolio Activity (AO5)

Create a short booklet for ICT pupils in a school describing the possible future developments of the Internet. To assess its validity, evaluate the sources you use.

1   Research the possible future developments of the Internet and keep a detailed bibliography (use at least four different sources).
2   Using your research (from at least four different sources), discuss the possible future developments of the Internet.
3   From this discussion, make predictions about what you realistically believe will happen in the future. Support each prediction with sound reasoning and justify it with information from your research.
4   For each of the sources you have used, evaluate its validity. State who has written it and whether they should be trusted. For example, if it is statement on a forum it is likely to be a personal opinion.

Pass – Candidates complete a **basic** search for possible future developments of the Internet. They explore the results of their search and produce **some limited** predictions. They use at least **two** sources. They complete a **limited** evaluation of their sources.

Merit – Candidates complete a **detailed** search for possible future developments of the Internet. They explore the results of their search and produce **some appropriate** predictions. They use at least **three** sources. They complete **some** appropriate evaluation of their sources.

Distinction – Candidates complete a **comprehensive** search for possible future developments of the Internet. They explore the results of their search and produce **some well-reasoned** and **well-developed** predictions. They use at least **four** sources. They complete a **well-reasoned** evaluation of their sources.

Index